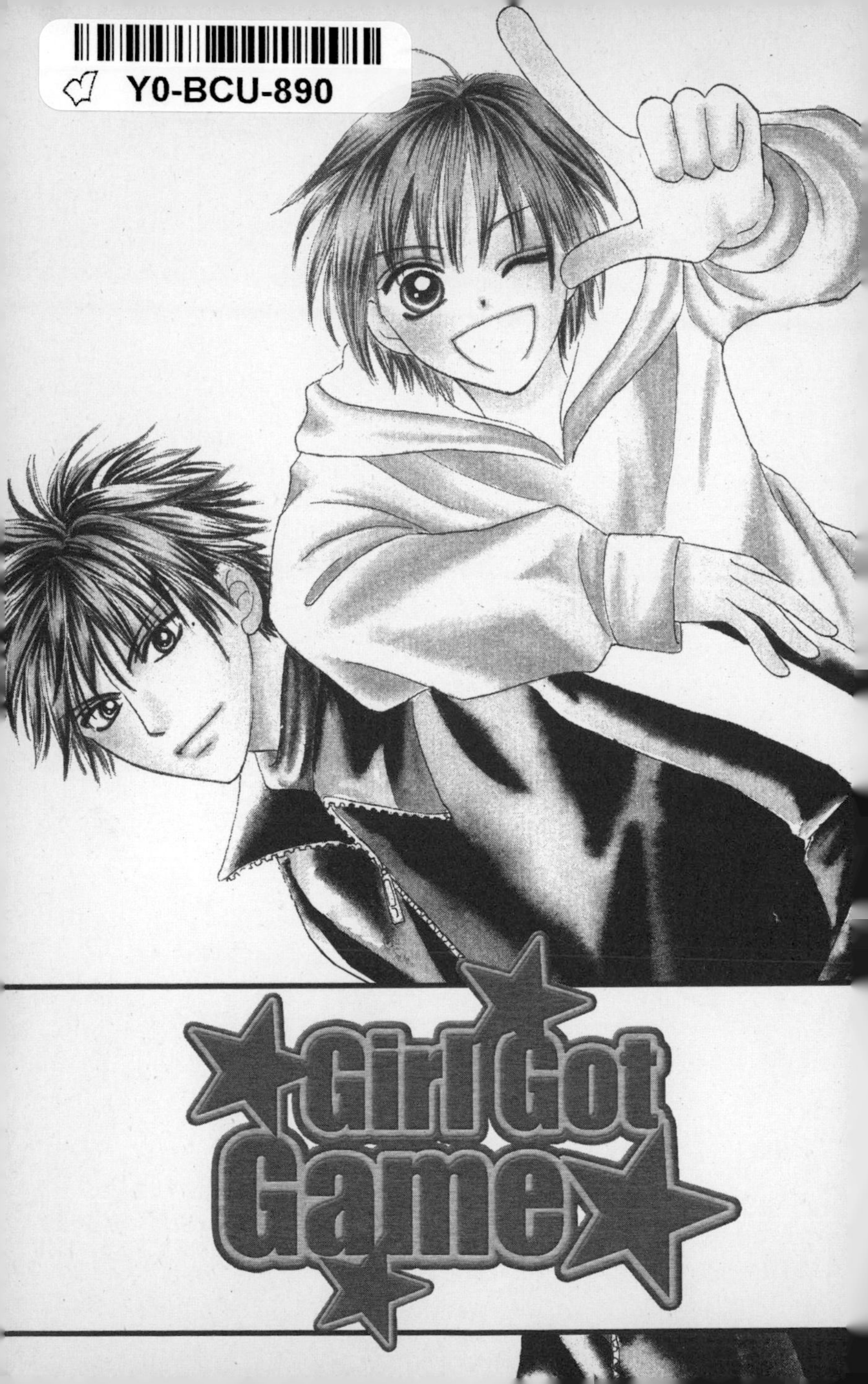

Girl Got Game

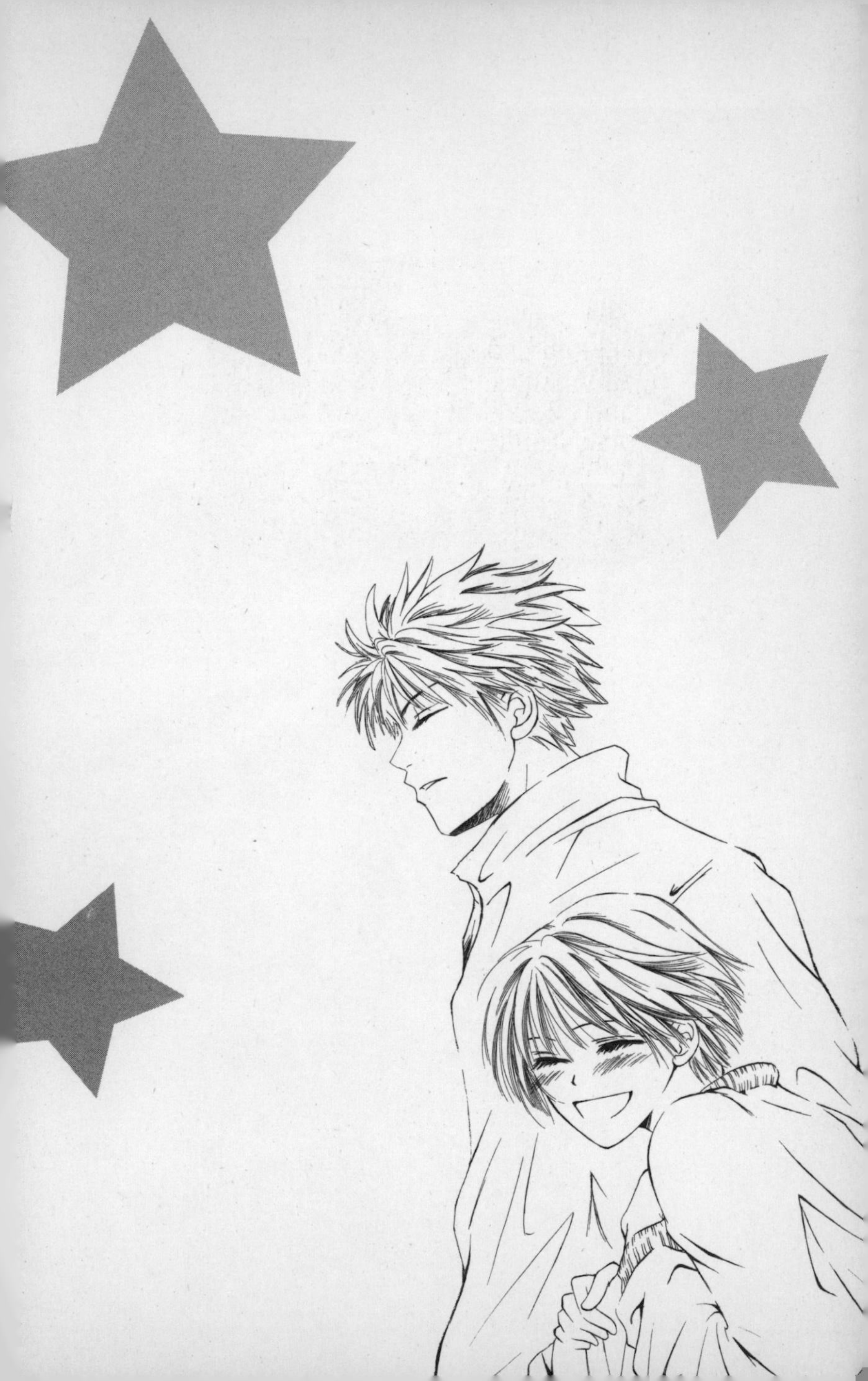

Girl Got Game

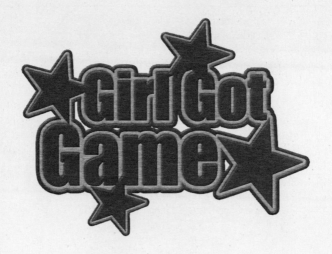

Girl Got Game Vol. 10
created by Shizuru Seino

Translation - Louie Kawamoto
English Adaptation - Kelly Sue DeConnick
Copy Editor - Suzanne Waldman
Retouch and Lettering - Benchcomix
Production Artist - Gloria Wu
Cover Artist - Al-Insan Lashley

Editor - Rob Tokar
Digital Imaging Manager - Chris Buford
Production Managers - Jennifer Miller and Mutsumi Miyazaki
Managing Editor - Jill Freshney
VP of Production - Ron Klamert
Publisher and E.I.C. - Mike Kiley
President and C.O.O. - John Parker
C.E.O. - Stuart Levy

A  Manga

TOKYOPOP Inc.
5900 Wilshire Blvd. Suite 2000
Los Angeles, CA 90036

E-mail: info@TOKYOPOP.com
Come visit us online at www.TOKYOPOP.com

ISBN: 1-59182-989-5

First TOKYOPOP printing: August 2005
10 9 8 7 6 5 4 3 2 1
Printed in the USA

Girl Got Game

by Shizuru Seino
Volume 10

HAMBURG // LONDON // LOS ANGELES // TOKYO

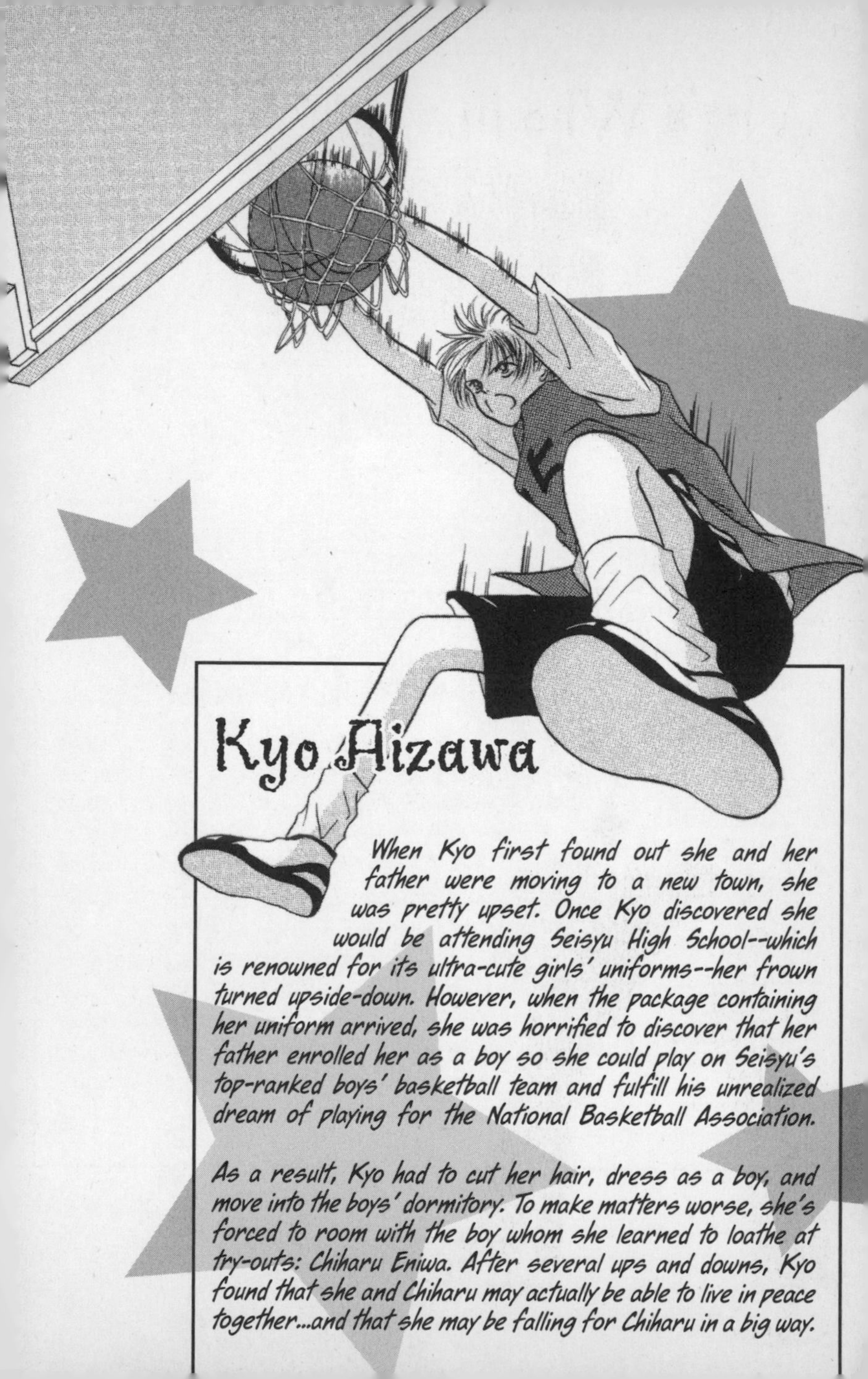

Kyo Aizawa

When Kyo first found out she and her father were moving to a new town, she was pretty upset. Once Kyo discovered she would be attending Seisyu High School--which is renowned for its ultra-cute girls' uniforms--her frown turned upside-down. However, when the package containing her uniform arrived, she was horrified to discover that her father enrolled her as a boy so she could play on Seisyu's top-ranked boys' basketball team and fulfill his unrealized dream of playing for the National Basketball Association.

As a result, Kyo had to cut her hair, dress as a boy, and move into the boys' dormitory. To make matters worse, she's forced to room with the boy whom she learned to loathe at try-outs: Chiharu Eniwa. After several ups and downs, Kyo found that she and Chiharu may actually be able to live in peace together...and that she may be falling for Chiharu in a big way.

Who's Who in...

★Girl Got Game★

Chiharu Eniwa

Kyo's teammate on the court and roommate in the dorms, Chiharu has a well-deserved reputation as a hard-nosed tough guy. Chiharu was at his most abrasive during his first meeting with Kyo, but his taunts and jibes drove Kyo to really show her best moves at tryouts.

Though a private person, Chiharu has opened up to Kyo about some of the problems that have plagued him. Kyo has made several attempts to aid Chiharu who has shown his appreciation by taking care of Kyo in return.

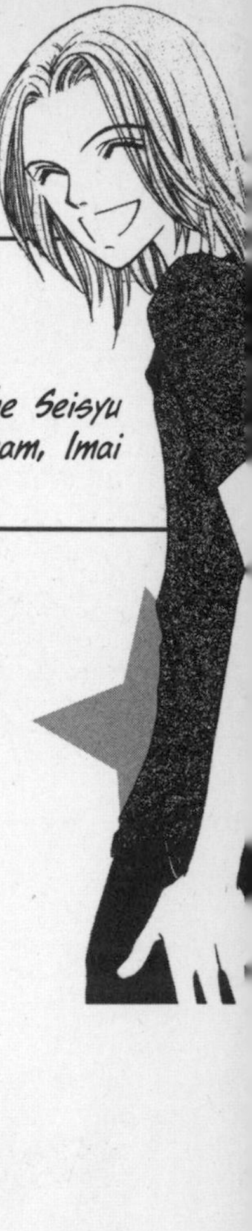

Hisashi Imai

The ever-friendly captain of the Seisyu High School boys' basketball team, Imai lives in room 310.

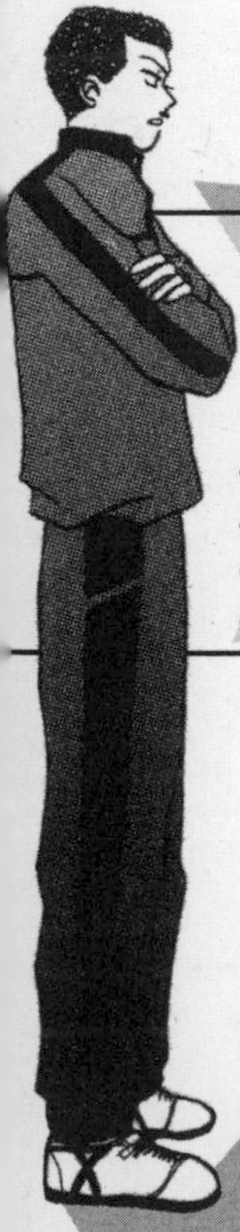

Coach

The coach of the Seisyu High School boys' basketball team comes complete with the wild mood swings and irritability that are essential to anyone working with teen athletes.

Mr. Aizawa

Kyo's father was once a great basketball player who aspired to play for the NBA. Unfortunately, a torn achilles tendon ended his career before it even started. Despite his disappointment, he passed his love of the game--and his moves--to Kyo.

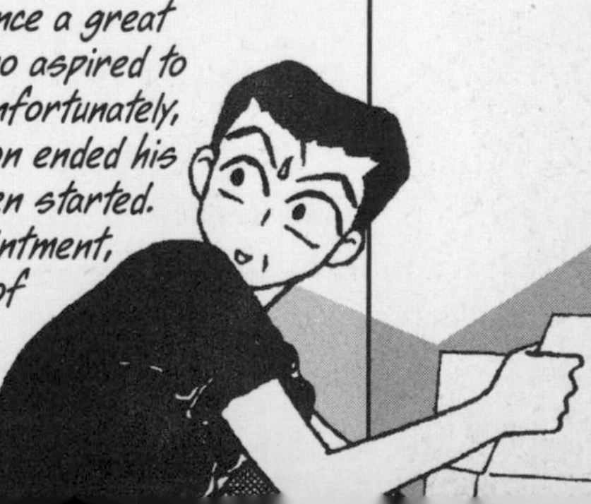

HI, I'M AYAHA. I'M THE HOUSE MOM.

Ayaha

"House Mom" of the Seisyu High School boys' dormitory, Ayaha was a great basketball player when she was a student. Unfortunately, a knee injury ended her playing career prematurely.

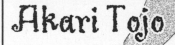

Akari Tojo

Manager of the Seisyu High School boys' basketball team.

Shinji Hamaya

A fellow freshman on the Seisyu High School boys' basketball team.

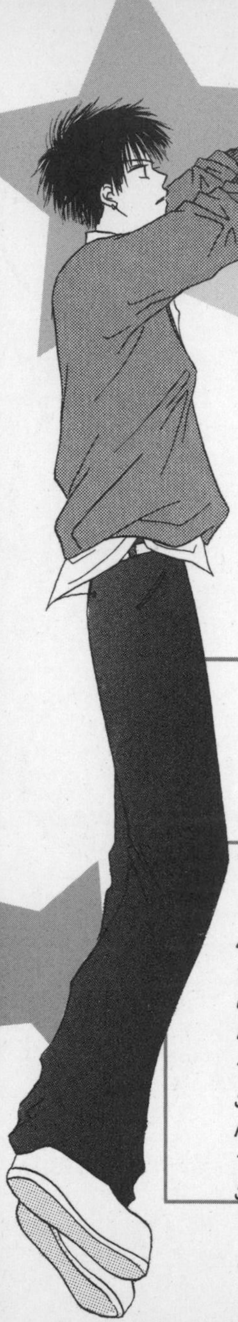

Kensuke Yura

A former member of the Seisyu High boys' basketball team. Yura thought Kyo was a girl when they first met. Though he had a hard time believing her, they still hit it off as friends. When Yura's dark side took over and he kidnapped Kyo, she confessed that she had lied about being a boy. Since Kyo's confession (and Yura's recovery), Yura has expressed an interest in dating her!

Tsuyaka Himejima

A girl who transferred to Seisyu High School so that she could play basketball with Kyo again. Despite Kyo's desire to remain on the boys' team, Tsuyaka still tried to force Kyo onto the girls' basketball team. When her plan failed, Tsuyaka tore Kyo's shirt open, revealing Kyo's gender to Chiharu.

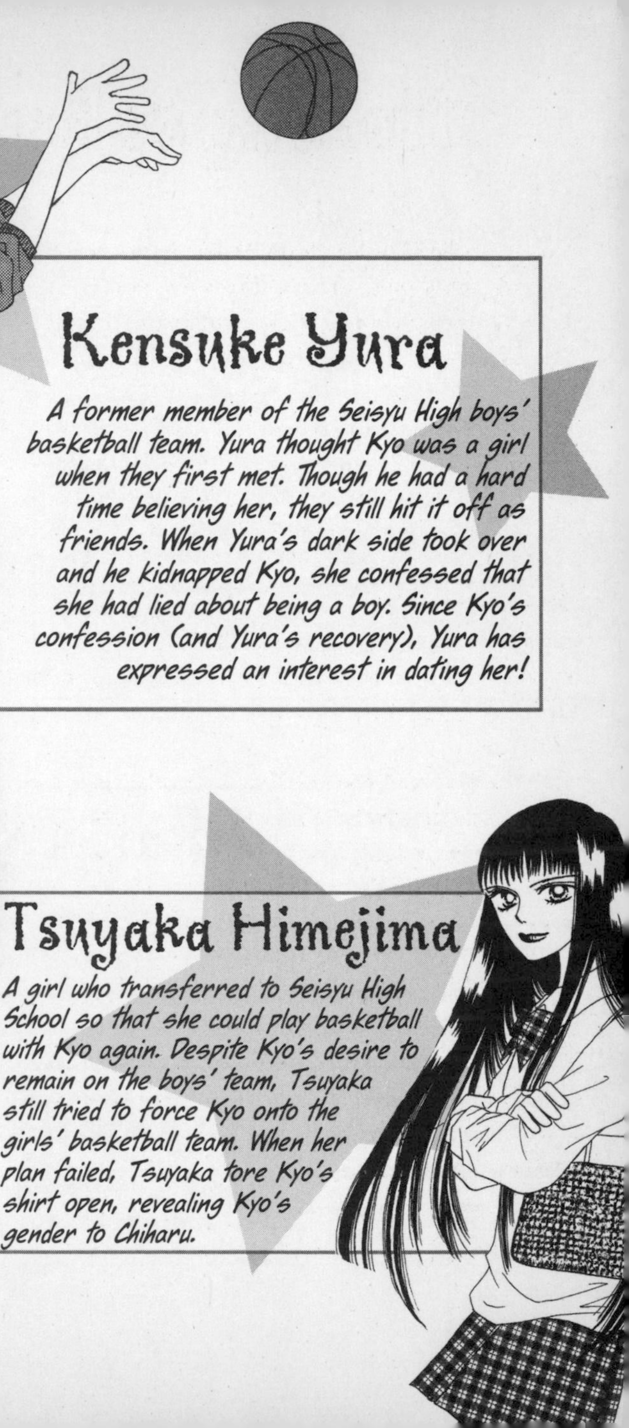

The Story So Far

Kyo Aizawa

Chiharu Eniwa

Hisashi Imai

Shinji Hamaya

Some people will do anything to realize their dreams...even if it means disguising a girl as a boy so she can play on a famous boys' basketball team. If you don't believe it, just imagine how Kyo Aizawa feels--her dad's the one who cooked up this crazy scheme!

Kyo's father was once a great basketball player who aspired to play for the NBA. Unfortunately, an injury ended his career before it even started. Despite his disappointment, he passed his love of the game--and his moves--to his daughter.

Kyo wanted to date a boy, not become one, and she was not happy about her father's kooky plan...until she met Chiharu Eniwa, the boy who was to be her teammate on the court...and her roommate in the dorms!

As luck would have it, Kyo and Chiharu got on each other's nerves right from the start, but Kyo's attempts to get past Chiharu's gruff, sullen exterior eventually made the two of them friends. In turn, Chiharu's thoughtful kindness also swept Kyo off her feet...and she wondered if she might have some serious feelings for him.

Kyo and Chiharu's peaceful coexistence was cut painfully short when an old friend of Kyo's named Tsuyaka Himejima arrived on the scene. Tsuyaka knew Kyo from her previous school and transferred to Seisyu so they could play on the same team again. When Tsuyaka learned Kyo was masquerading as a boy, she concocted a scheme that would maintain Kyo's cover but still a llow Kyo to play on the girls' basketball team.

Despite Kyo's protestations, Tsuyaka challenged Chiharu to a one-on-one game of hoops with Kyo as the prize. Surprised by Tsuyaka's moves, Chiharu lost and Kyo was forced to leave the boy's team and join the girls'. Determined to win Kyo back, Chiharu used Kyo's knowledge of Tsuyaka's style to eventually defeat Tsuyaka fair and square.

Ever the sore loser, Tsuyaka tore open Kyo's shirt in front of Chiharu, revealing Kyo's breasts! Though Chiharu didn't tell Kyo's secret, he did tell Kyo that they couldn't room together anymore. Distraught, Kyo left the dorm and tried to return home. Unfortunately, her father had gone to America for the N.B.A. season and she had to spend a night in a cardboard box in the park. Luckily, Chiharu went looking for Kyo just as Kyo realized she had to return to the dorm and the two quickly reconciled.

Just as life seemed like it was going to return to "normal," Kyo literally stumbled across Kensuke Yura on her way to practice. Yura, it turns out, is one of the best players on the Seisyu High basketball team, but he hadn't shown up for practice or any games since before Kyo became a member. After getting to know the friendless young man, Kyo eventually managed to form a bond of trust with Yura and bring him back to the team...though she had to reveal her secret to him in the process.

Later, Yura discovered that his friendship with Kyo made Chiharu jealous...and Yura's questions about Chiharu's feelings for Kyo certainly didn't help. To further complicate things, while Kyo was complaining about Chiharu to Yura, Yura expressed an interest in dating her. Kyo's confusion turned to dismay when she discovered that the entire team was going away for basketball boot camp...and she was assigned to room with Chiharu, Hamaya, and Yura!

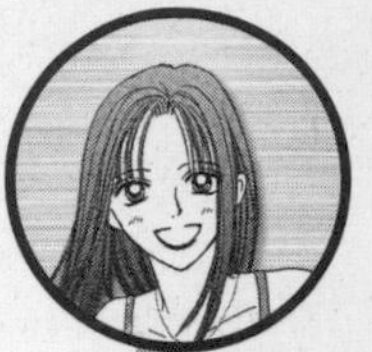

Ayaha

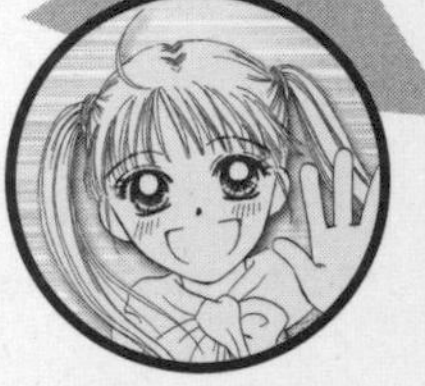

Akari Tojo

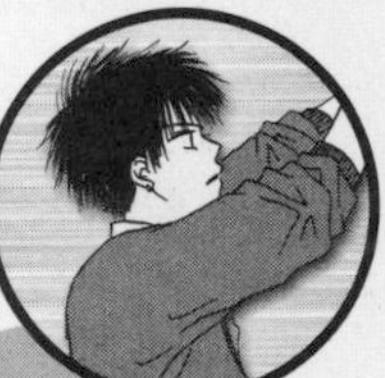

Kensuke Yura

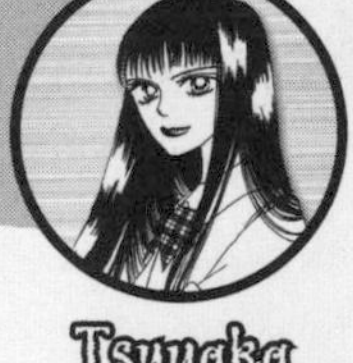

Tsuyaka Himejima

At the basketball boot camp, team captain Hisashi Imai made plenty of time for the ever-popular pastime of mushroom gathering, but Kyo, Chiharu and Hamaya accidentally gathered and ingested the kind of mushrooms that mess with your mind! Hamaya ended up naked, but Chiharu and Kyo were even more revealing as they confessed their love for each other. As it turned out, Yura was only coming on to Kyo to make Chiharu jealous, but the young couple was unsure of where their relationship should go and how it would get there.

In order to have an actual date, Kyo told Chiharu to meet her at an off-campus location... where he didn't even recognize her because she was dressed and made-up as a girl.

Before their first date could get started, they bumped into their perpetually pervy teammate Hamaya. As a cover, they told Hamaya that Kyo was actually Chiharu's sister Kyoko. When Hamaya wouldn't stop hitting on Kyo/Kyoko, Chiharu phoned Imai to get some help. Imai brought Tsuyaka with him and Tsuyaka saw through Kyo's disguise. Rather than expose Kyo, Tsuyaka used her commanding personality and karaoke to try to get Chiharu and Kyo/Kyoko to kiss.

Though that plan went somewhat awry, Chiharu and Kyo planned another date. Before they could go on the date, Kyo's true gender was exposed to the entire team and she ran away in fear and shame. After a week of hiding, Kyo returned to explain herself and proposed to earn her way back onto the team by challenging the entire group to face her on the court.

Chiharu thought the idea was crazy, but Imai approved it. After spreading out on the court, Kyo managed to make it past almost every member of the team, including Chiharu and Yura. The only one remaining is team captain Imai himself... and he's ready to play his best!

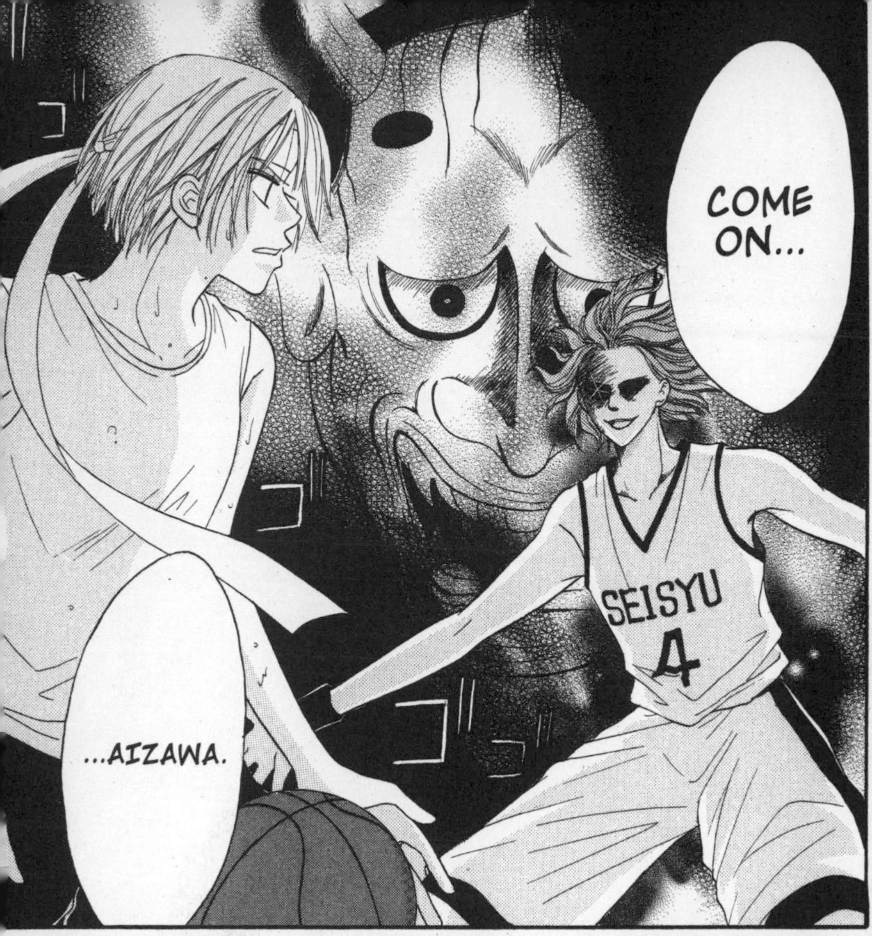
COME ON...
...AIZAWA.

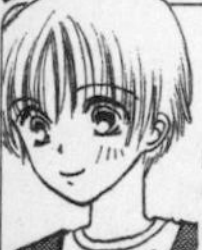

KYO AIZAWA
To please her father, she is forced to disguise herself as a guy and attend Seisyu High, a school famous for its men's basketball team.

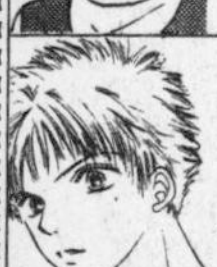

CHIHARU ENIWA
Seisyu High's best freshman player and Kyo's roommate. Kind of obnoxious.

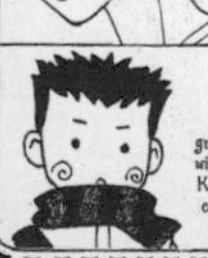

SHINJI HAMAYA
The oddball of the group, poor HAMAYA witnessed the scene where KYO and CHIHARU confessed their feelings for one another.

Our story so far...

KYO AIZAWA transferred to Seisyu High and dressed like a guy in order to join the men's basketball team and realize her father's dreams.

* She and her roommate, CHIHARU, managed to overcome personality conflicts and attraction to finally make an uneasy peace.

* The peace only lasted until their teammates happened into the clubroom when KYO was changing--and they found out her secret!!

* KYO ran away and found a job in construction. CHIHARU and others searched for her tirelessly, CHIHARU especially. Something at the construction site touched KYO's heart and she decided to go back and face her team.

* KYO challenges all 24 teammates to successive one-on-one games. She had to cheat to do it, but she managed to beat 23 people, leaving team Captain, Imai-san as her final opponent!!

Girl Got Game

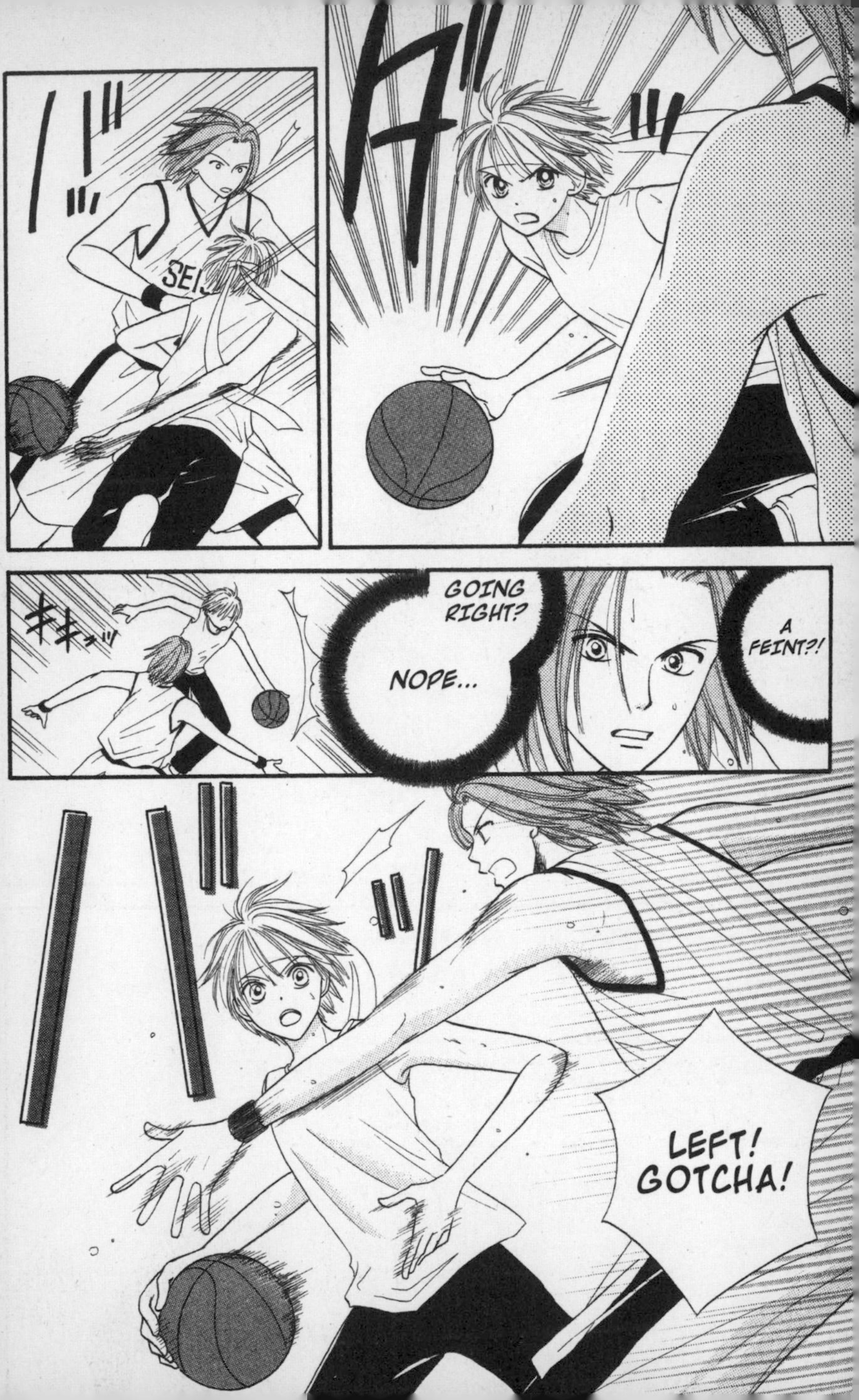
A FEINT?!
GOING RIGHT?
NOPE...
LEFT! GOTCHA!

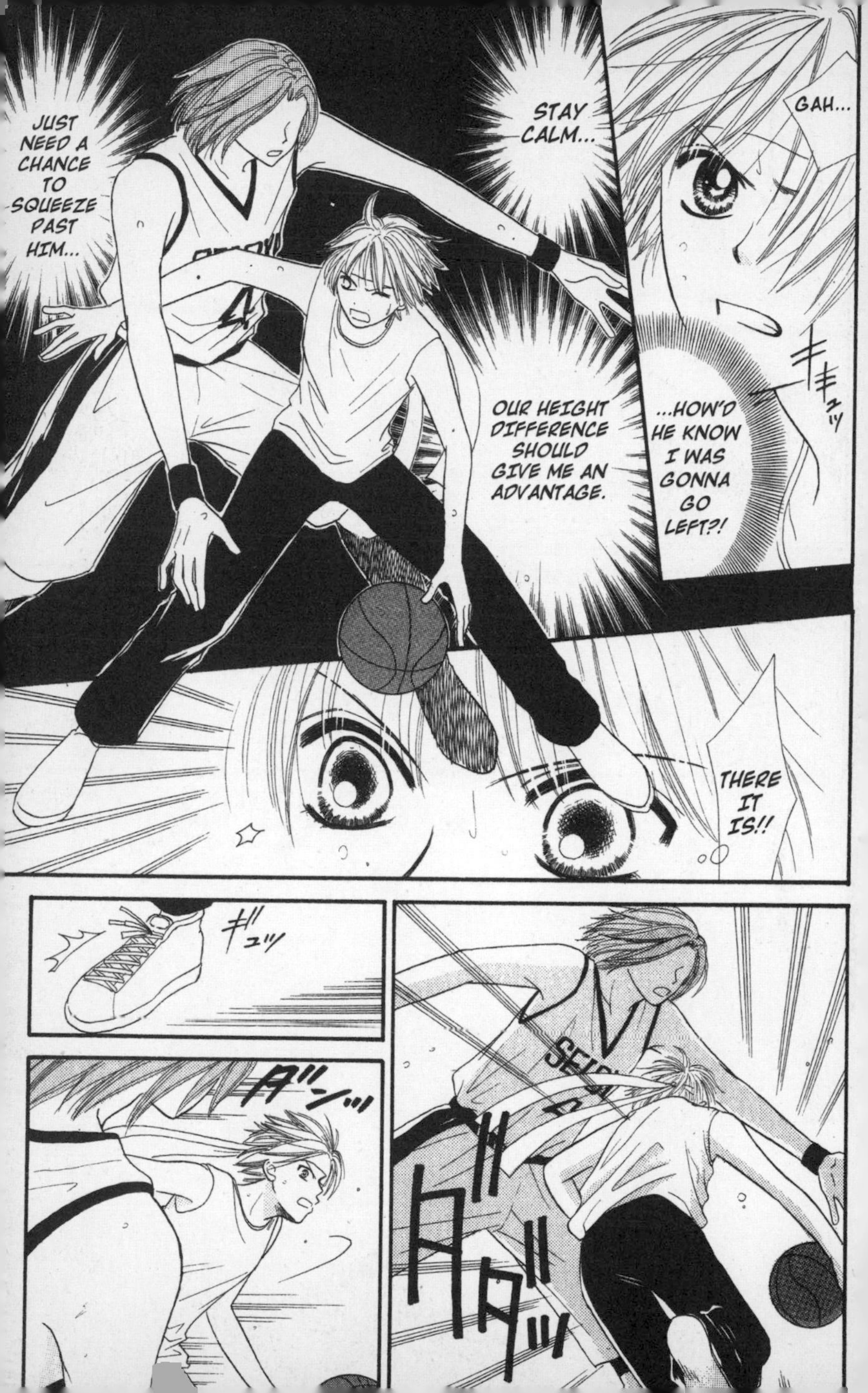
GAH...
...HOW'D HE KNOW I WAS GONNA GO LEFT?!
STAY CALM...
OUR HEIGHT DIFFERENCE SHOULD GIVE ME AN ADVANTAGE.
JUST NEED A CHANCE TO SQUEEZE PAST HIM...
THERE IT IS!!
ギュッ
ダンッ

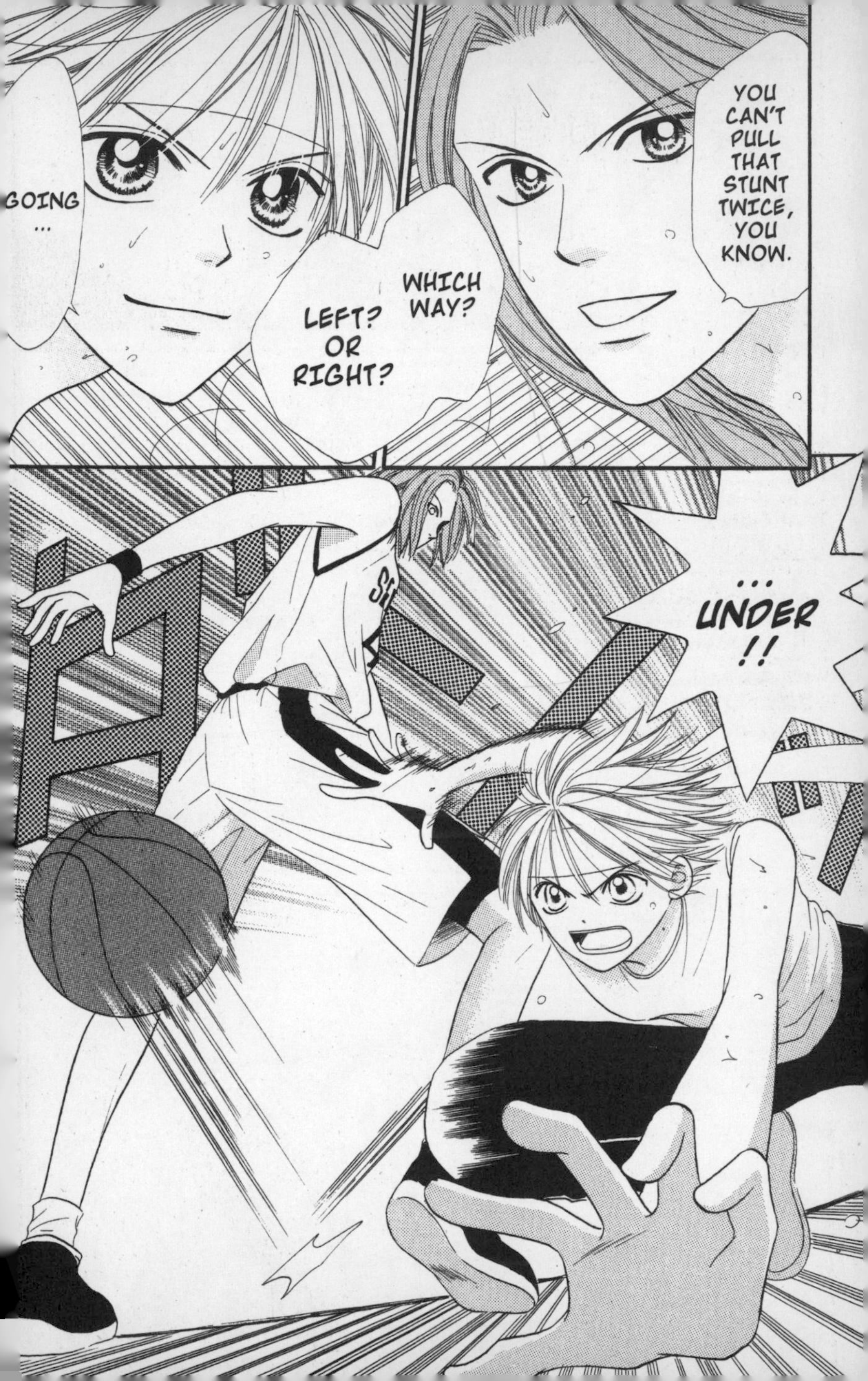
YOU CAN'T PULL THAT STUNT TWICE, YOU KNOW.
WHICH WAY?
LEFT? OR RIGHT?
GOING ...
... UNDER !!

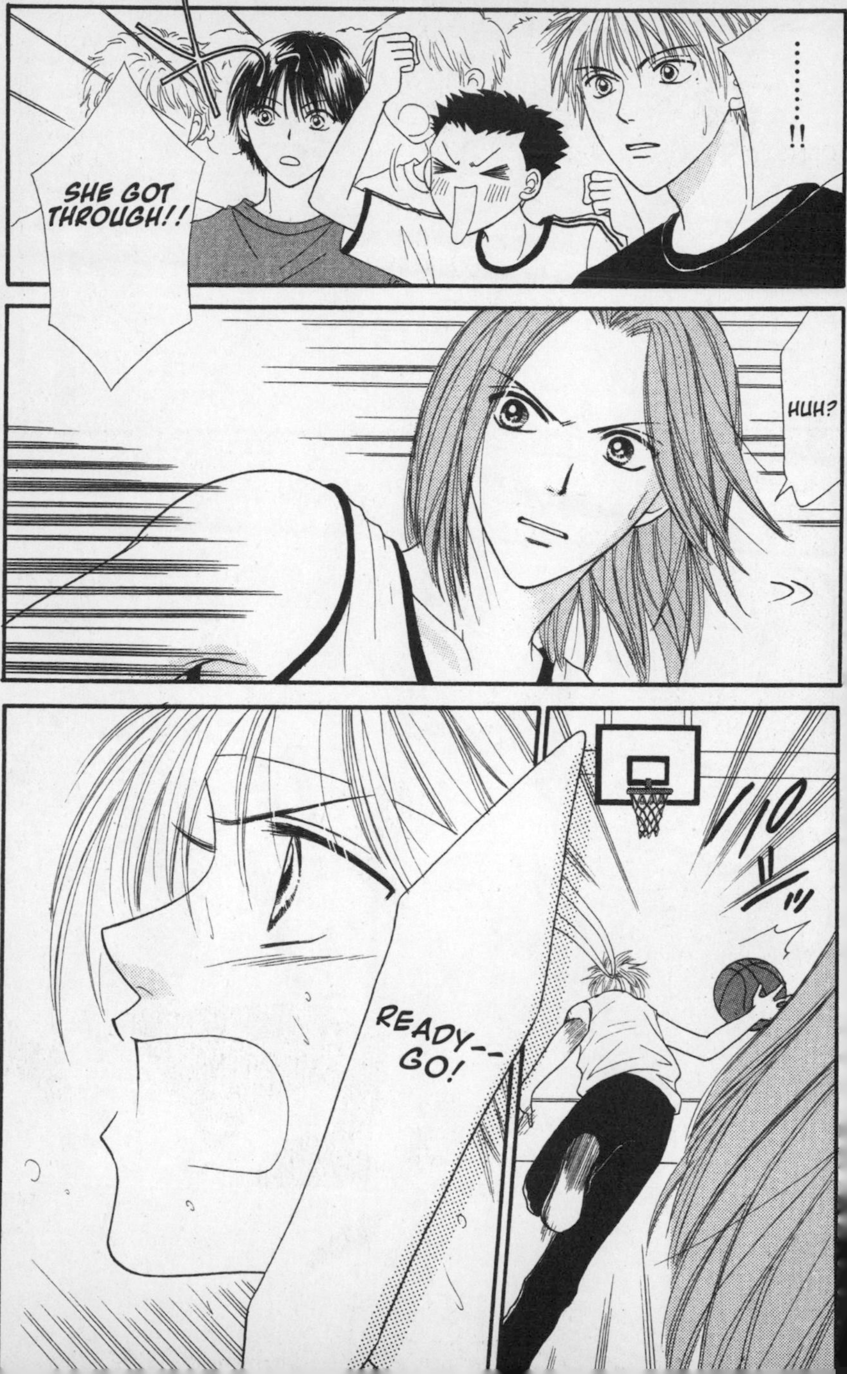
......!!
SHE GOT THROUGH!!
HUH?
READY-- GO!

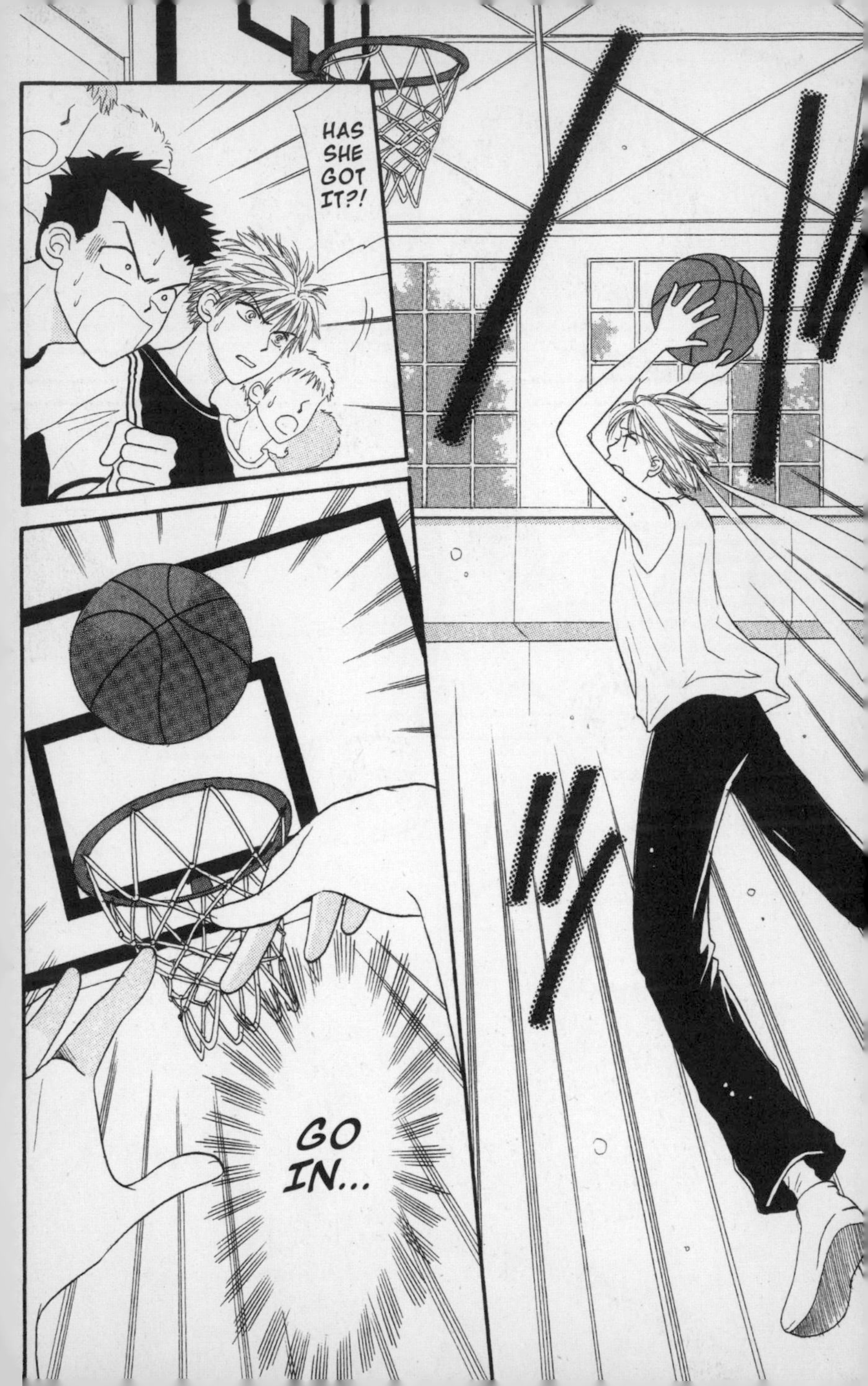
HAS SHE GOT IT?!
GO IN...

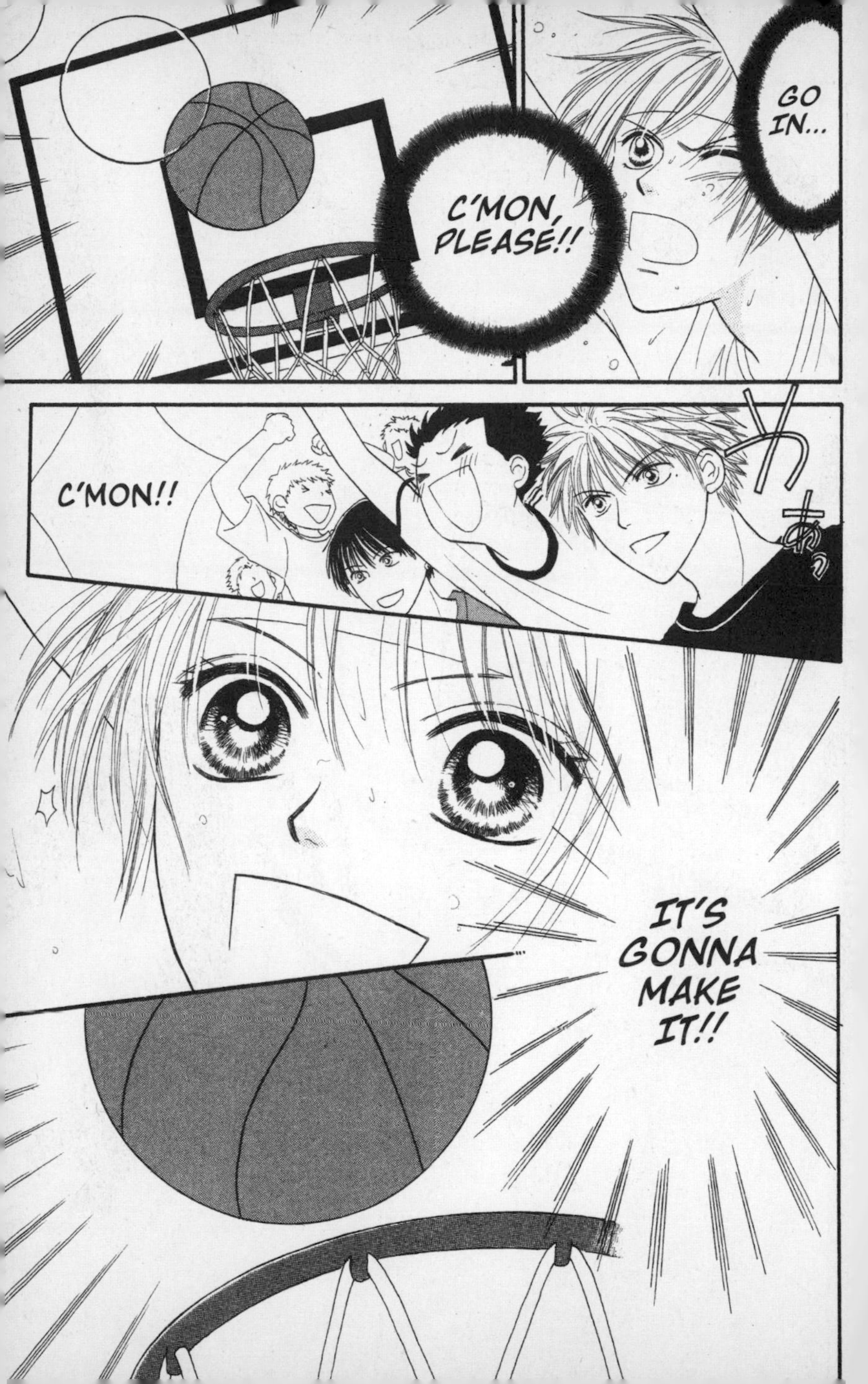
GO IN...
C'MON, PLEASE!!
C'MON!!
IT'S GONNA MAKE IT!!

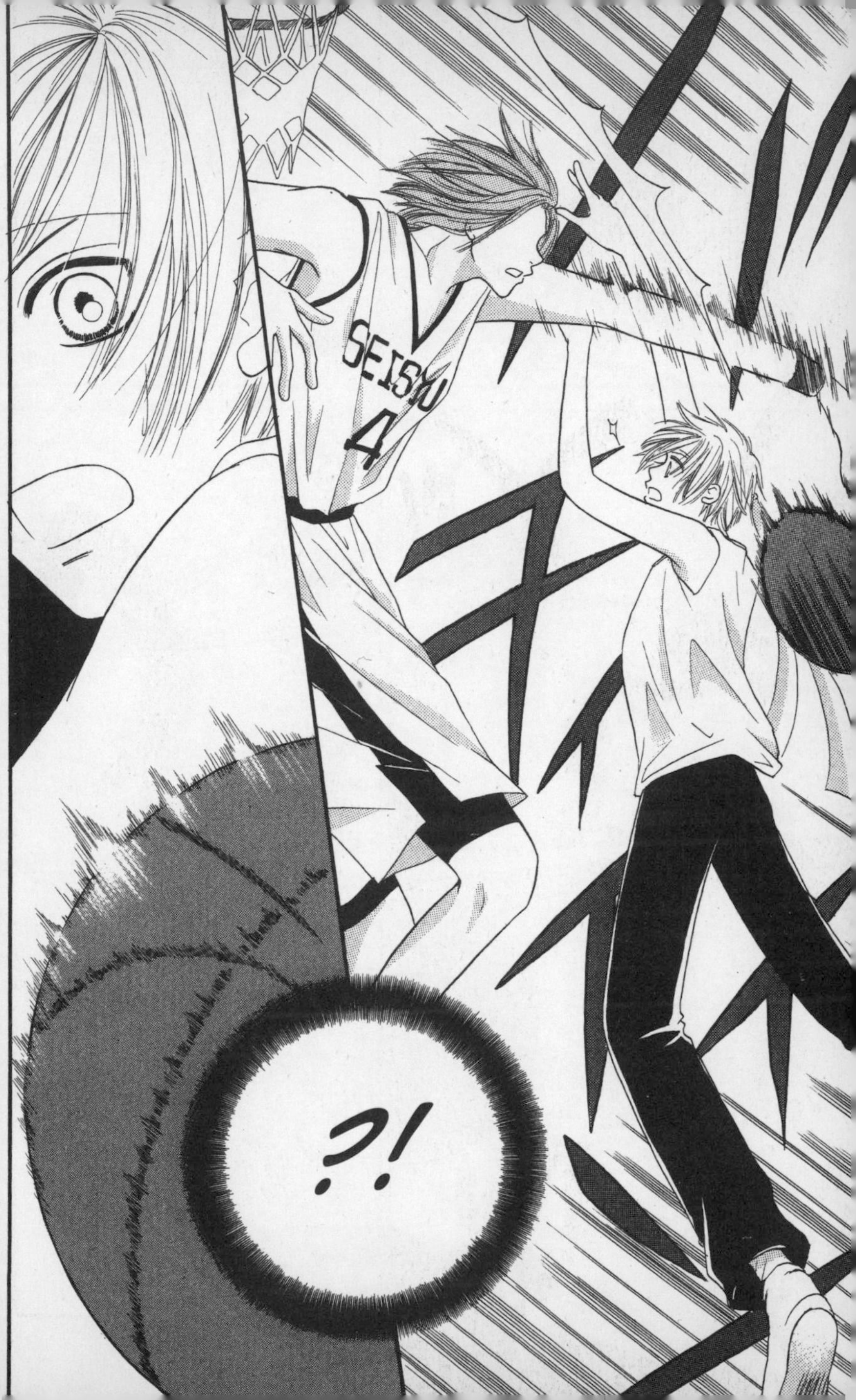
SEISYU
4
?!

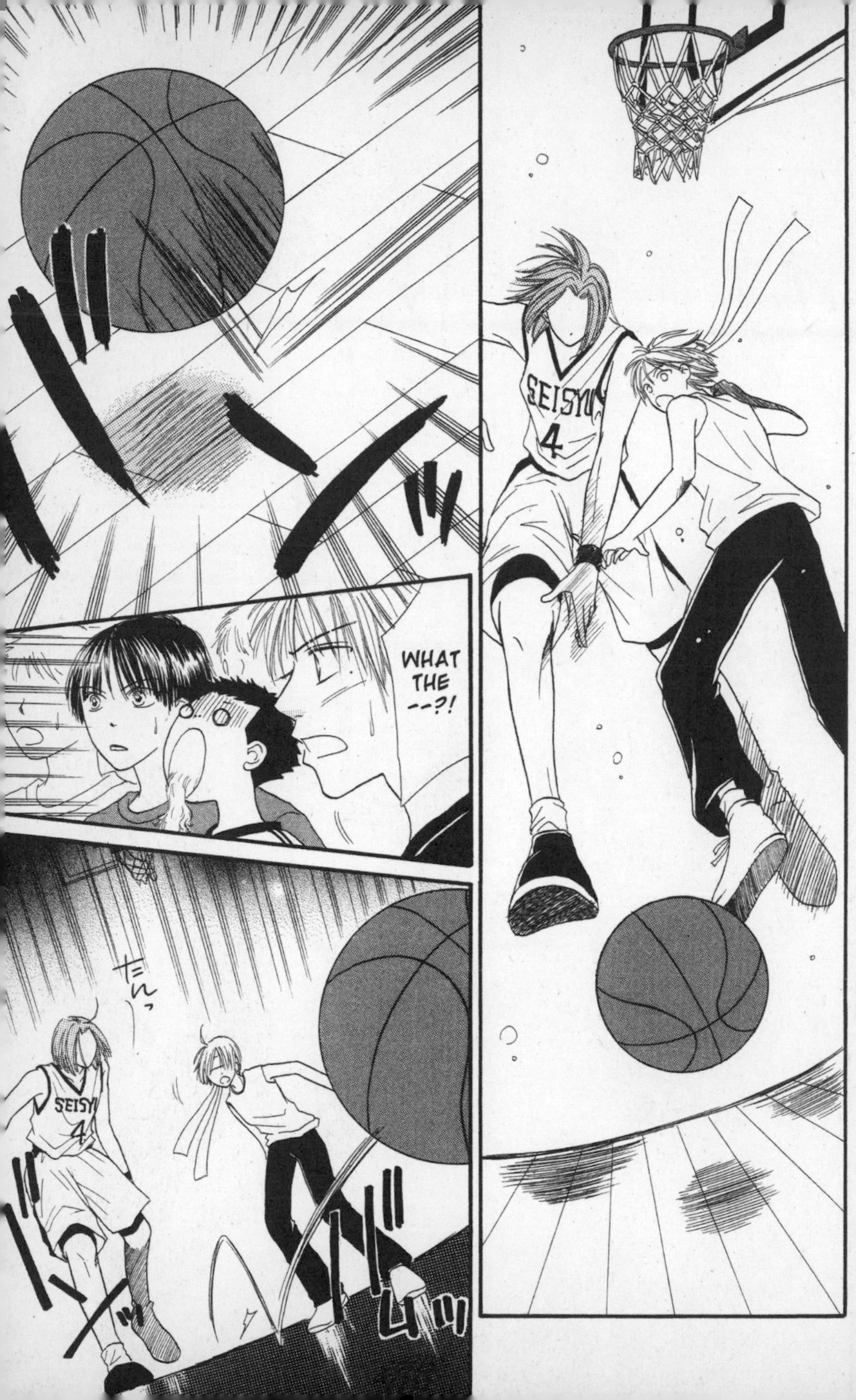
WHAT THE --?!
たんっ

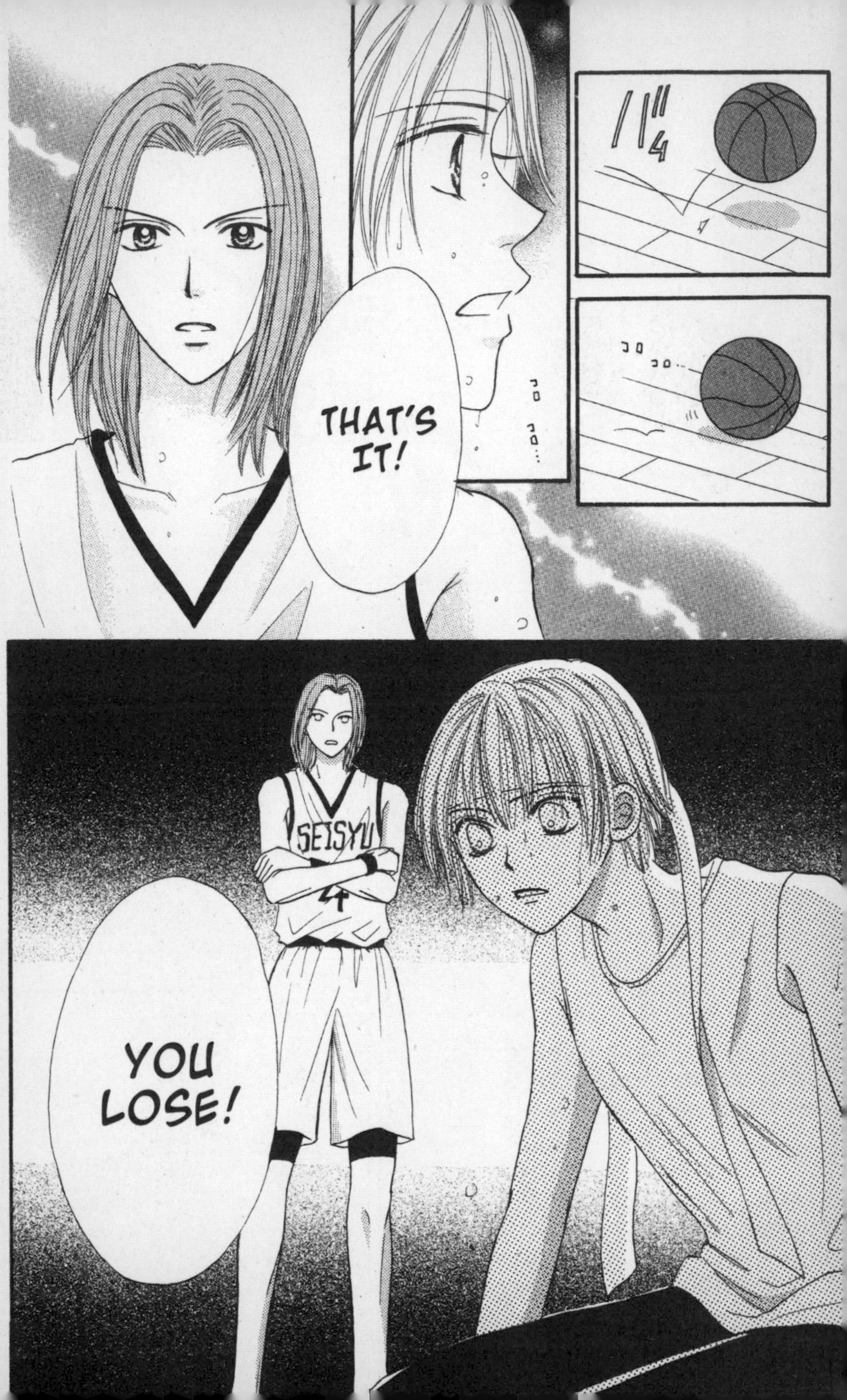
THAT'S IT!
YOU LOSE!

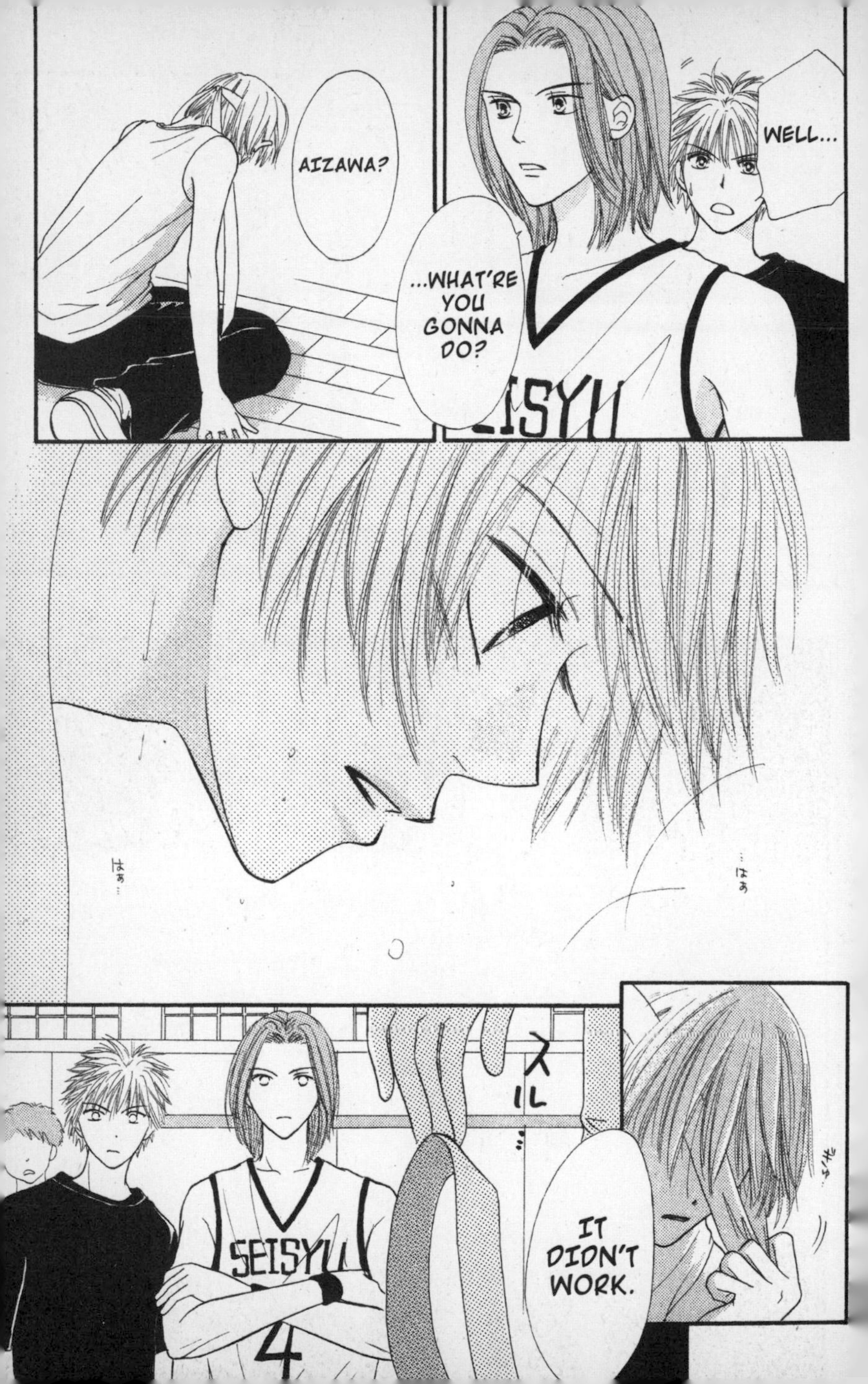
WELL...
...WHAT'RE YOU GONNA DO?
SEISYU
AIZAWA?
はぁ…
はぁ…
IT DIDN'T WORK.
スル
SEISYU
4

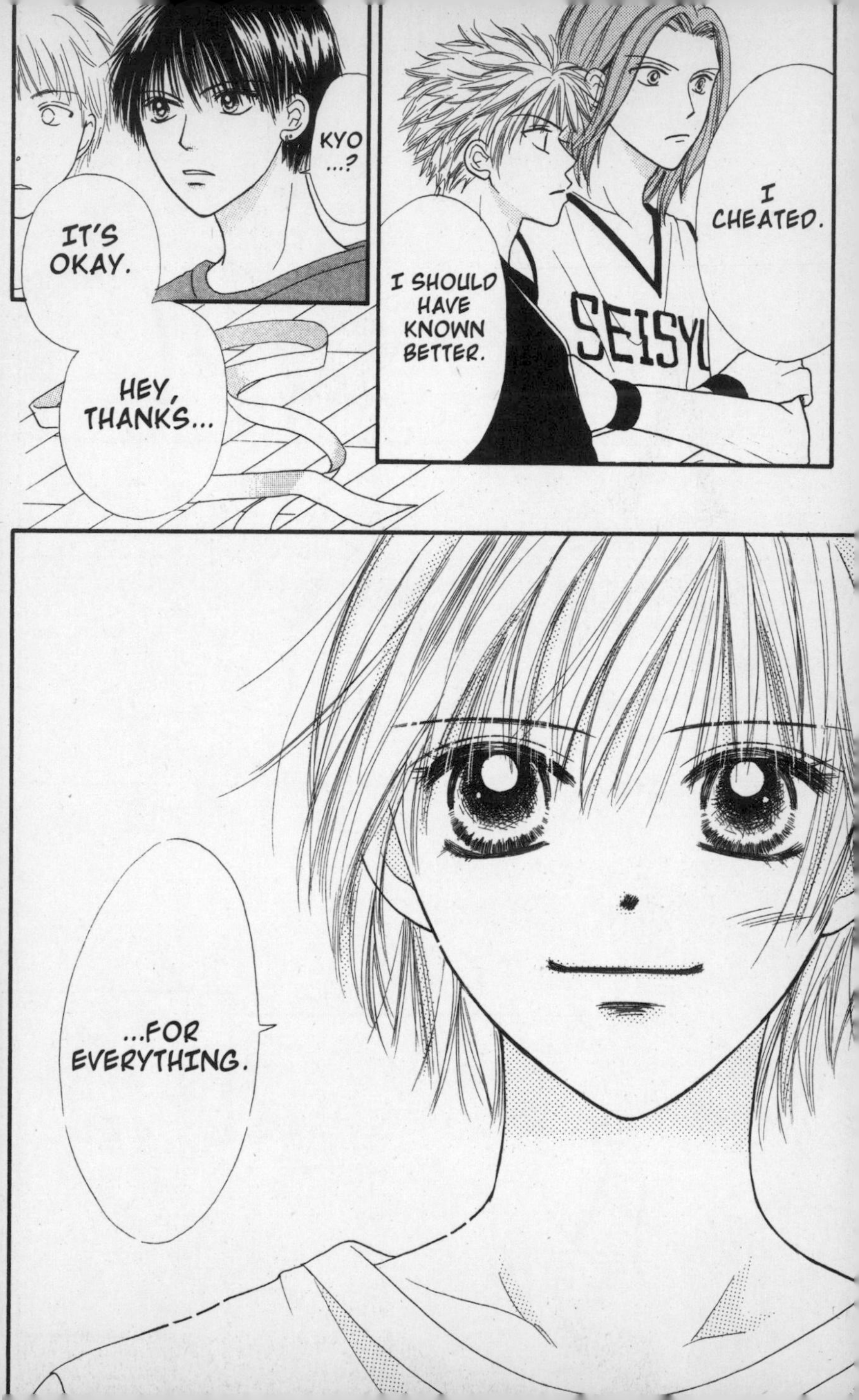
I CHEATED.
I SHOULD HAVE KNOWN BETTER.
KYO ...?
IT'S OKAY.
HEY, THANKS...
...FOR EVERYTHING.

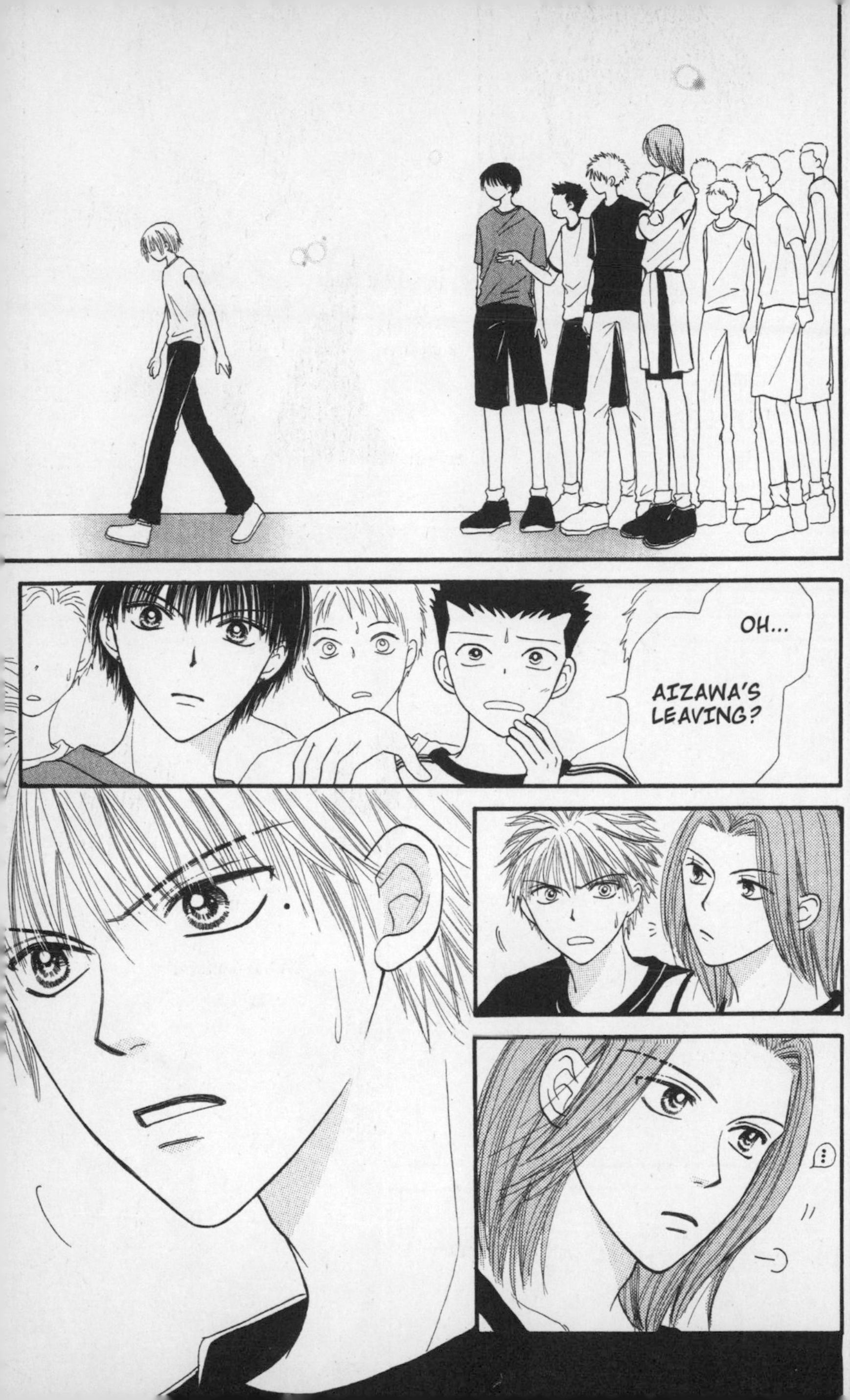
OH...
AIZAWA'S LEAVING?
...

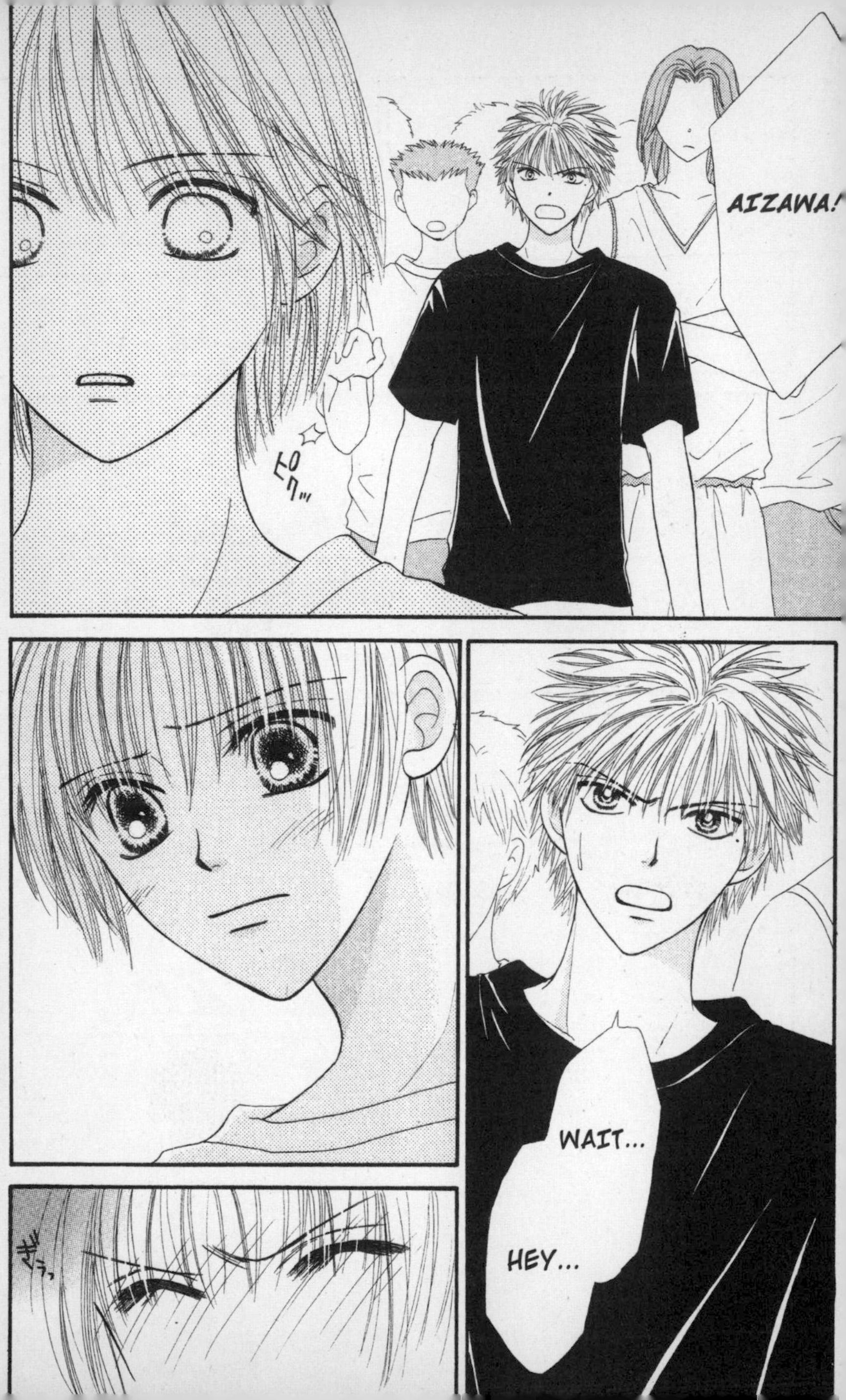
AIZAWA!
ピクッ
WAIT...
HEY...

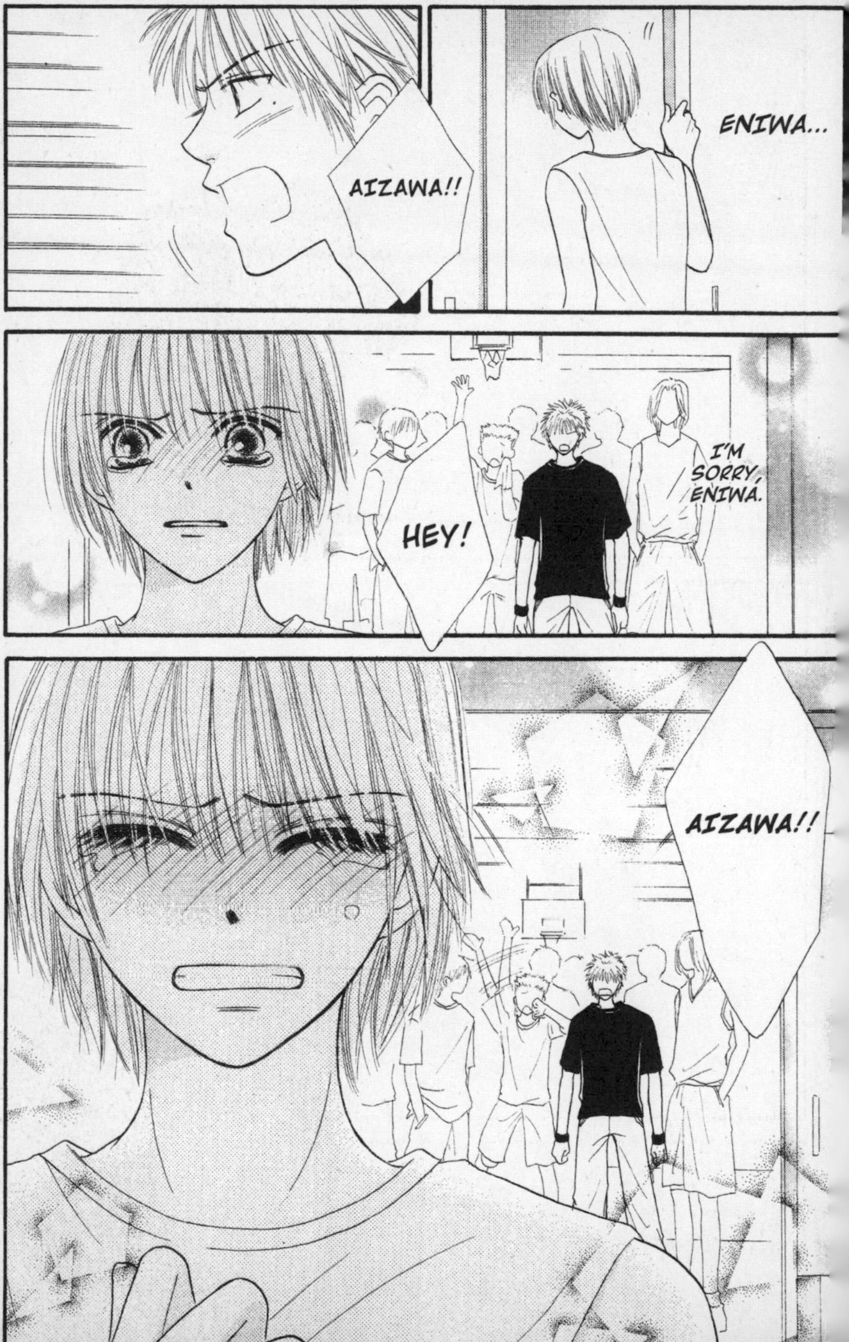
ENIWA...
AIZAWA!!
I'M SORRY, ENIWA.
HEY!
AIZAWA!!

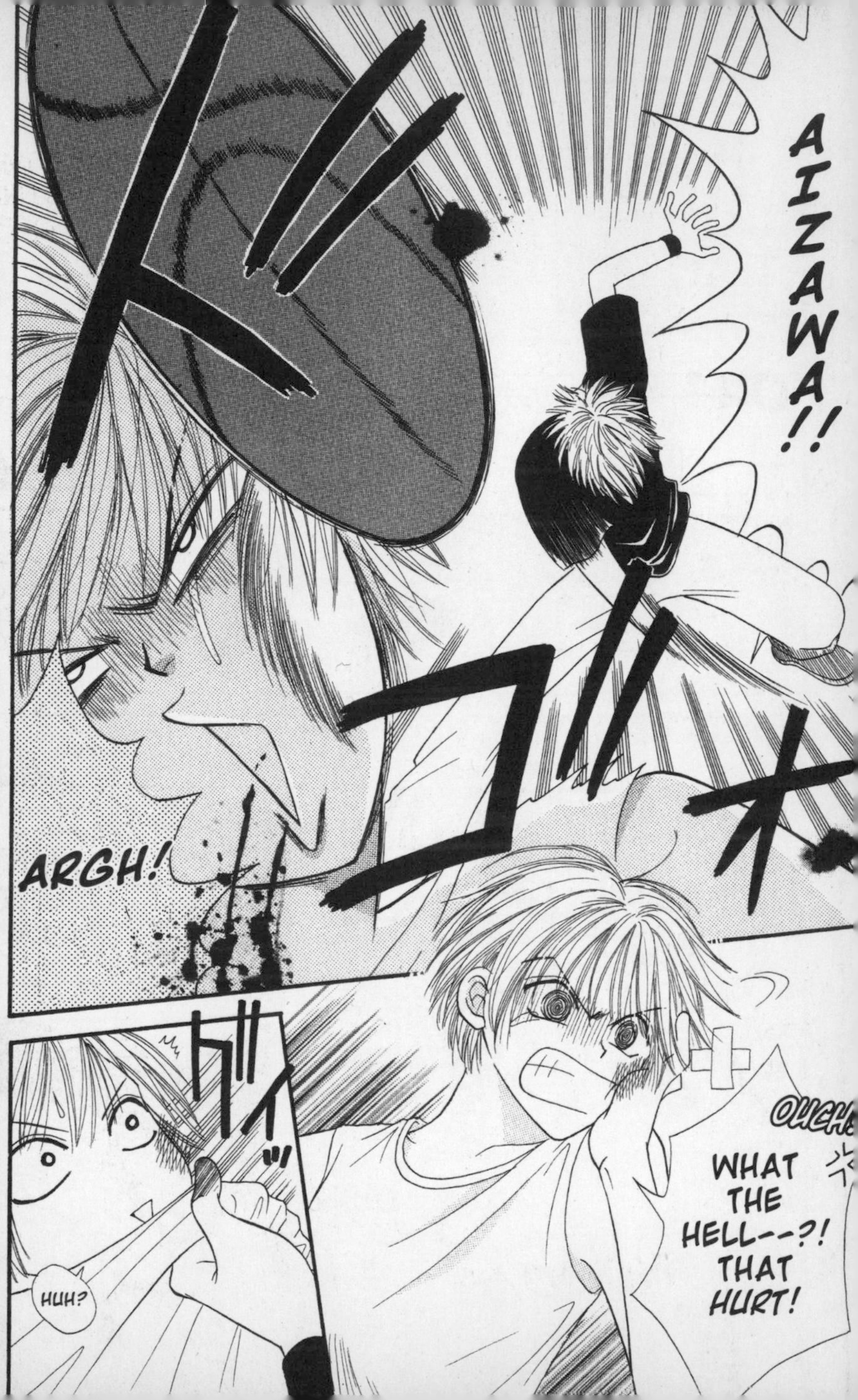
AIZAWA!!
ARGH!
OUCH
WHAT THE HELL--?! THAT HURT!
HUH?

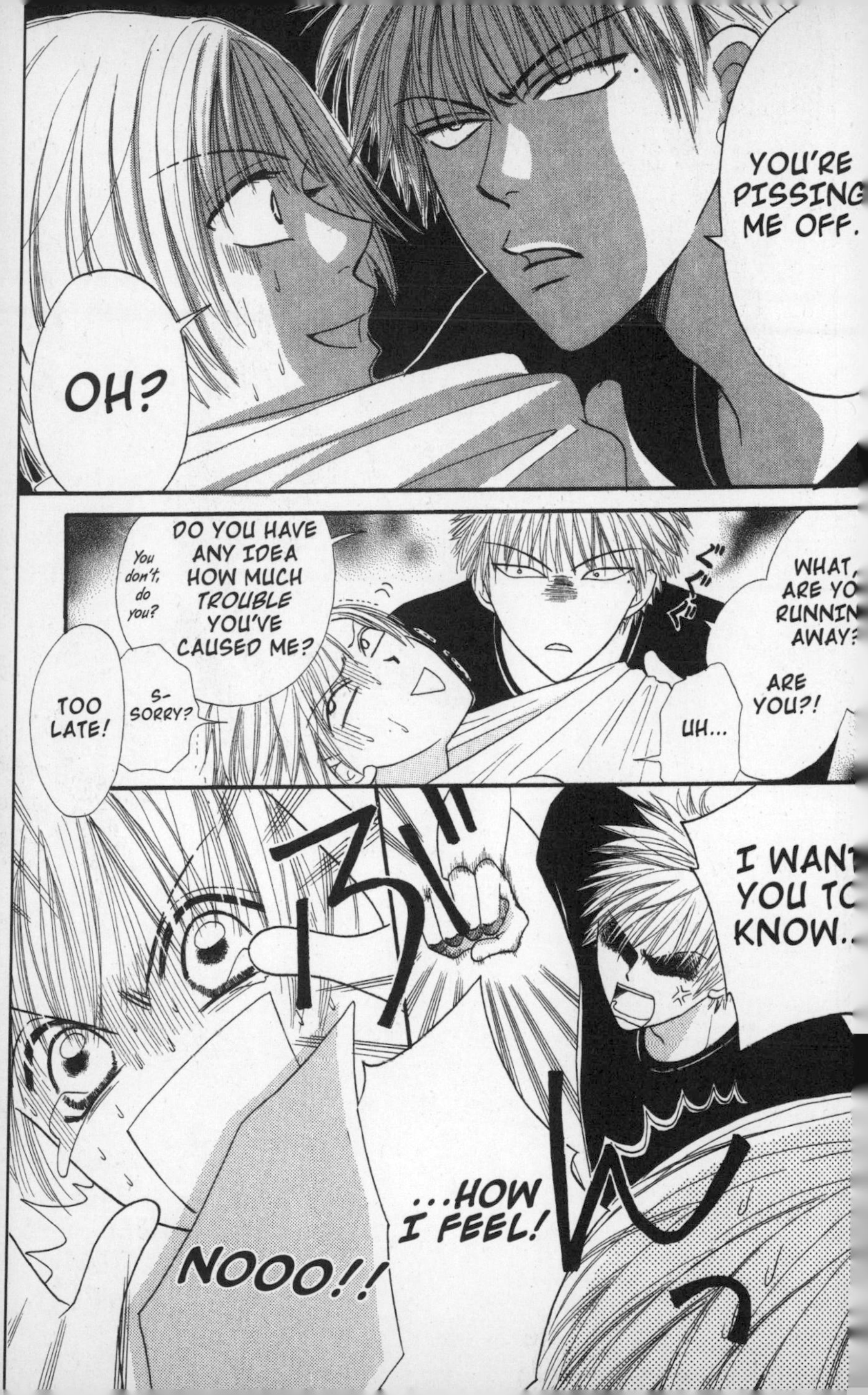
YOU'RE PISSING ME OFF.
OH?
WHAT, ARE YO RUNNIN AWAY?
ARE YOU?!
UH...
DO YOU HAVE ANY IDEA HOW MUCH TROUBLE YOU'VE CAUSED ME?
You don't, do you?
S-SORRY?
TOO LATE!
I WAN YOU T KNOW..
...HOW I FEEL!
NOOO!!

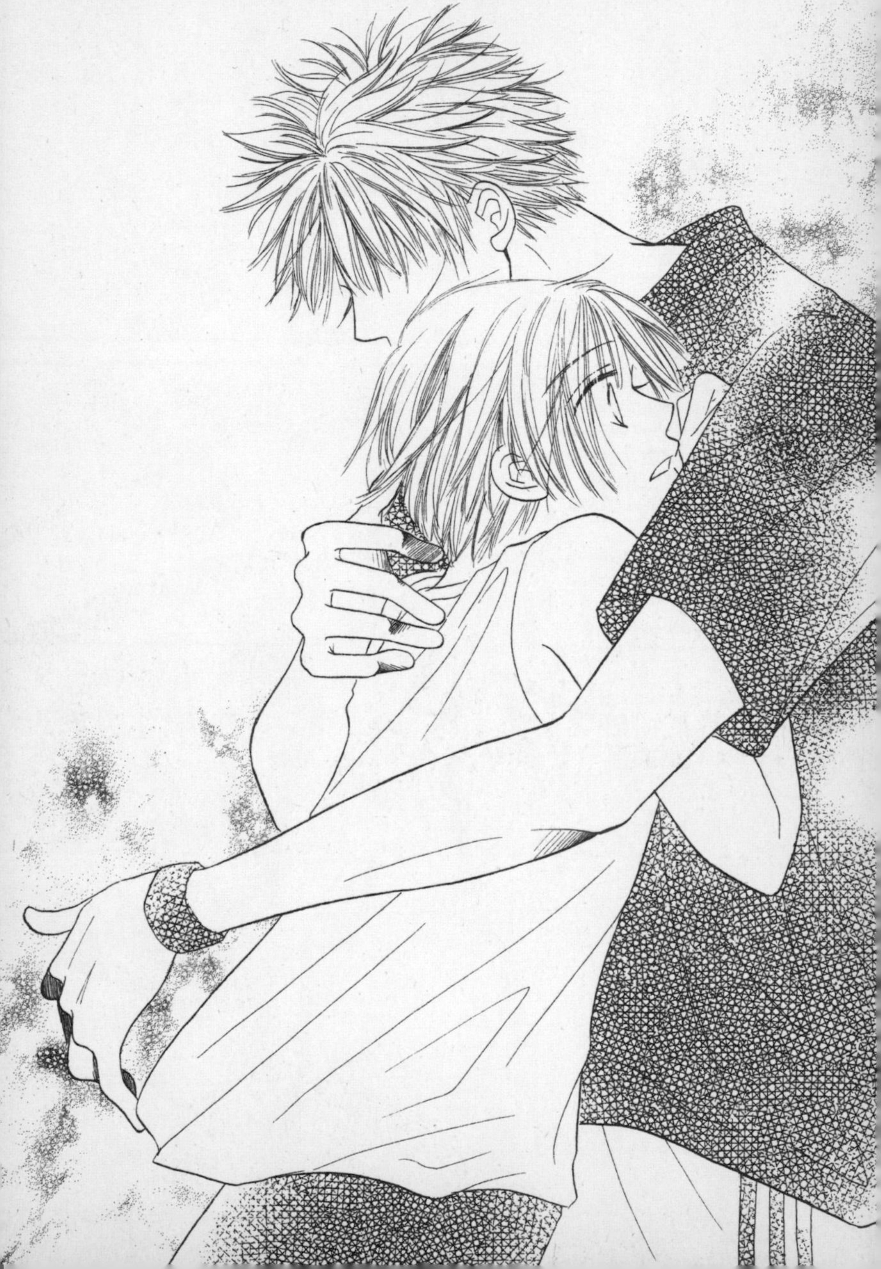

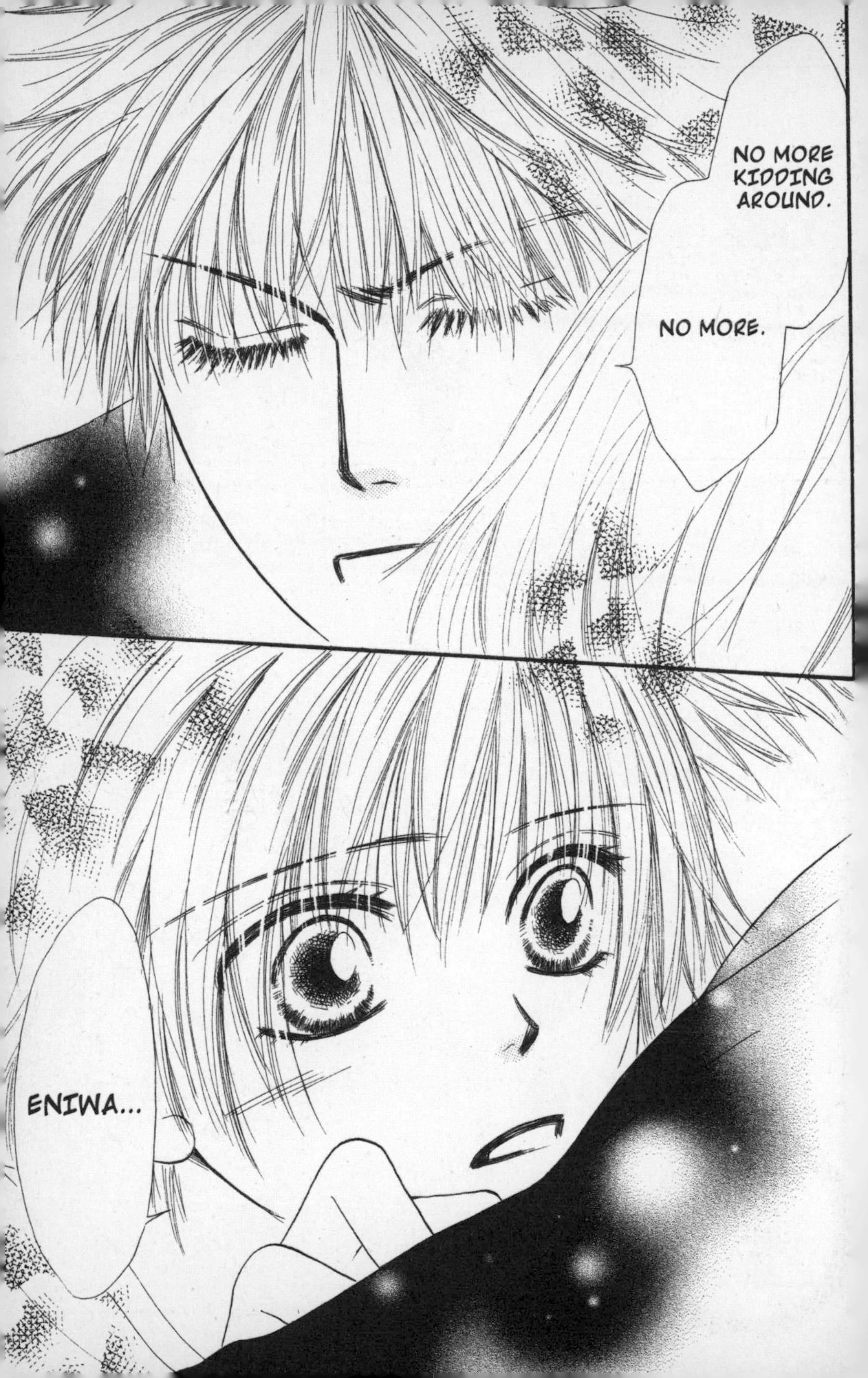
NO MORE KIDDING AROUND.
NO MORE.
ENIWA...

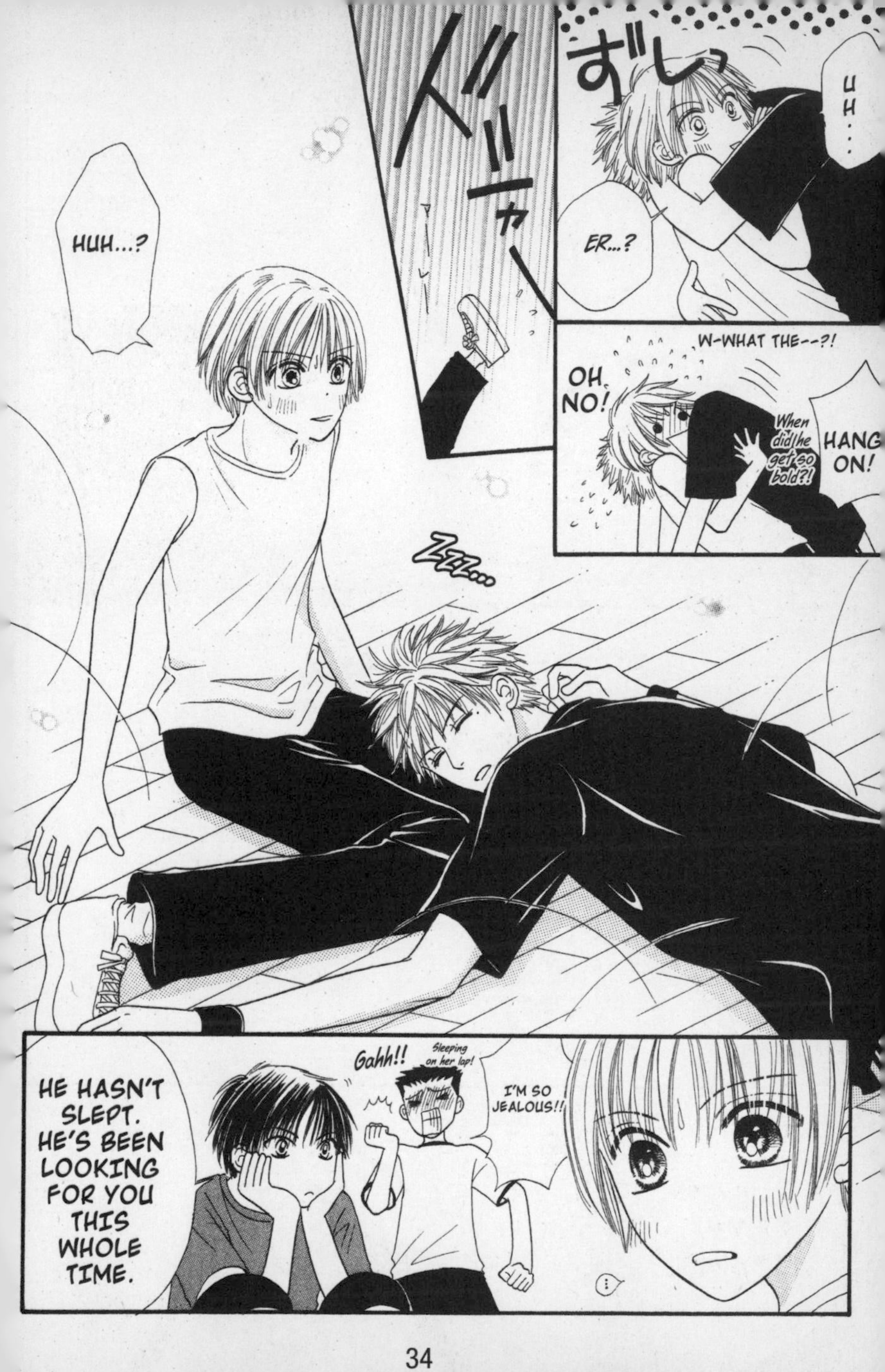
ずしっ
UH...
ER...?
W-WHAT THE--?!
HANG ON!
When did he get so bold?!
OH NO!
HUH...?
ZZZ...
...
I'M SO JEALOUS!!
Sleeping on her lap!
Gahh!!
HE HASN'T SLEPT. HE'S BEEN LOOKING FOR YOU THIS WHOLE TIME.

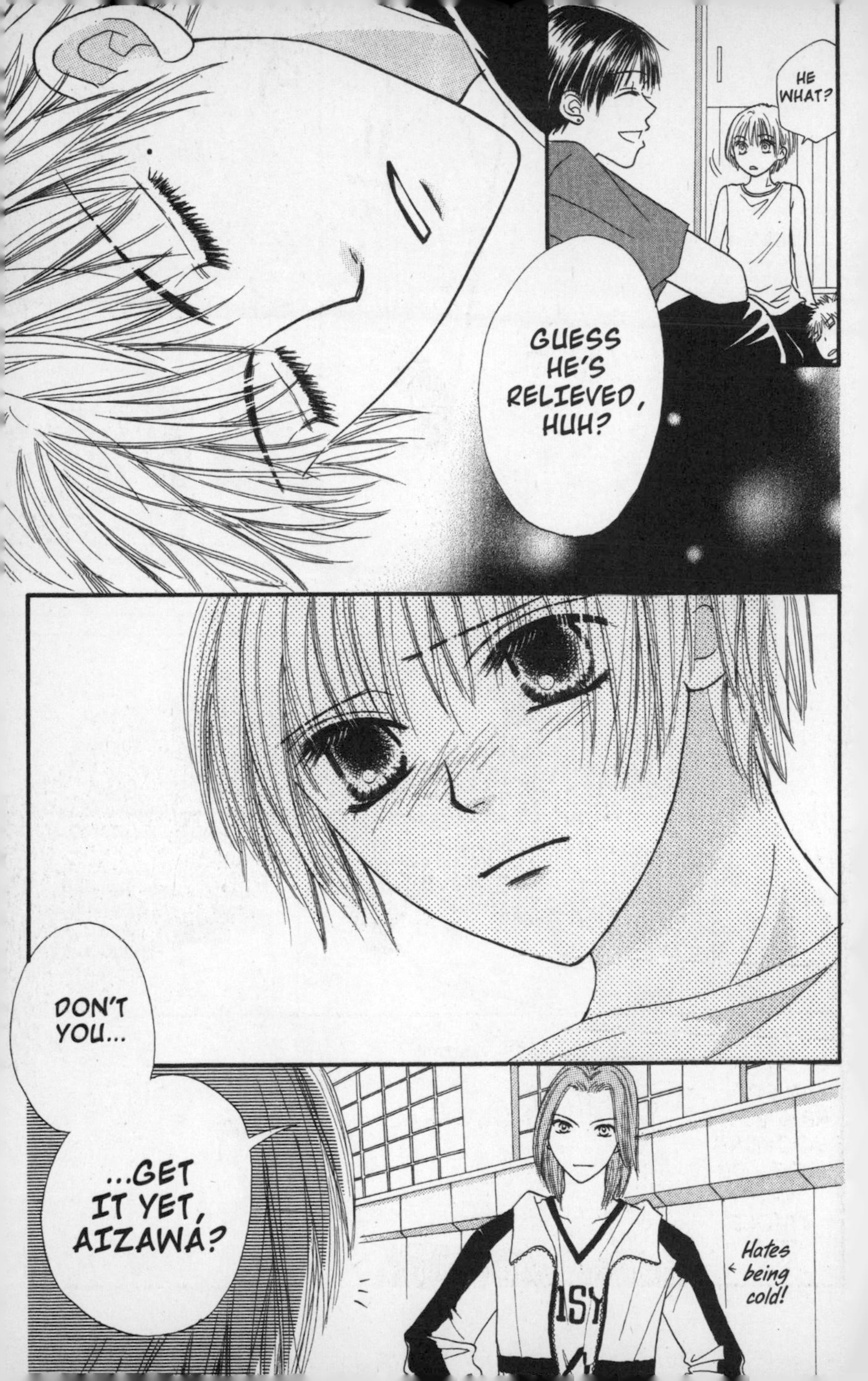
HE WHAT?
GUESS HE'S RELIEVED, HUH?
DON'T YOU...
...GET IT YET, AIZAWA?
Hates being cold!

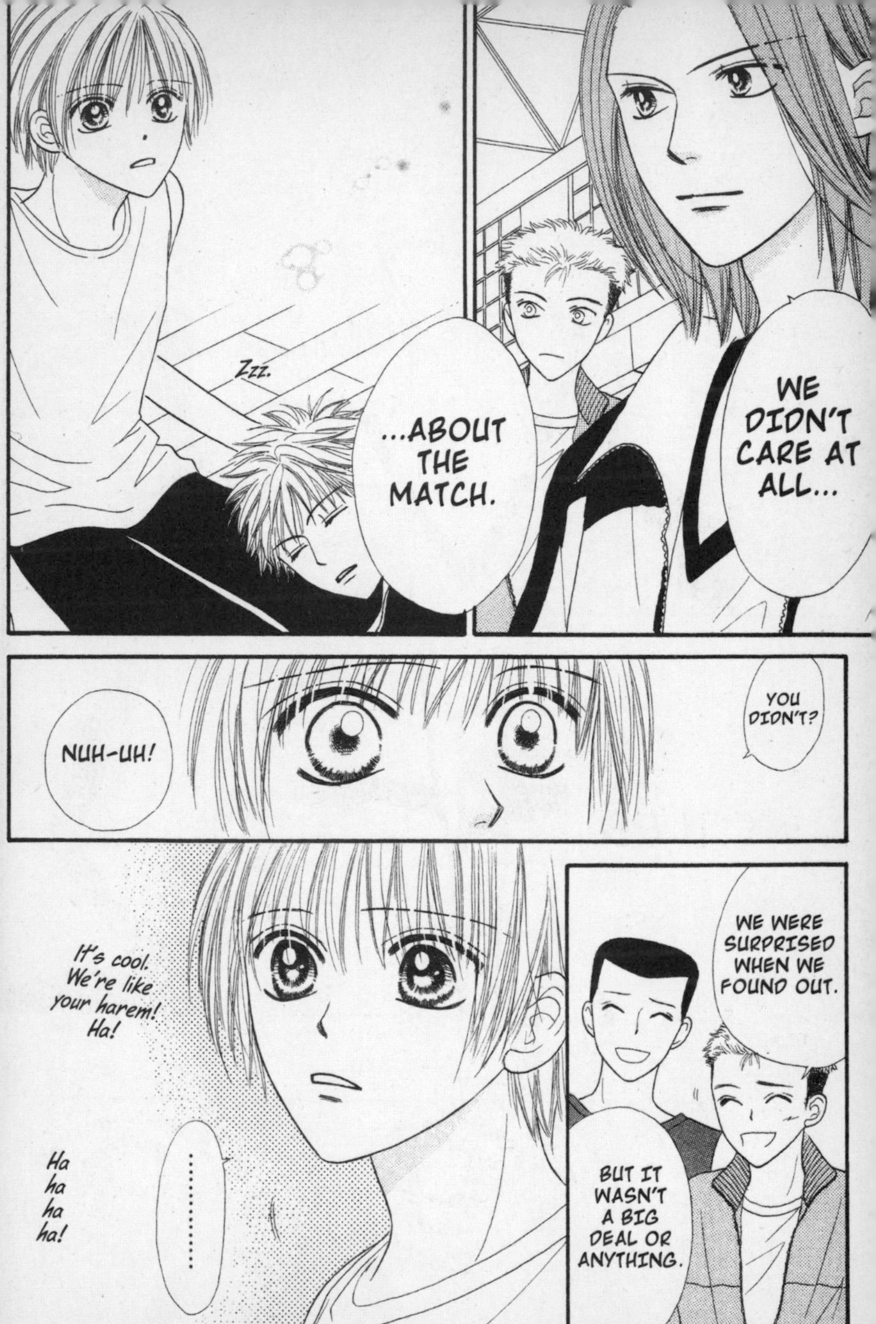
WE DIDN'T CARE AT ALL...
...ABOUT THE MATCH.
Zzz.
YOU DIDN'T?
NUH-UH!
WE WERE SURPRISED WHEN WE FOUND OUT.
BUT IT WASN'T A BIG DEAL OR ANYTHING.
It's cool. We're like your harem! Ha!
Ha ha ha ha!
....

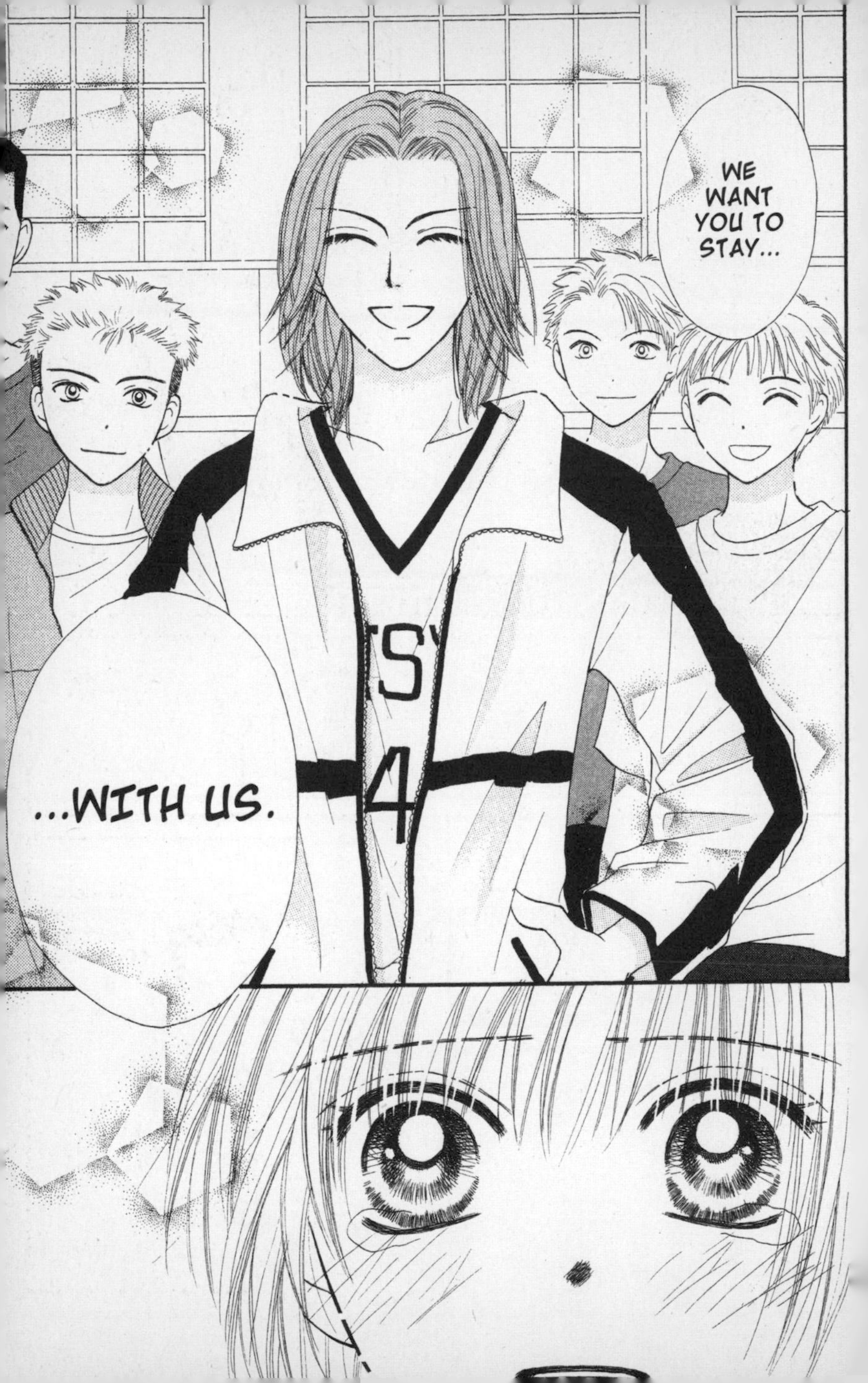
WE WANT YOU TO STAY...
...WITH US.

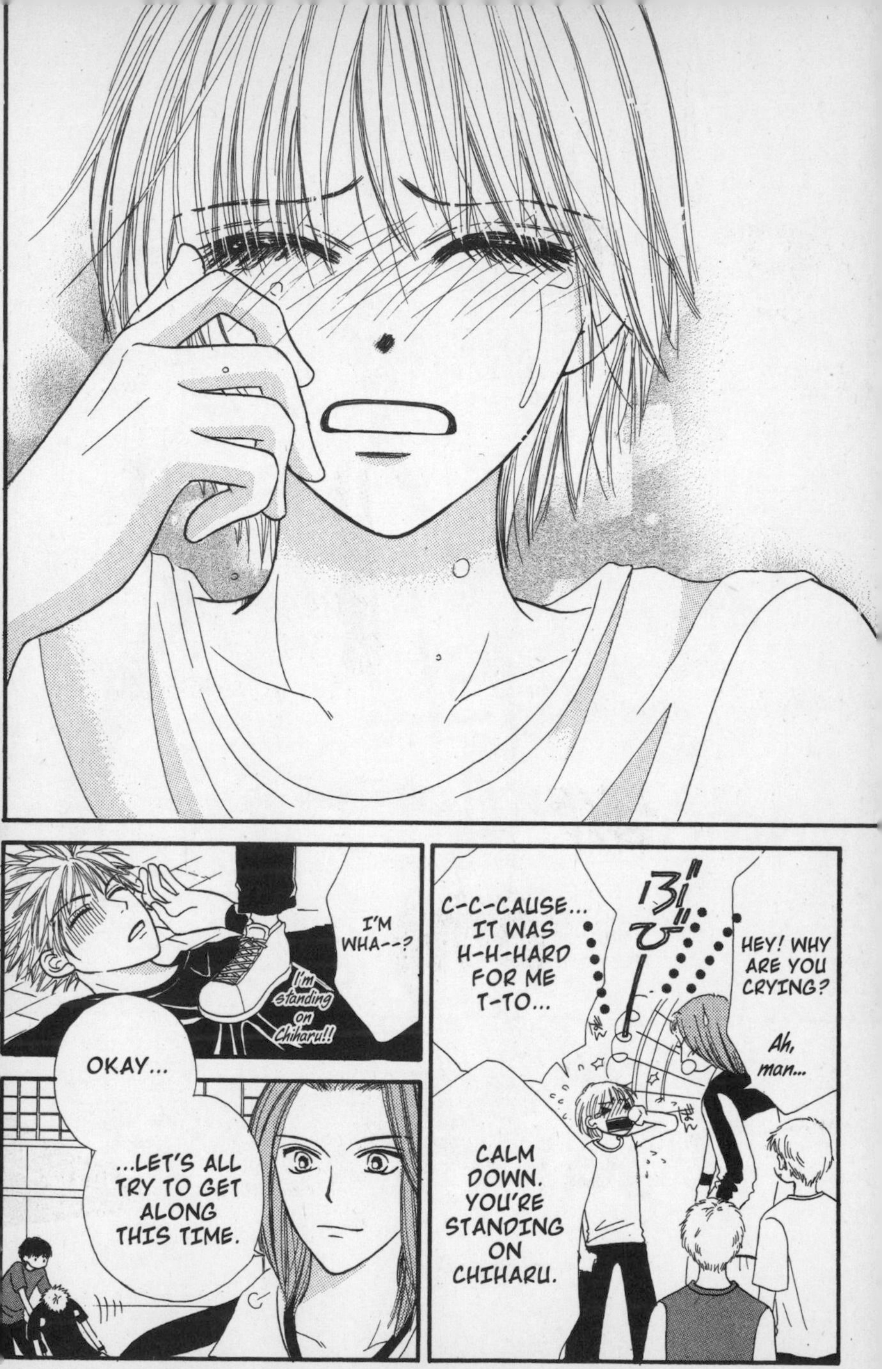
HEY! WHY ARE YOU CRYING?
Ah, man...
C-C-CAUSE... IT WAS H-H-HARD FOR ME T-TO...
CALM DOWN. YOU'RE STANDING ON CHIHARU.
I'M WHA--?
I'm standing on Chiharu!!
OKAY...
...LET'S ALL TRY TO GET ALONG THIS TIME.

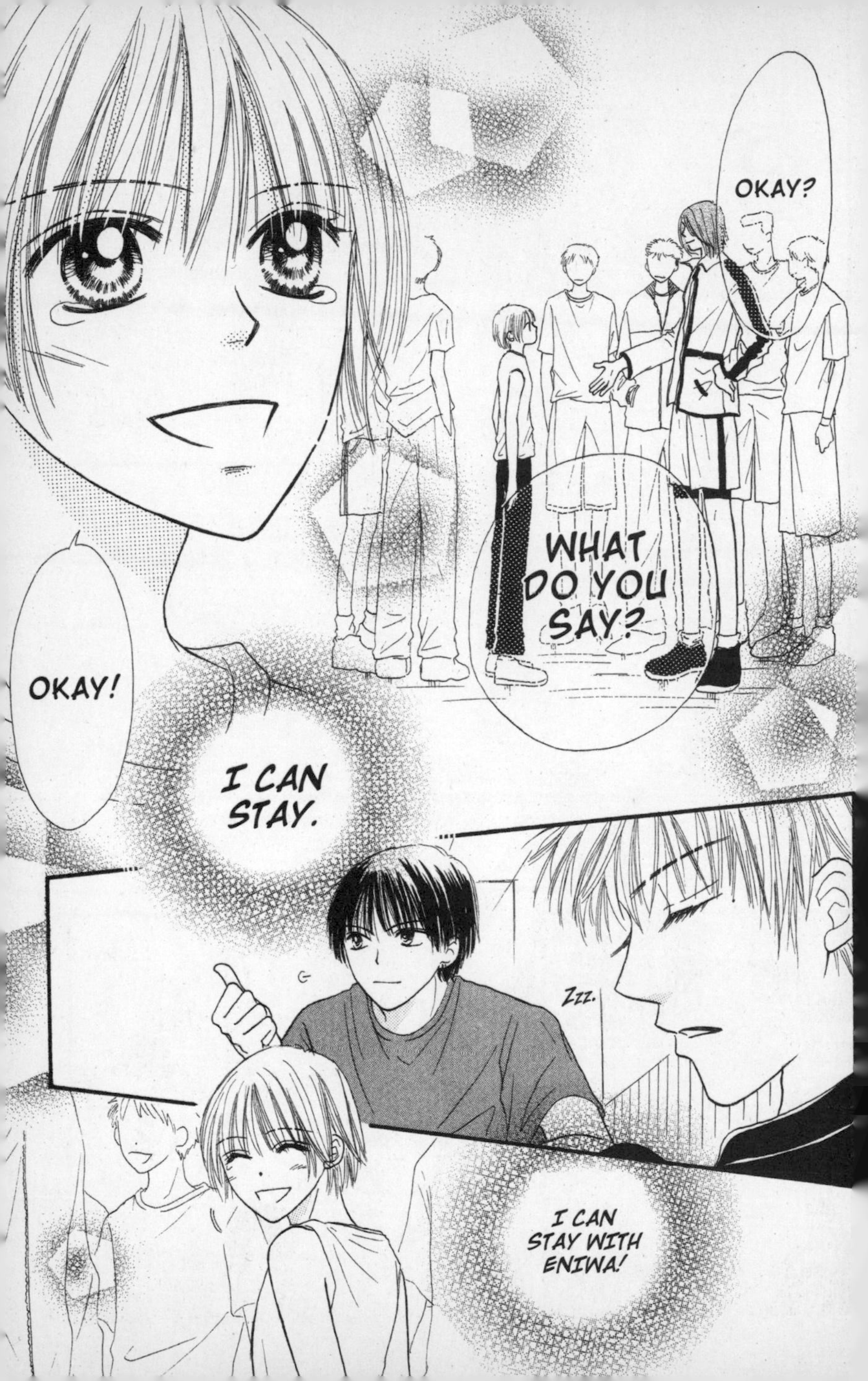
OKAY?
WHAT DO YOU SAY?
OKAY!
I CAN STAY.
Zzz.
I CAN STAY WITH ENIWA!

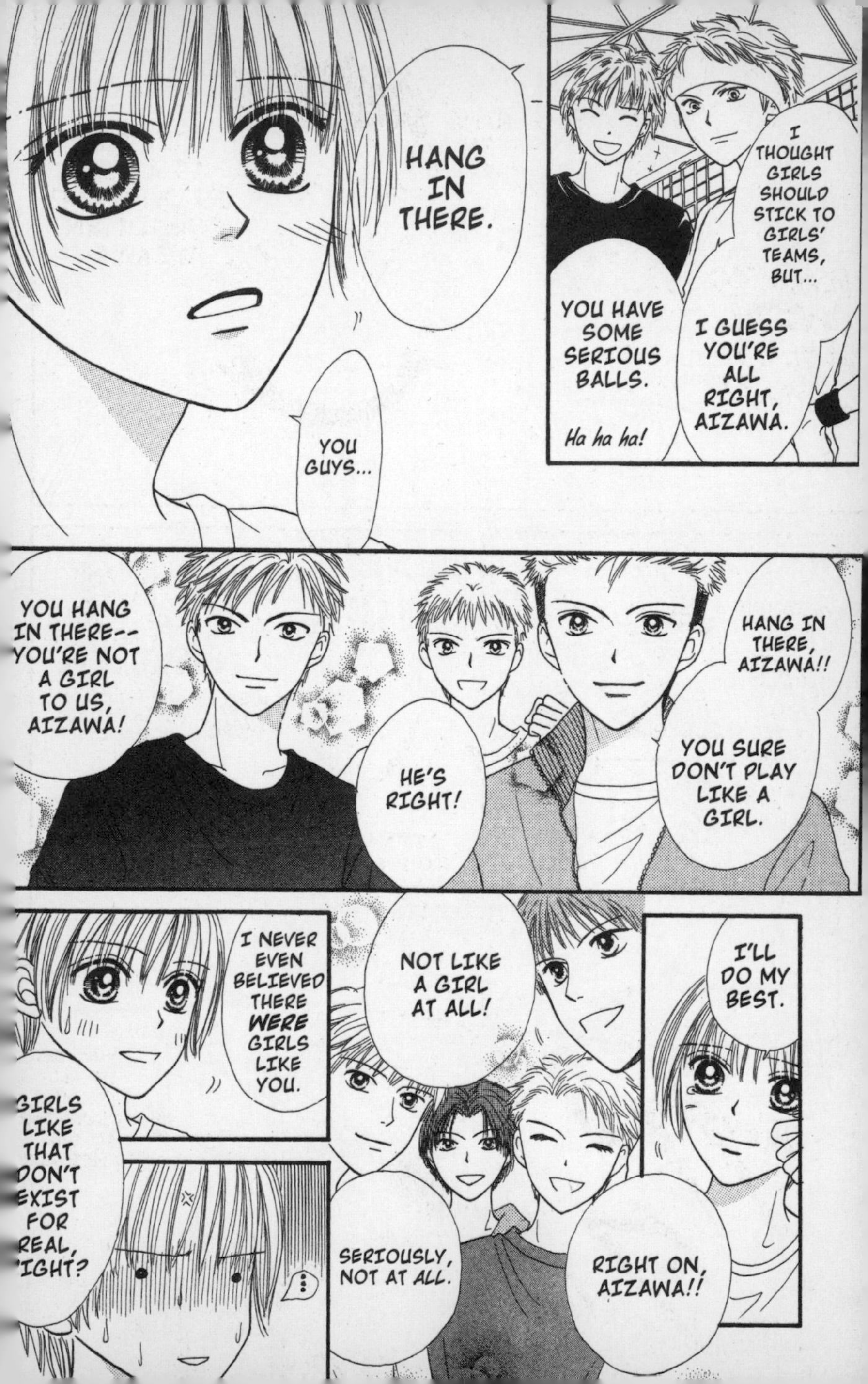
I THOUGHT GIRLS SHOULD STICK TO GIRLS' TEAMS, BUT...
I GUESS YOU'RE ALL RIGHT, AIZAWA.
YOU HAVE SOME SERIOUS BALLS.
Ha ha ha!
HANG IN THERE.
YOU GUYS...
HANG IN THERE, AIZAWA!!
YOU SURE DON'T PLAY LIKE A GIRL.
HE'S RIGHT!
YOU HANG IN THERE-- YOU'RE NOT A GIRL TO US, AIZAWA!
I'LL DO MY BEST.
NOT LIKE A GIRL AT ALL!
RIGHT ON, AIZAWA!!
SERIOUSLY, NOT AT ALL.
I NEVER EVEN BELIEVED THERE WERE GIRLS LIKE YOU.
GIRLS LIKE THAT DON'T EXIST FOR REAL, RIGHT?
...

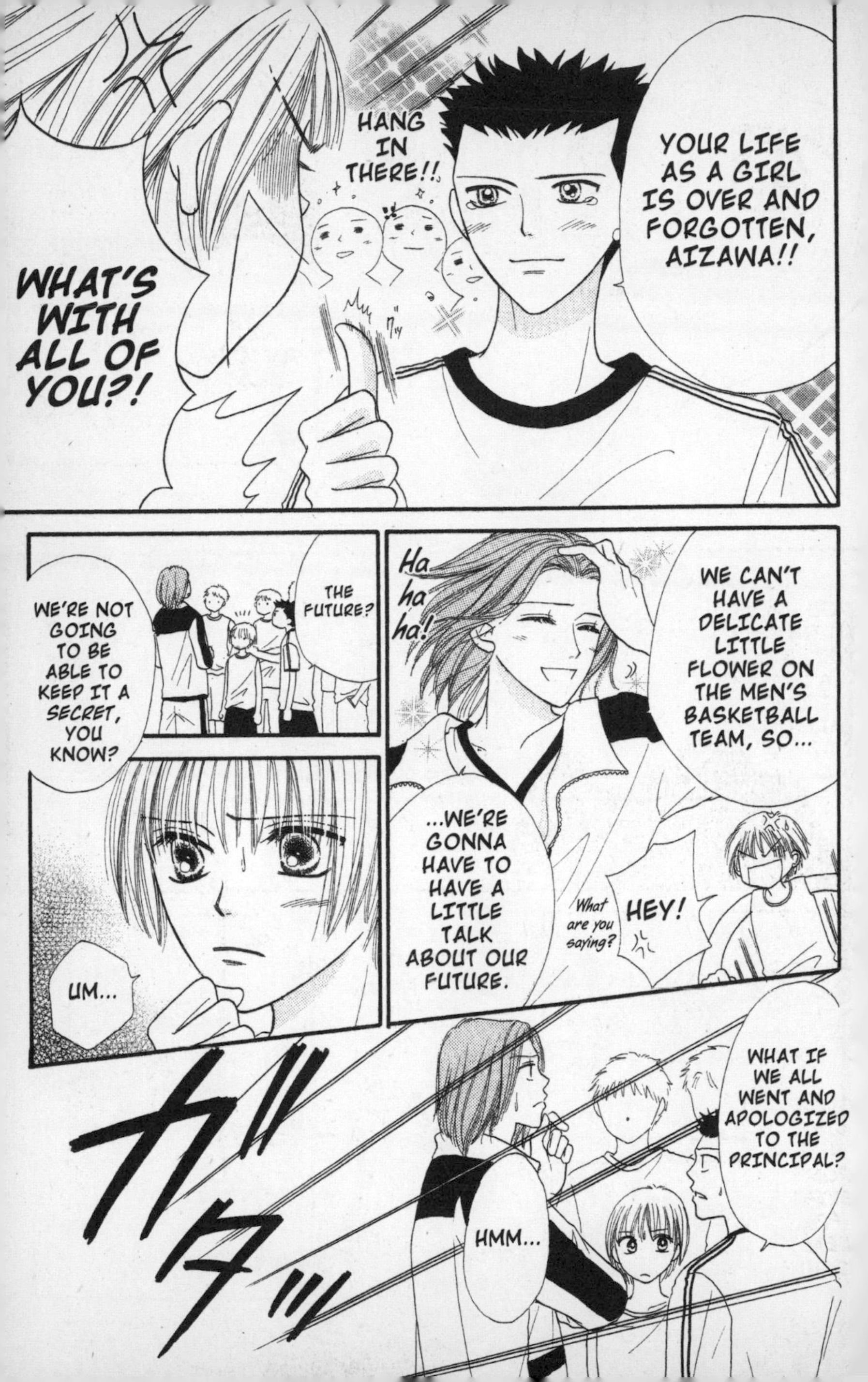

YOUR LIFE AS A GIRL IS OVER AND FORGOTTEN, AIZAWA!!
HANG IN THERE!!
WHAT'S WITH ALL OF YOU?!
WE CAN'T HAVE A DELICATE LITTLE FLOWER ON THE MEN'S BASKETBALL TEAM, SO...
Ha ha ha!
HEY!
What are you saying?
...WE'RE GONNA HAVE TO HAVE A LITTLE TALK ABOUT OUR FUTURE.
THE FUTURE?
WE'RE NOT GOING TO BE ABLE TO KEEP IT A SECRET, YOU KNOW?
UM...
WHAT IF WE ALL WENT AND APOLOGIZED TO THE PRINCIPAL?
HMM...
ガタッ

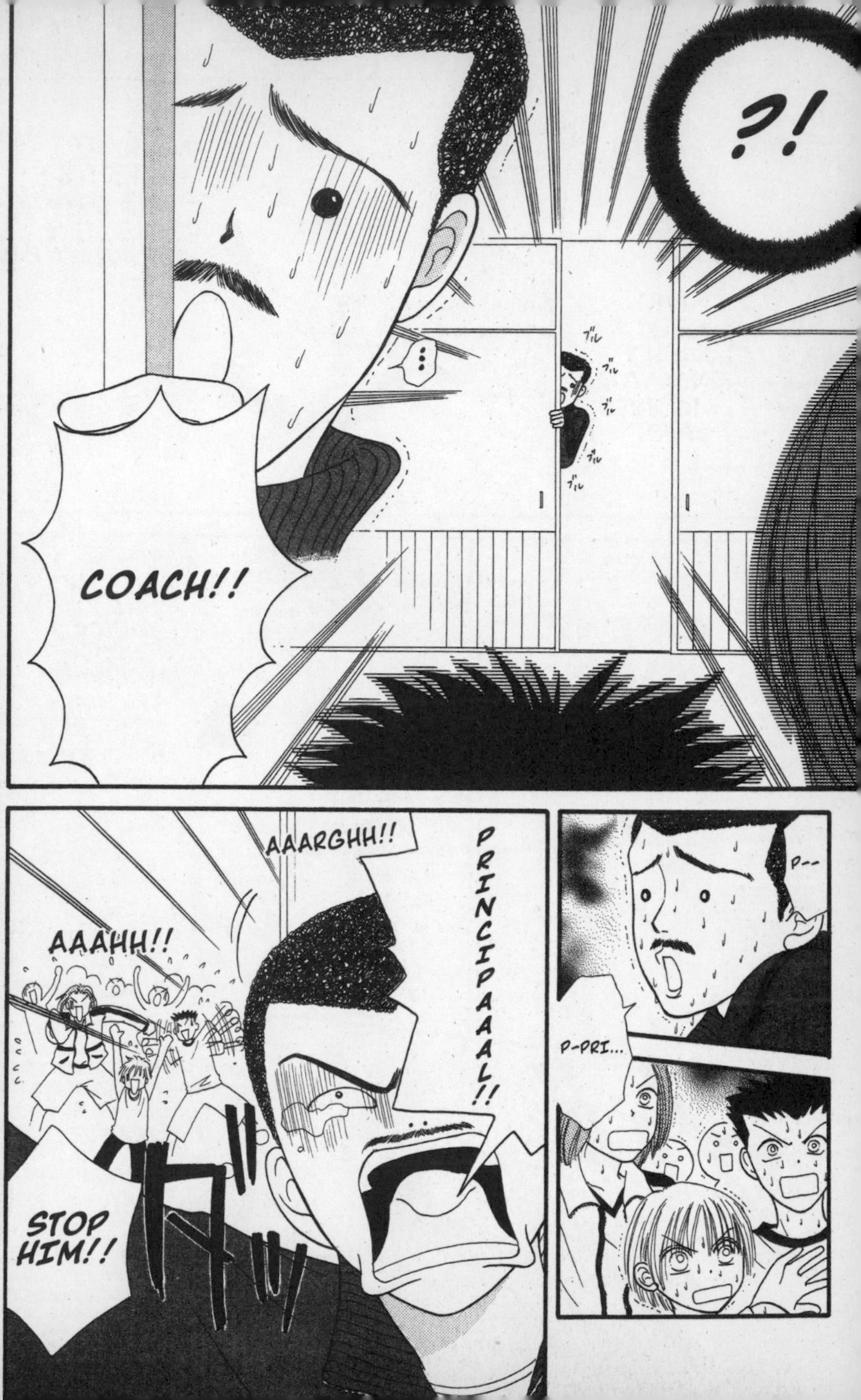
?!
...
COACH!!
P--
P-PRI...
PRINCIPAAAL!!
AAARGHH!!
AAAHH!!
STOP HIM!!

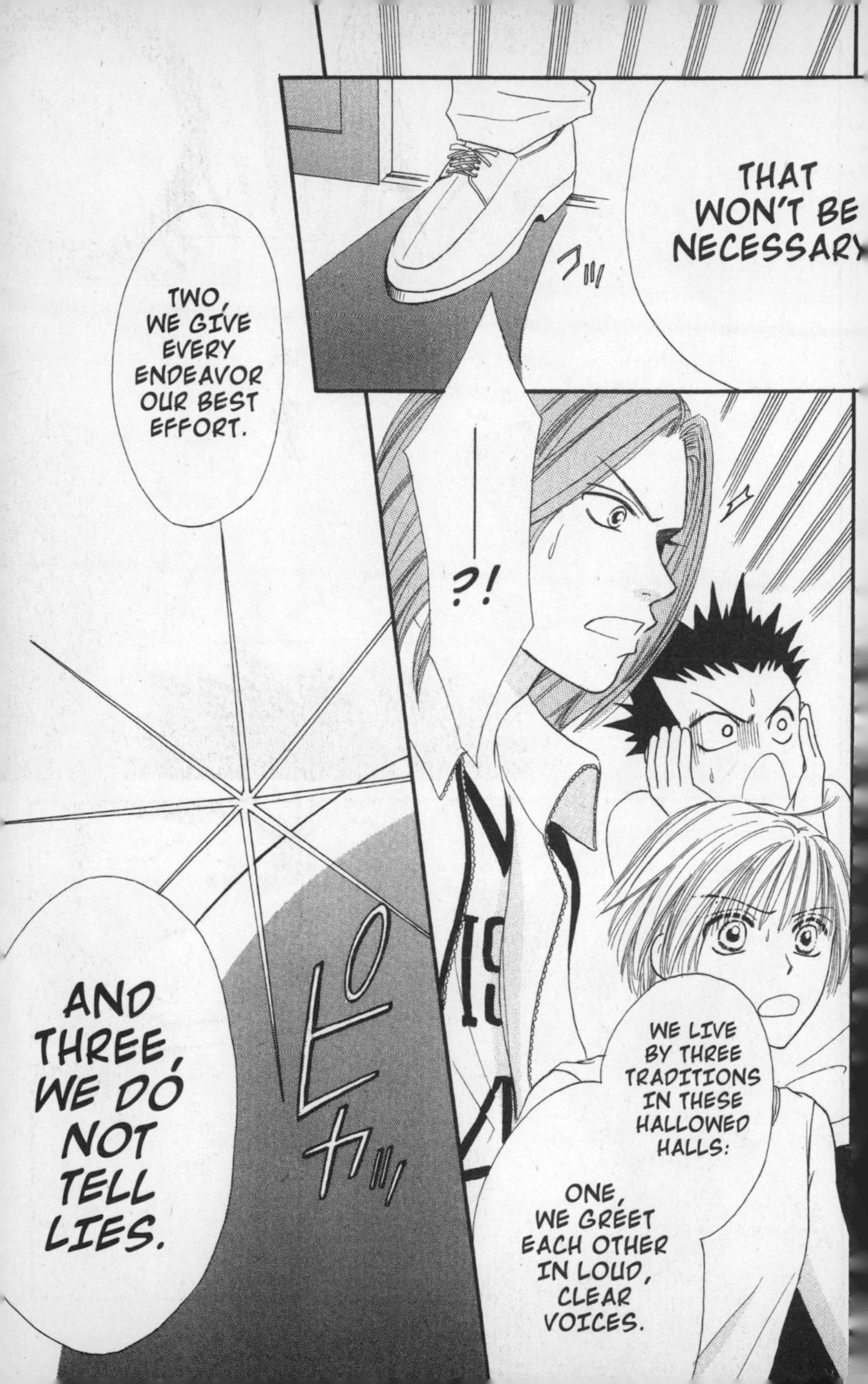
THAT WON'T BE NECESSARY
フッ
?!
WE LIVE BY THREE TRADITIONS IN THESE HALLOWED HALLS:
ONE, WE GREET EACH OTHER IN LOUD, CLEAR VOICES.
TWO, WE GIVE EVERY ENDEAVOR OUR BEST EFFORT.
ピカッ
AND THREE, WE DO NOT TELL LIES.

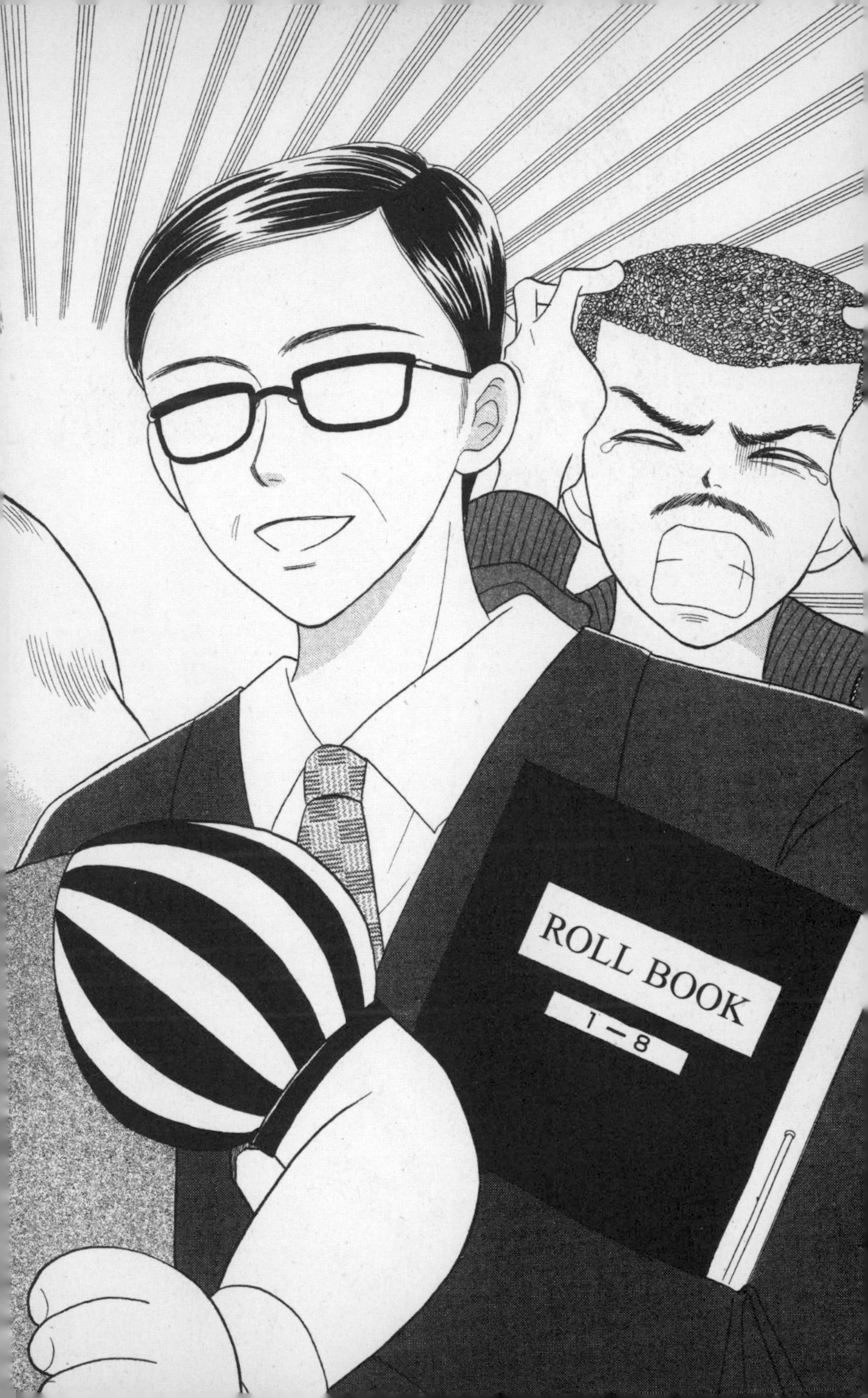
ROLL BOOK
1—8

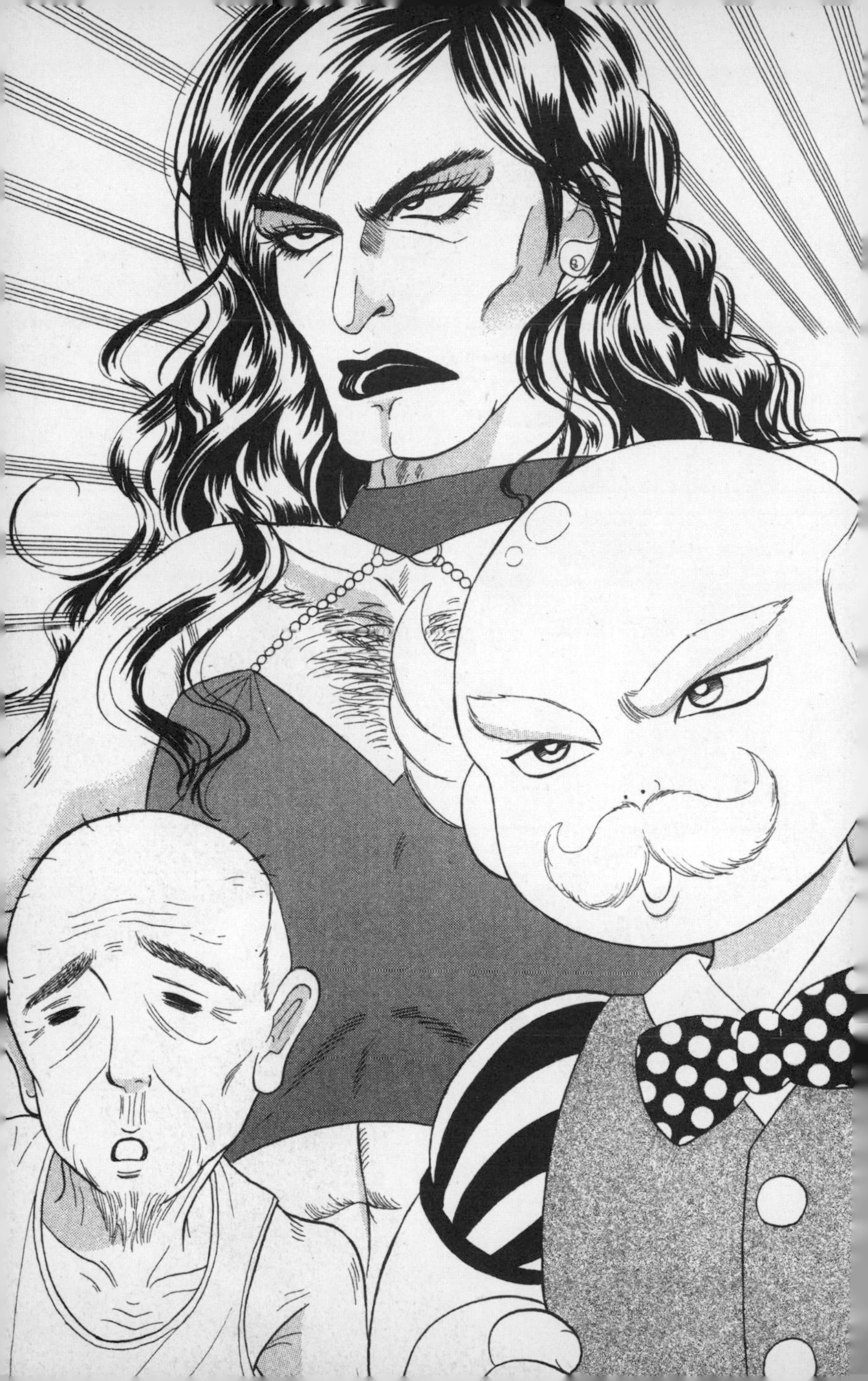

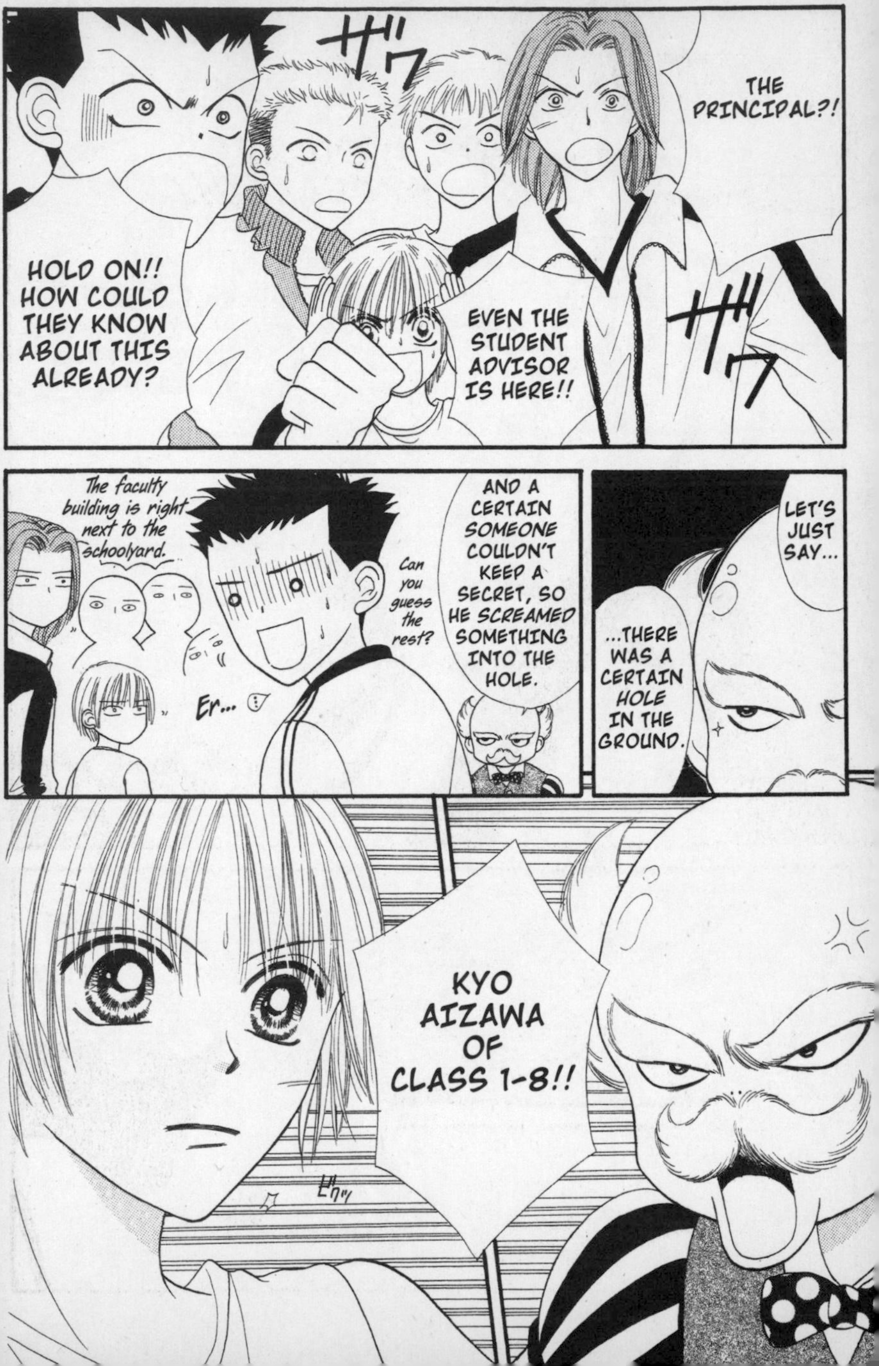
THE PRINCIPAL?!
ザワ
EVEN THE STUDENT ADVISOR IS HERE!!
ザワ
HOLD ON!! HOW COULD THEY KNOW ABOUT THIS ALREADY?
LET'S JUST SAY...
...THERE WAS A CERTAIN HOLE IN THE GROUND.
AND A CERTAIN SOMEONE COULDN'T KEEP A SECRET, SO HE SCREAMED SOMETHING INTO THE HOLE.
Can you guess the rest?
The faculty building is right next to the schoolyard.
Er...
KYO AIZAWA OF CLASS 1-8!!

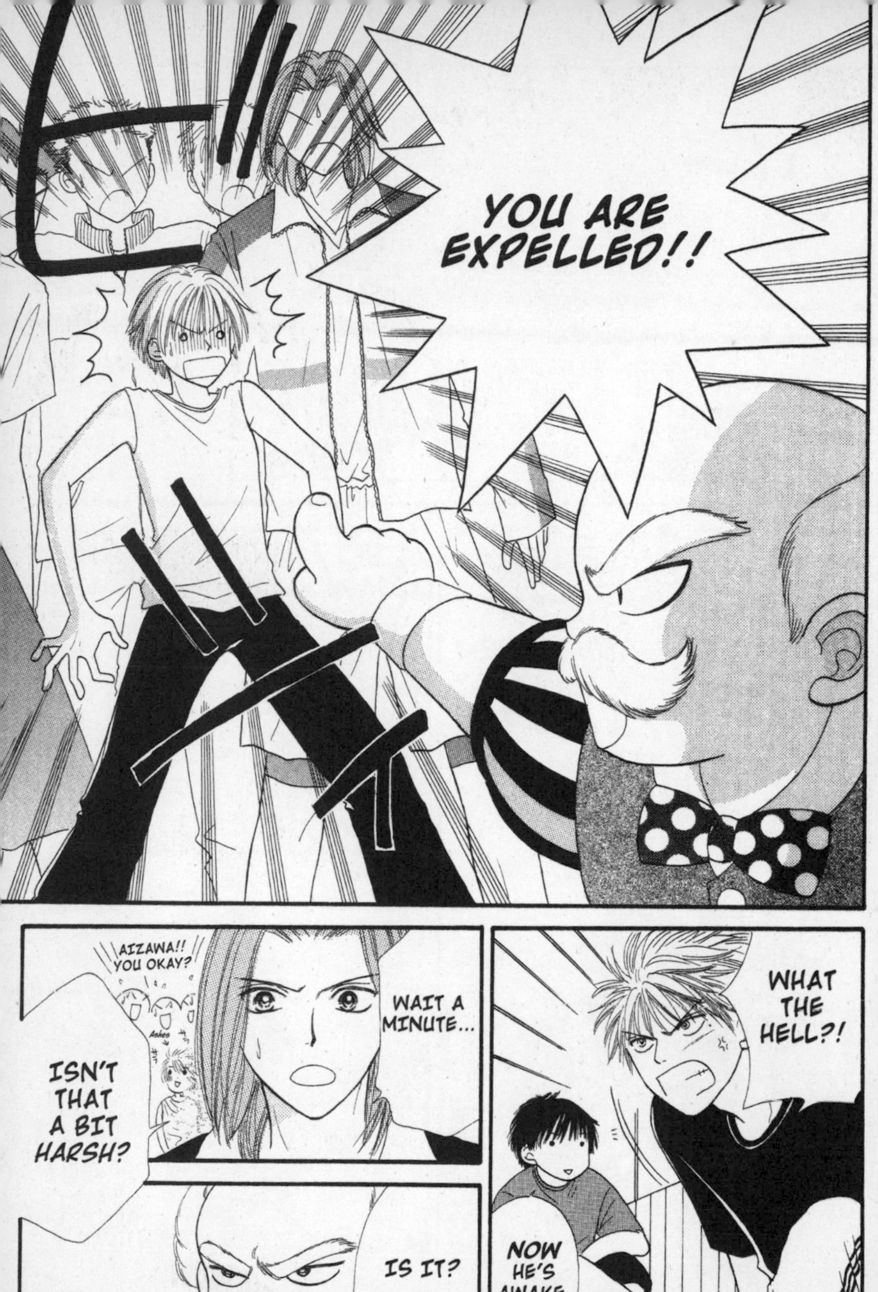
YOU ARE EXPELLED!!
WHAT THE HELL?!
NOW HE'S AWAKE.
WAIT A MINUTE...
AIZAWA!! YOU OKAY?
ISN'T THAT A BIT HARSH?
IS IT?

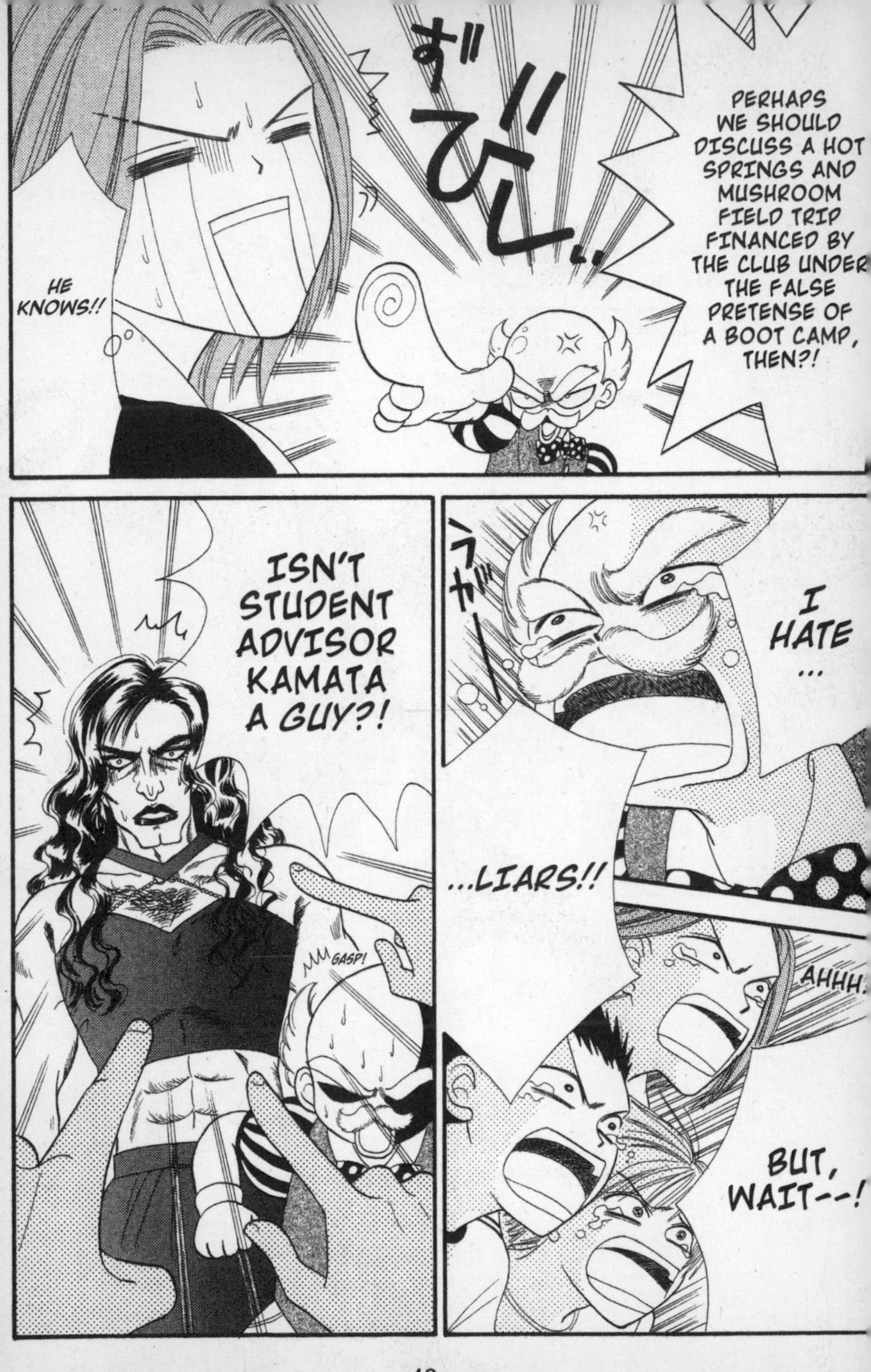

PERHAPS WE SHOULD DISCUSS A HOT SPRINGS AND MUSHROOM FIELD TRIP FINANCED BY THE CLUB UNDER THE FALSE PRETENSE OF A BOOT CAMP, THEN?!
ずびし..
HE KNOWS!!
ウガー
I HATE...
...LIARS!!
AHHH
BUT, WAIT--!
ISN'T STUDENT ADVISOR KAMATA A GUY?!
GASP!

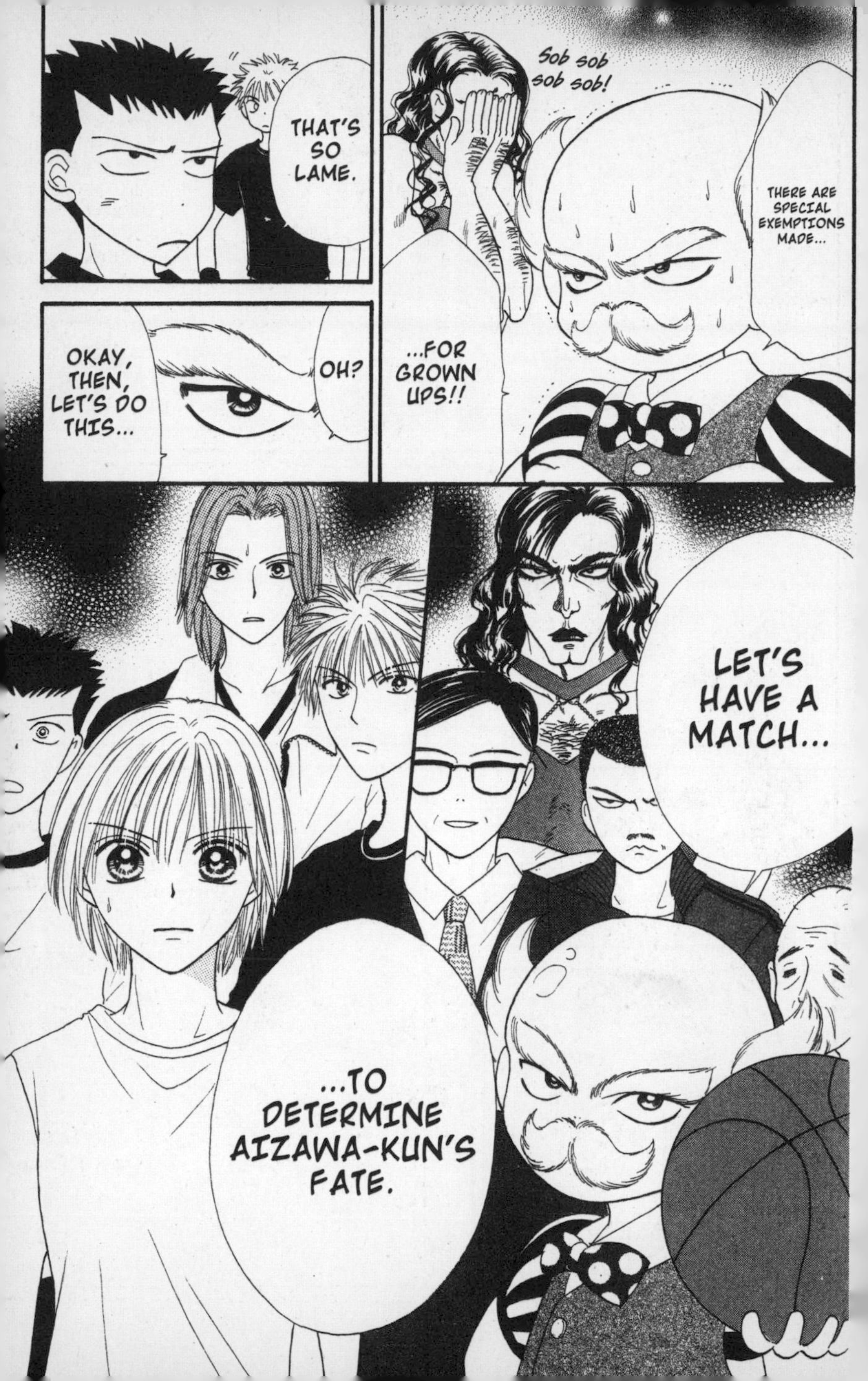
Sob sob sob sob!
THERE ARE SPECIAL EXEMPTIONS MADE...
...FOR GROWN UPS!!
THAT'S SO LAME.
OH?
OKAY, THEN, LET'S DO THIS...
LET'S HAVE A MATCH...
...TO DETERMINE AIZAWA-KUN'S FATE.

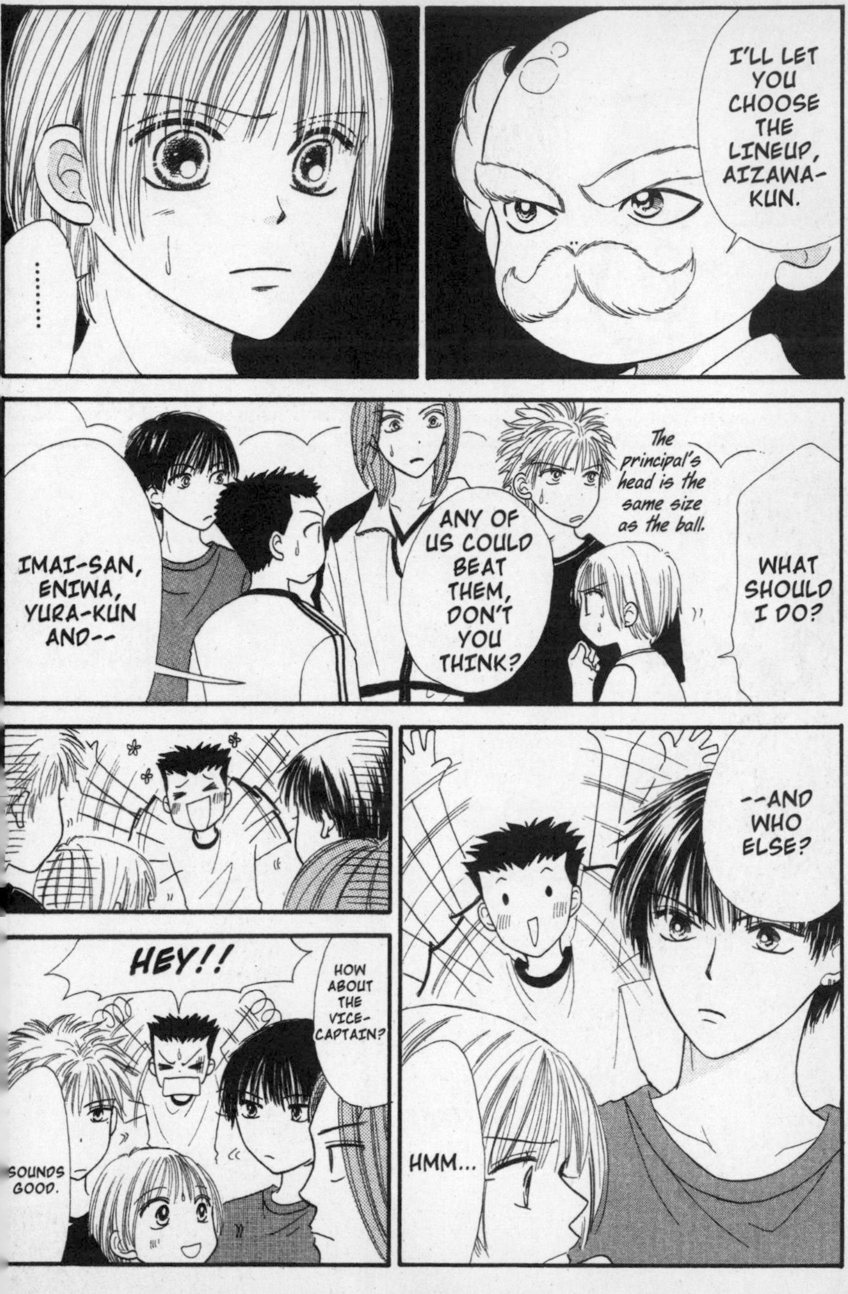
I'LL LET YOU CHOOSE THE LINEUP, AIZAWA-KUN.
......
WHAT SHOULD I DO?
The principal's head is the same size as the ball.
ANY OF US COULD BEAT THEM, DON'T YOU THINK?
IMAI-SAN, ENIWA, YURA-KUN AND--
--AND WHO ELSE?
HMM...
HOW ABOUT THE VICE-CAPTAIN?
HEY!!
SOUNDS GOOD.

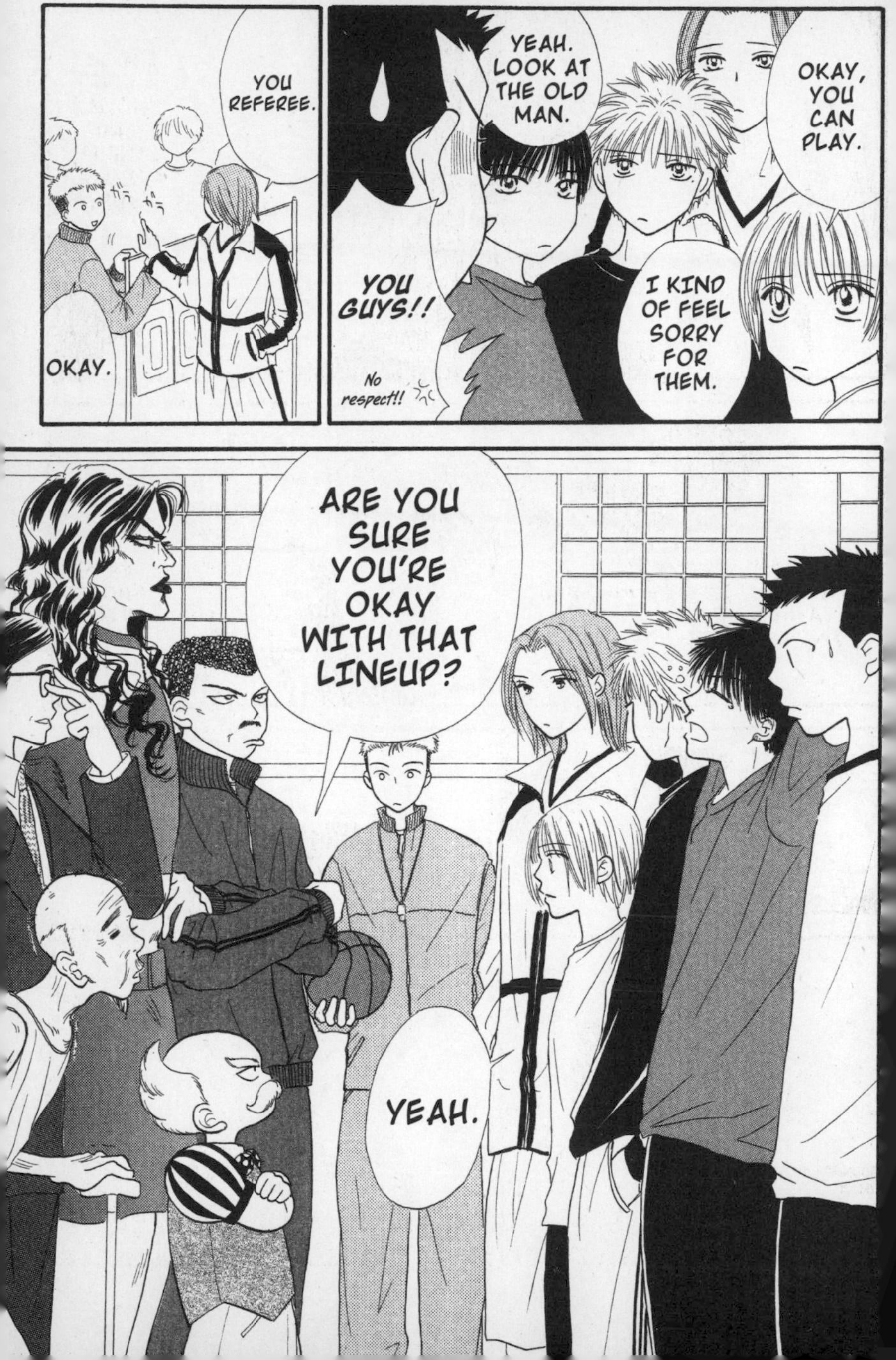
OKAY, YOU CAN PLAY.
YEAH. LOOK AT THE OLD MAN.
I KIND OF FEEL SORRY FOR THEM.
YOU GUYS!!
No respect!!
YOU REFEREE.
OKAY.
ARE YOU SURE YOU'RE OKAY WITH THAT LINEUP?
YEAH.

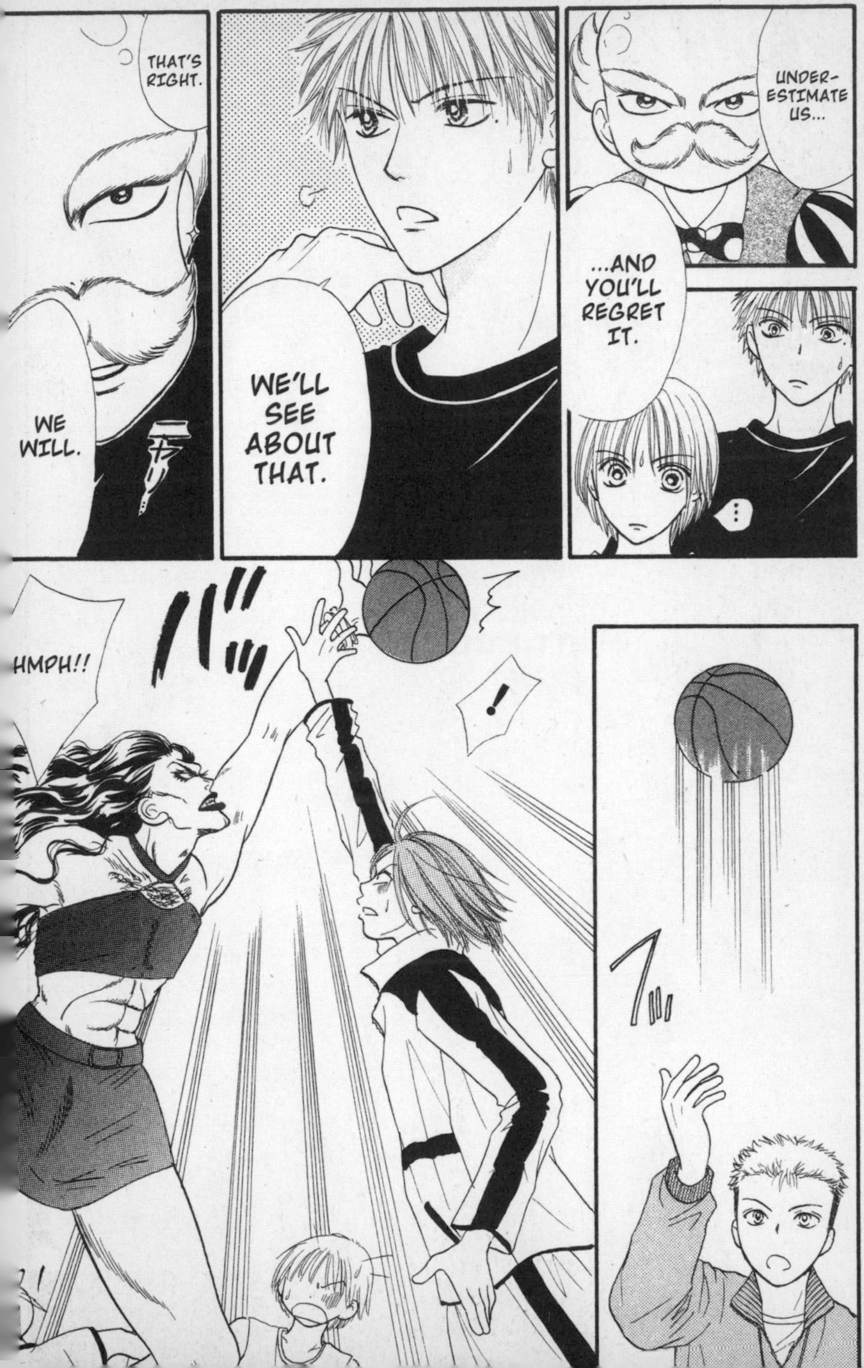
UNDER-ESTIMATE US...
...AND YOU'LL REGRET IT.
...
WE'LL SEE ABOUT THAT.
THAT'S RIGHT.
WE WILL.
!
HMPH!!

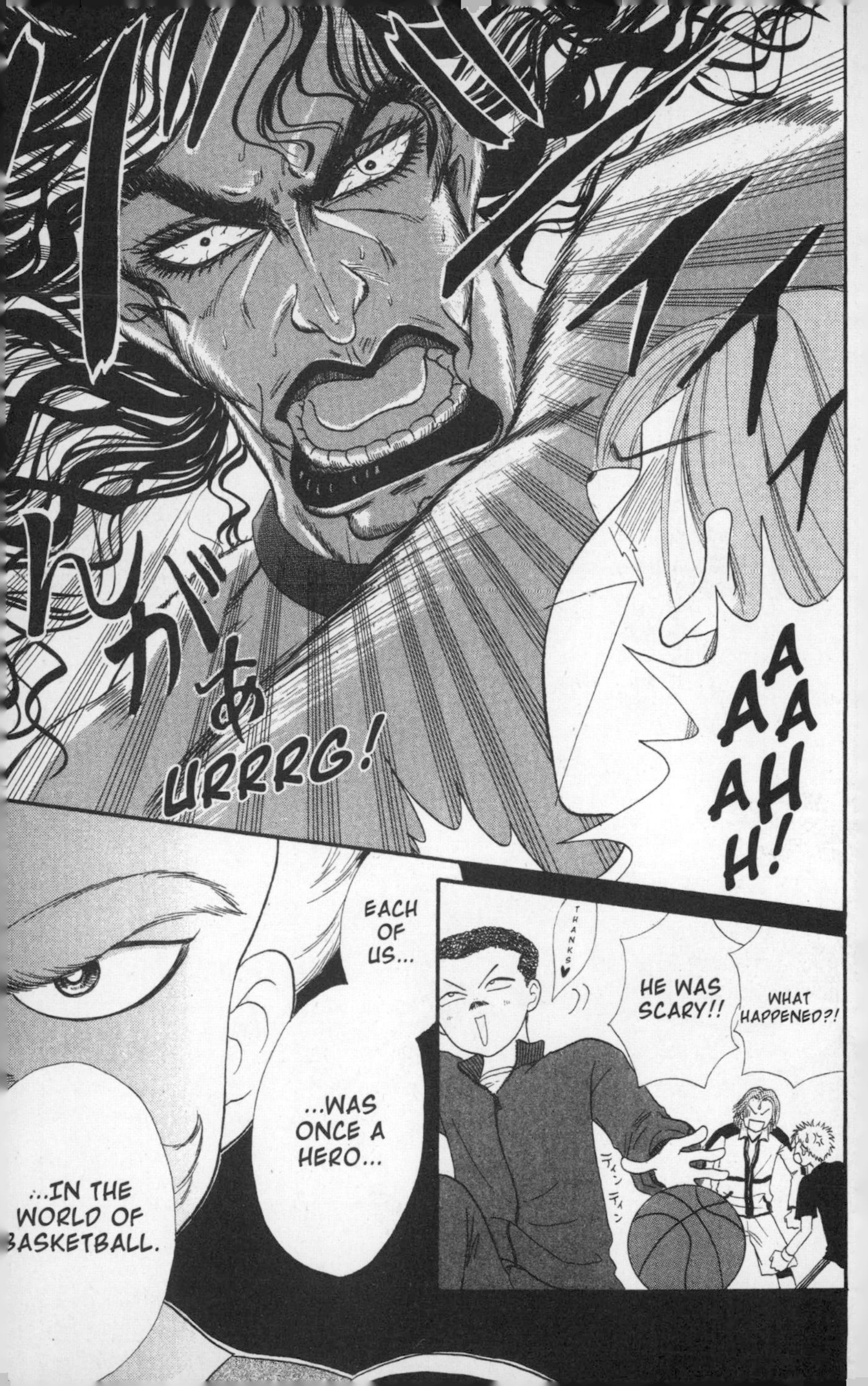
AAAAHH!
んがぁ
URRRG!
WHAT HAPPENED?!
HE WAS SCARY!!
THANKS
ティン ティン
EACH OF US...
...WAS ONCE A HERO...
...IN THE WORLD OF BASKETBALL.

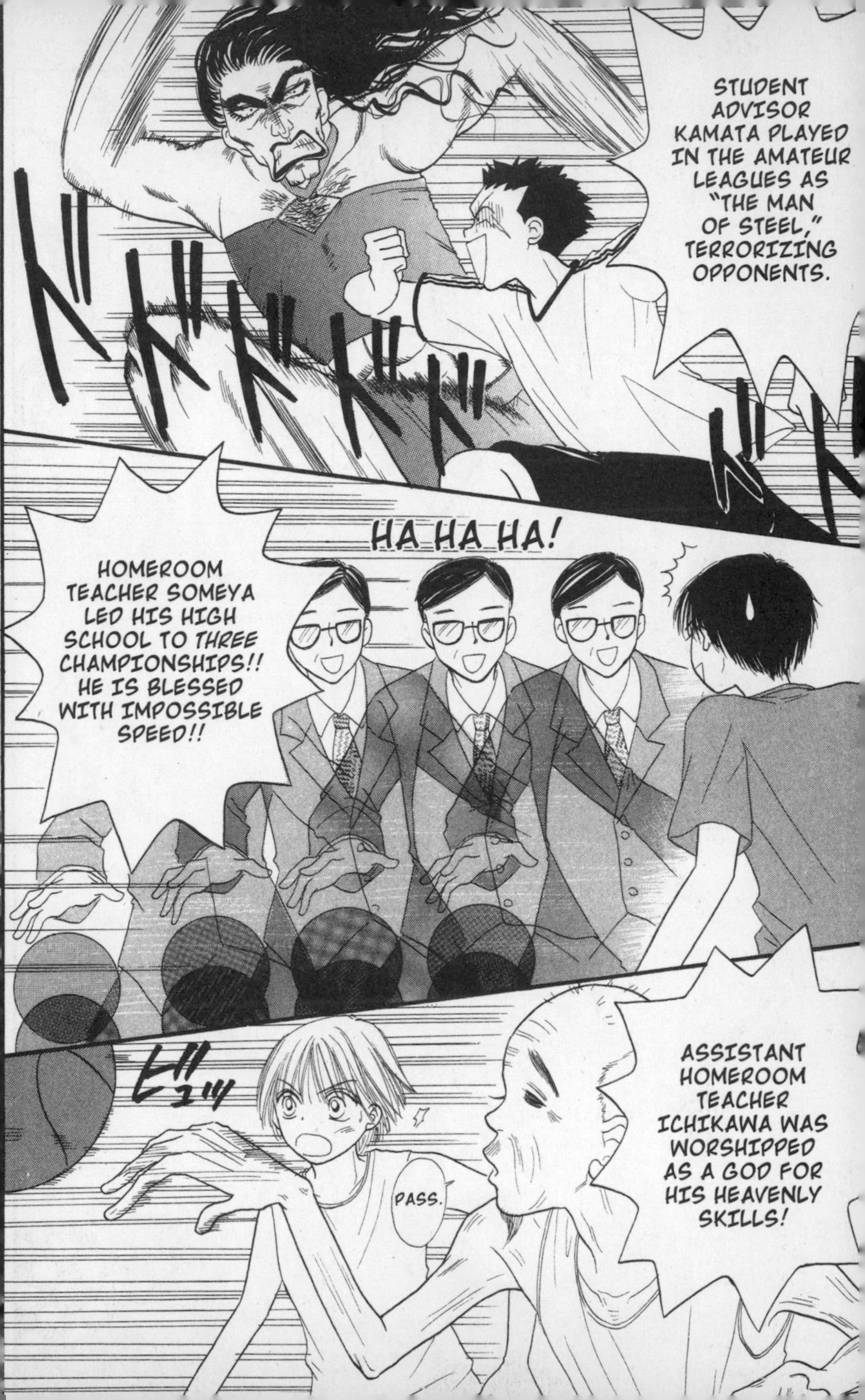
STUDENT ADVISOR KAMATA PLAYED IN THE AMATEUR LEAGUES AS "THE MAN OF STEEL," TERRORIZING OPPONENTS.
HA HA HA!
HOMEROOM TEACHER SOMEYA LED HIS HIGH SCHOOL TO THREE CHAMPIONSHIPS!! HE IS BLESSED WITH IMPOSSIBLE SPEED!!
ASSISTANT HOMEROOM TEACHER ICHIKAWA WAS WORSHIPPED AS A GOD FOR HIS HEAVENLY SKILLS!
PASS.

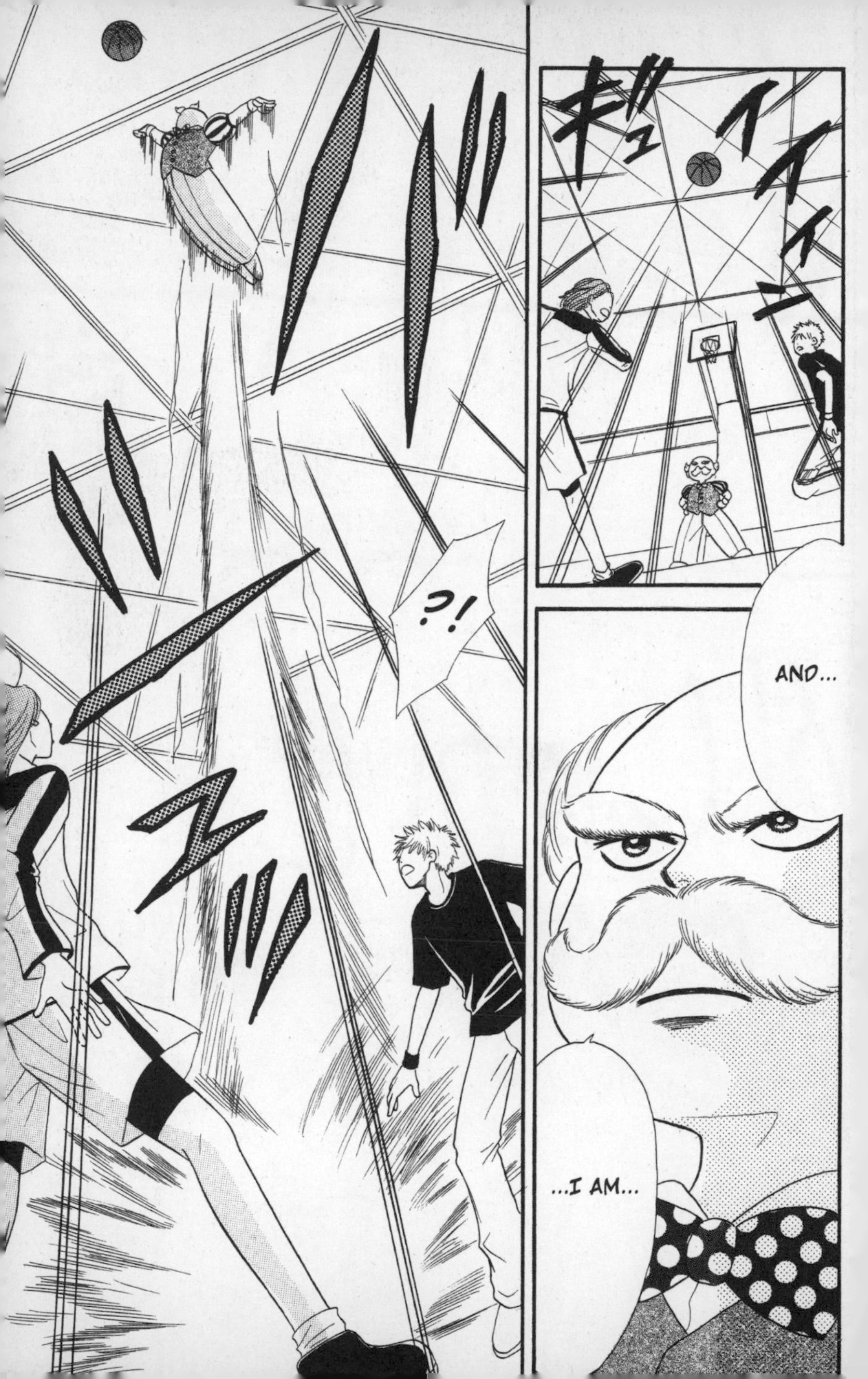
ギュイイイー
AND...
...I AM...
?!

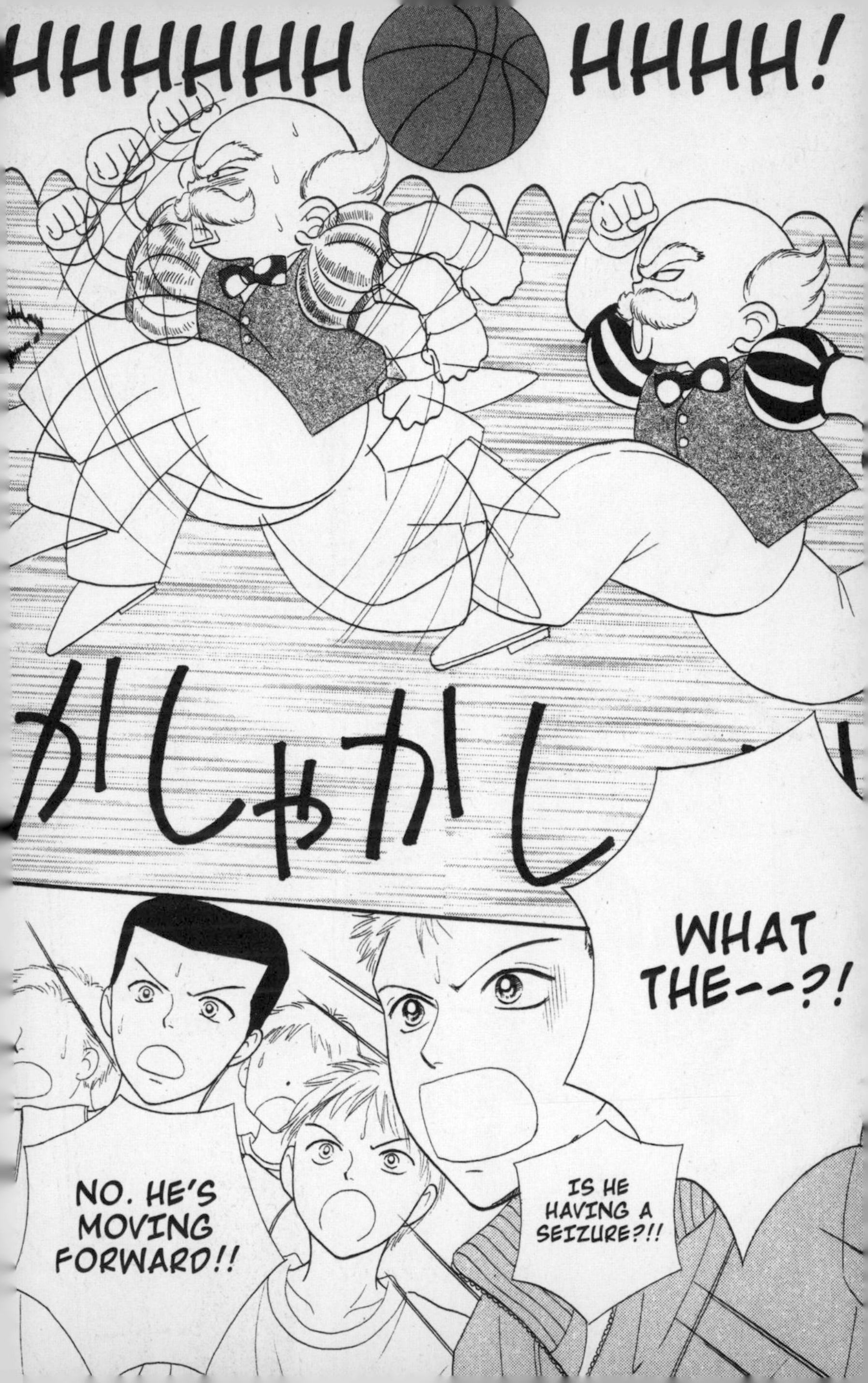
HHHHHH HHHH!
かしゃかし
WHAT THE--?!
IS HE HAVING A SEIZURE?!!
NO. HE'S MOVING FORWARD!!

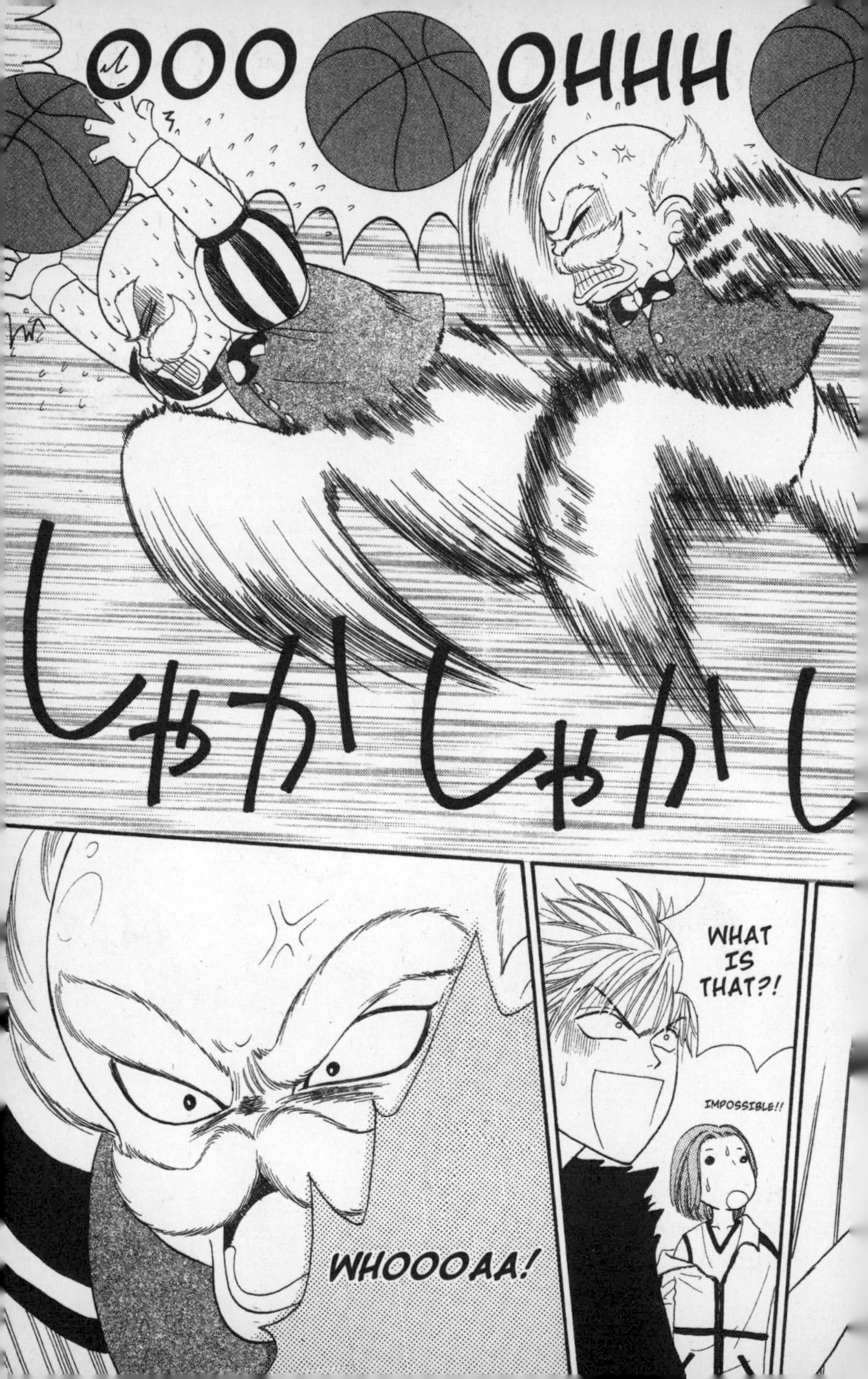
OOOOHHH
しゃかしゃかし
WHAT IS THAT?!
IMPOSSIBLE!!
WHOOOAA!

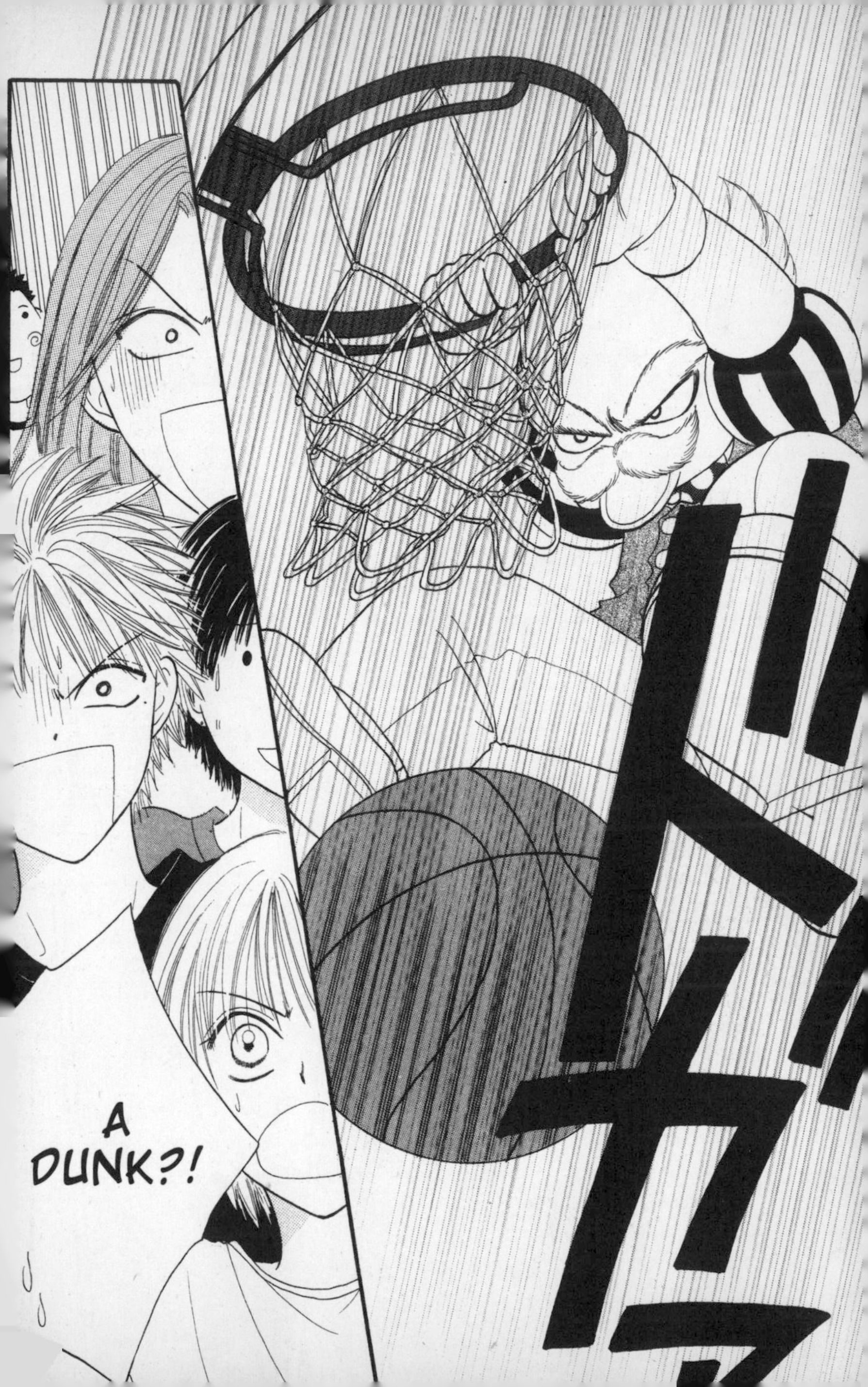
A DUNK?!

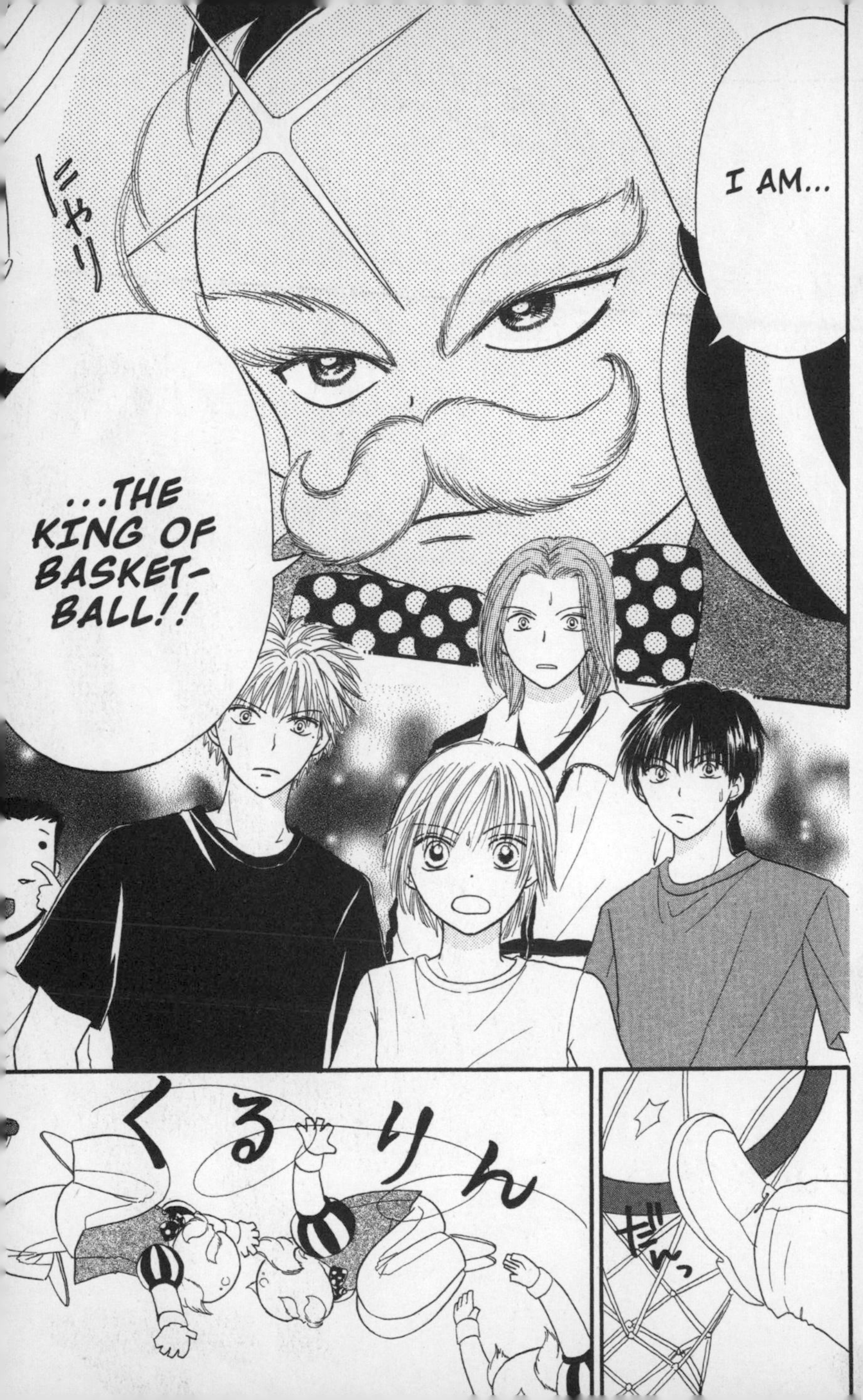
I AM...
にやり
...THE KING OF BASKET-BALL!!
だんっ
くるりん

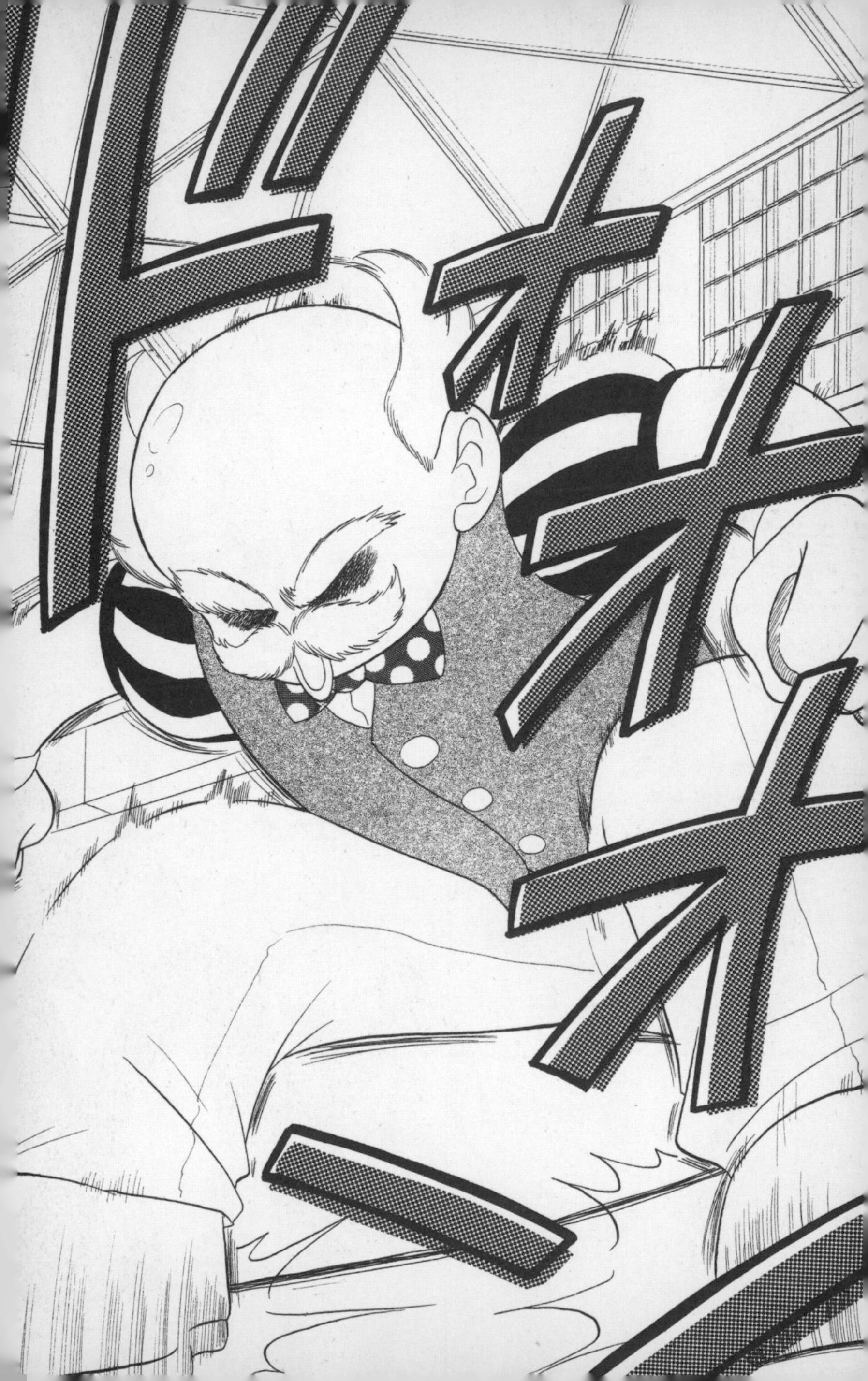
ドオオオー

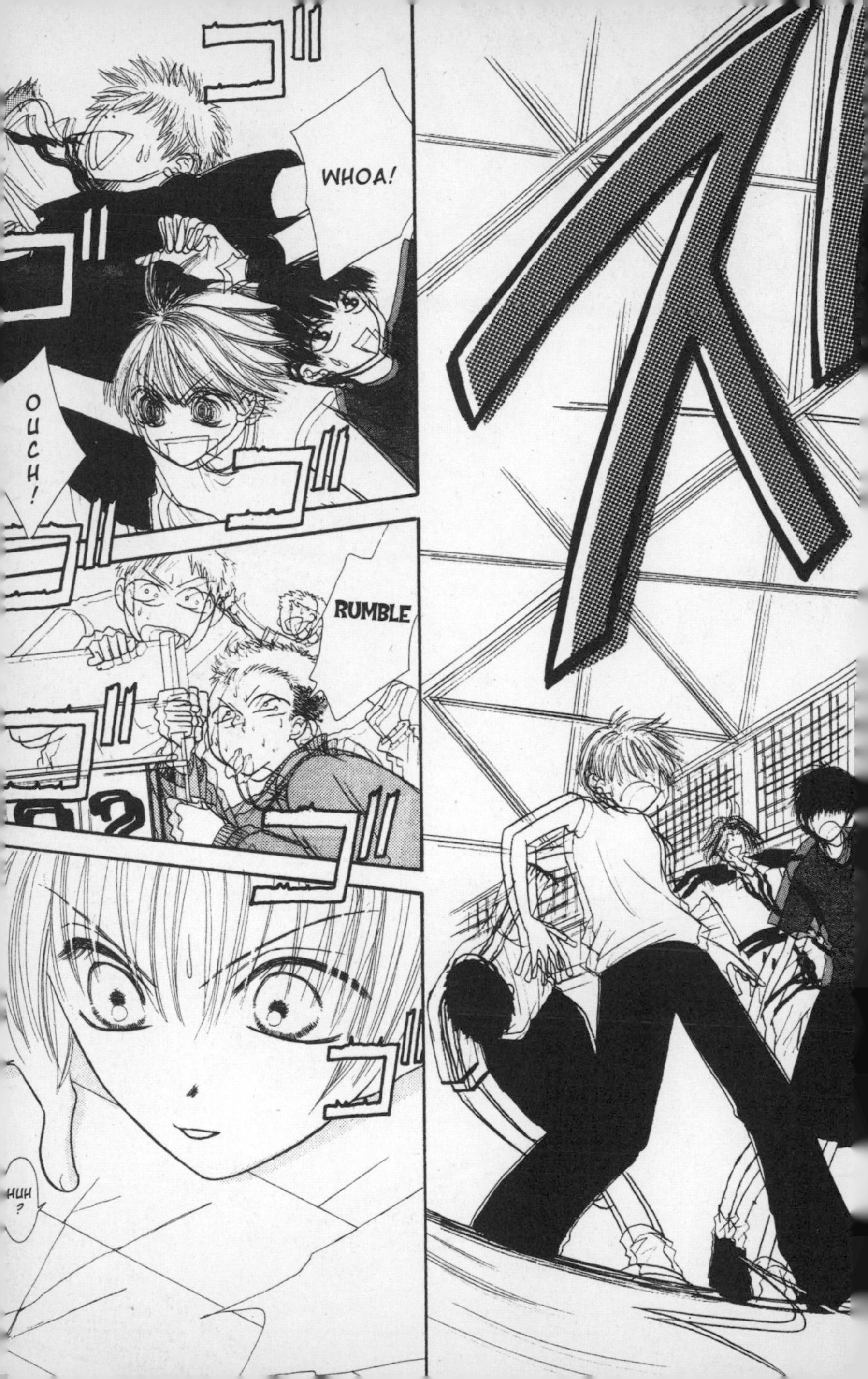
WHOA!
OUCH!
RUMBLE
HUH?

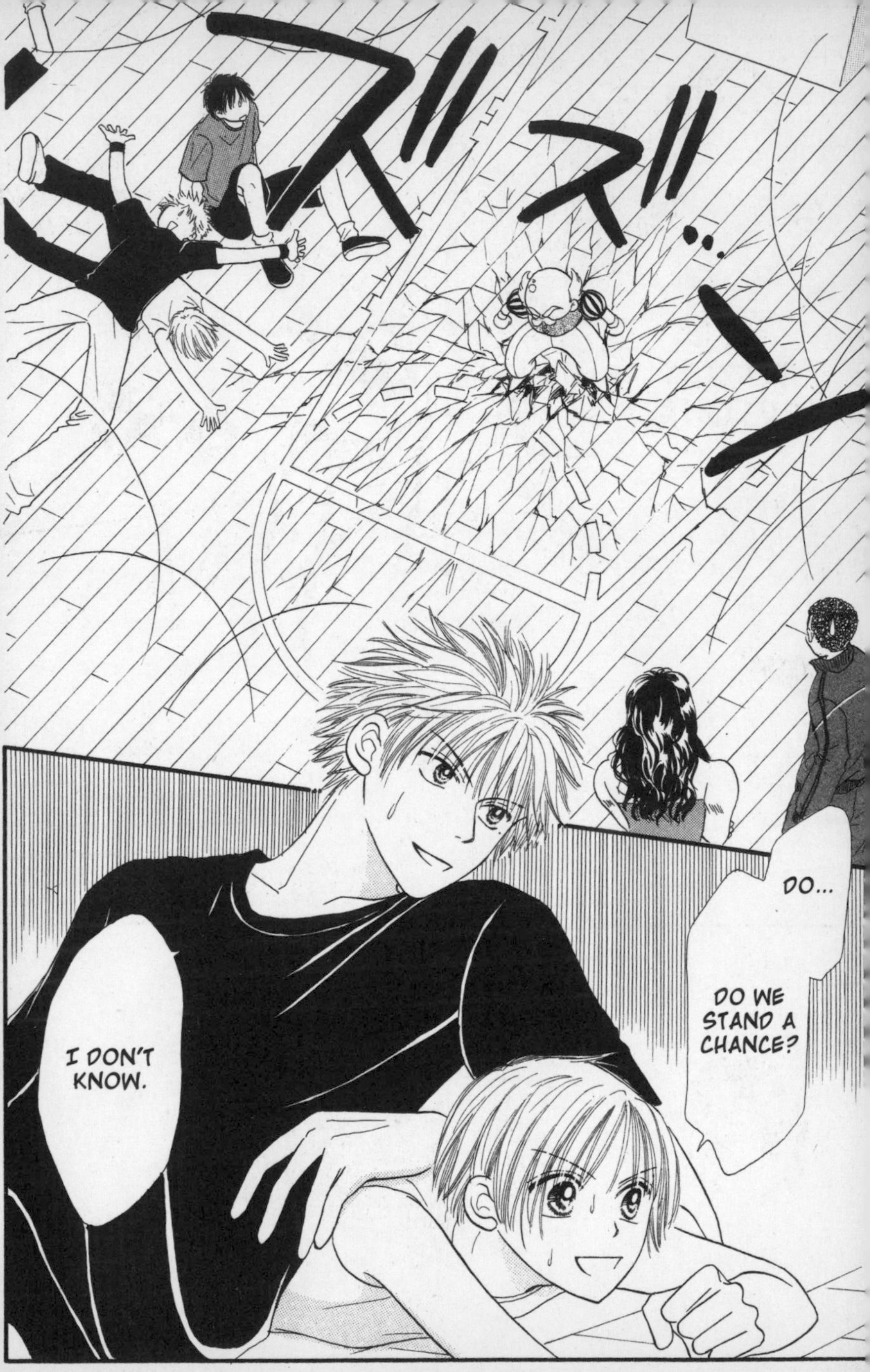
ズズ…
DO...
DO WE STAND A CHANCE?
I DON'T KNOW.

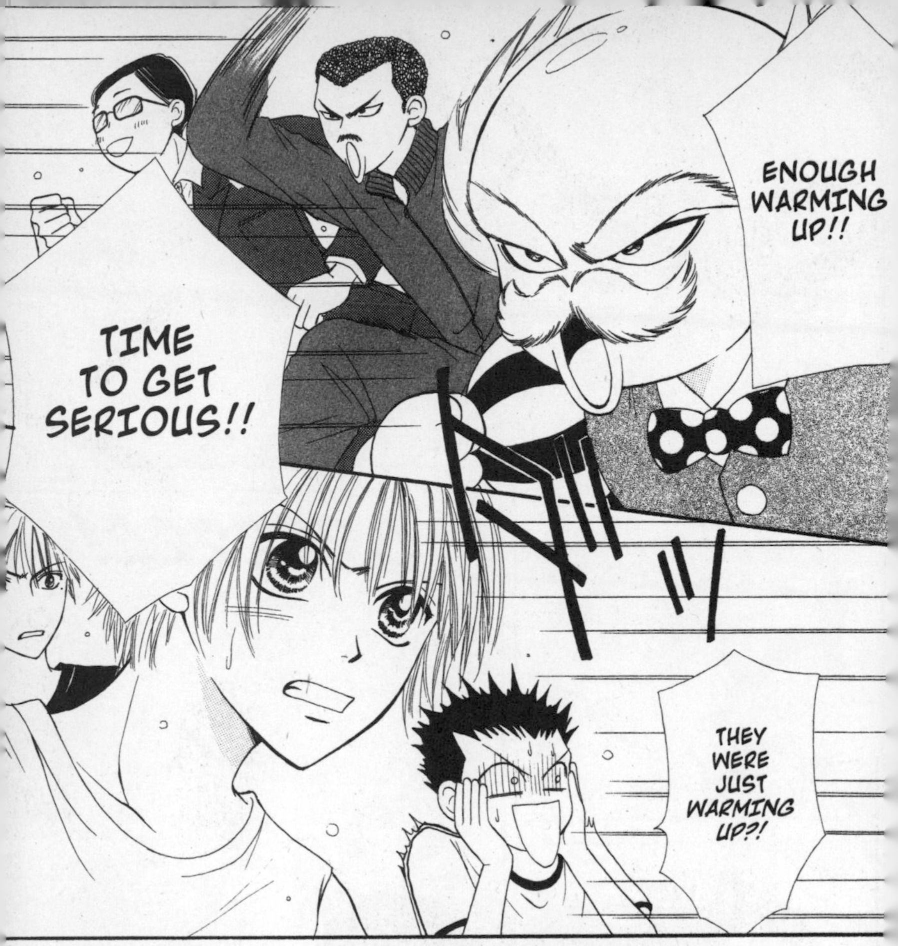
ENOUGH WARMING UP!!
TIME TO GET SERIOUS!!
THEY WERE JUST WARMING UP?!

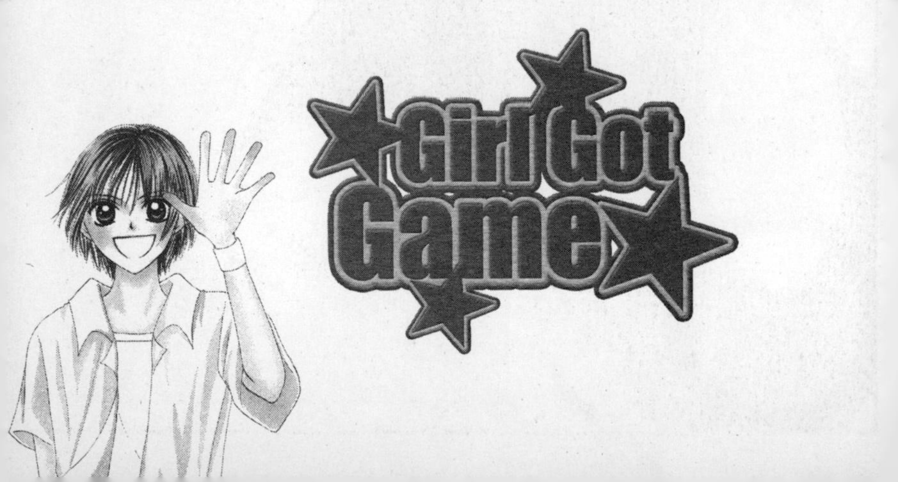
Girl Got Game

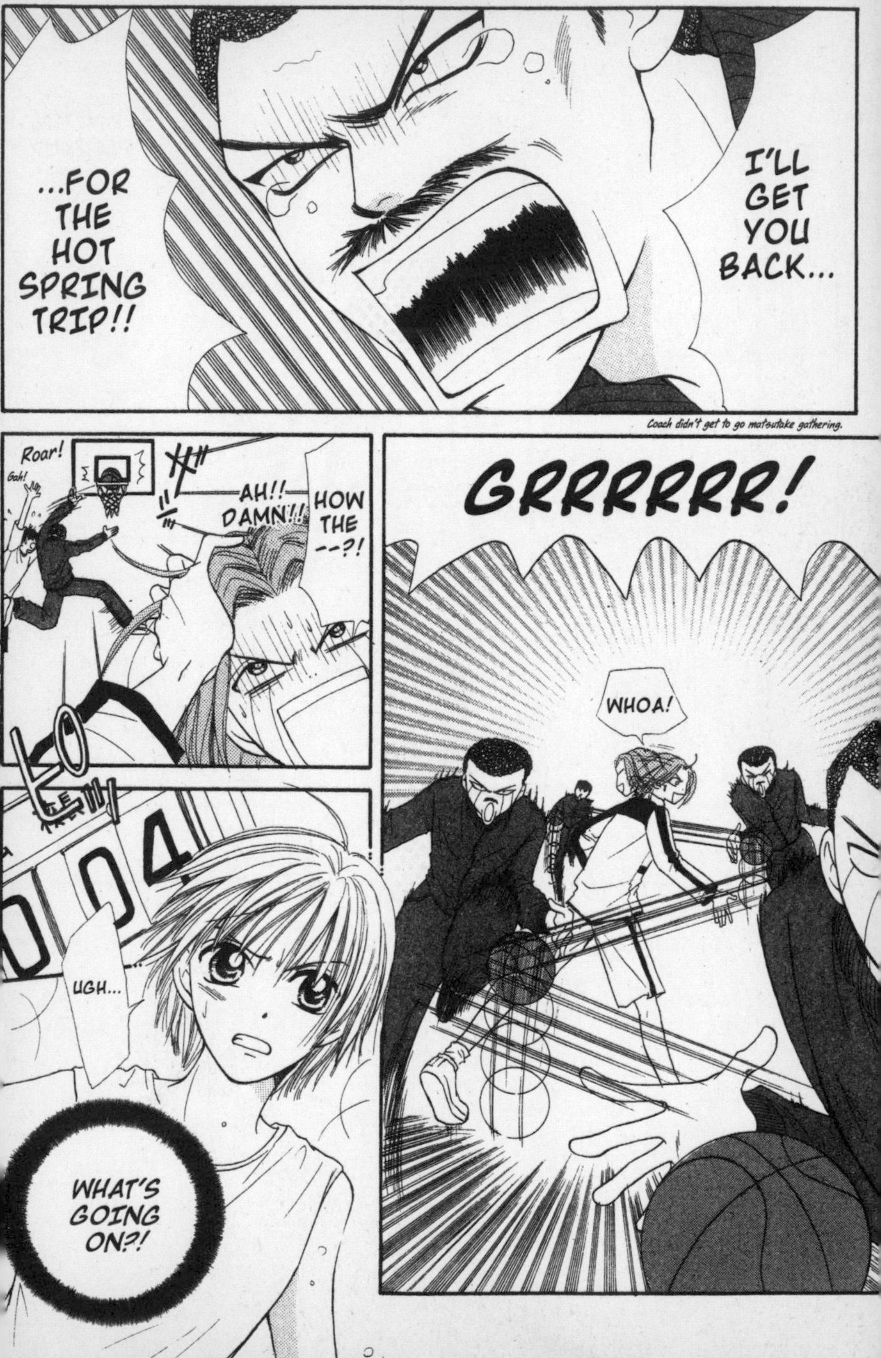
I'LL GET YOU BACK...
...FOR THE HOT SPRING TRIP!!
Coach didn't get to go matsutake gathering.
GRRRRRRR!
WHOA!
HOW THE --?!
AH!! DAMN!!
Roar!
Gah!
UGH...
WHAT'S GOING ON?!

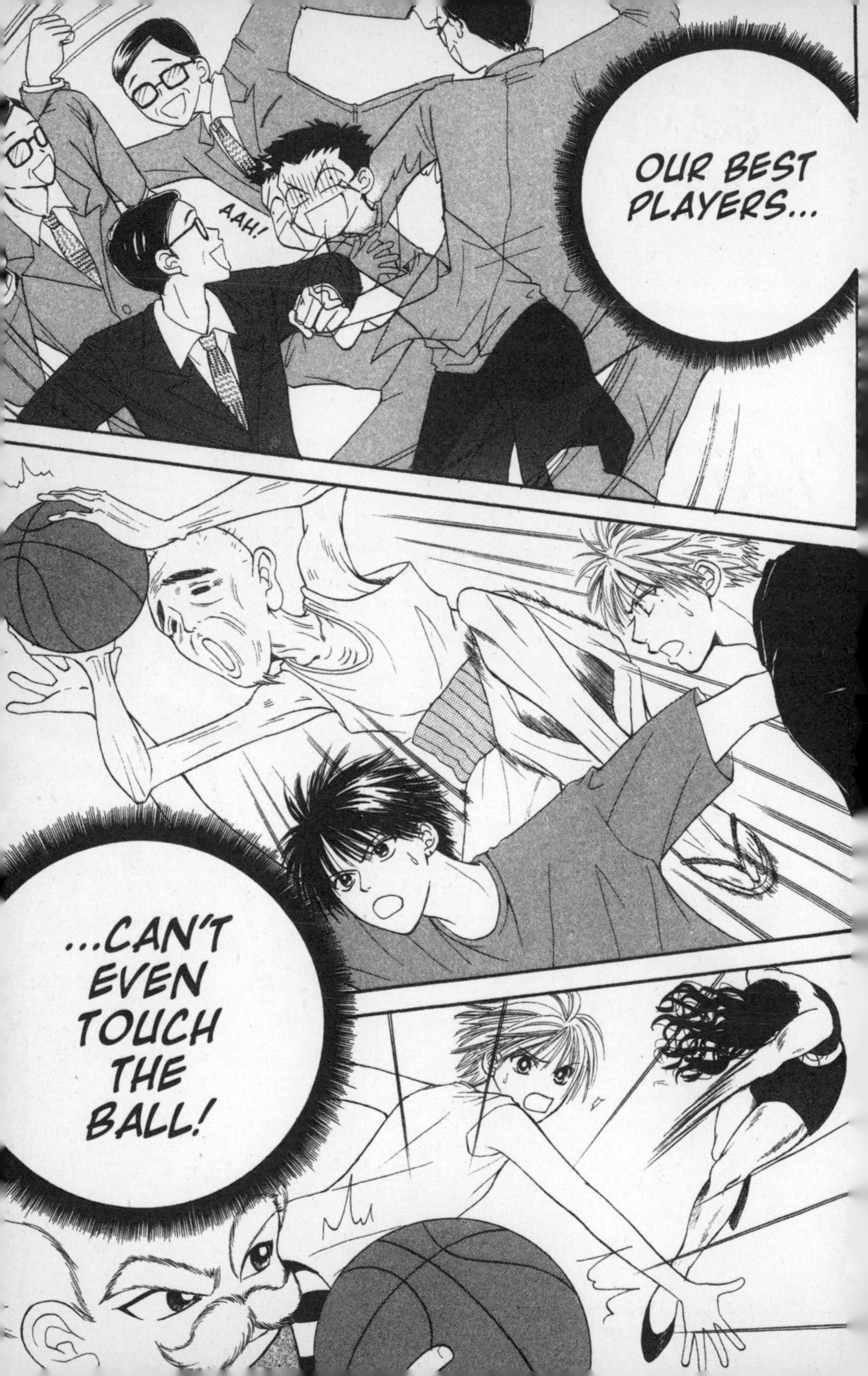
OUR BEST PLAYERS...
AAH!
...CAN'T EVEN TOUCH THE BALL!

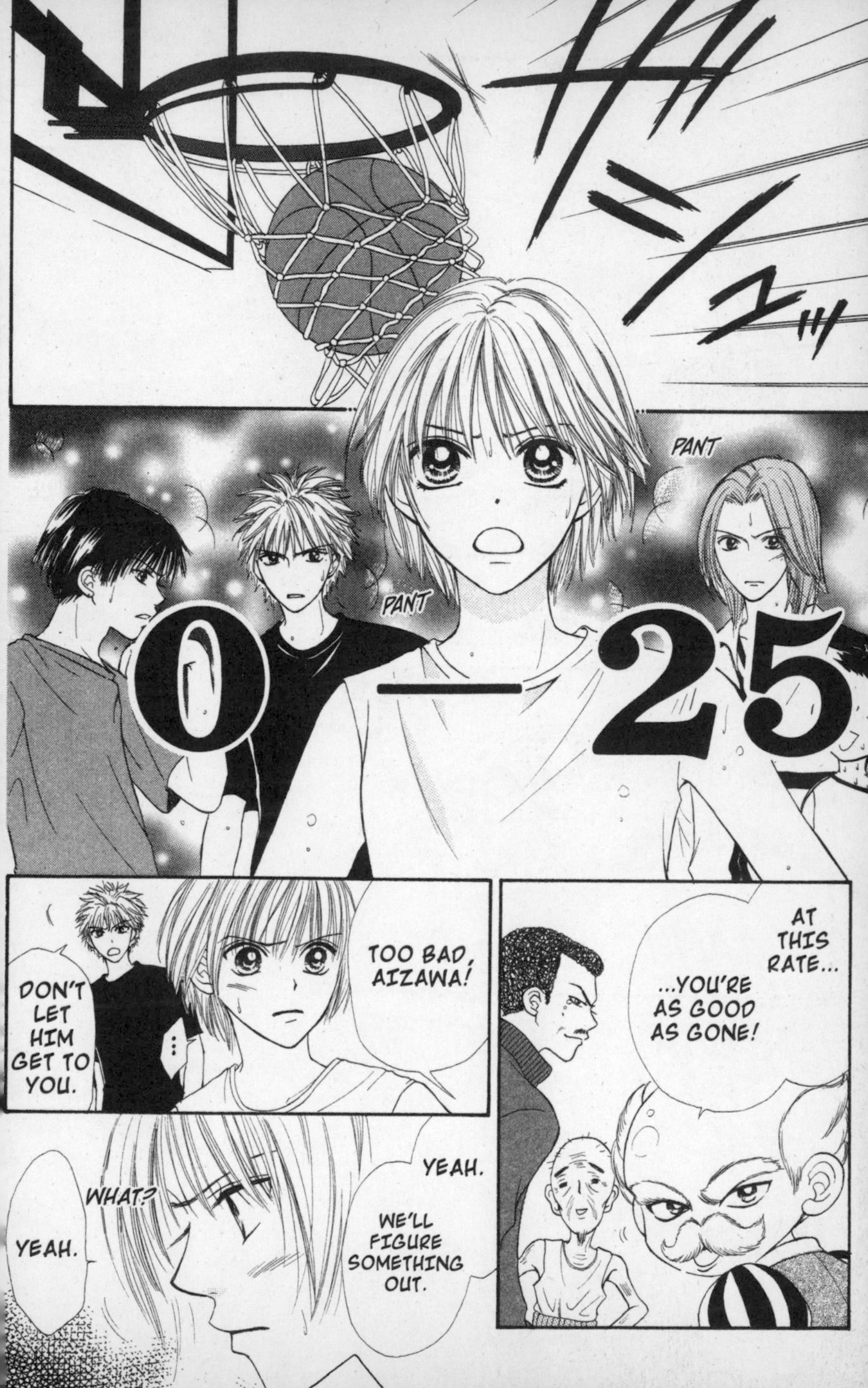
PANT
PANT
0—25
AT THIS RATE...
...YOU'RE AS GOOD AS GONE!
TOO BAD, AIZAWA!
DON'T LET HIM GET TO YOU.
YEAH.
WE'LL FIGURE SOMETHING OUT.
WHAT?
YEAH.

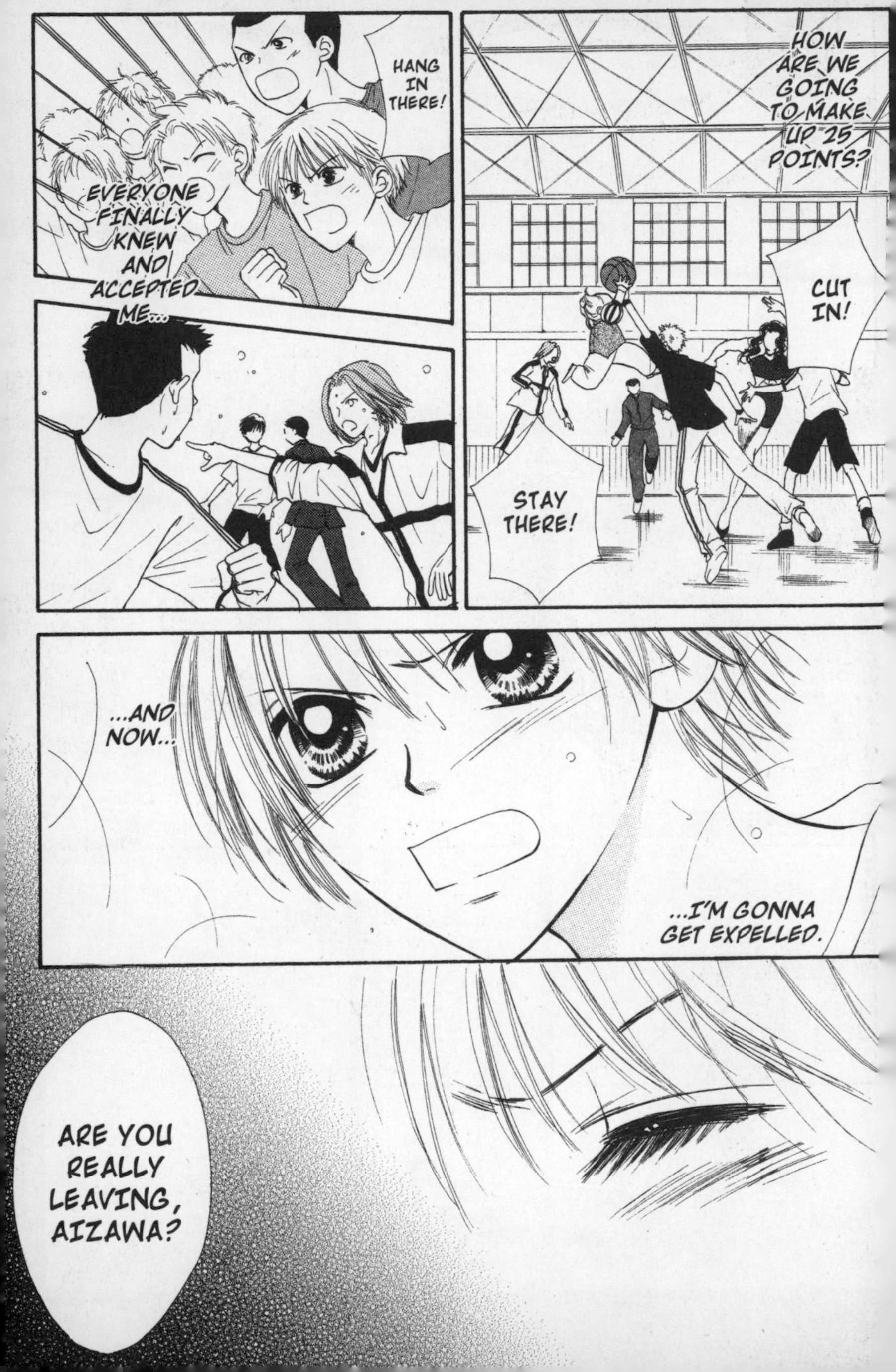
HOW ARE WE GOING TO MAKE UP 25 POINTS?
CUT IN!
STAY THERE!
HANG IN THERE!
EVERYONE FINALLY KNEW AND ACCEPTED ME...
...AND NOW...
...I'M GONNA GET EXPELLED.
ARE YOU REALLY LEAVING, AIZAWA?

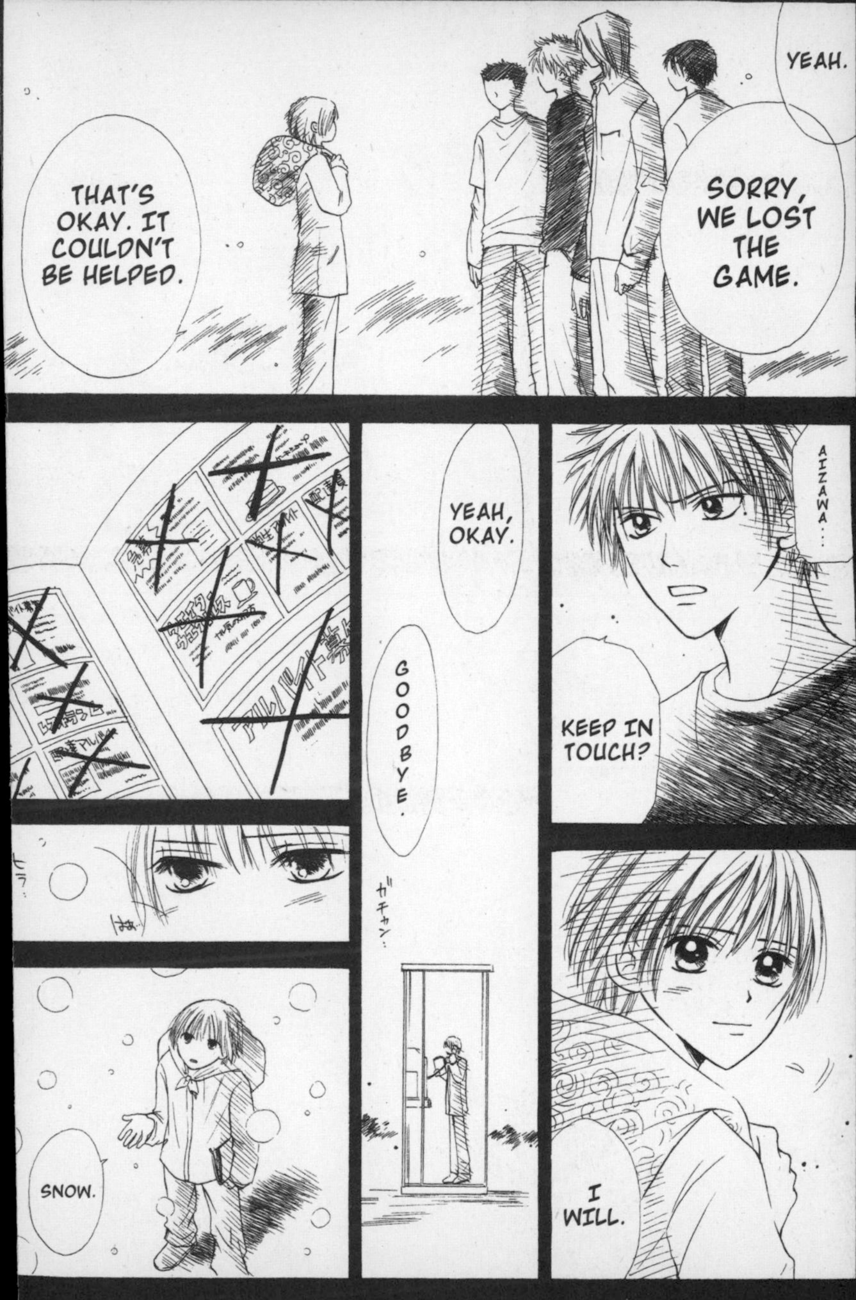
YEAH.
SORRY, WE LOST THE GAME.
THAT'S OKAY. IT COULDN'T BE HELPED.
AIZAWA...
KEEP IN TOUCH?
I WILL.
YEAH, OKAY.
GOODBYE.
ガチャン…
ヒラ…
はぁ…
SNOW.

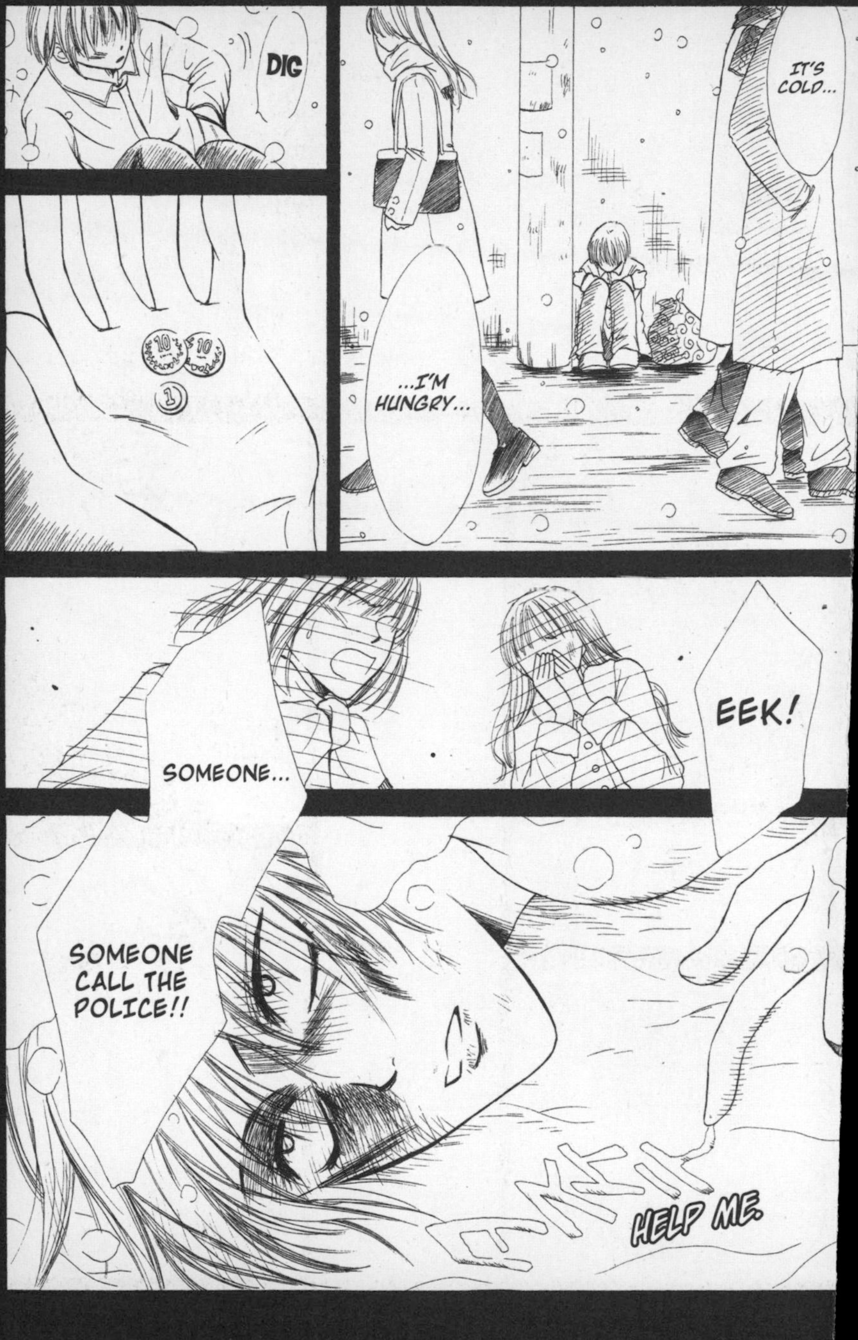
IT'S COLD...
...I'M HUNGRY...
DIG
EEK!
SOMEONE...
SOMEONE CALL THE POLICE!!
HELP ME.

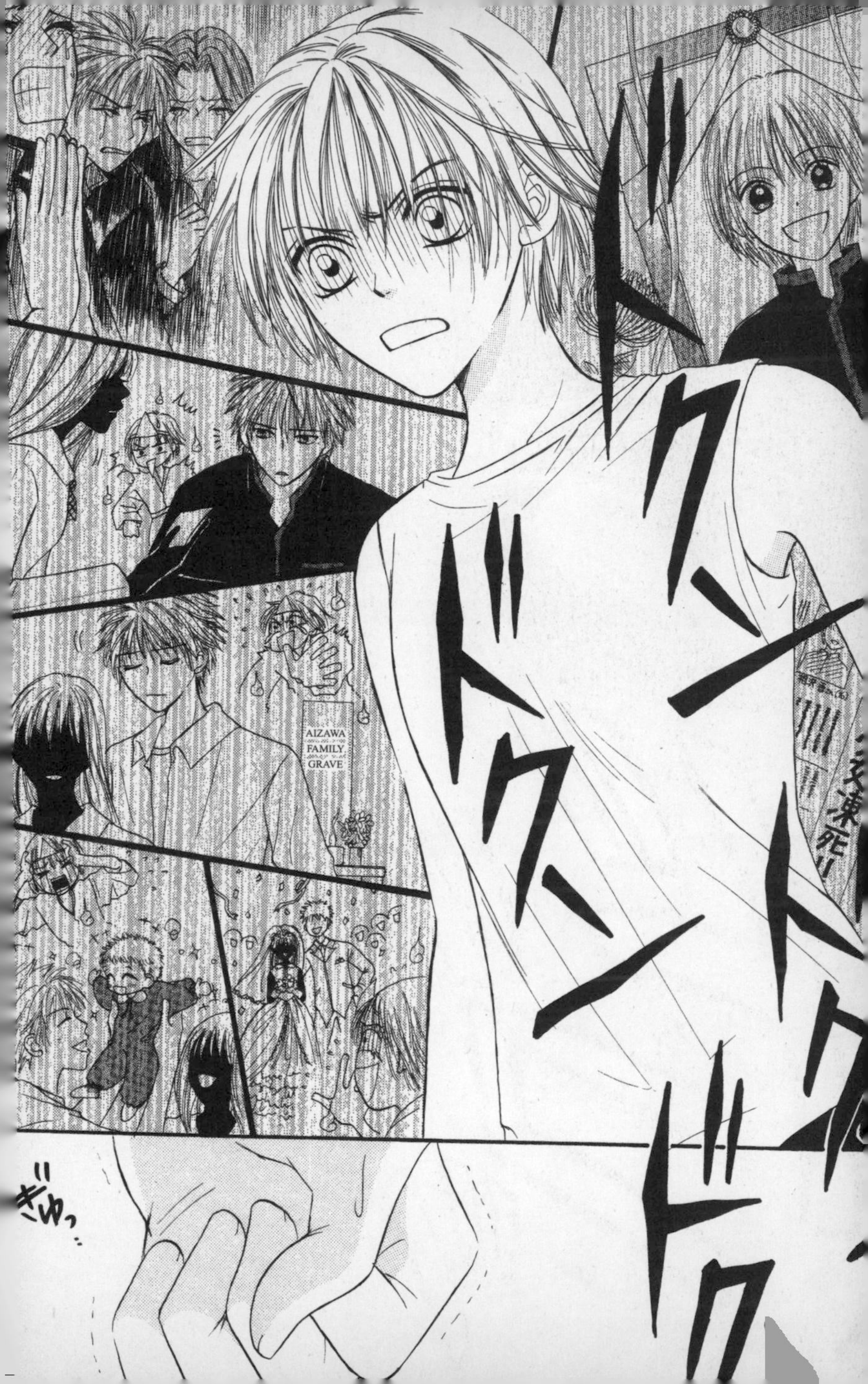
ドクン
ドクン
父凍死!!
AIZAWA FAMILY GRAVE
ドクン
ぎゅっ…

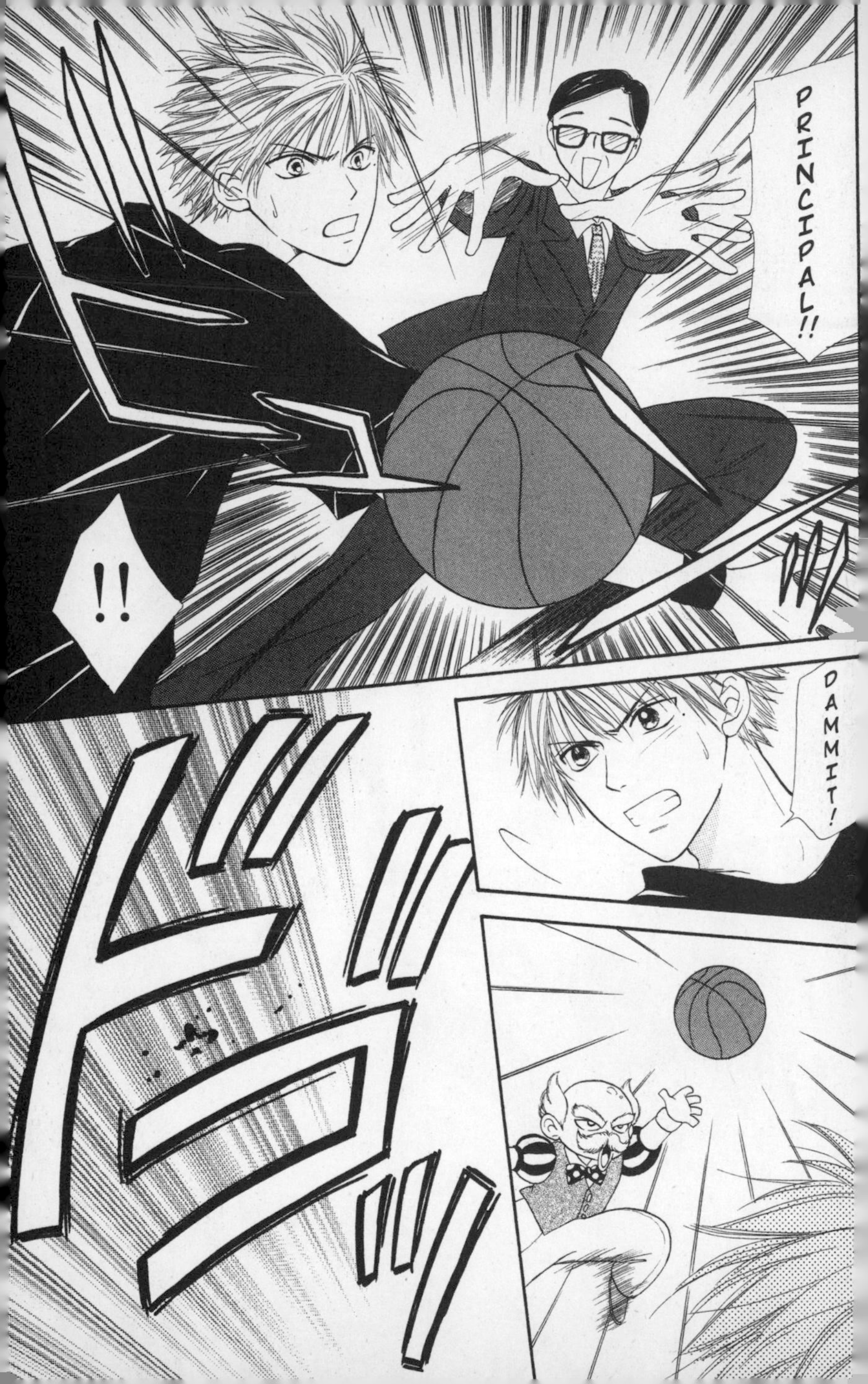
PRINCIPAL!!
!!
DAMMIT!

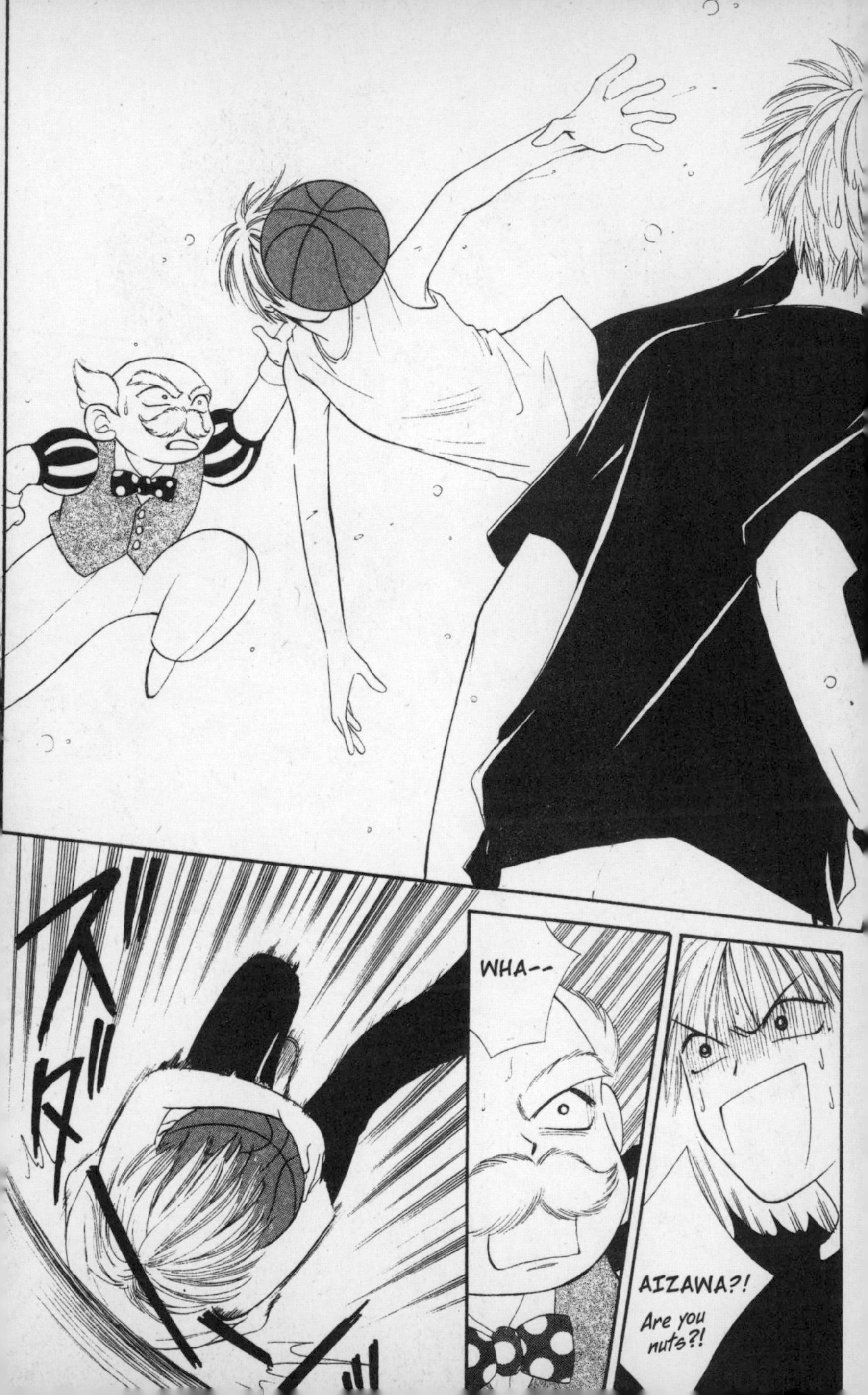
AIZAWA?!
Are you nuts?!
WHA--
ズダ

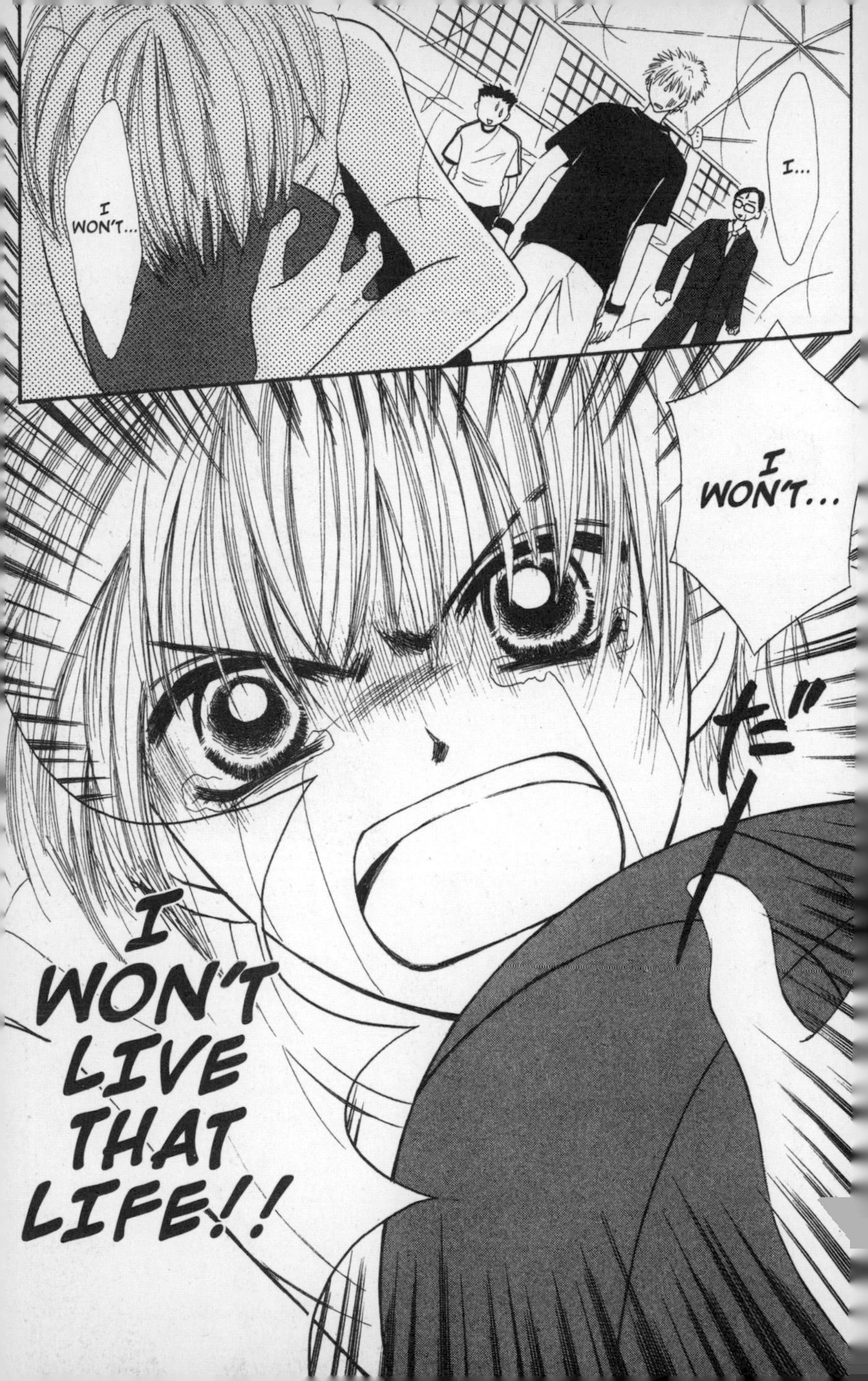
I...
I WON'T...
I WON'T...
だ
I WON'T LIVE THAT LIFE!!

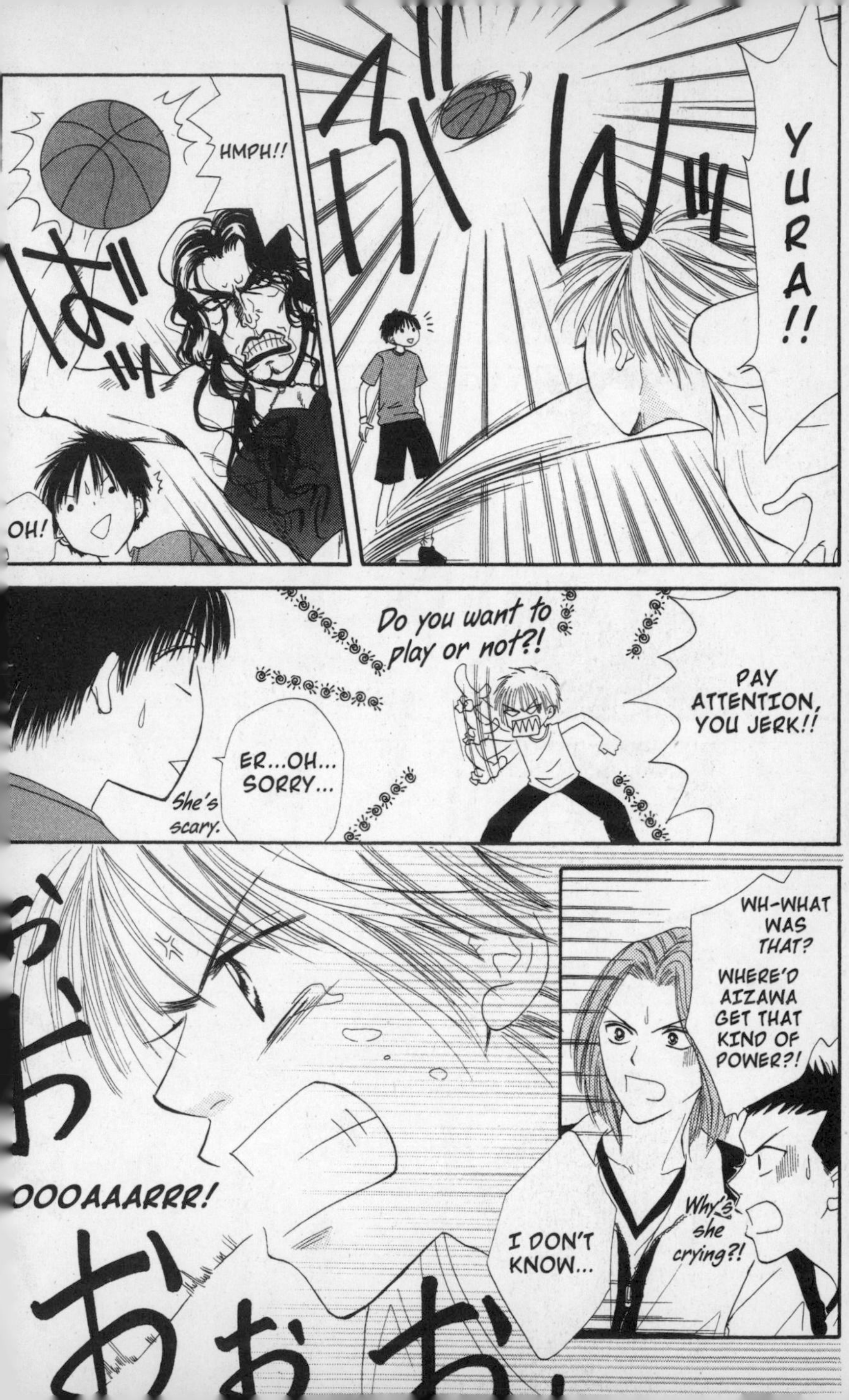
YURA!!
HMPH!!
OH!
PAY ATTENTION, YOU JERK!!
Do you want to play or not?!
ER...OH... SORRY...
She's scary.
WH-WHAT WAS THAT?
WHERE'D AIZAWA GET THAT KIND OF POWER?!
Why's she crying?!
I DON'T KNOW...
OOOAAARRR!

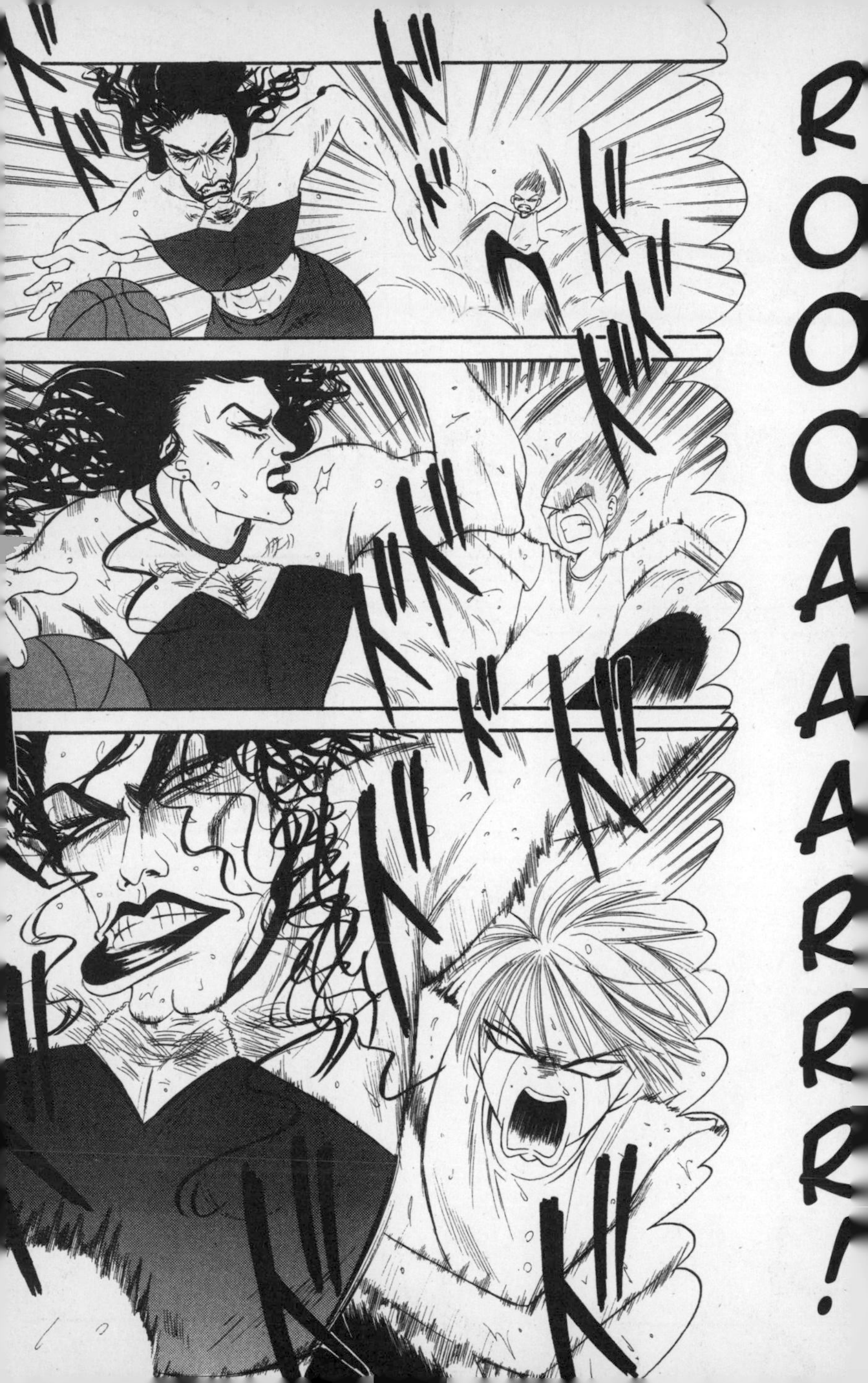
ROOOAAARRR!

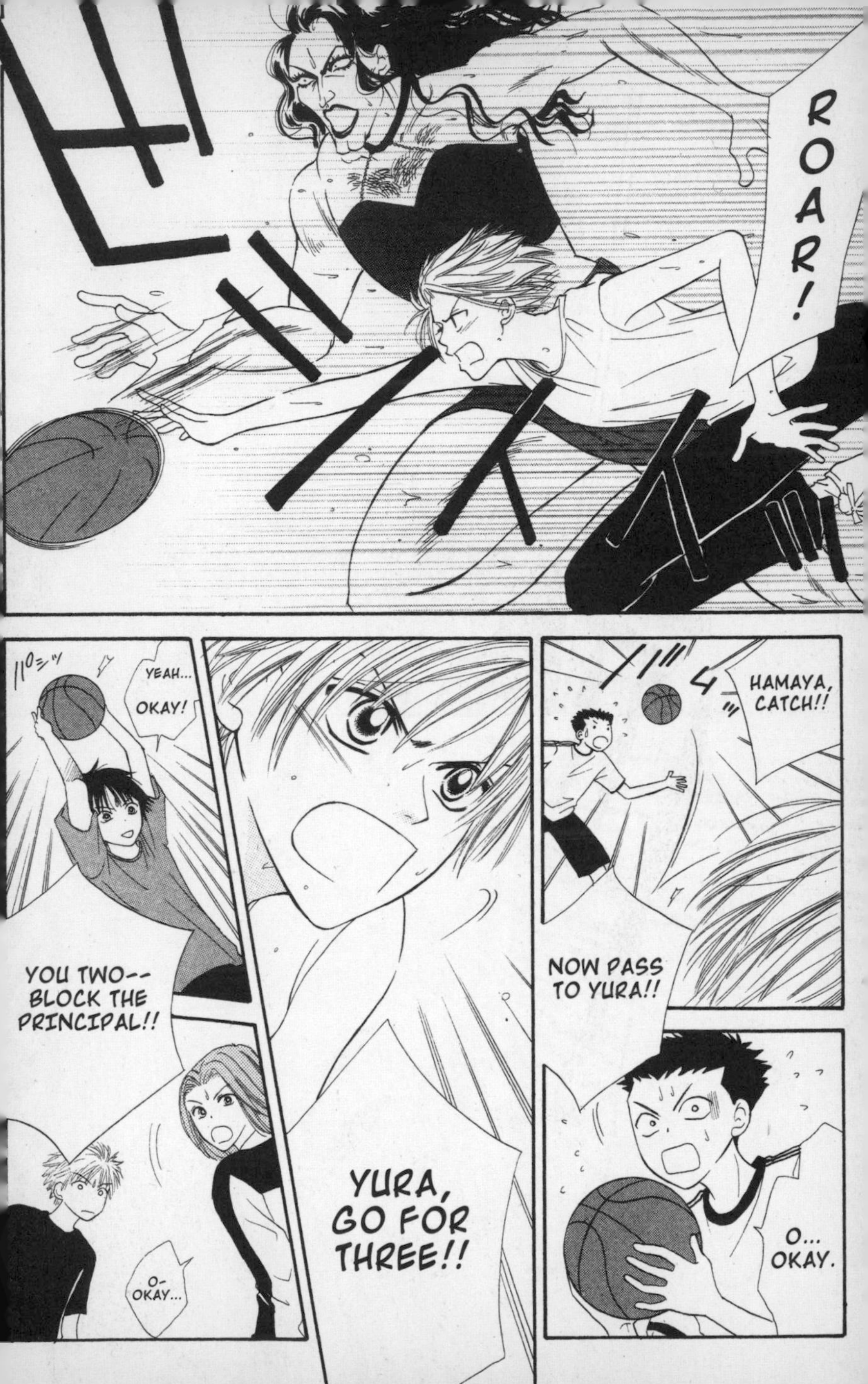
ROAR!
HAMAYA, CATCH!!
NOW PASS TO YURA!!
O... OKAY.
YURA, GO FOR THREE!!
YEAH... OKAY!
YOU TWO-- BLOCK THE PRINCIPAL!!
O- OKAY...

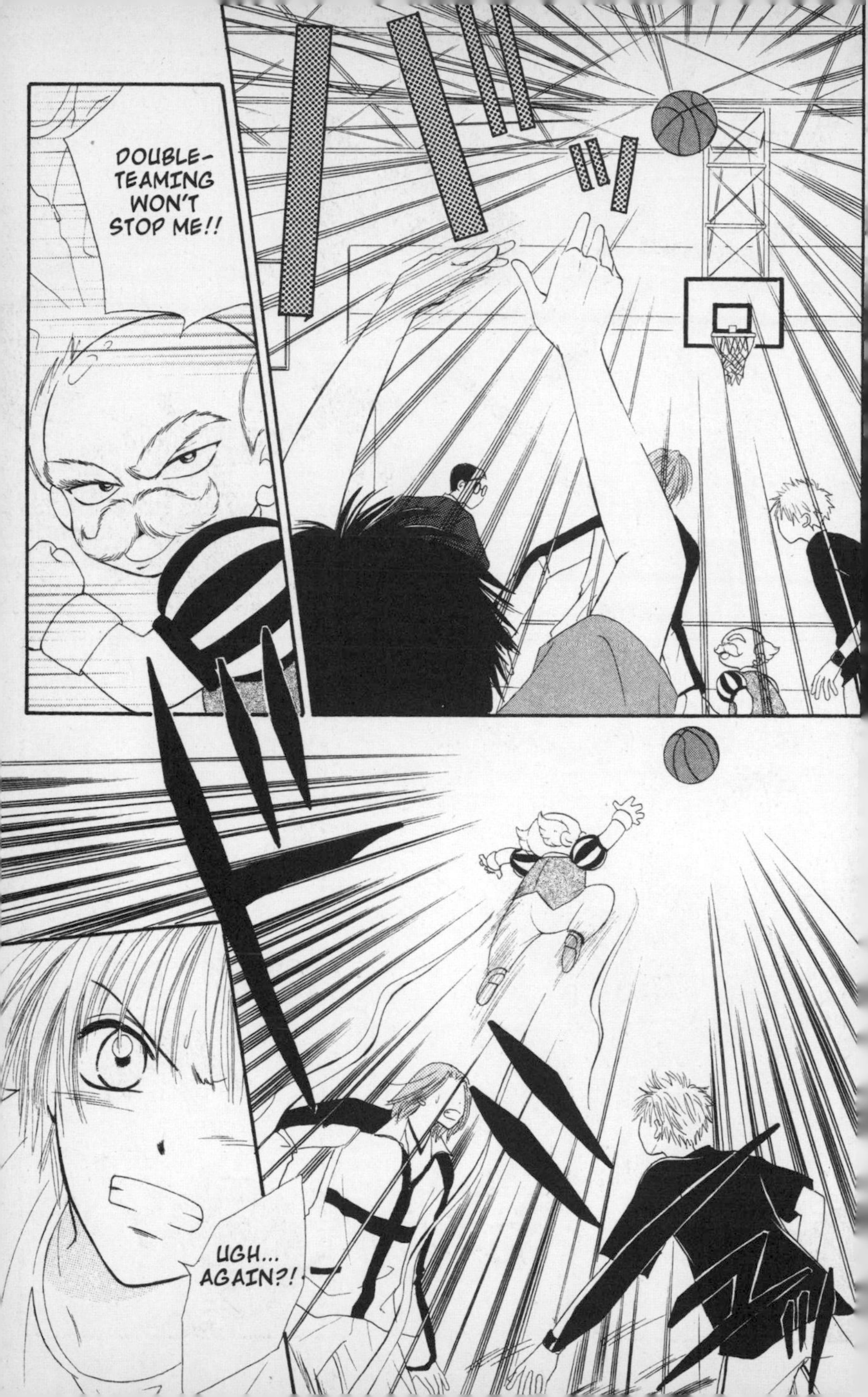
DOUBLE-TEAMING WON'T STOP ME!!
UGH... AGAIN?!

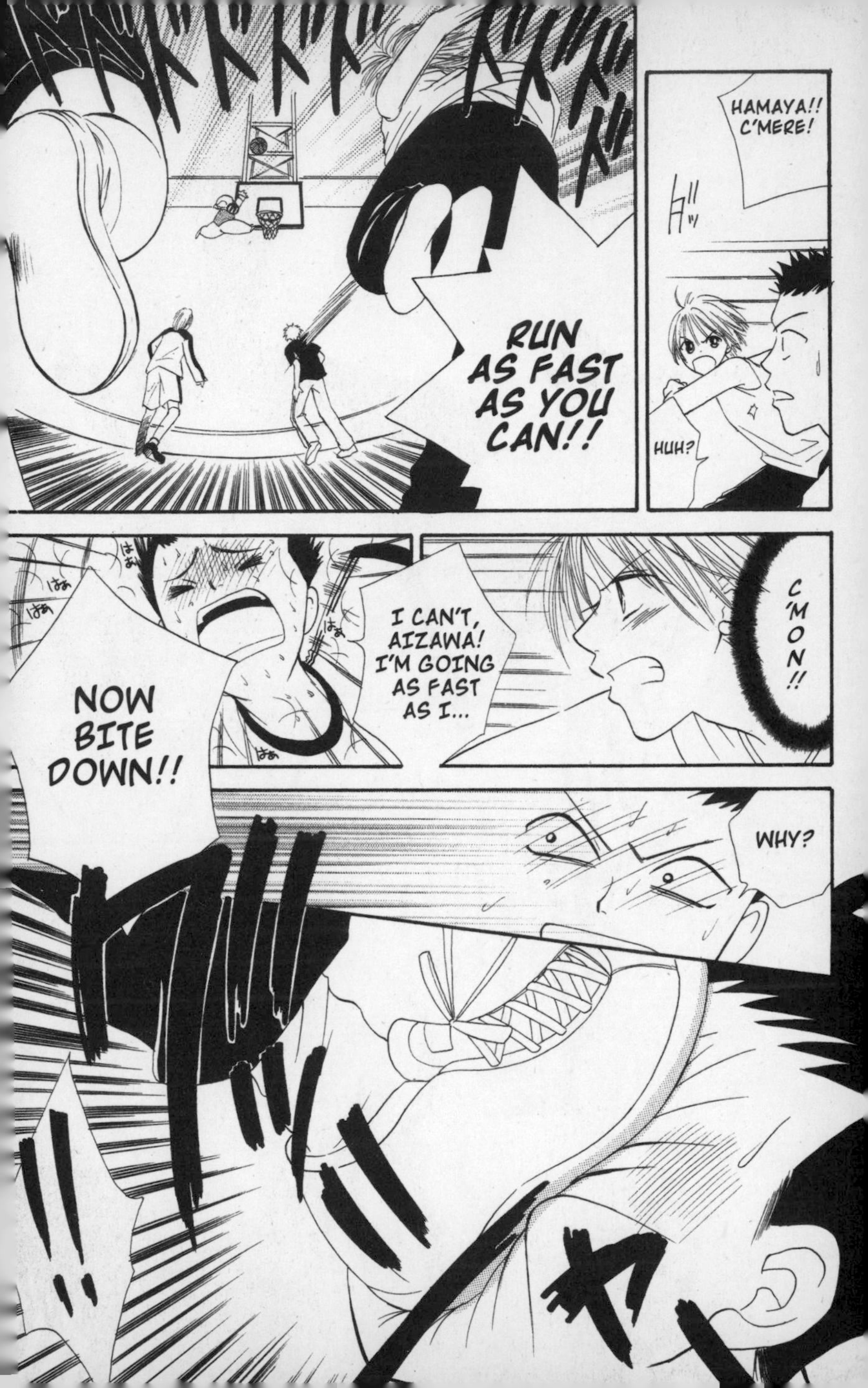
HAMAYA!! C'MERE!
HUH?
RUN AS FAST AS YOU CAN!!
C'MON!!
I CAN'T, AIZAWA! I'M GOING AS FAST AS I...
NOW BITE DOWN!!
WHY?

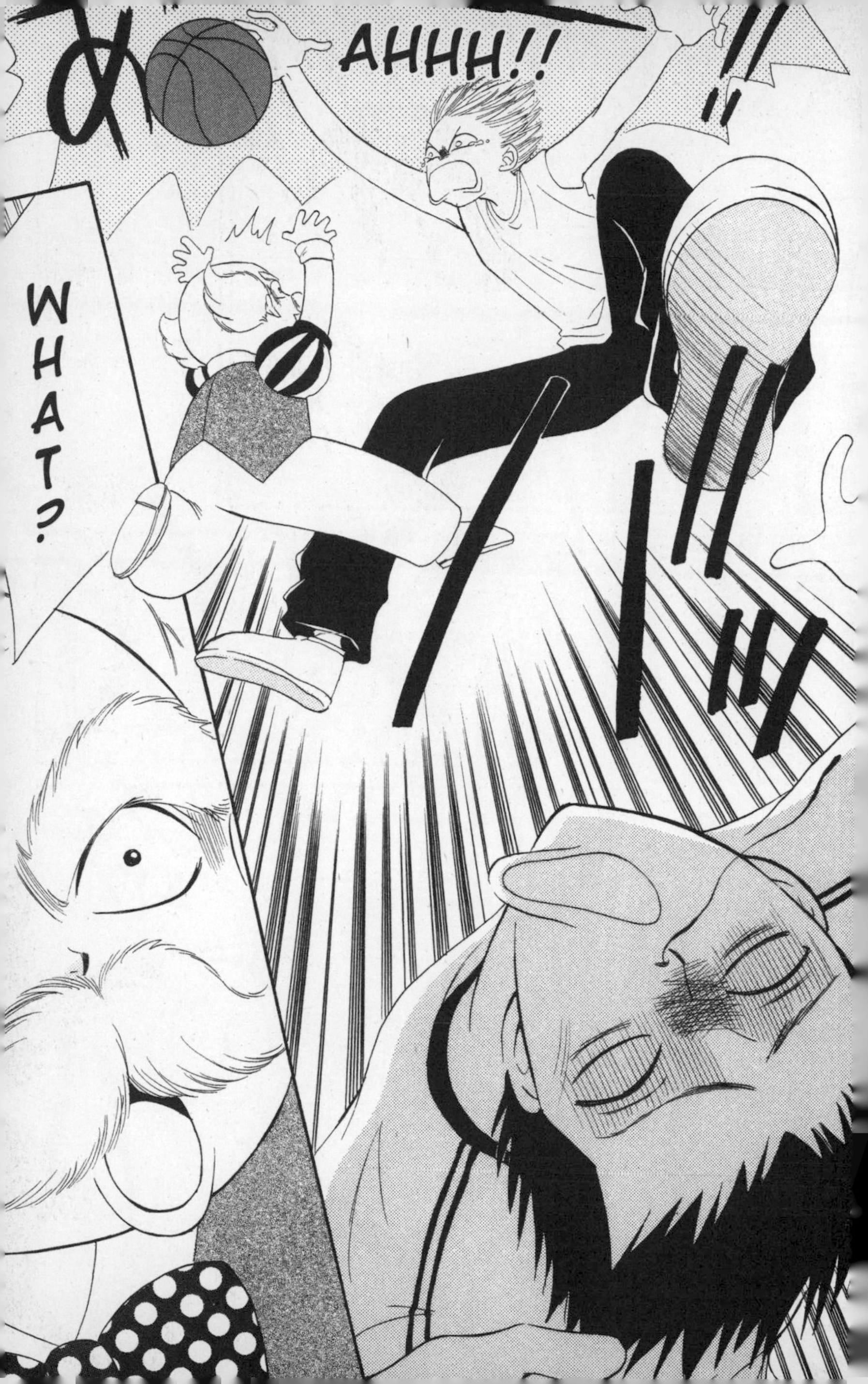
AHHH!!
ぬ
WHAT?

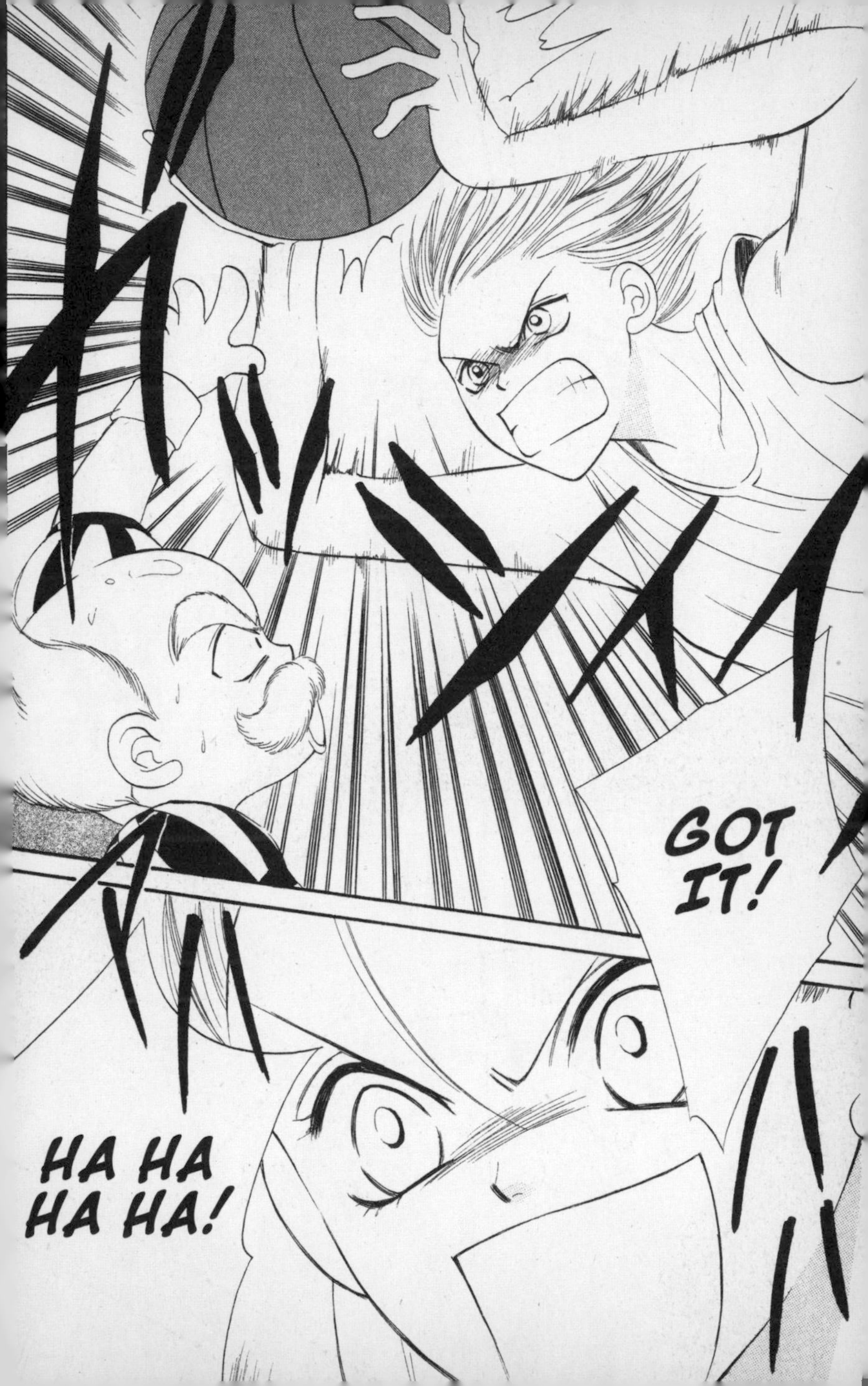
GOT IT!
HA HA HA HA!

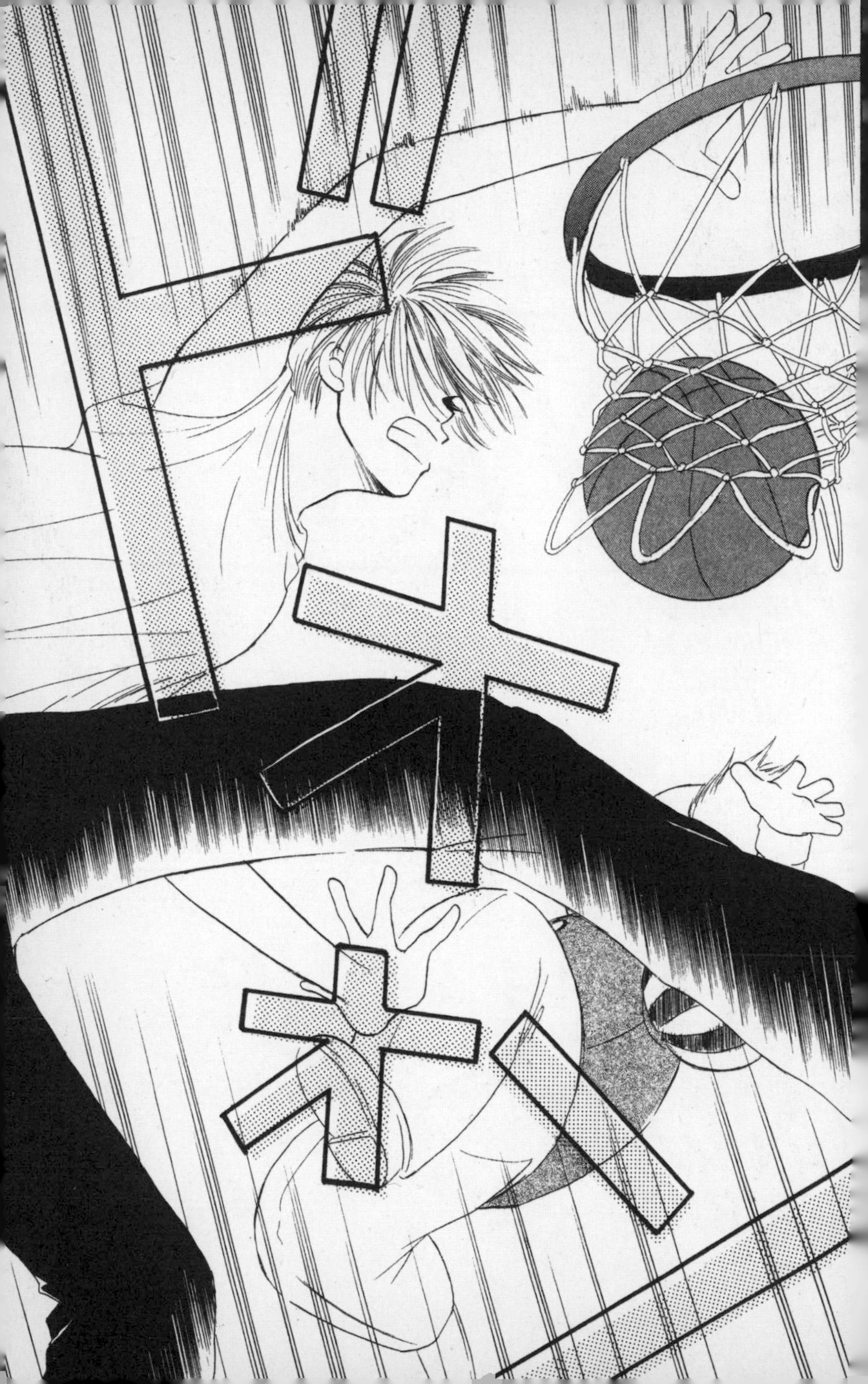

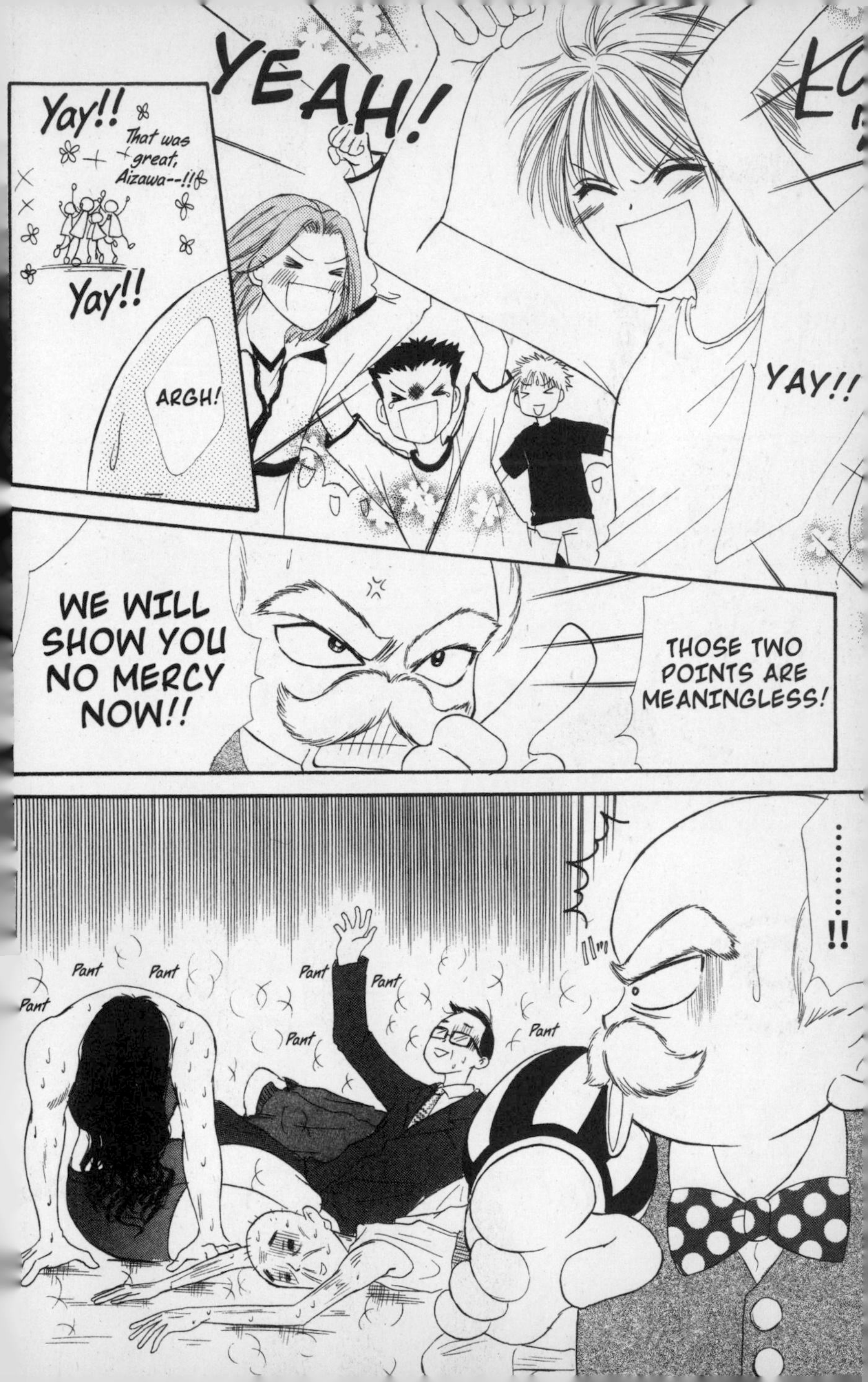
YEAH!
YAY!!
Yay!!
That was great, Aizawa--!!
Yay!!
ARGH!
THOSE TWO POINTS ARE MEANINGLESS!
WE WILL SHOW YOU NO MERCY NOW!!
......!!
Pant
Pant
Pant
Pant
Pant
Pant
Pant

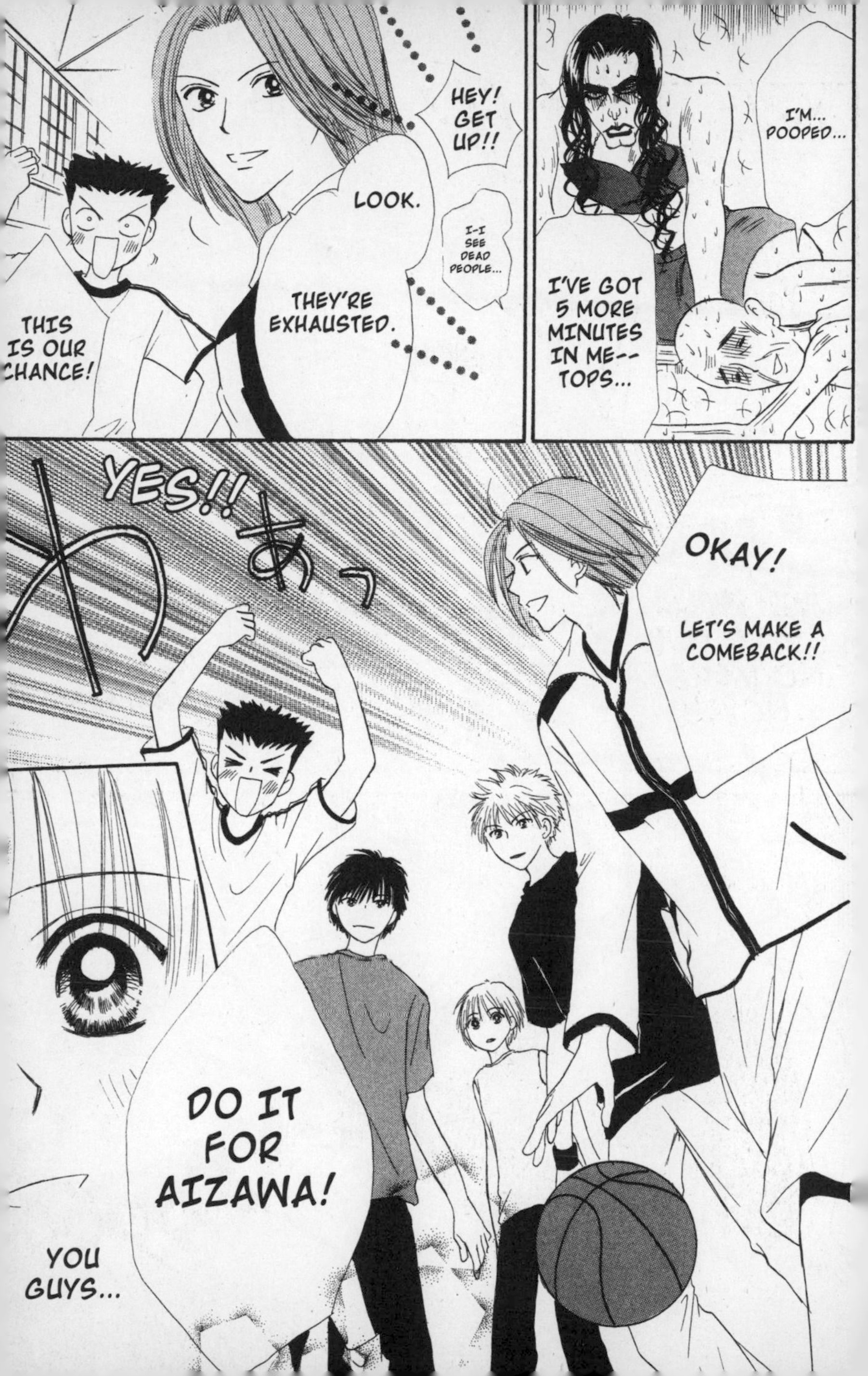
I'M... POOPED...
I'VE GOT 5 MORE MINUTES IN ME-- TOPS...
HEY! GET UP!!
I-I SEE DEAD PEOPLE...
LOOK.
THEY'RE EXHAUSTED.
THIS IS OUR CHANCE!
OKAY!
LET'S MAKE A COMEBACK!!
YES!!
やあっ
DO IT FOR AIZAWA!
YOU GUYS...

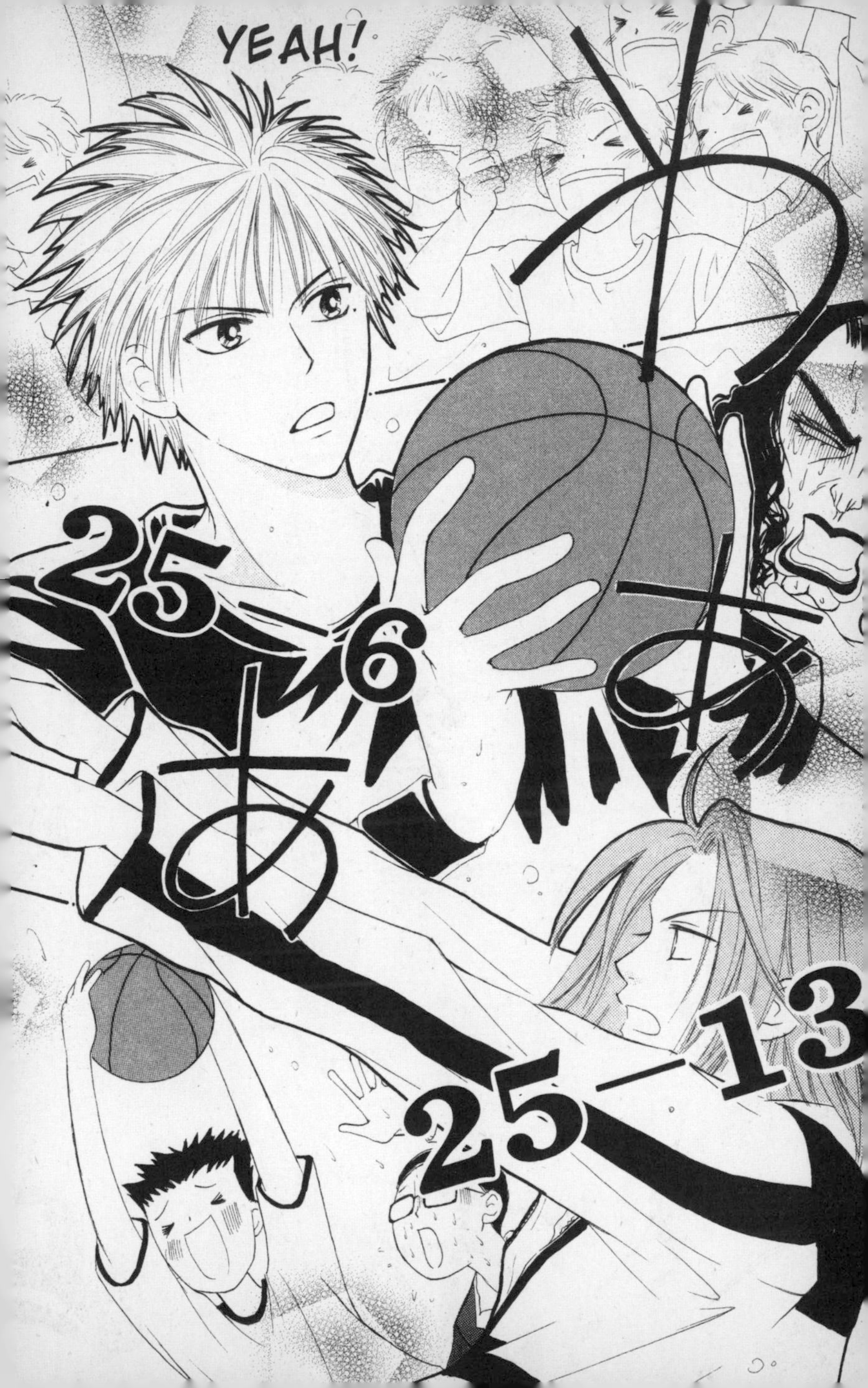
YEAH!
25–6
25–13

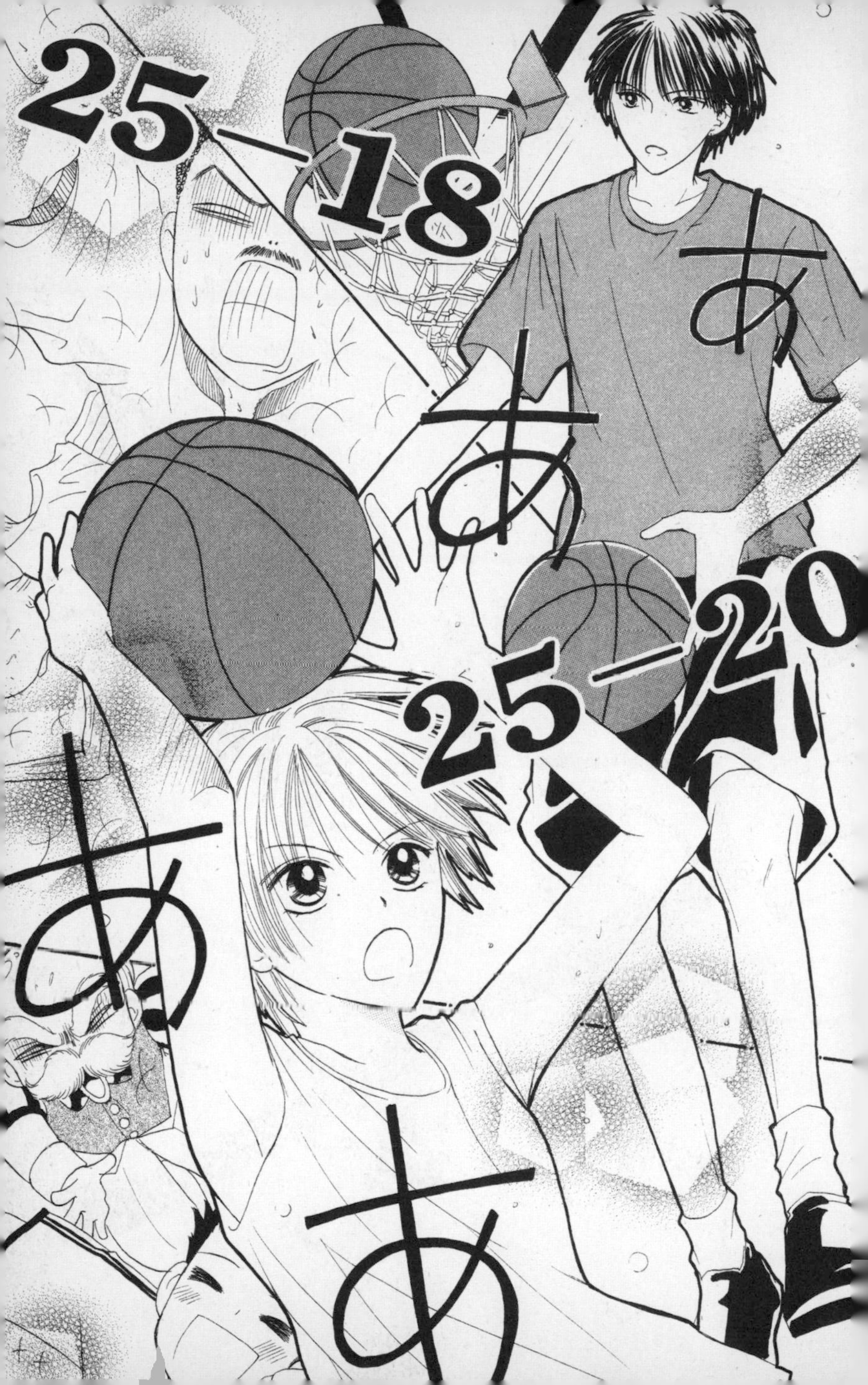
25-18
25-20
あ
あ
あ
あ

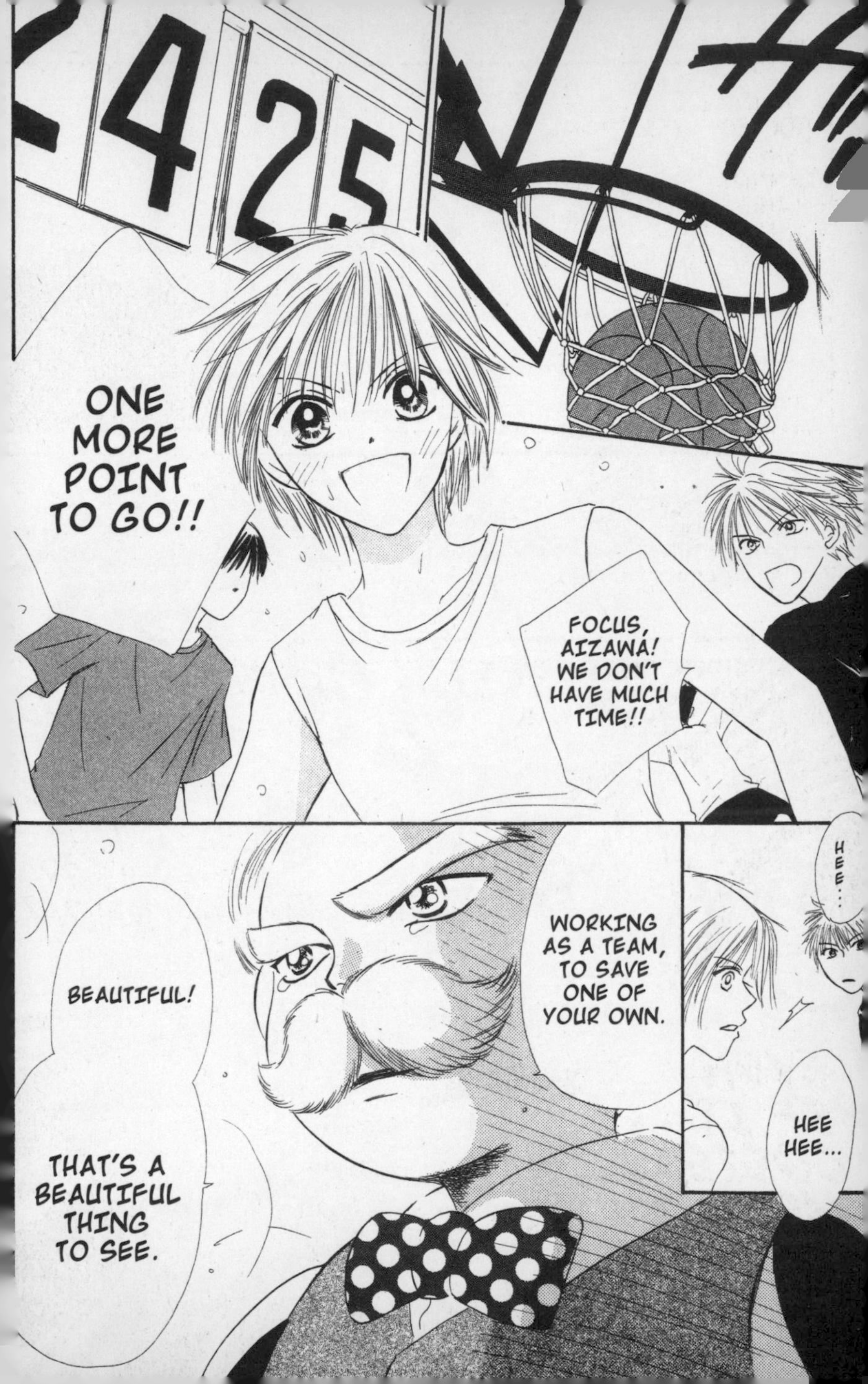
FOCUS, AIZAWA! WE DON'T HAVE MUCH TIME!!
ONE MORE POINT TO GO!!
HEE...
HEE HEE...
WORKING AS A TEAM, TO SAVE ONE OF YOUR OWN.
BEAUTIFUL!
THAT'S A BEAUTIFUL THING TO SEE.

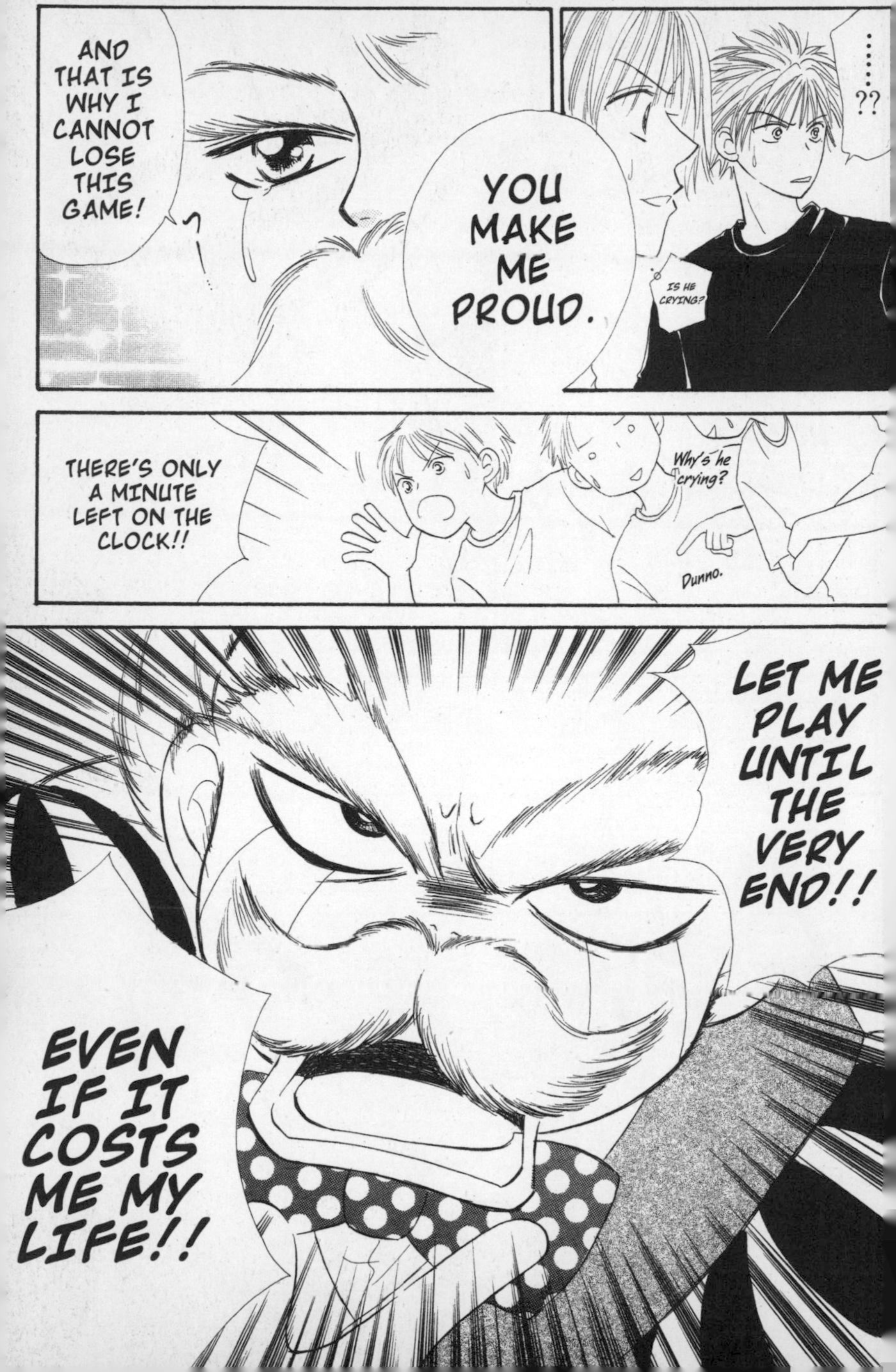
......??
YOU MAKE ME PROUD.
IS HE CRYING?
AND THAT IS WHY I CANNOT LOSE THIS GAME!
Why's he crying?
Dunno.
THERE'S ONLY A MINUTE LEFT ON THE CLOCK!!
LET ME PLAY UNTIL THE VERY END!!
EVEN IF IT COSTS ME MY LIFE!!

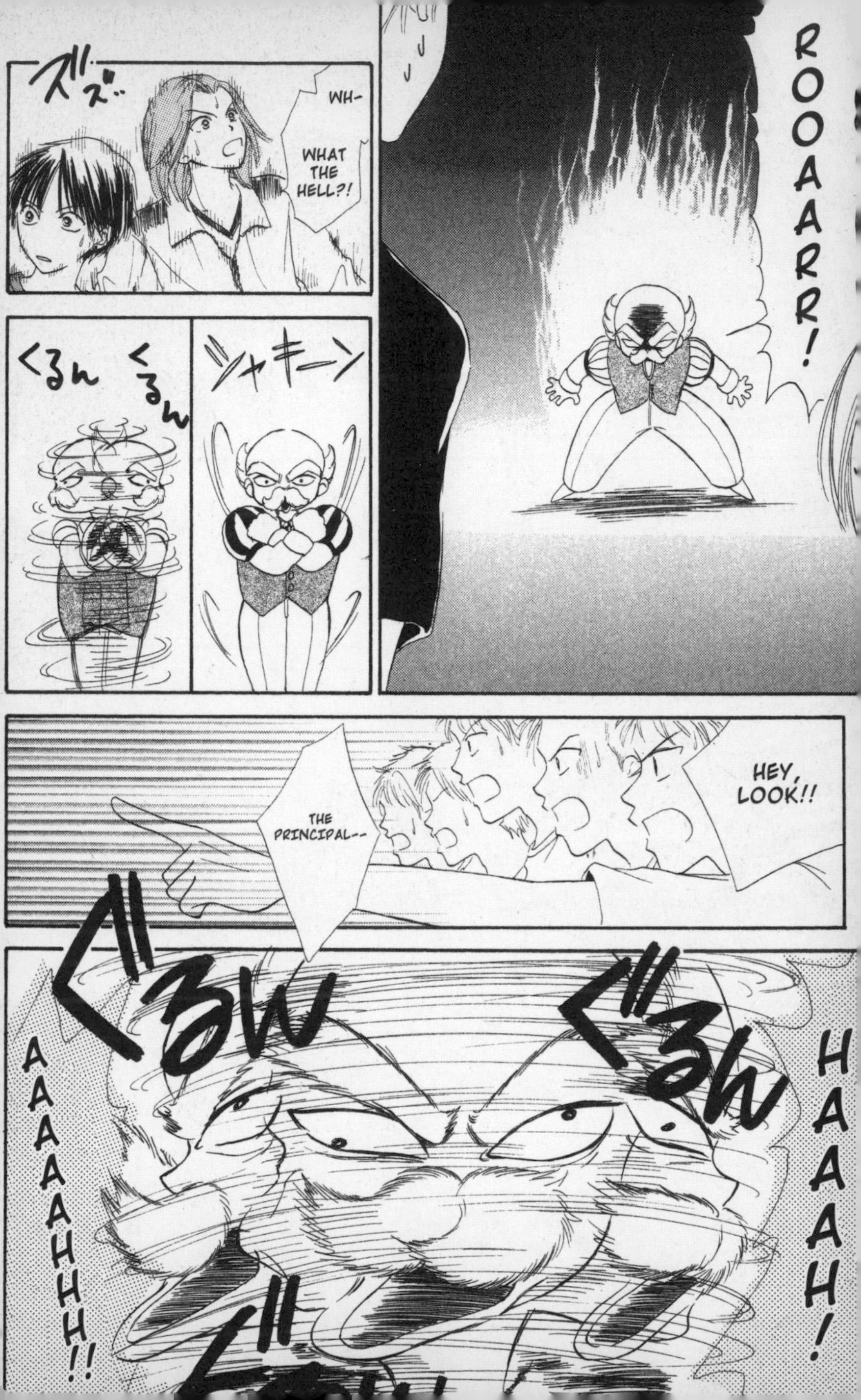
ROOAARR!
ズズ
WH-
WHAT THE HELL?!
シャキーン
くるん くるん
HEY, LOOK!!
THE PRINCIPAL--
HAAAAH!
ぐるん
ぐるん
AAAAAHHH!!

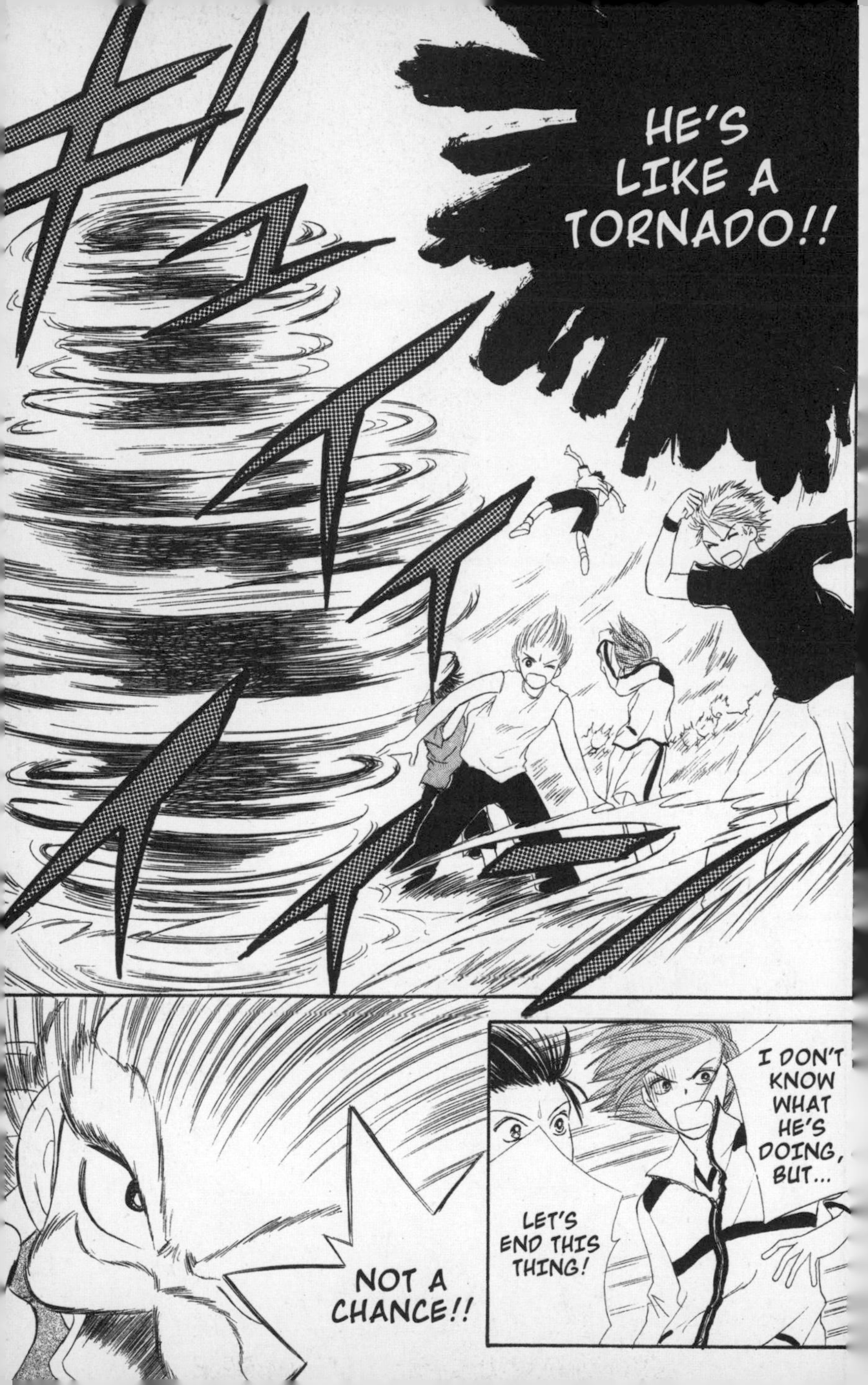
HE'S LIKE A TORNADO!!
I DON'T KNOW WHAT HE'S DOING, BUT...
LET'S END THIS THING!
NOT A CHANCE!!

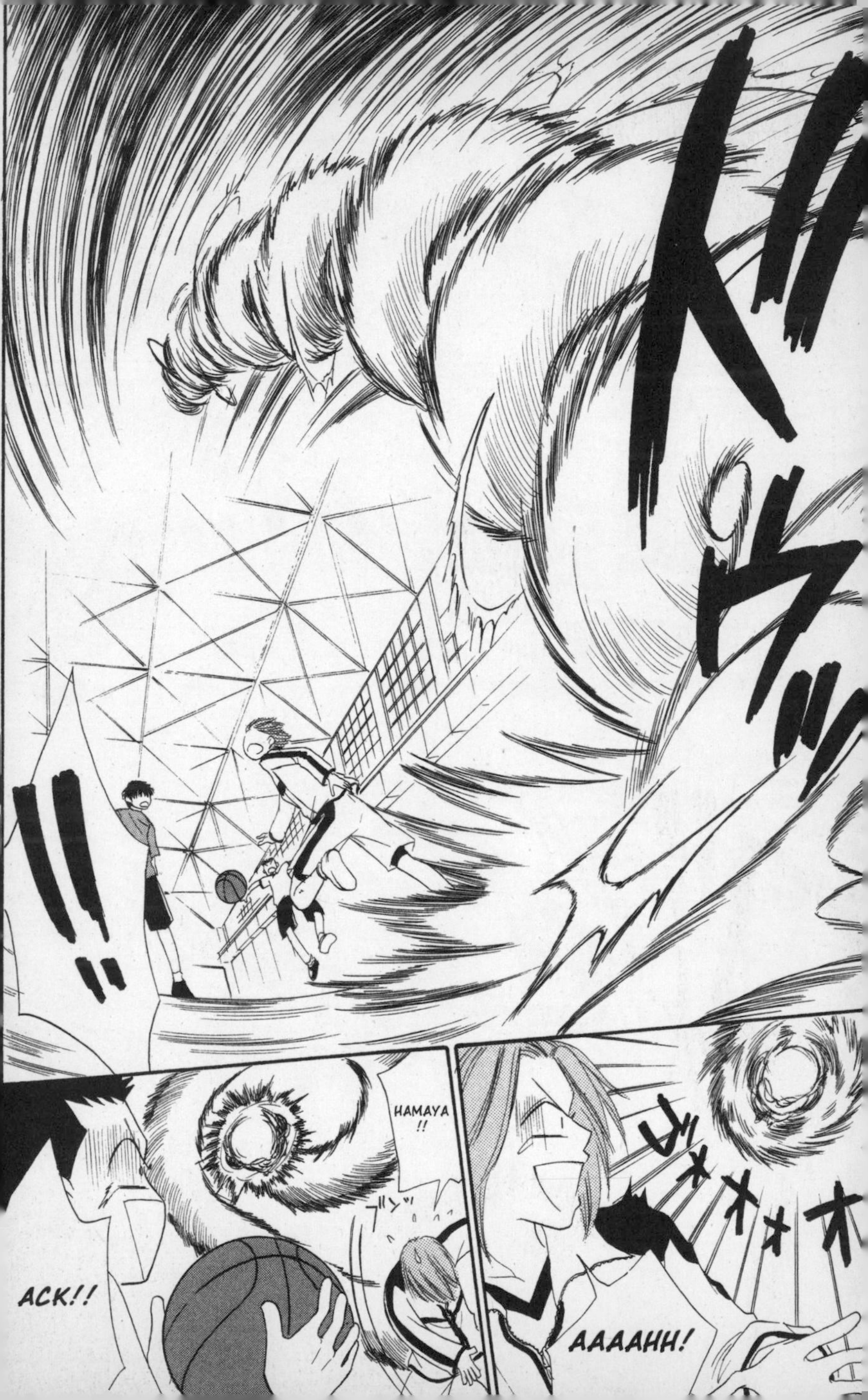
AAAAHH!
HAMAYA !!
ACK!!

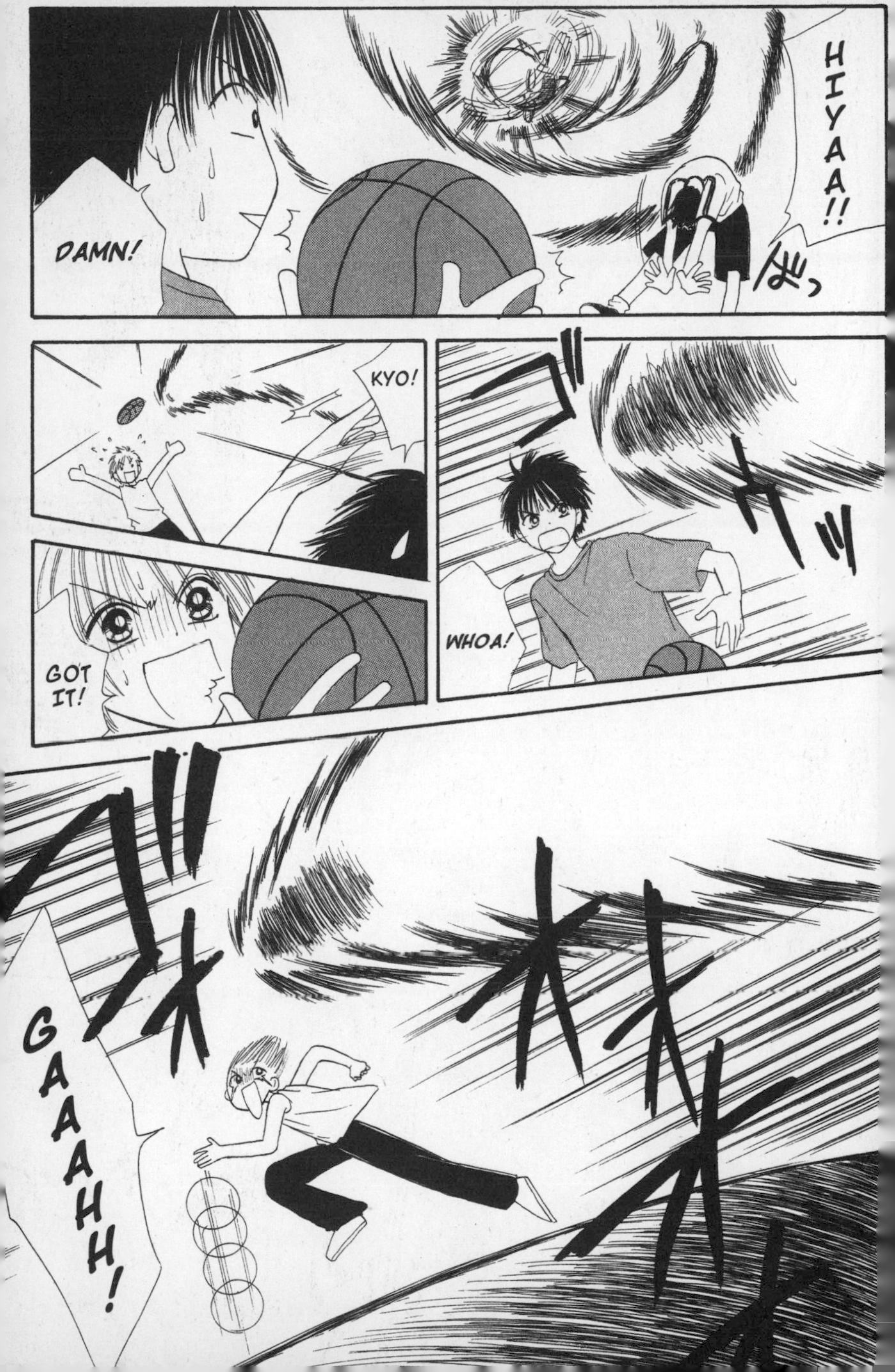
HIYAAA!!
ぱっ
DAMN!
WHOA!
KYO!
GOT IT!
GAAAHH!

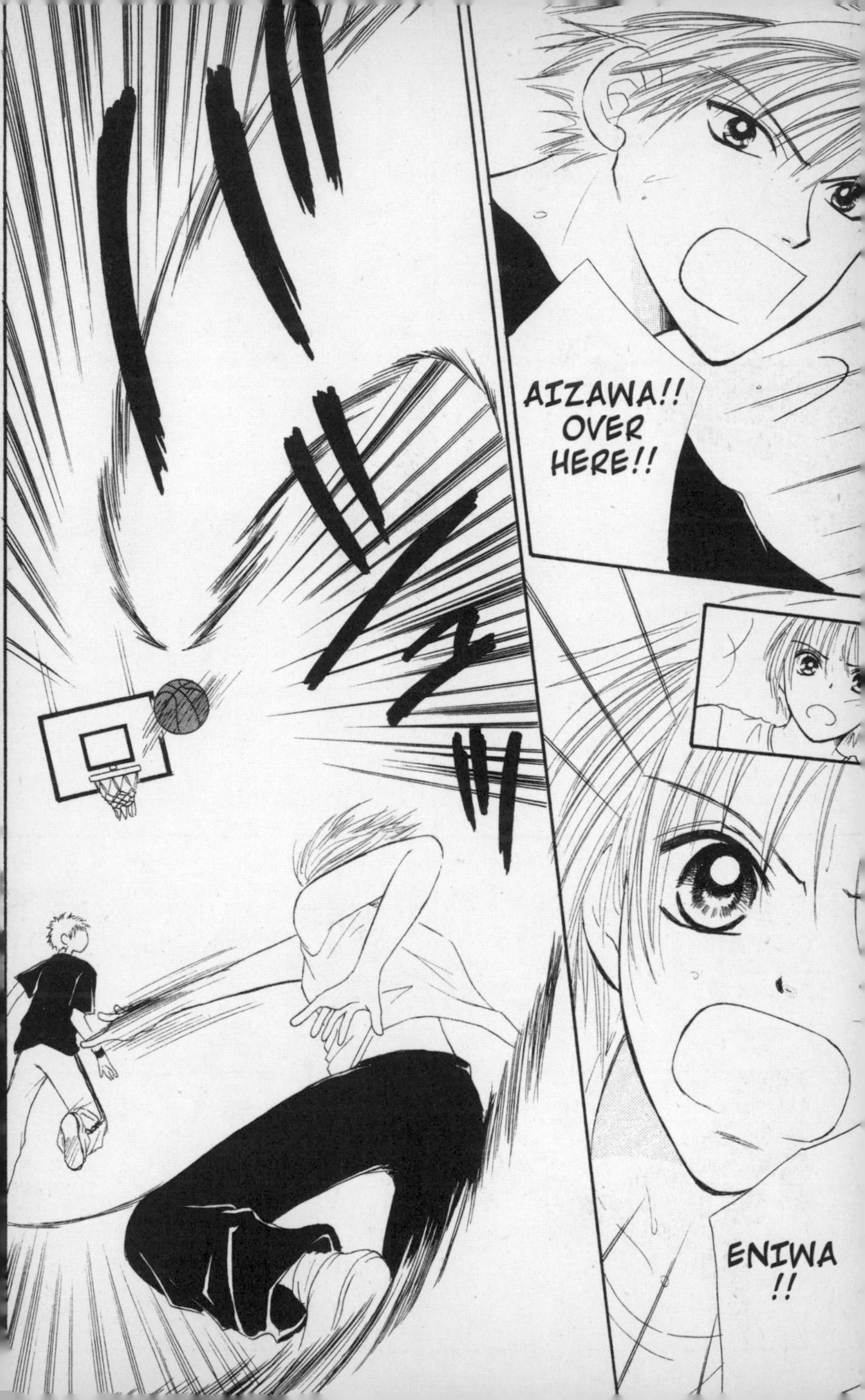
AIZAWA!! OVER HERE!!
ENIWA !!

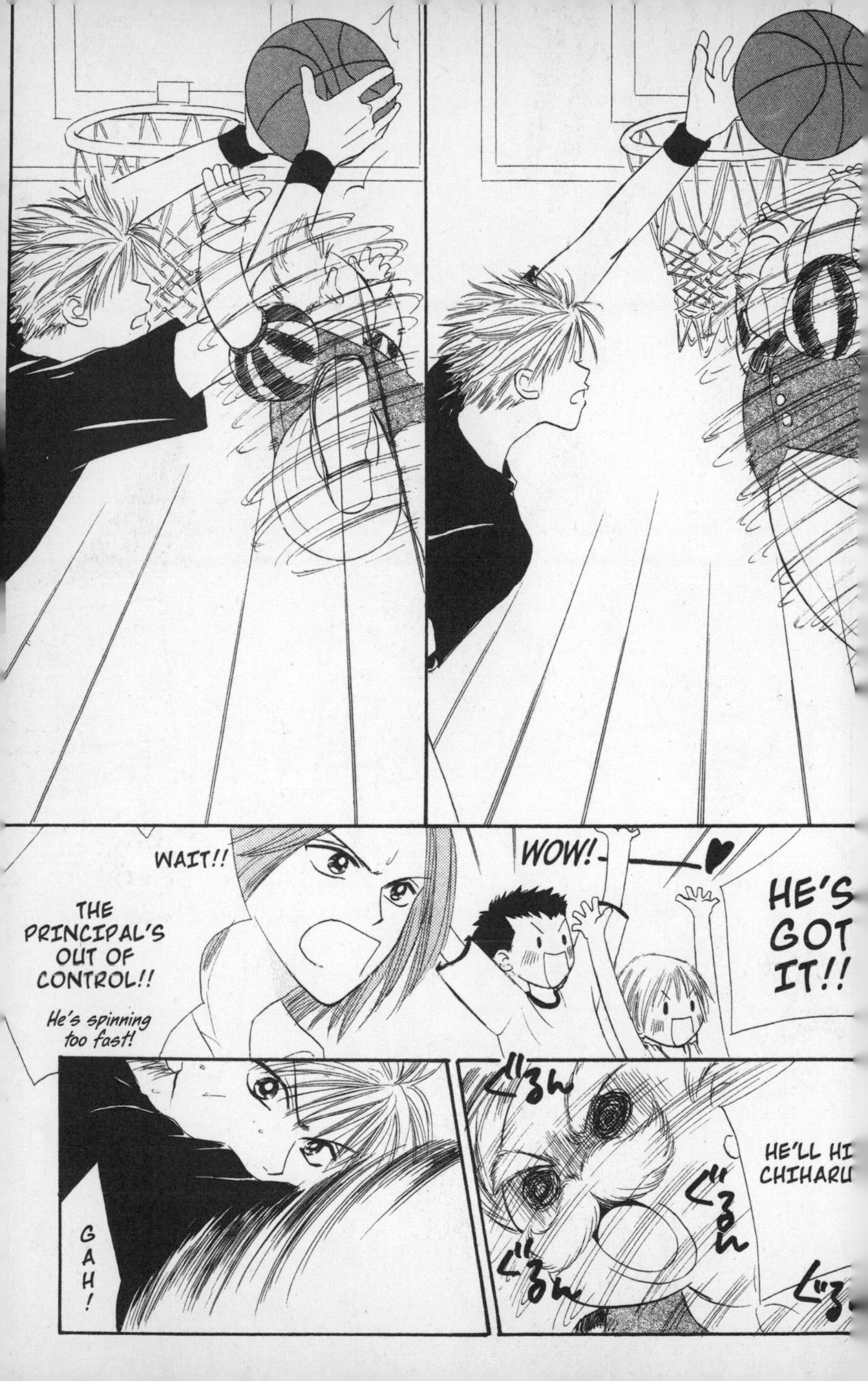
HE'S GOT IT!!
WOW!—♥
WAIT!!
THE PRINCIPAL'S OUT OF CONTROL!!
He's spinning too fast!
ぐるん
HE'LL HI
CHIHARU
ぐるん
ぐるん
ぐる
GAH!

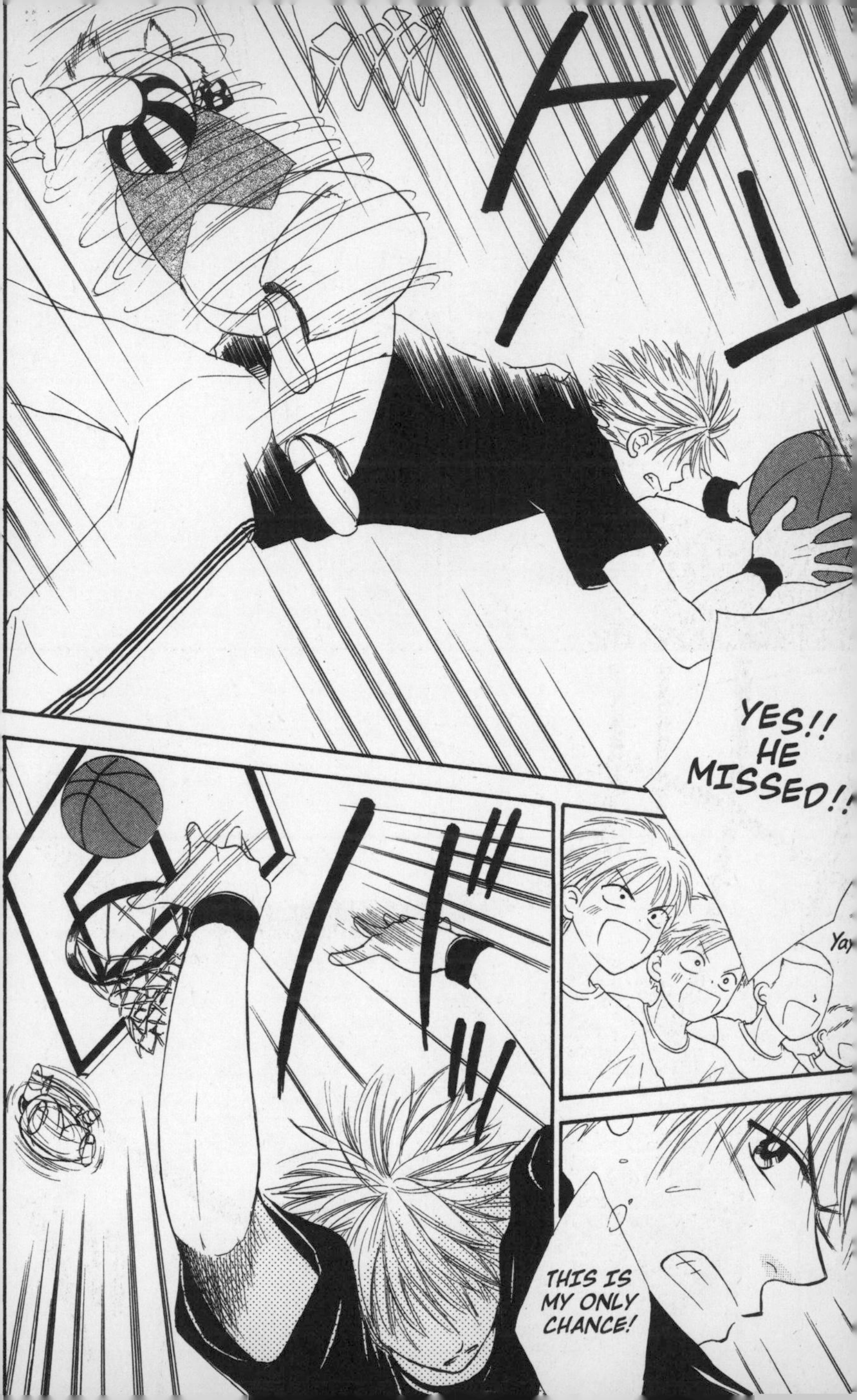
YES!! HE MISSED!!
THIS IS MY ONLY CHANCE!

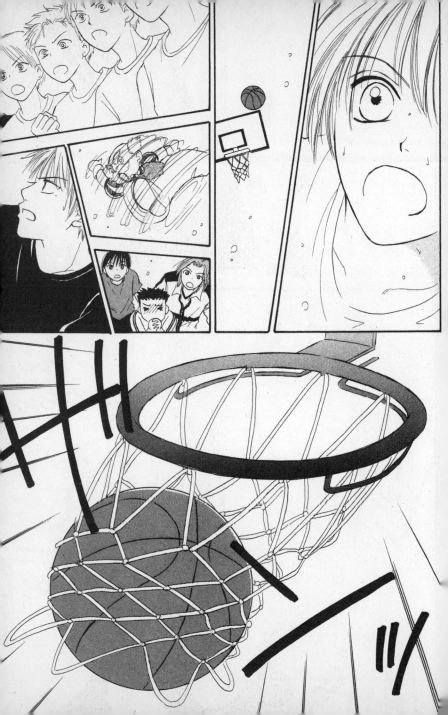

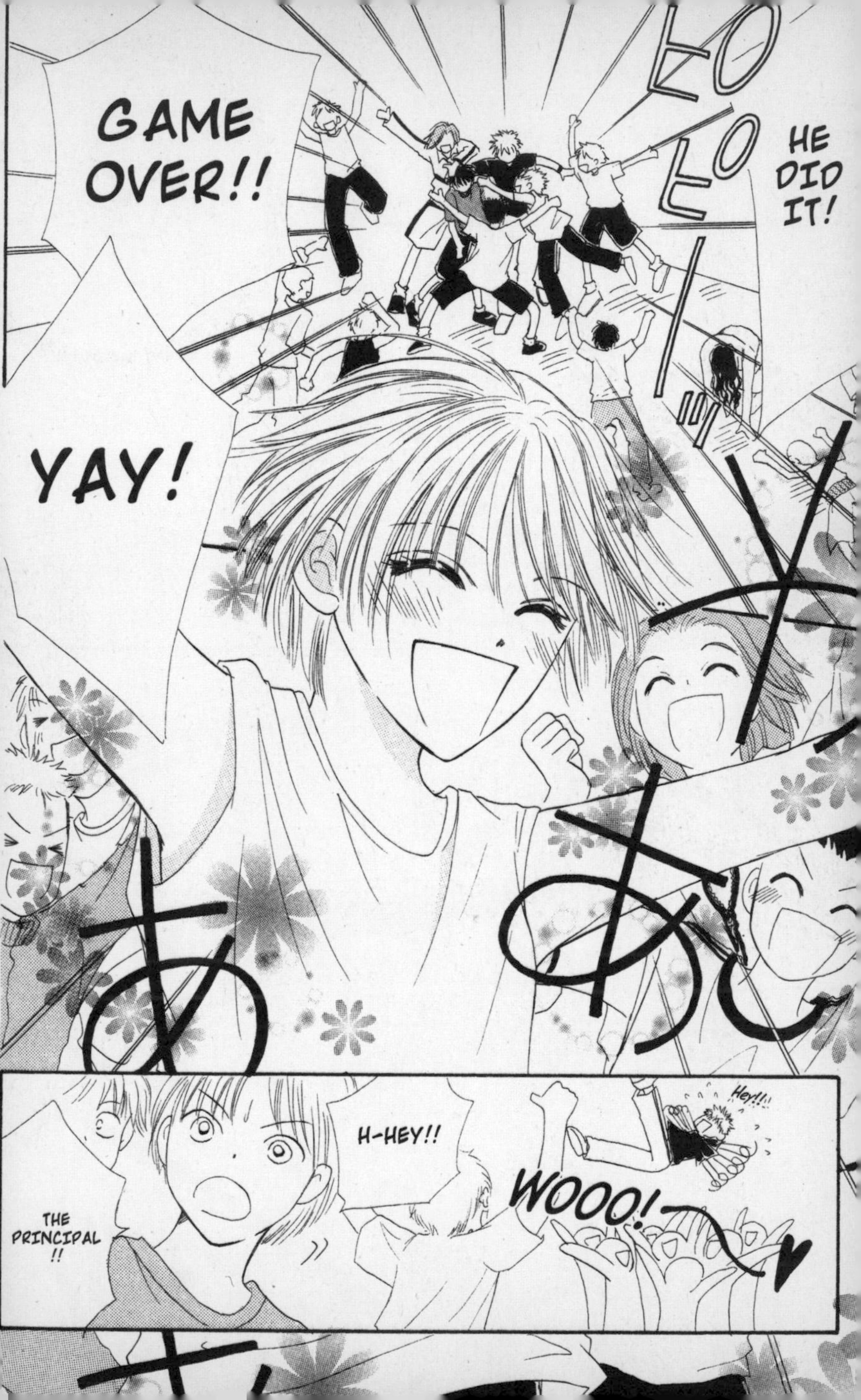
HE DID IT!
GAME OVER!!
YAY!
Hey!!
WOOO!
H-HEY!!
THE PRINCIPAL!!

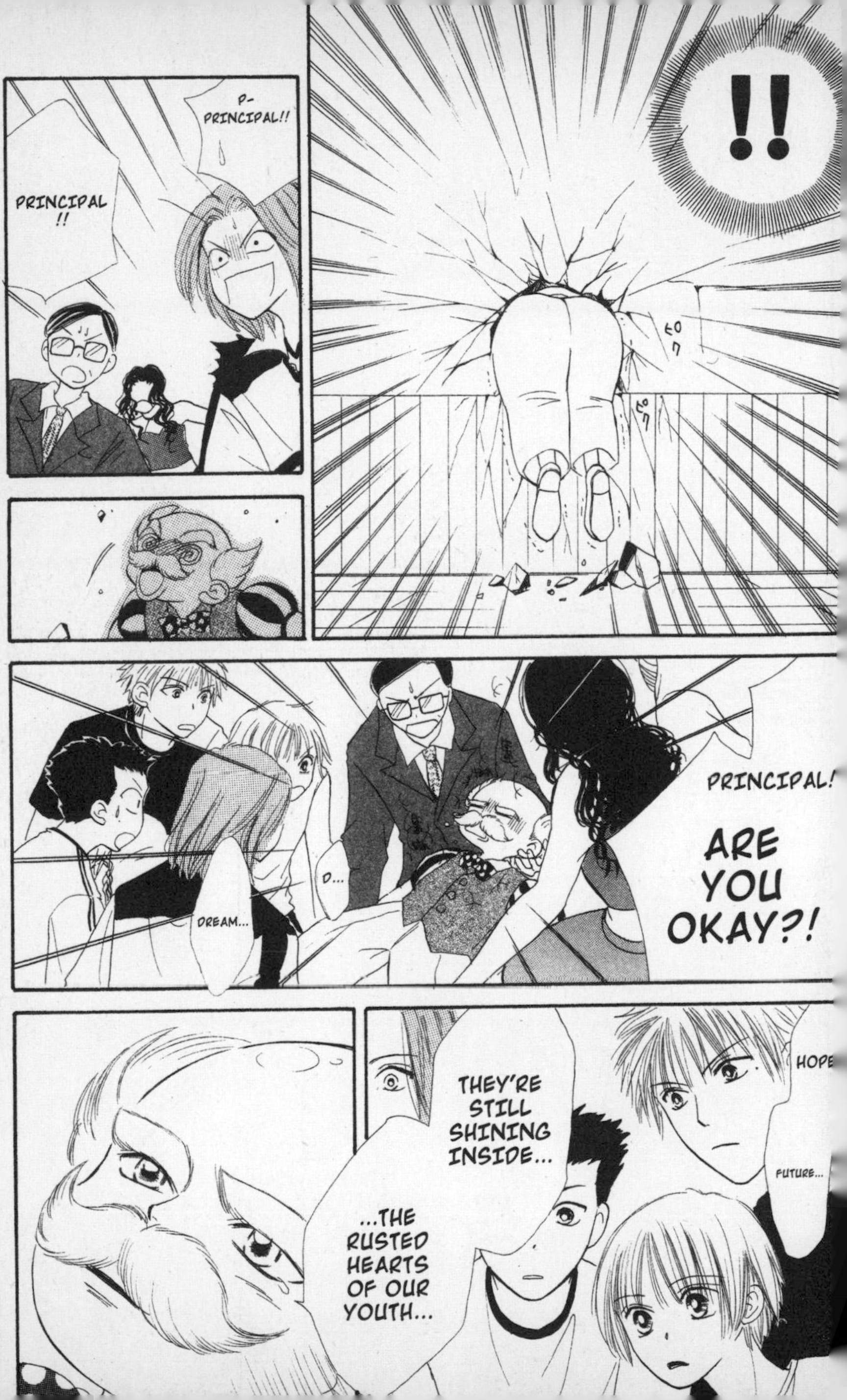
!!
P-
PRINCIPAL!!
PRINCIPAL
!!
PRINCIPAL!
ARE YOU OKAY?!
D...
DREAM...
HOPE
FUTURE...
THEY'RE STILL SHINING INSIDE...
...THE RUSTED HEARTS OF OUR YOUTH...

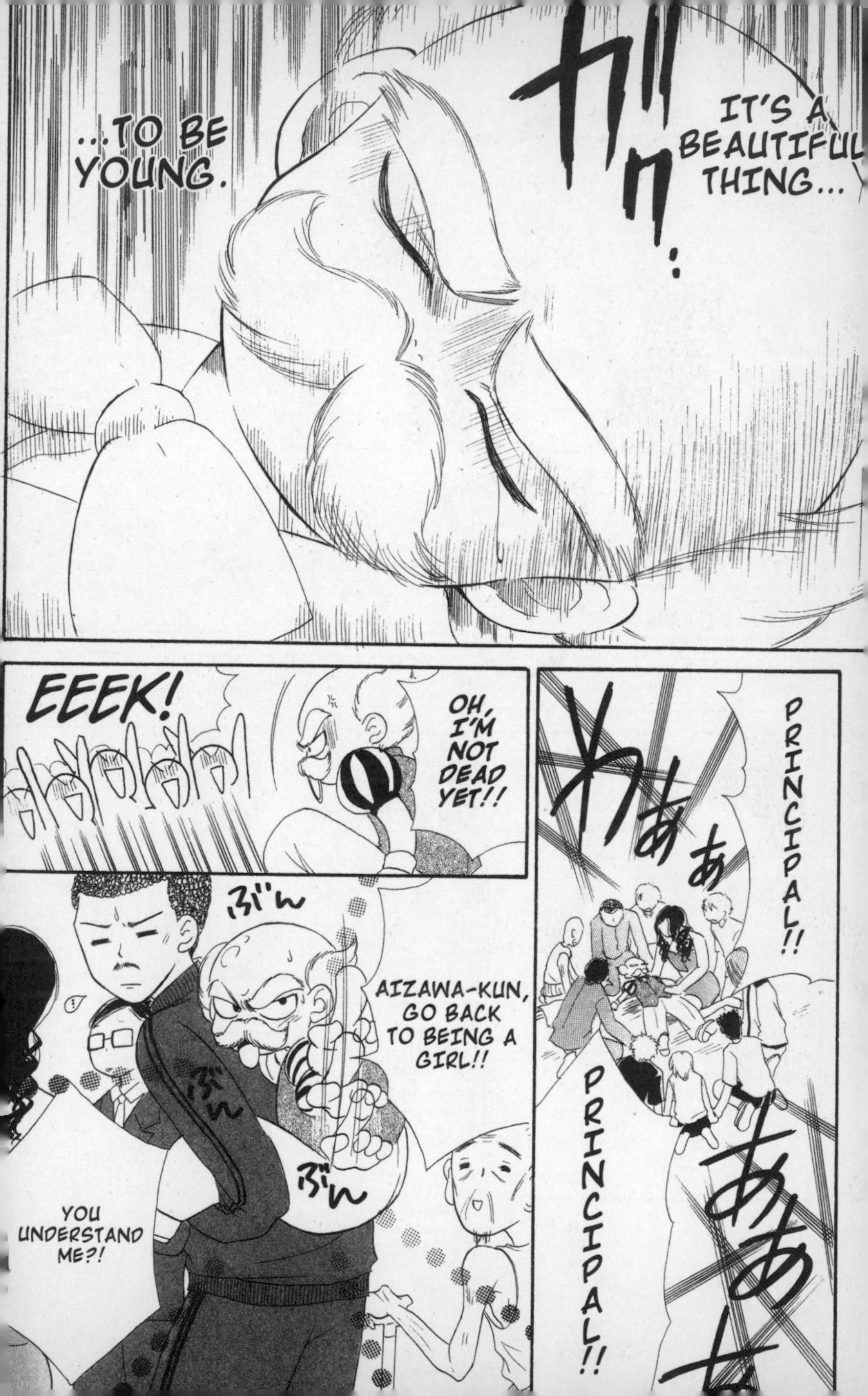
カリ
IT'S A BEAUTIFUL THING...
...TO BE YOUNG.
わぁぁぁぁぁ
PRINCIPAL!!
PRINCIPAL!!
EEEK!
OH, I'M NOT DEAD YET!!
ぶん
AIZAWA-KUN, GO BACK TO BEING A GIRL!!
ぶん
ぶん
YOU UNDERSTAND ME?!

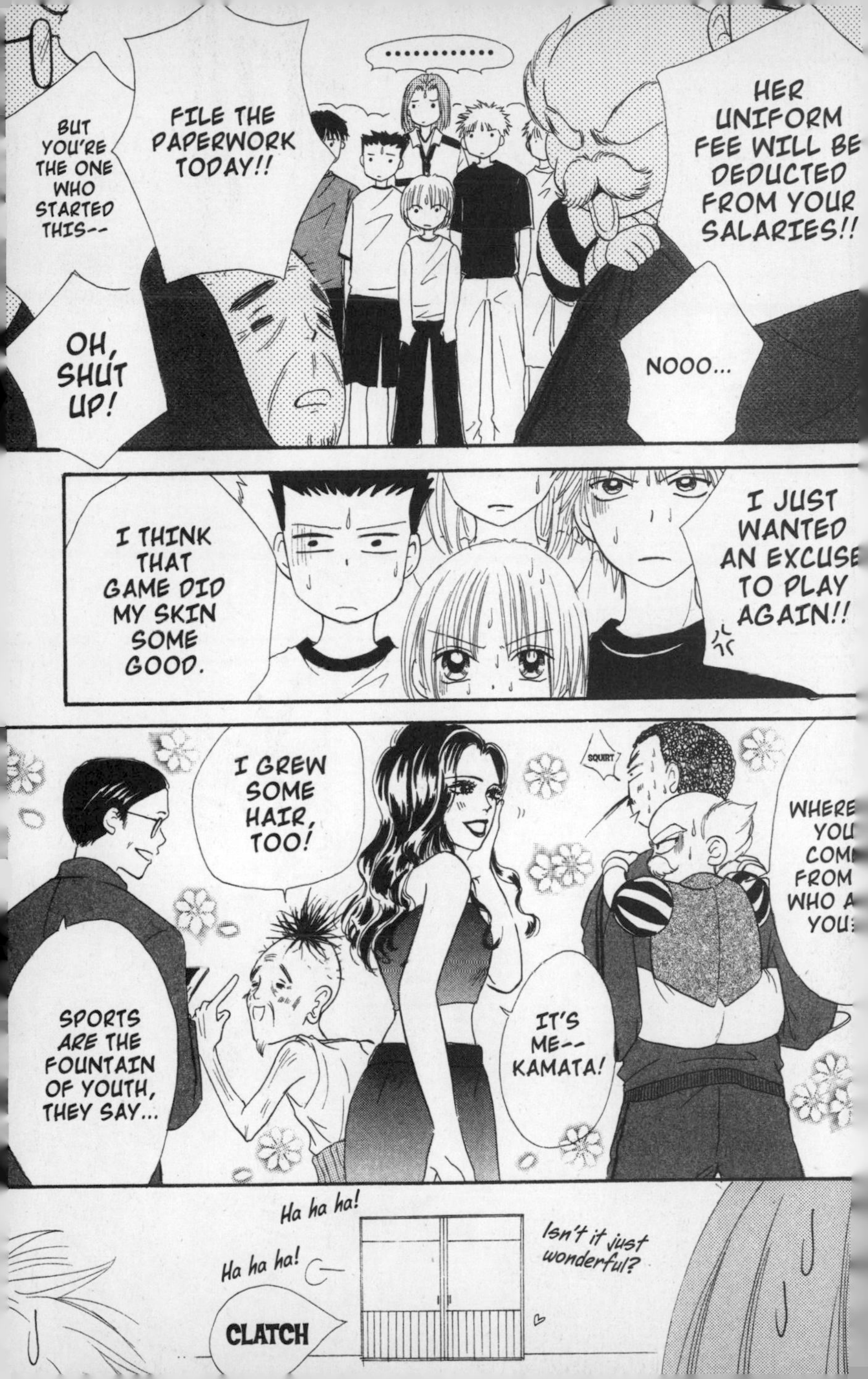
HER UNIFORM FEE WILL BE DEDUCTED FROM YOUR SALARIES!!
....
FILE THE PAPERWORK TODAY!!
BUT YOU'RE THE ONE WHO STARTED THIS--
NOOO...
OH, SHUT UP!
I JUST WANTED AN EXCUSE TO PLAY AGAIN!!
I THINK THAT GAME DID MY SKIN SOME GOOD.
WHERE YOU COM FROM WHO A YOU
SQUIRT
IT'S ME--KAMATA!
I GREW SOME HAIR, TOO!
SPORTS ARE THE FOUNTAIN OF YOUTH, THEY SAY...
Isn't it just wonderful?
Ha ha ha!
Ha ha ha!
CLATCH

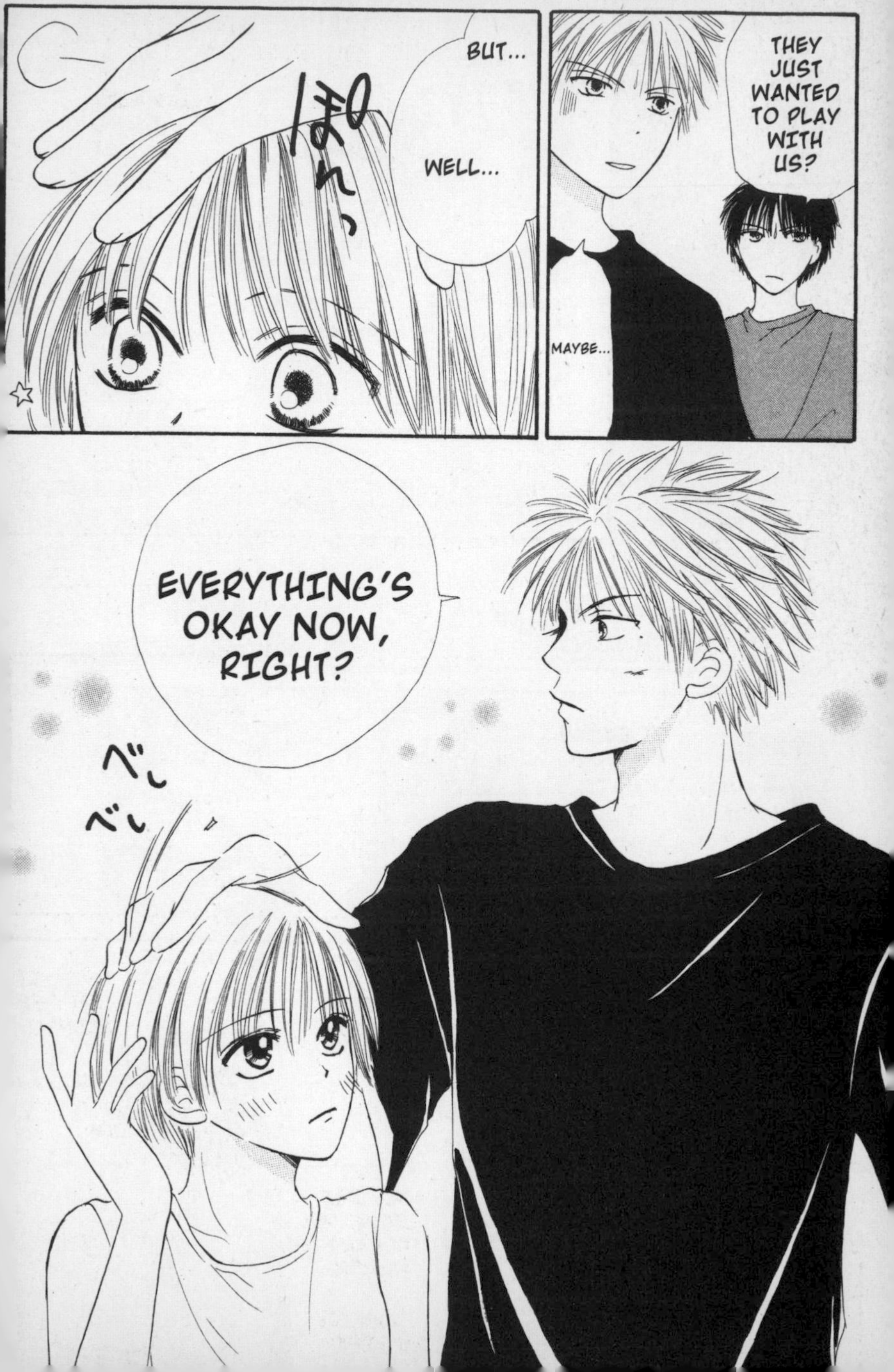
THEY JUST WANTED TO PLAY WITH US?
MAYBE...
BUT...
WELL...
ぽんっ
EVERYTHING'S OKAY NOW, RIGHT?
べしべし

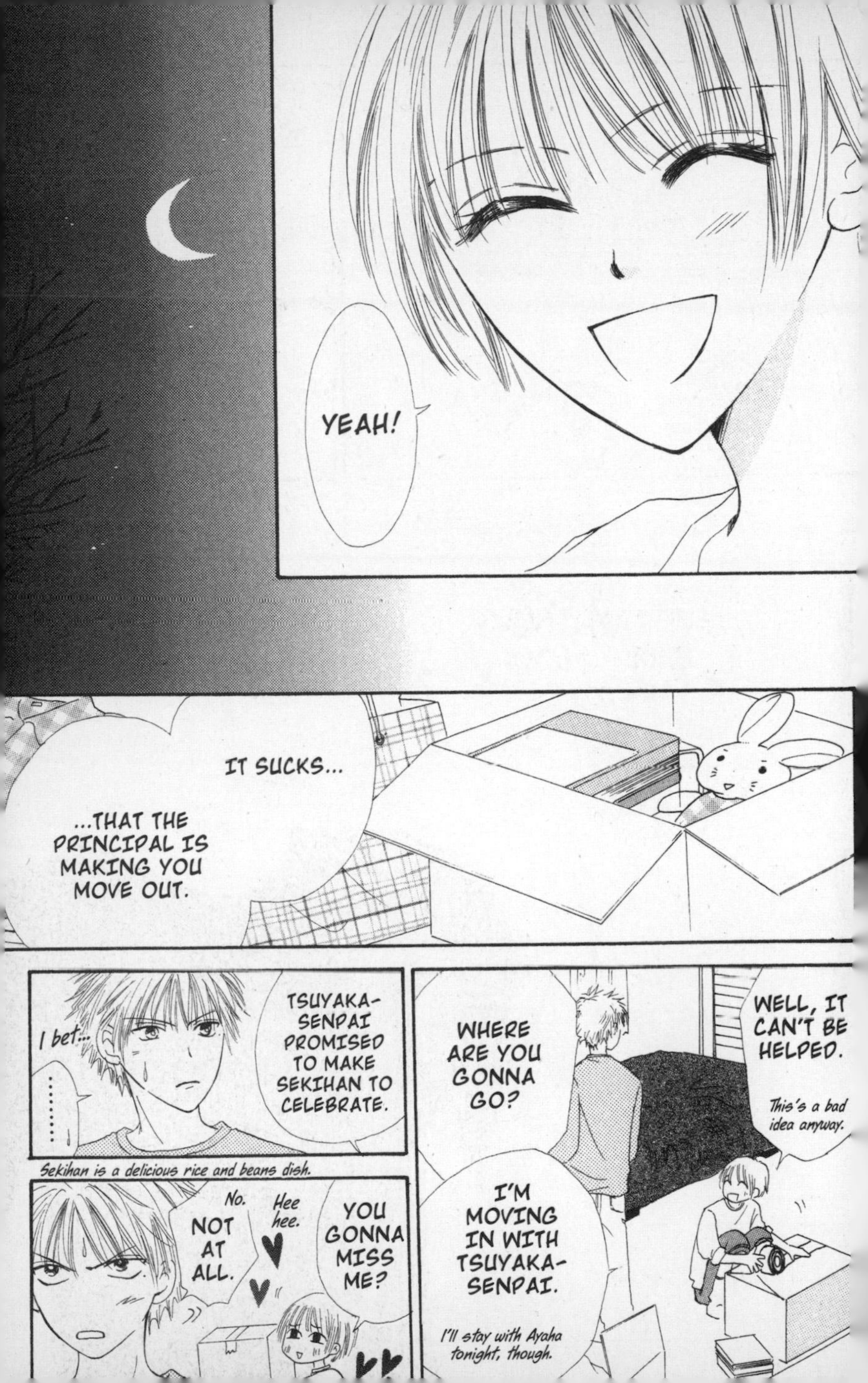
YEAH!
IT SUCKS...
...THAT THE PRINCIPAL IS MAKING YOU MOVE OUT.
WELL, IT CAN'T BE HELPED.
This's a bad idea anyway.
WHERE ARE YOU GONNA GO?
I'M MOVING IN WITH TSUYAKA-SENPAI.
I'll stay with Ayaha tonight, though.
TSUYAKA-SENPAI PROMISED TO MAKE SEKIHAN TO CELEBRATE.
I bet...
......
Sekihan is a delicious rice and beans dish.
YOU GONNA MISS ME?
Hee hee.
NOT AT ALL.
No.

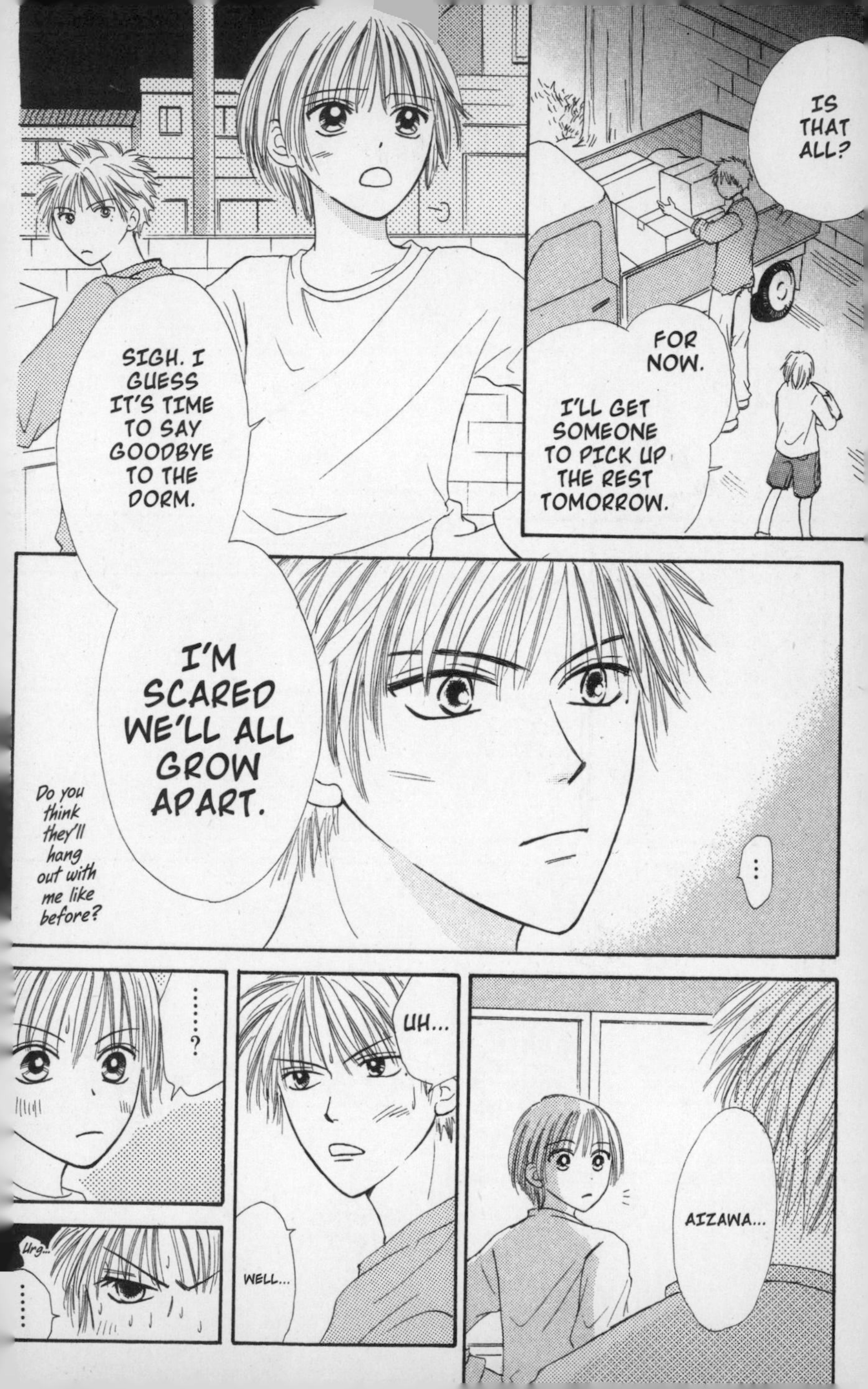
IS THAT ALL?
FOR NOW.
I'LL GET SOMEONE TO PICK UP THE REST TOMORROW.
SIGH. I GUESS IT'S TIME TO SAY GOODBYE TO THE DORM.
I'M SCARED WE'LL ALL GROW APART.
Do you think they'll hang out with me like before?
...
AIZAWA...
UH...
WELL...
......?
Urg...
......

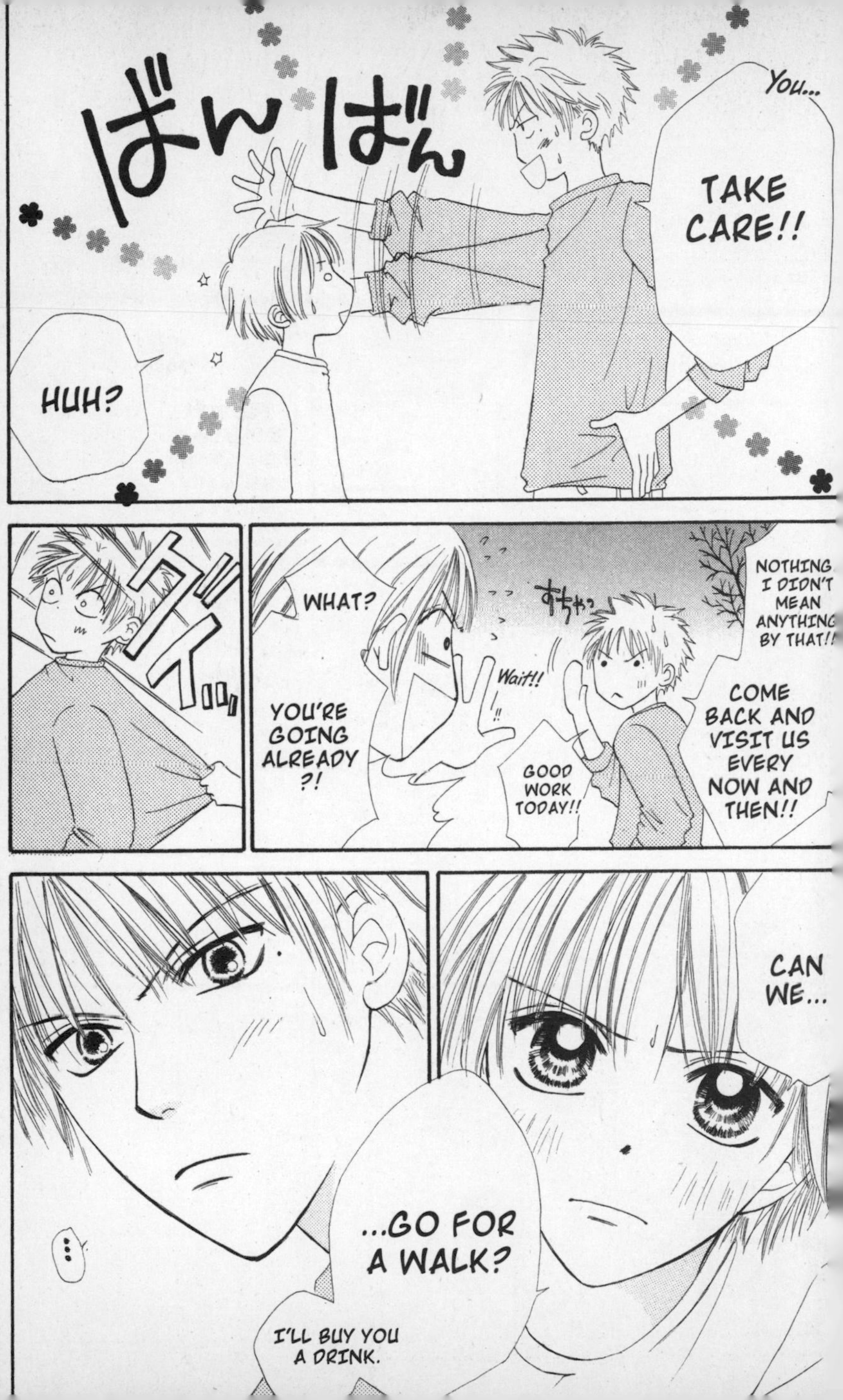
You...
TAKE CARE!!
ばんばん
HUH?
NOTHING. I DIDN'T MEAN ANYTHING BY THAT!!
COME BACK AND VISIT US EVERY NOW AND THEN!!
すちゃっ
WHAT?
Wait!!
GOOD WORK TODAY!!
YOU'RE GOING ALREADY?!
グイ
CAN WE...
...GO FOR A WALK?
I'LL BUY YOU A DRINK.
...

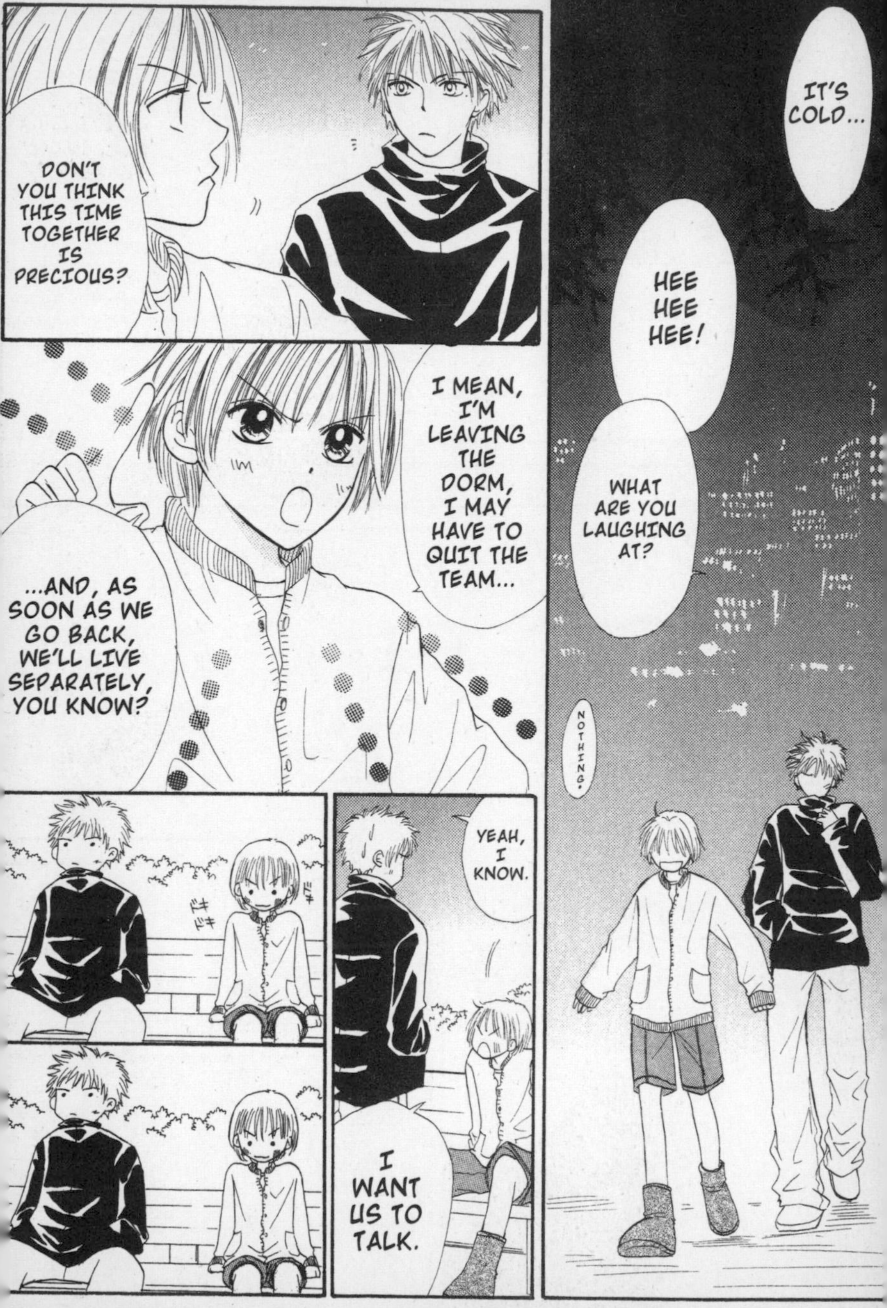
IT'S COLD...
HEE HEE HEE!
WHAT ARE YOU LAUGHING AT?
NOTHING.
DON'T YOU THINK THIS TIME TOGETHER IS PRECIOUS?
I MEAN, I'M LEAVING THE DORM, I MAY HAVE TO QUIT THE TEAM...
...AND, AS SOON AS WE GO BACK, WE'LL LIVE SEPARATELY, YOU KNOW?
YEAH, I KNOW.
I WANT US TO TALK.

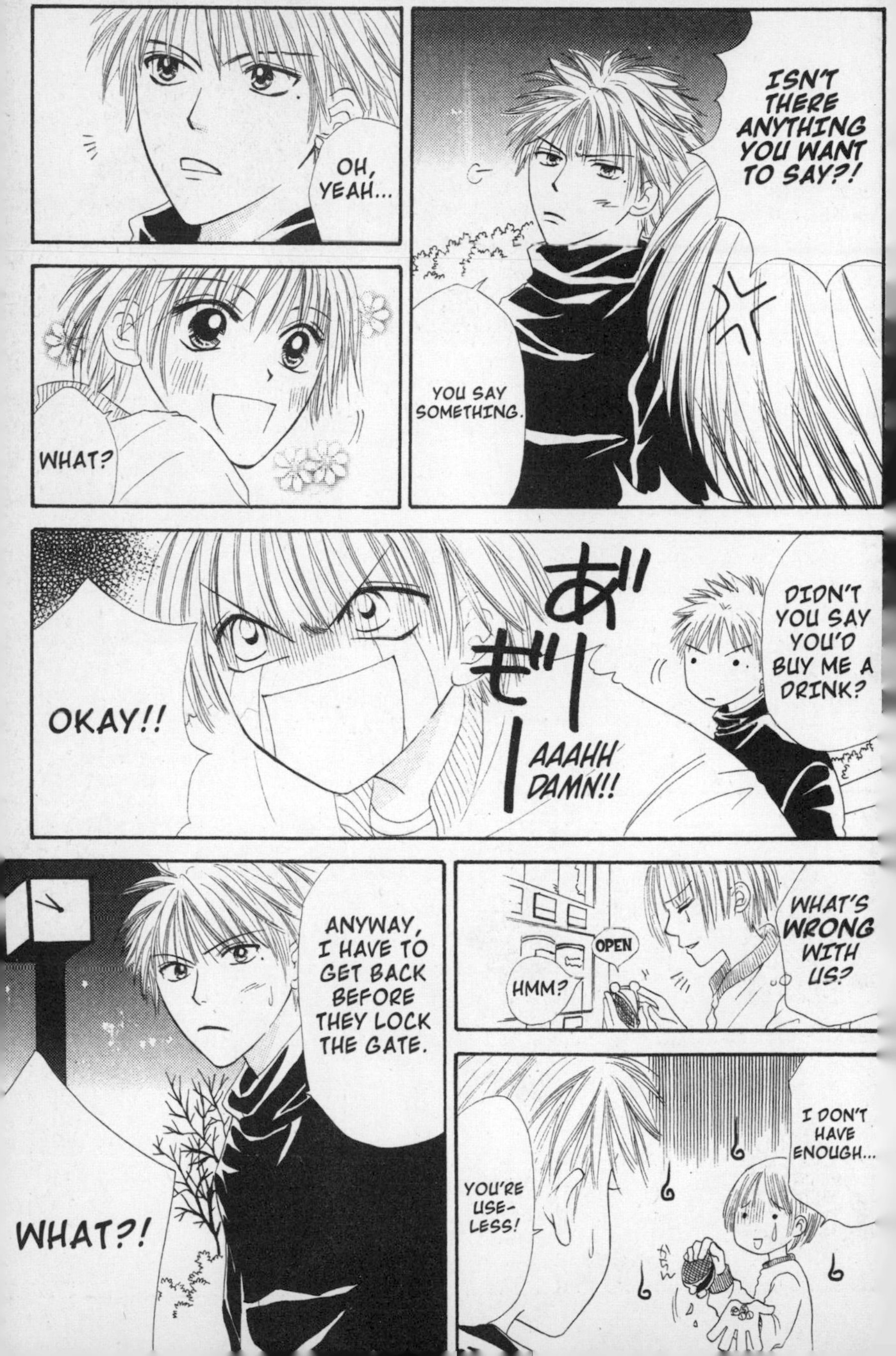
ISN'T THERE ANYTHING YOU WANT TO SAY?!
YOU SAY SOMETHING.
OH, YEAH...
WHAT?
DIDN'T YOU SAY YOU'D BUY ME A DRINK?
あ゛ー ぜ゛ー
AAAHH DAMN!!
OKAY!!
WHAT'S WRONG WITH US?
OPEN
HMM?
I DON'T HAVE ENOUGH...
YOU'RE USE-LESS!
ANYWAY, I HAVE TO GET BACK BEFORE THEY LOCK THE GATE.
WHAT?!

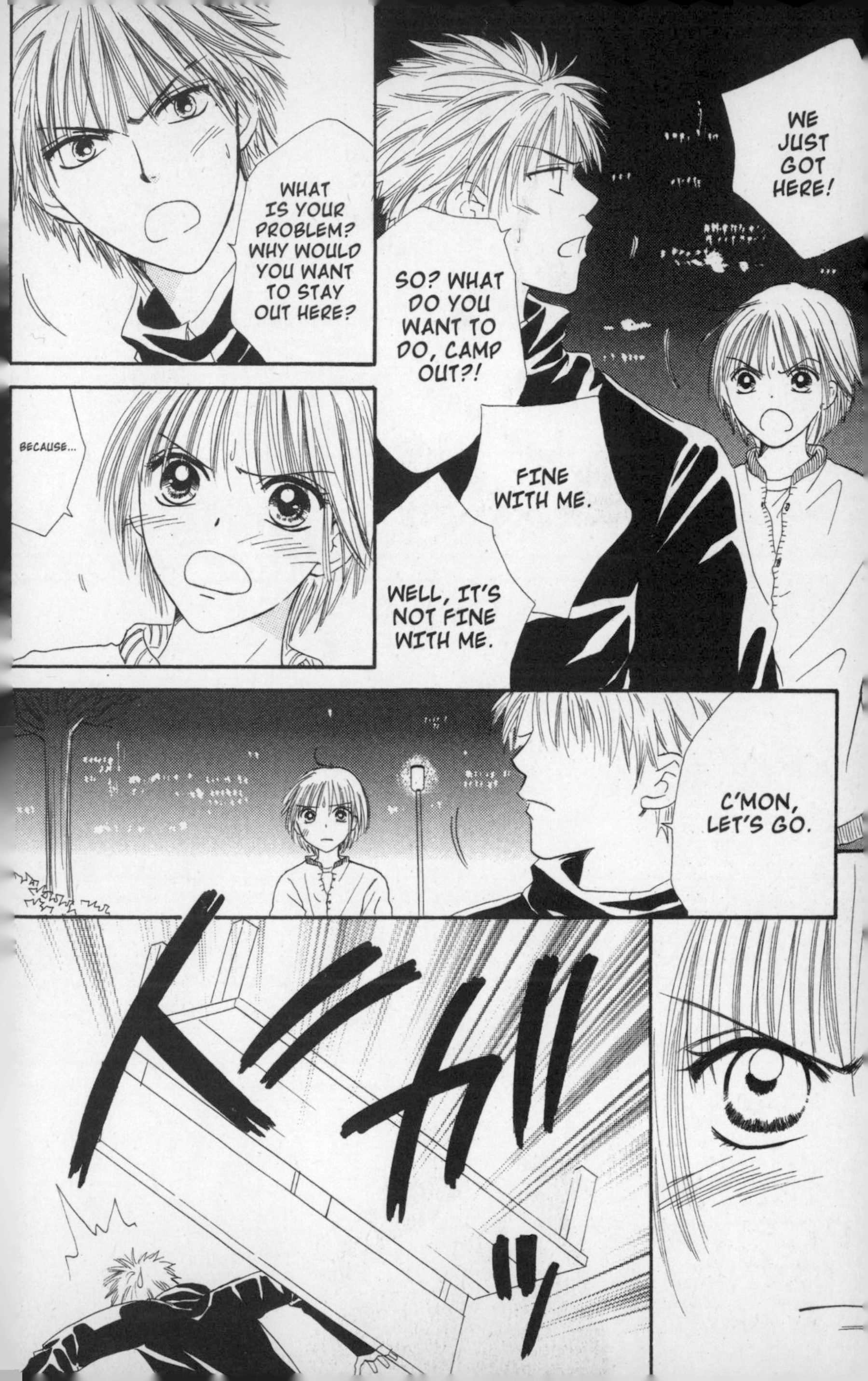
WE JUST GOT HERE!
SO? WHAT DO YOU WANT TO DO, CAMP OUT?!
FINE WITH ME.
WELL, IT'S NOT FINE WITH ME.
WHAT IS YOUR PROBLEM? WHY WOULD YOU WANT TO STAY OUT HERE?
BECAUSE...
C'MON, LET'S GO.

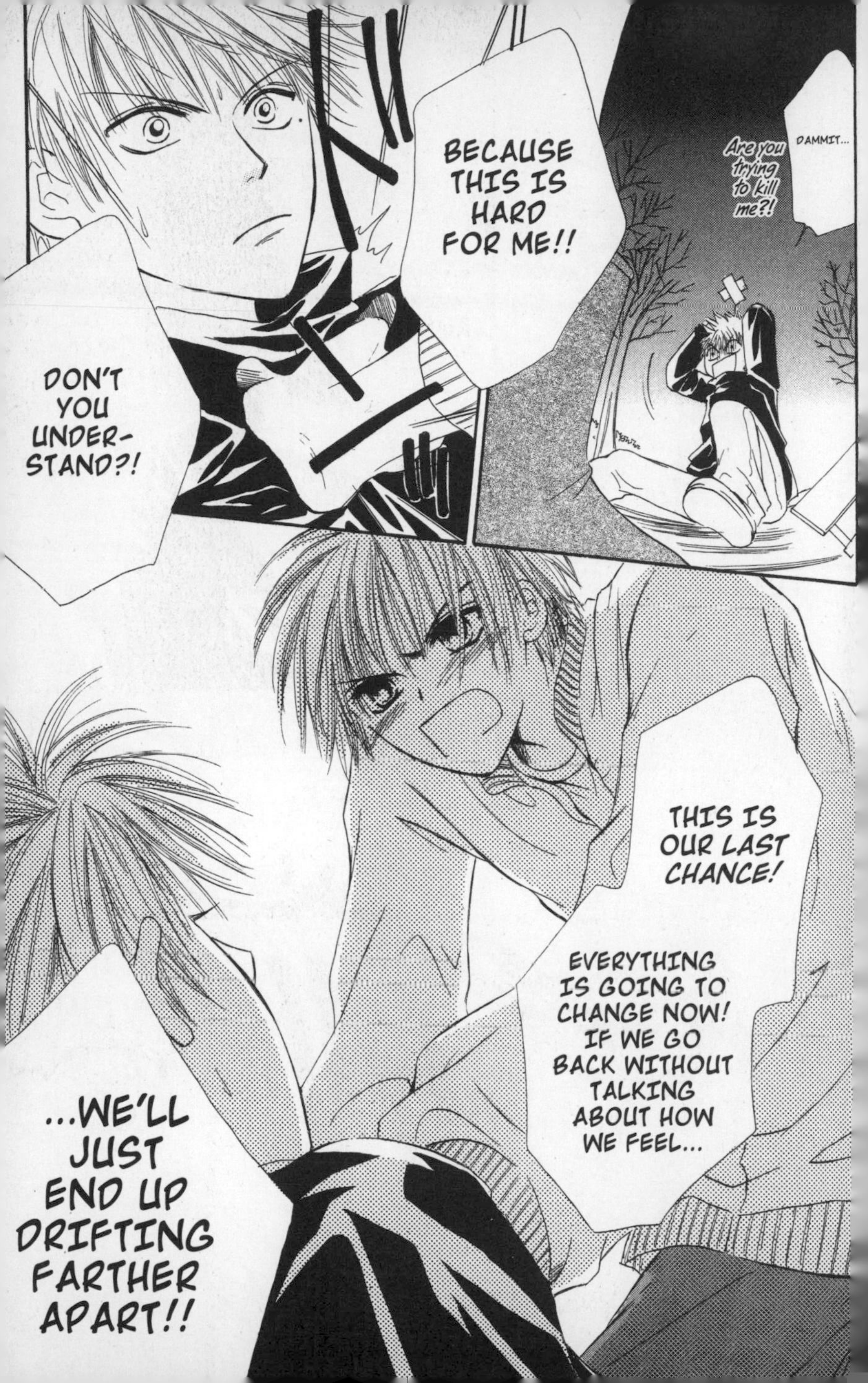
DAMMIT...
Are you trying to kill me?!
BECAUSE THIS IS HARD FOR ME!!
DON'T YOU UNDER-STAND?!
THIS IS OUR LAST CHANCE!
EVERYTHING IS GOING TO CHANGE NOW! IF WE GO BACK WITHOUT TALKING ABOUT HOW WE FEEL...
...WE'LL JUST END UP DRIFTING FARTHER APART!!

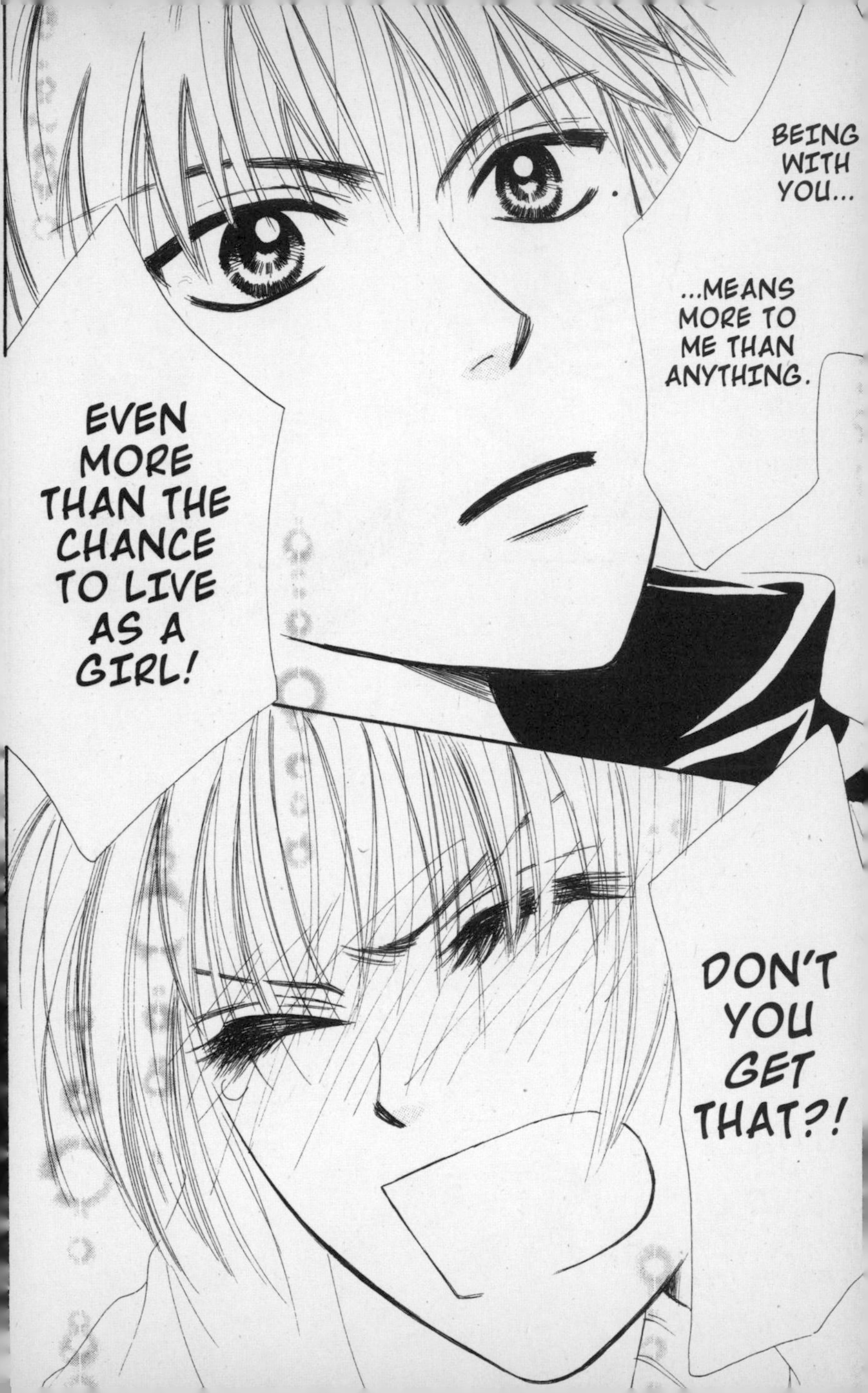
BEING WITH YOU...
...MEANS MORE TO ME THAN ANYTHING.
EVEN MORE THAN THE CHANCE TO LIVE AS A GIRL!
DON'T YOU GET THAT?!

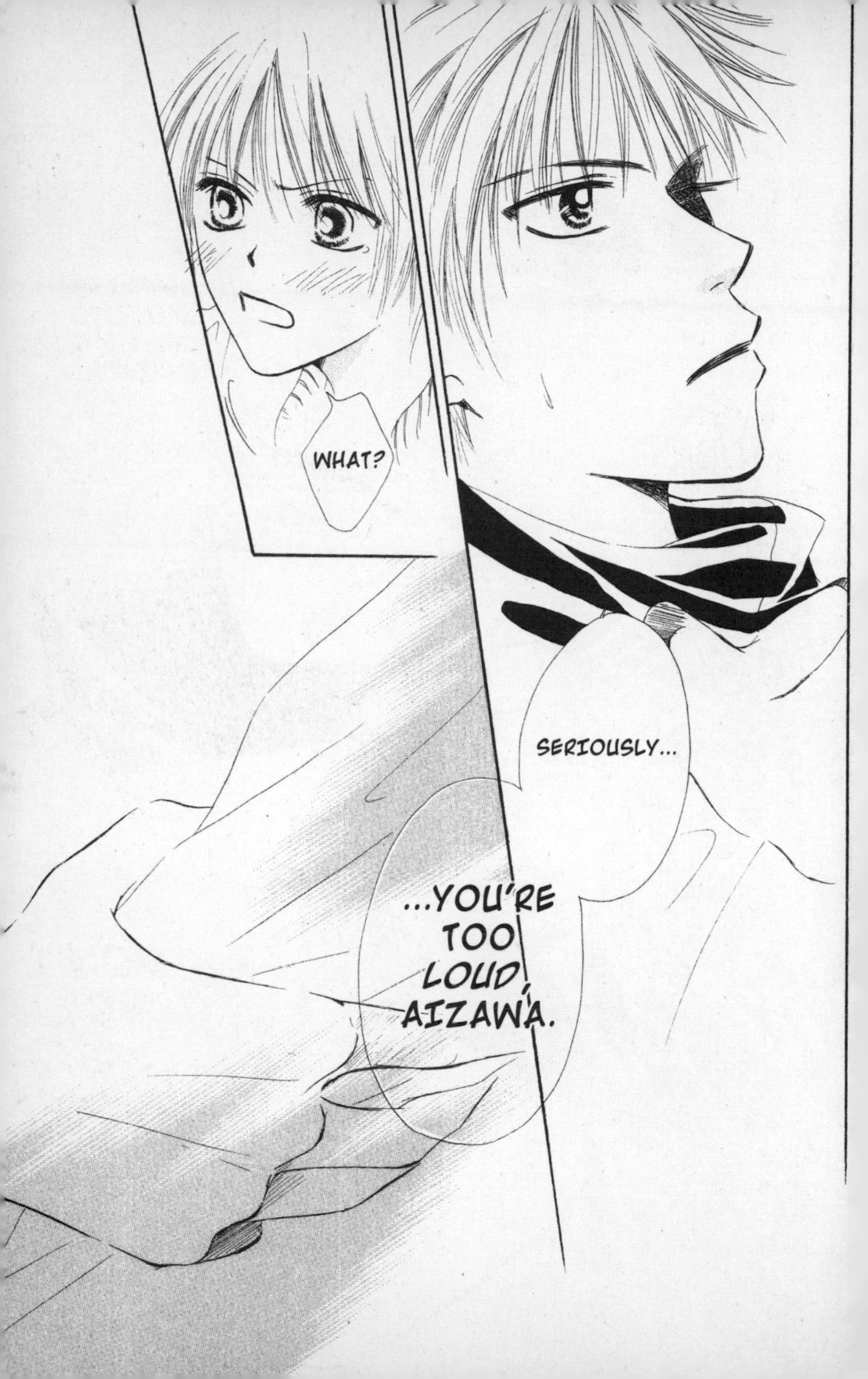
SERIOUSLY...
...YOU'RE TOO LOUD, AIZAWA.
WHAT?

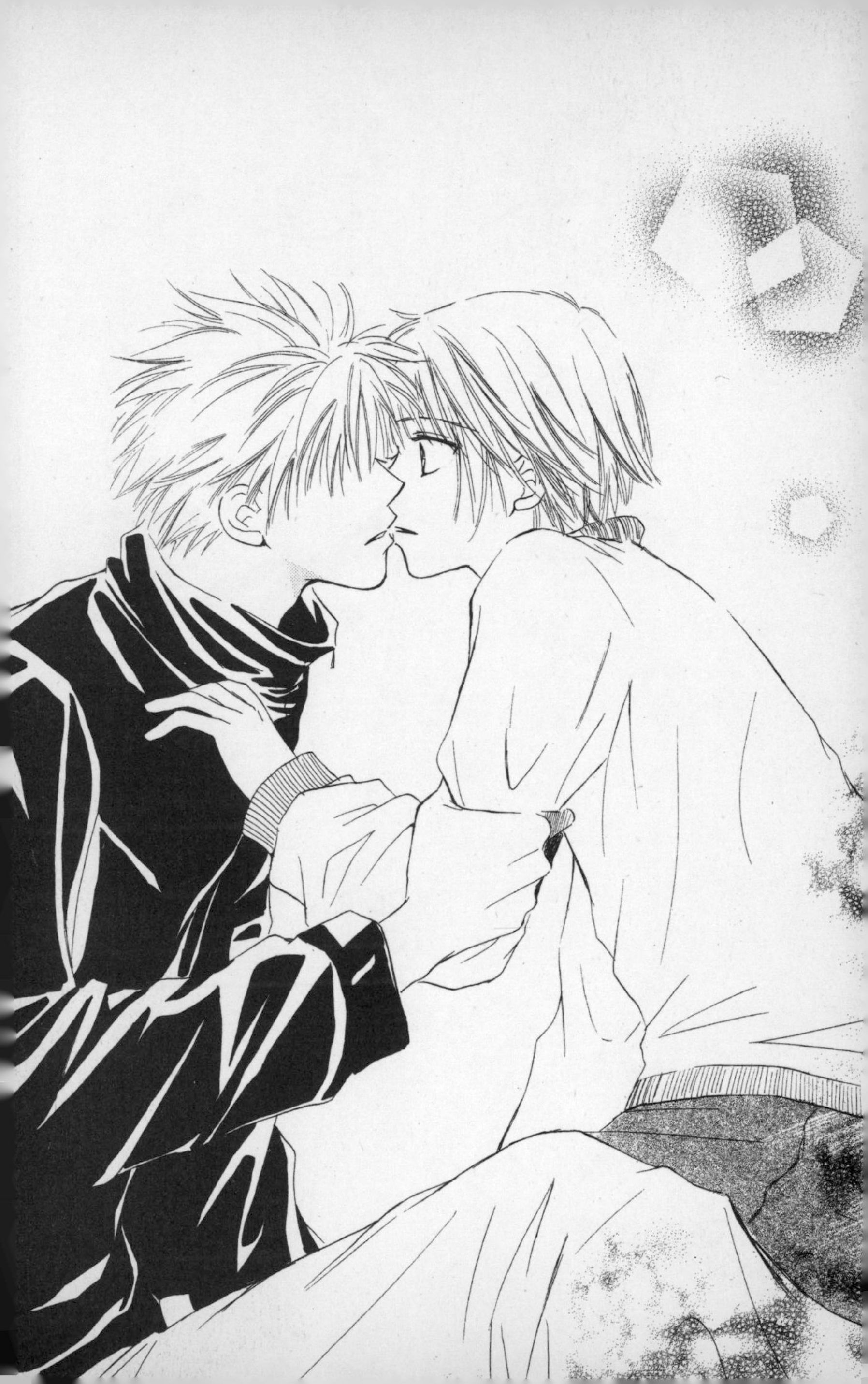

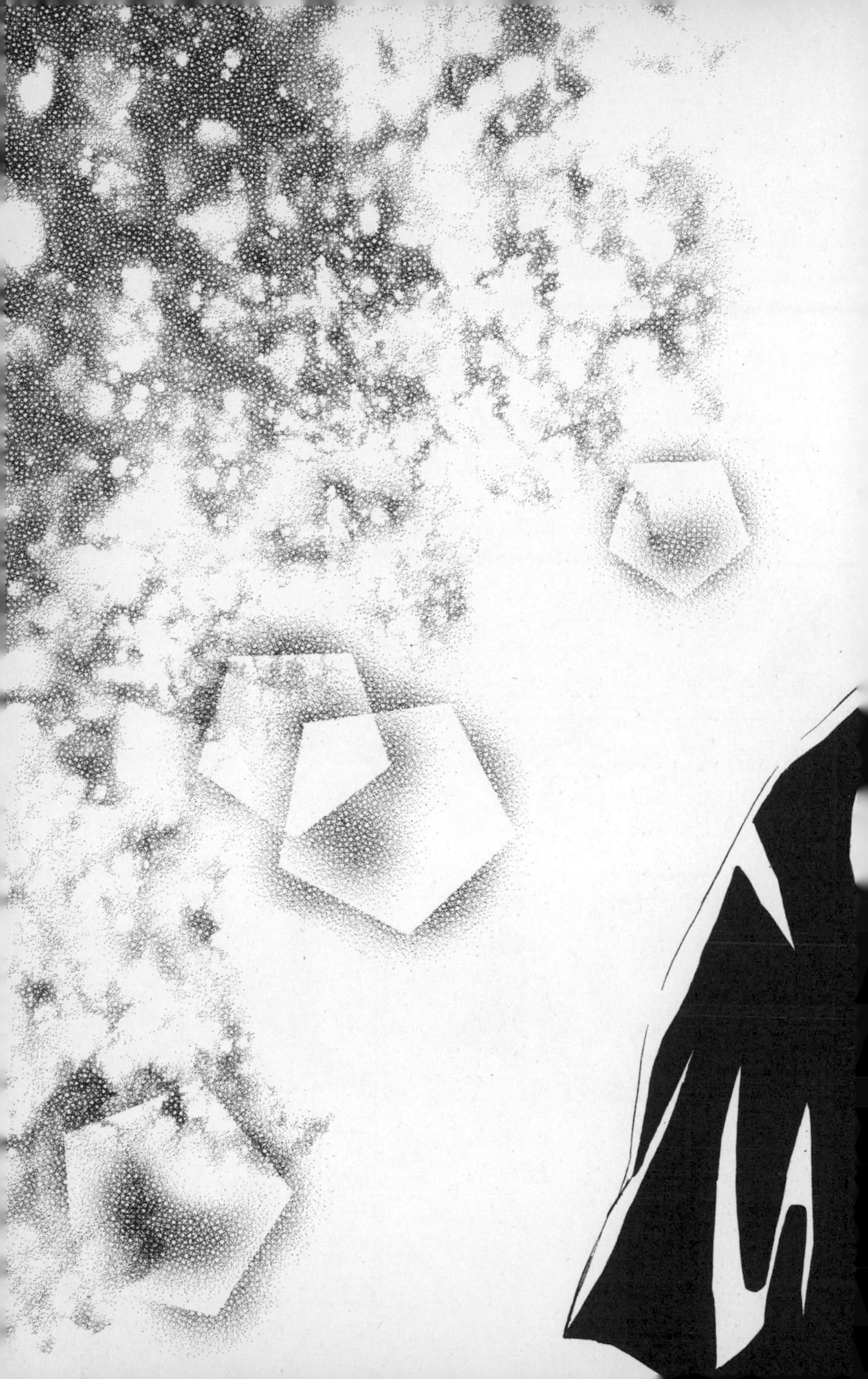

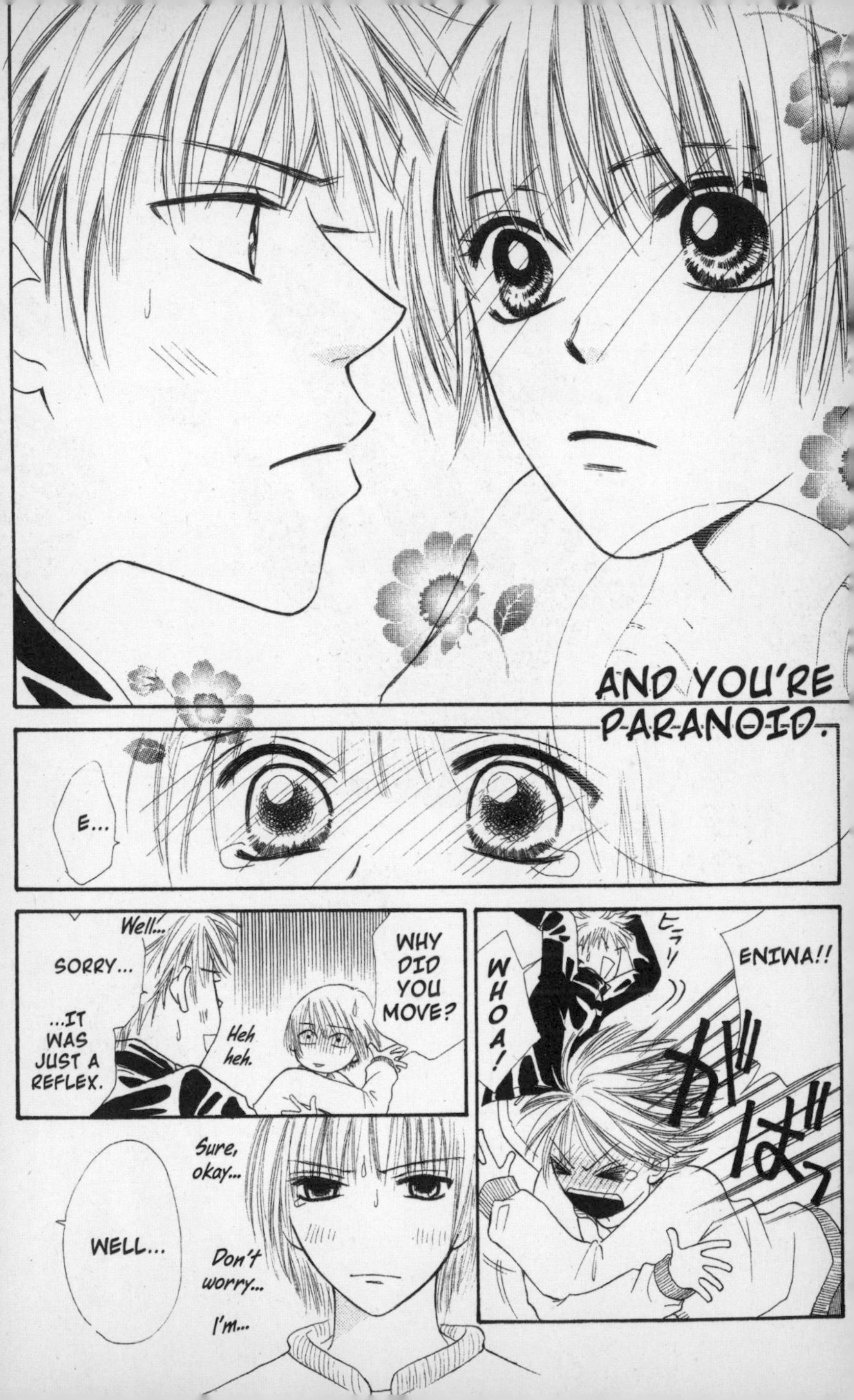
AND YOU'RE PARANOID.
E...
ENIWA!!
WHOA!
ガばっ
WHY DID YOU MOVE?
Heh heh.
Well...
SORRY...
...IT WAS JUST A REFLEX.
Sure, okay...
Don't worry...
I'm...
WELL...

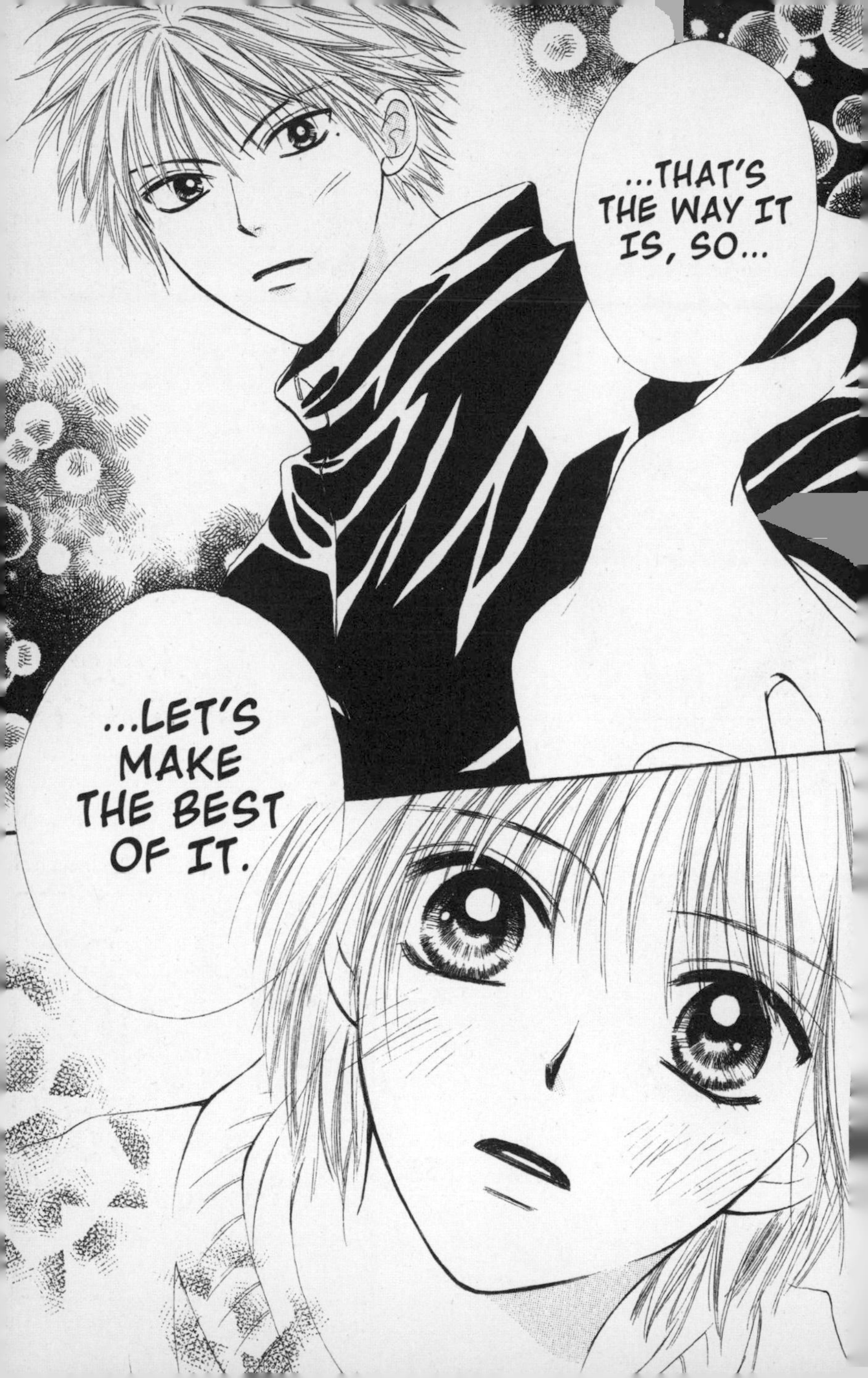
...THAT'S THE WAY IT IS, SO...
...LET'S MAKE THE BEST OF IT.

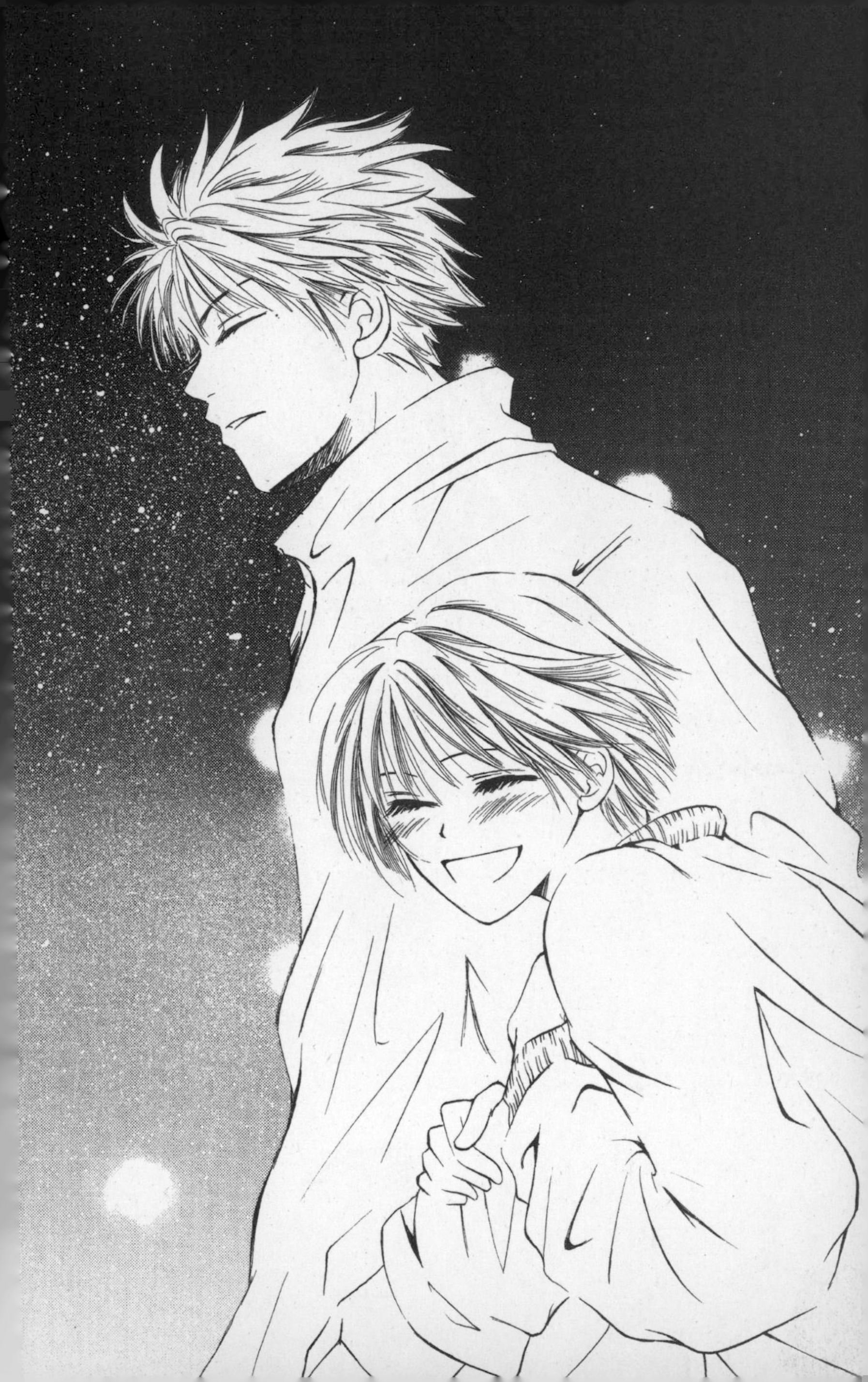

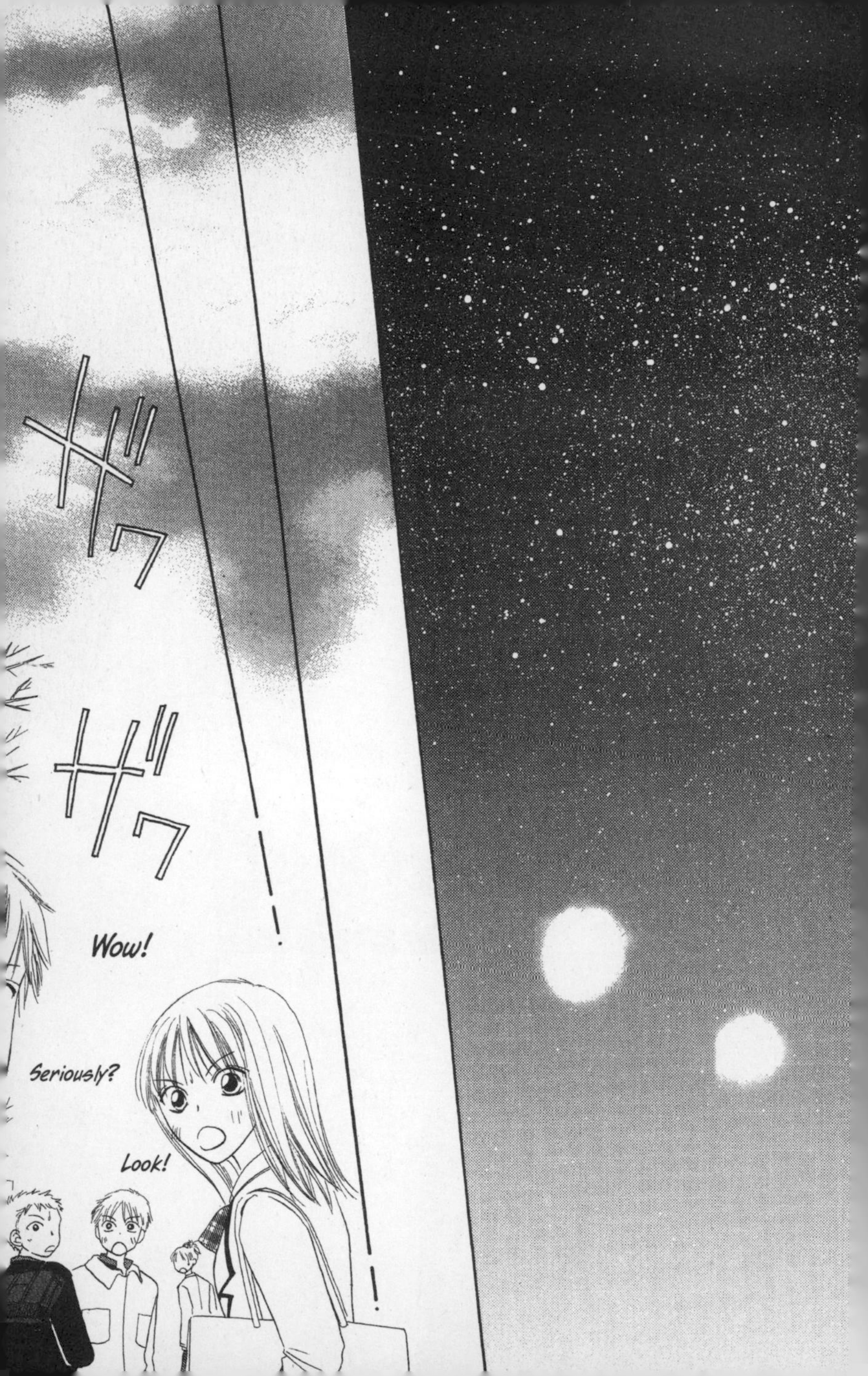
ザワ
ザワ
Wow!
Seriously?
Look!

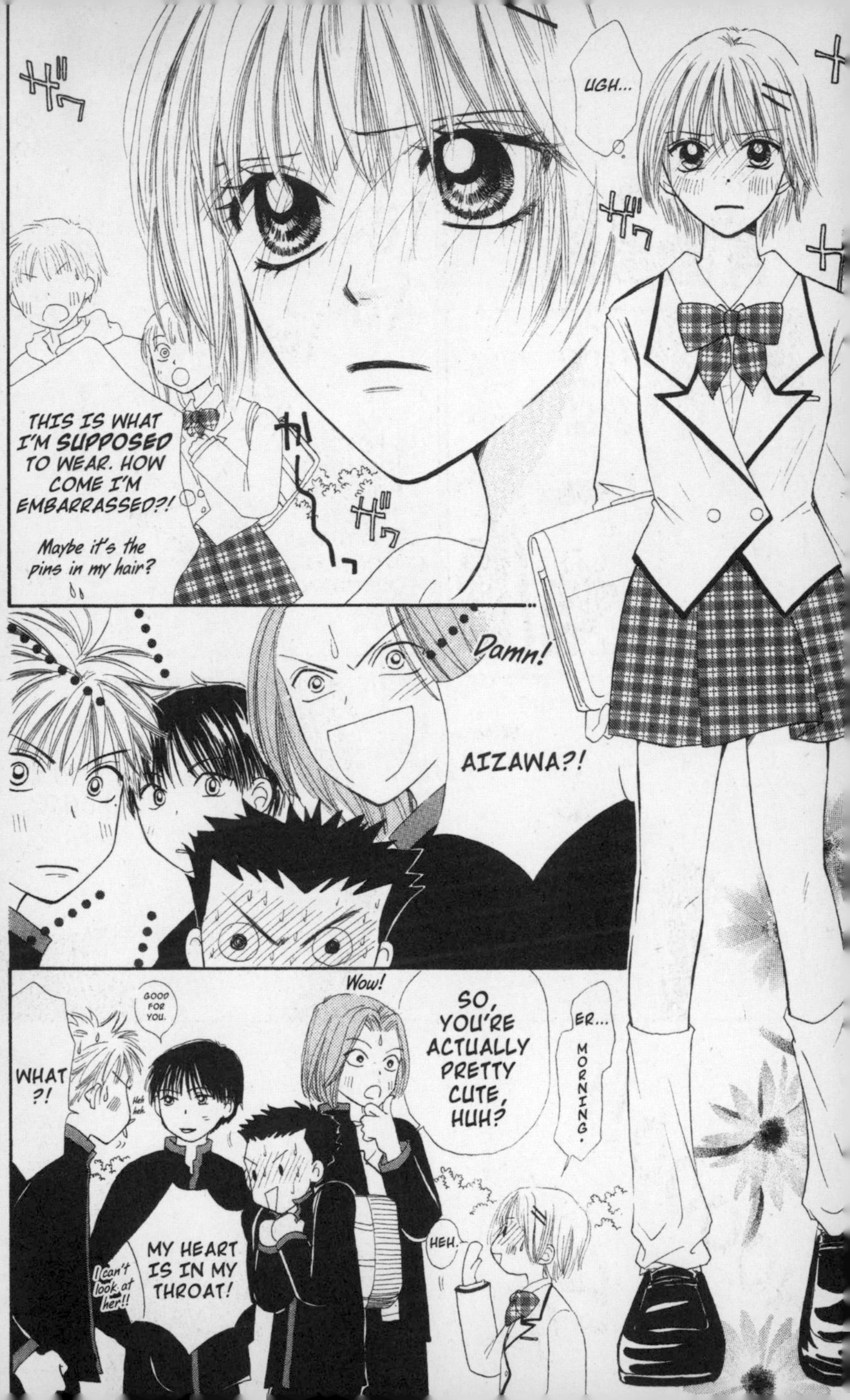
UGH...
THIS IS WHAT I'M SUPPOSED TO WEAR. HOW COME I'M EMBARRASSED?!
Maybe it's the pins in my hair?
Damn!
AIZAWA?!
ER... MORNING.
SO, YOU'RE ACTUALLY PRETTY CUTE, HUH?
Wow!
GOOD FOR YOU.
WHAT?!
Heh heh.
HEH.
MY HEART IS IN MY THROAT!
I can't look at her!!

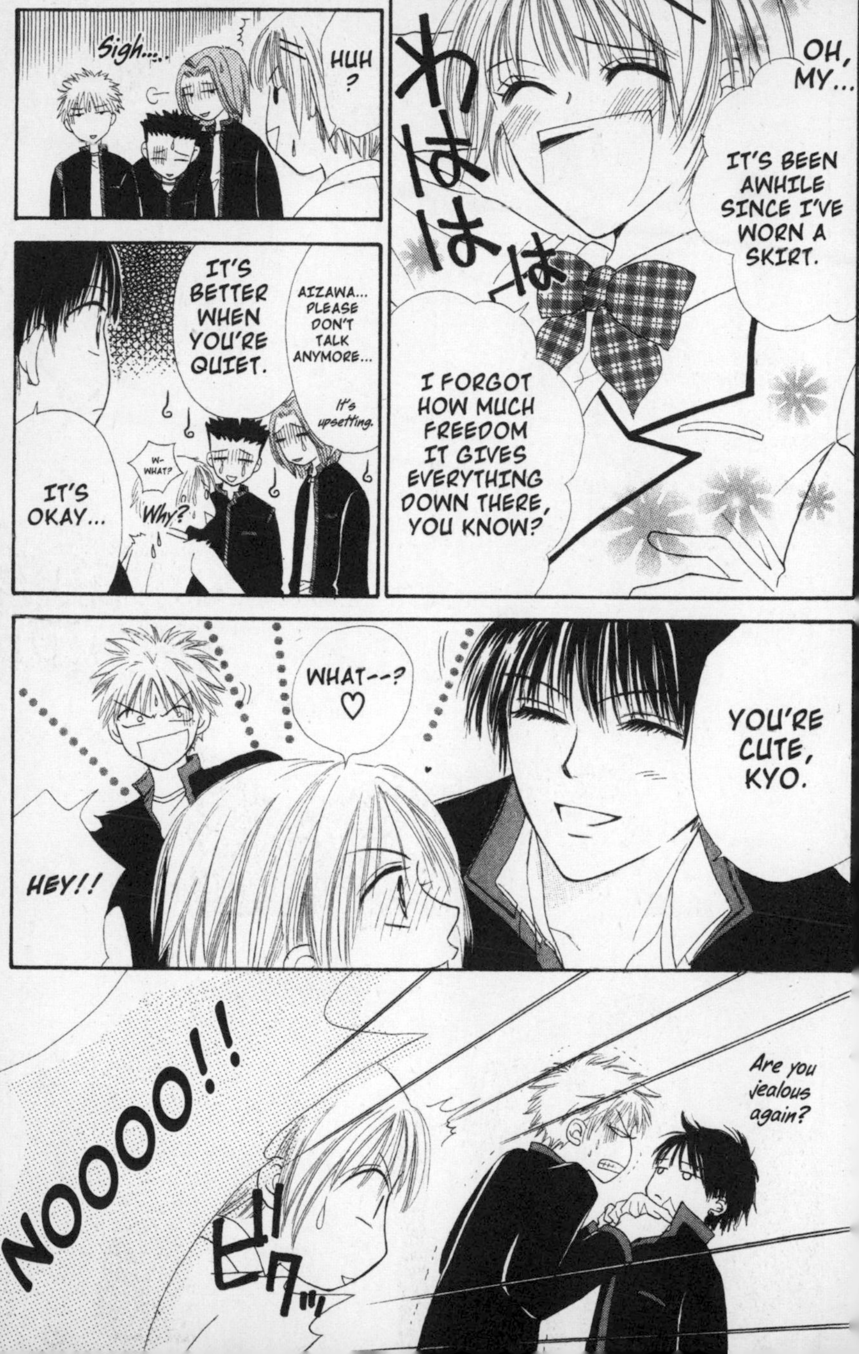
わははは
OH, MY...
IT'S BEEN AWHILE SINCE I'VE WORN A SKIRT.
I FORGOT HOW MUCH FREEDOM IT GIVES EVERYTHING DOWN THERE, YOU KNOW?
HUH?
Sigh...
IT'S BETTER WHEN YOU'RE QUIET.
AIZAWA... PLEASE DON'T TALK ANYMORE...
It's upsetting.
W-WHAT?
Why?
IT'S OKAY...
YOU'RE CUTE, KYO.
WHAT--? ♡
HEY!!
Are you jealous again?
NOOOO!!
ビクッ

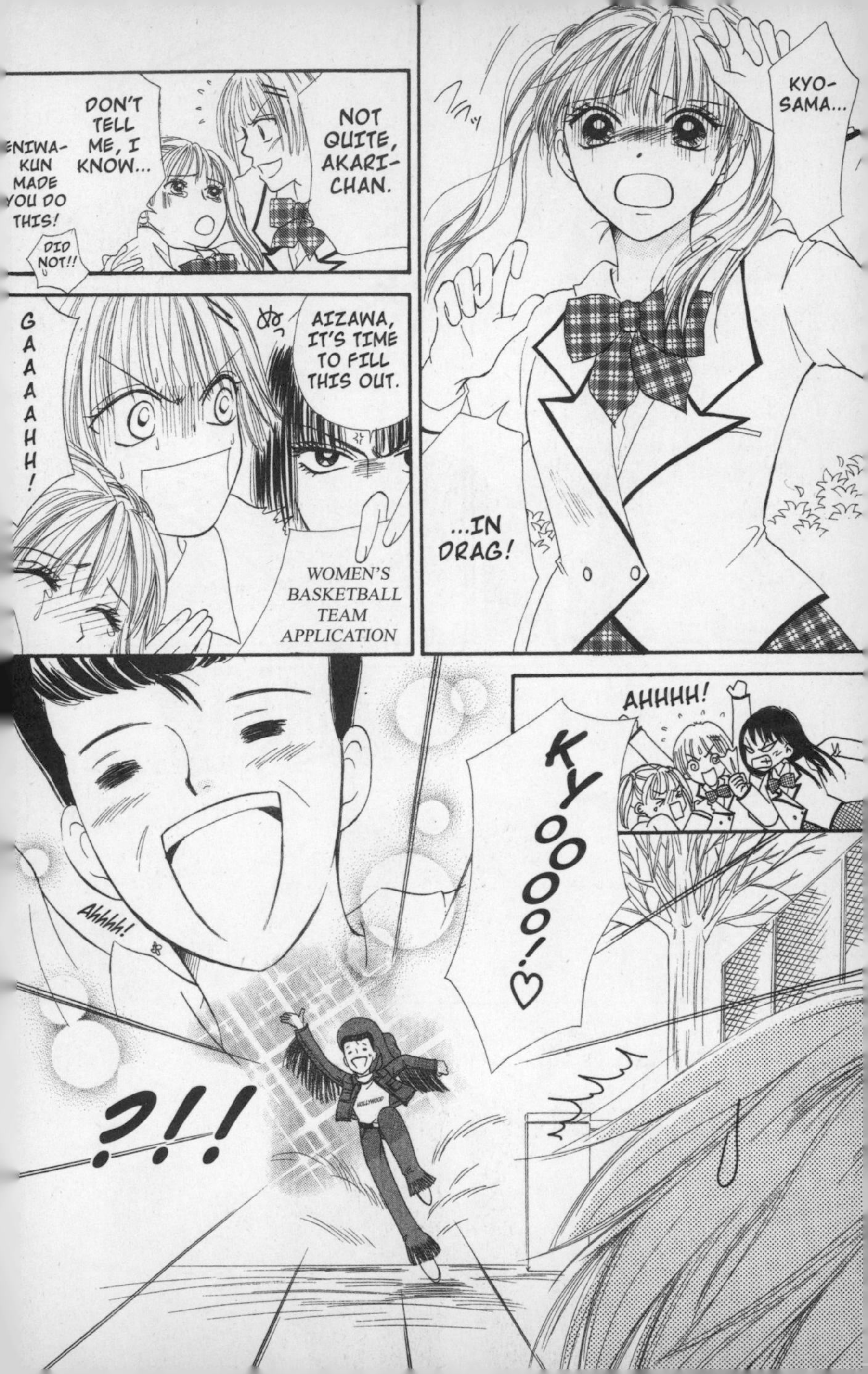
KYO-SAMA...
...IN DRAG!
NOT QUITE, AKARI-CHAN.
DON'T TELL ME, I KNOW...
ENIWA-KUN MADE YOU DO THIS!
DID NOT!!
AIZAWA, IT'S TIME TO FILL THIS OUT.
WOMEN'S BASKETBALL TEAM APPLICATION
GAAAAAHH!
AHHHH!
KYOOOOOO!♥
Ahhhh!
?!!

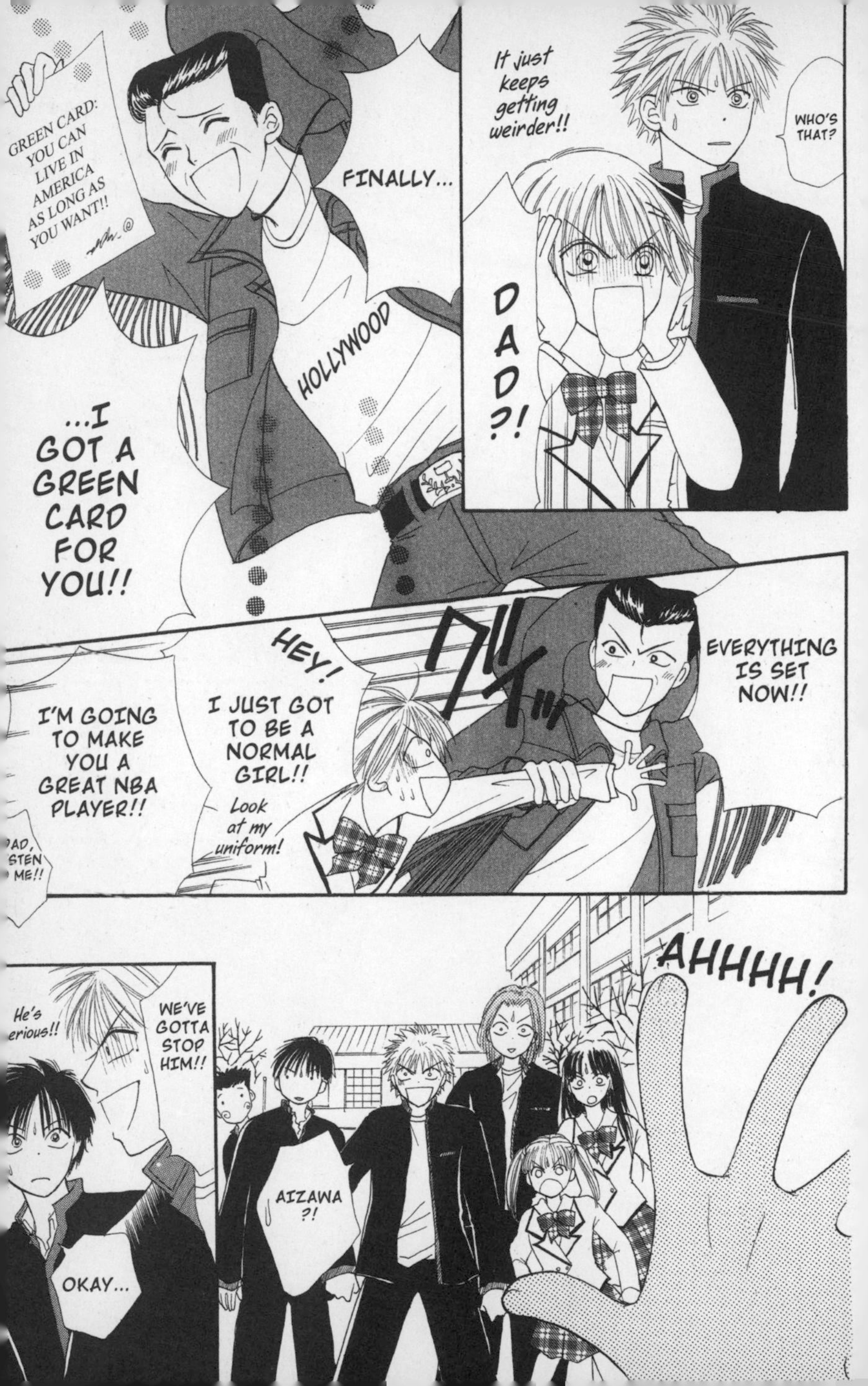
WHO'S THAT?
It just keeps getting weirder!!
DAD?!
FINALLY...
...I GOT A GREEN CARD FOR YOU!!
GREEN CARD: YOU CAN LIVE IN AMERICA AS LONG AS YOU WANT!!
HOLLYWOOD
EVERYTHING IS SET NOW!!
HEY!
I JUST GOT TO BE A NORMAL GIRL!!
Look at my uniform!
I'M GOING TO MAKE YOU A GREAT NBA PLAYER!!
AHHHH!
AIZAWA?!
WE'VE GOTTA STOP HIM!!
OKAY...

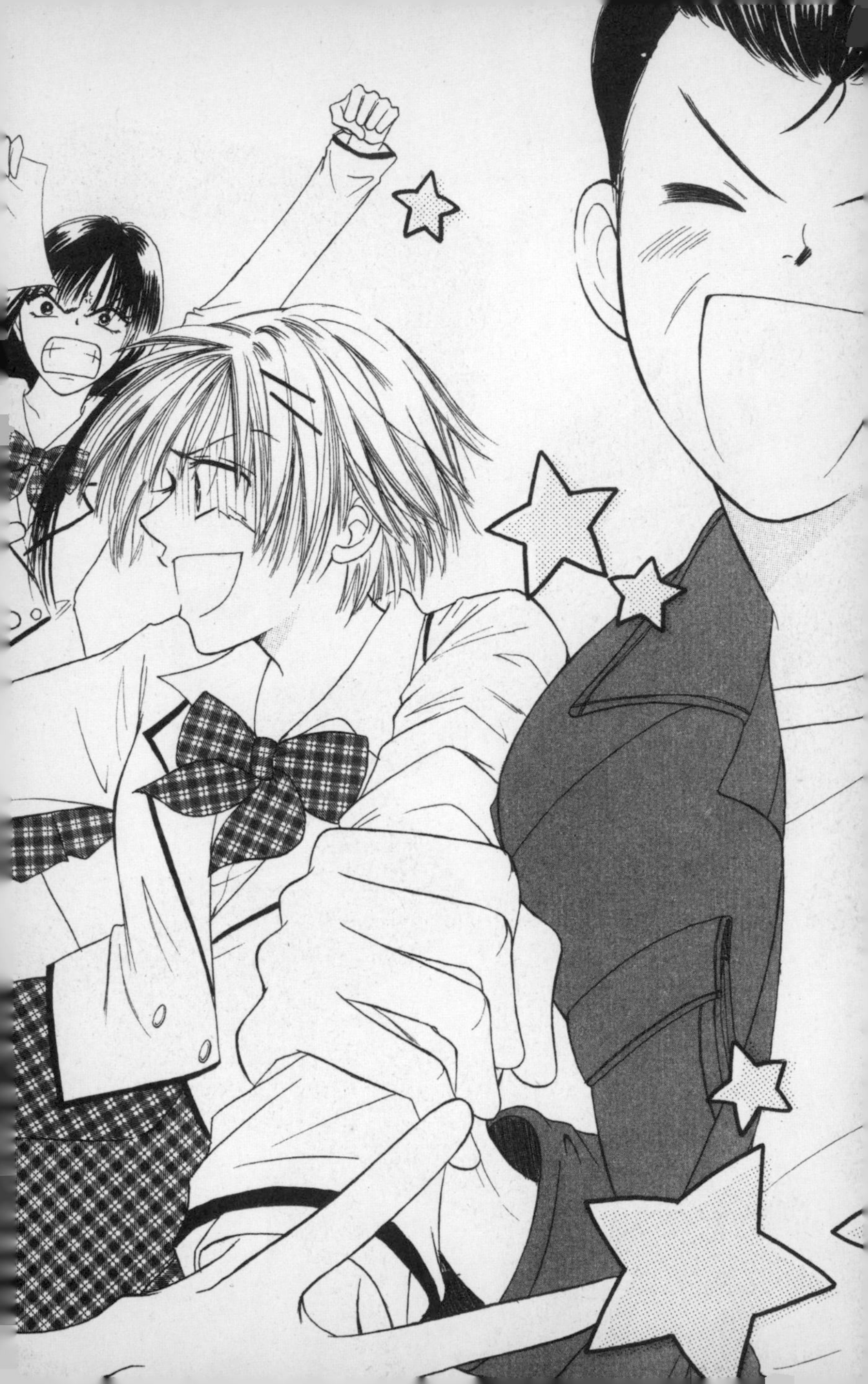

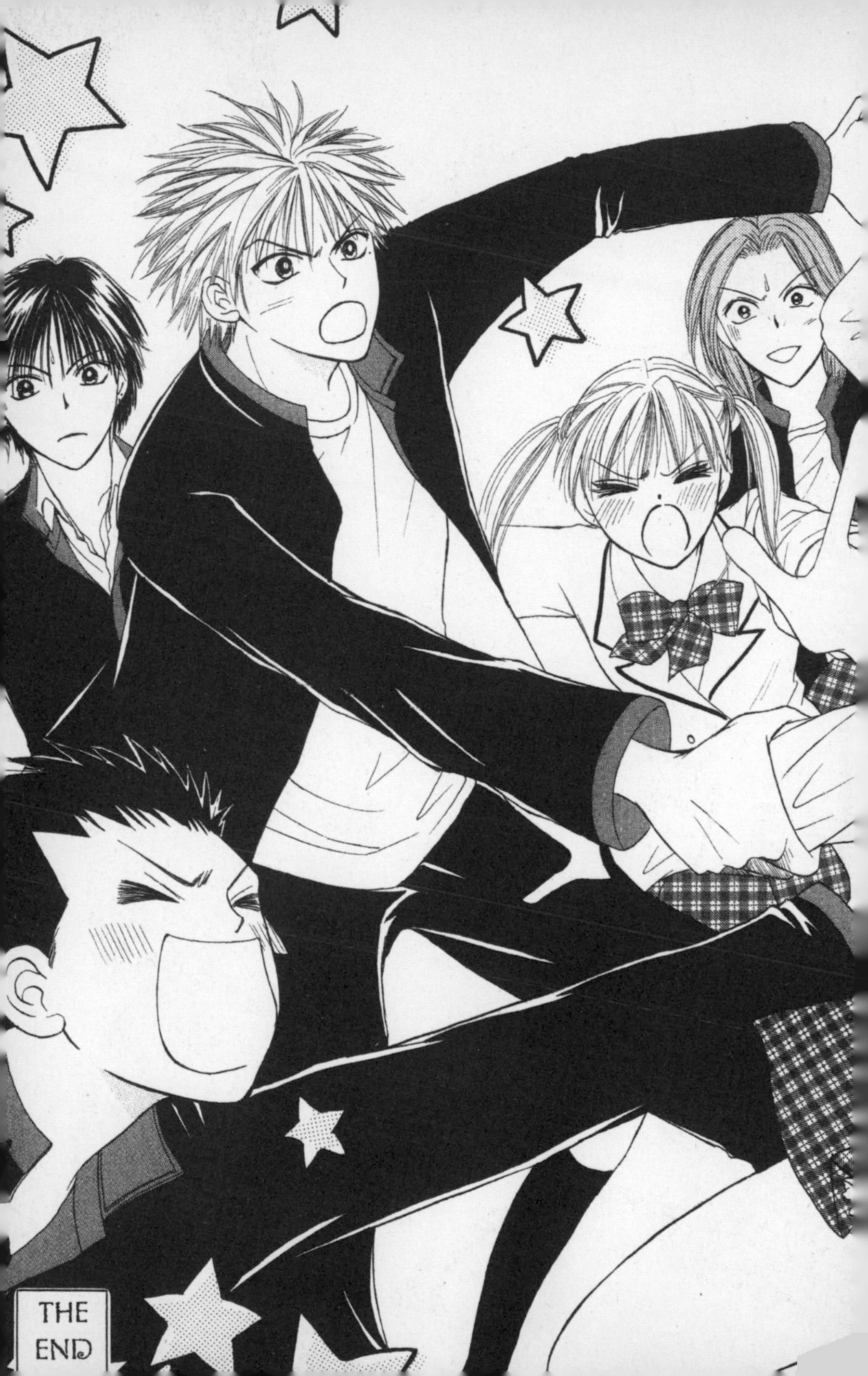
THE
END

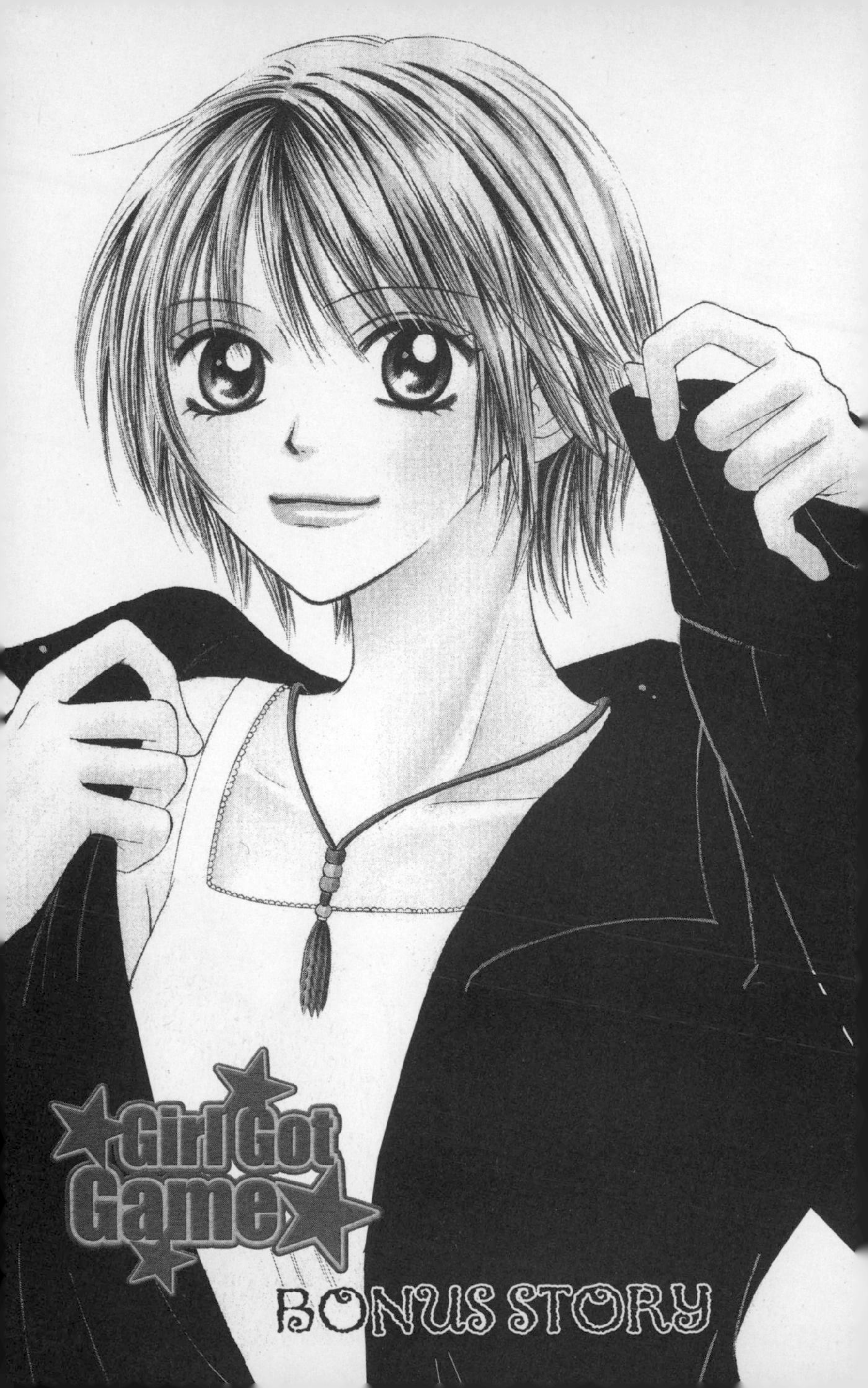
Girl Got Game
BONUS STORY

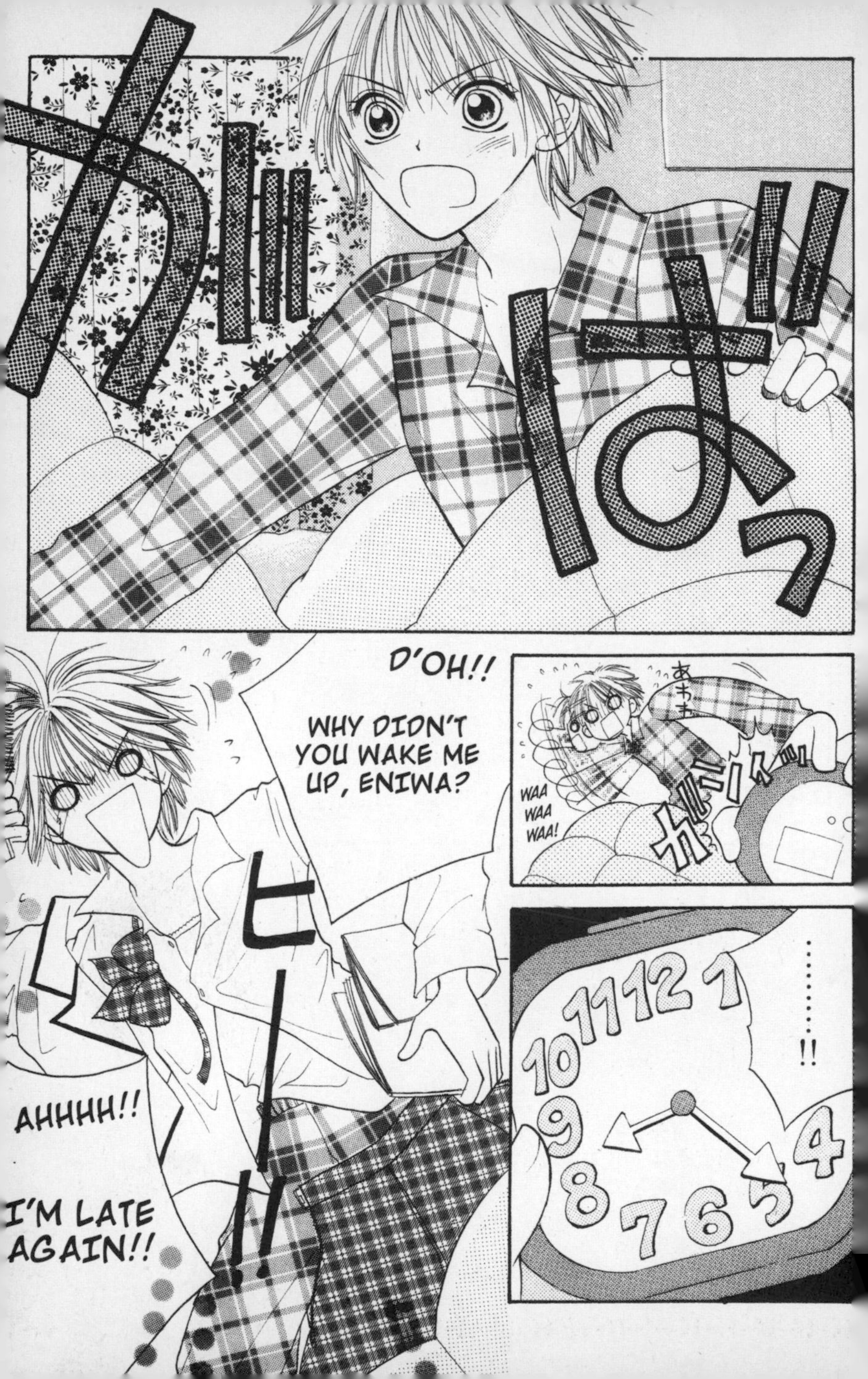
WAA WAA WAA!
......!!
D'OH!!
WHY DIDN'T YOU WAKE ME UP, ENIWA?
AHHHH!!
I'M LATE AGAIN!!

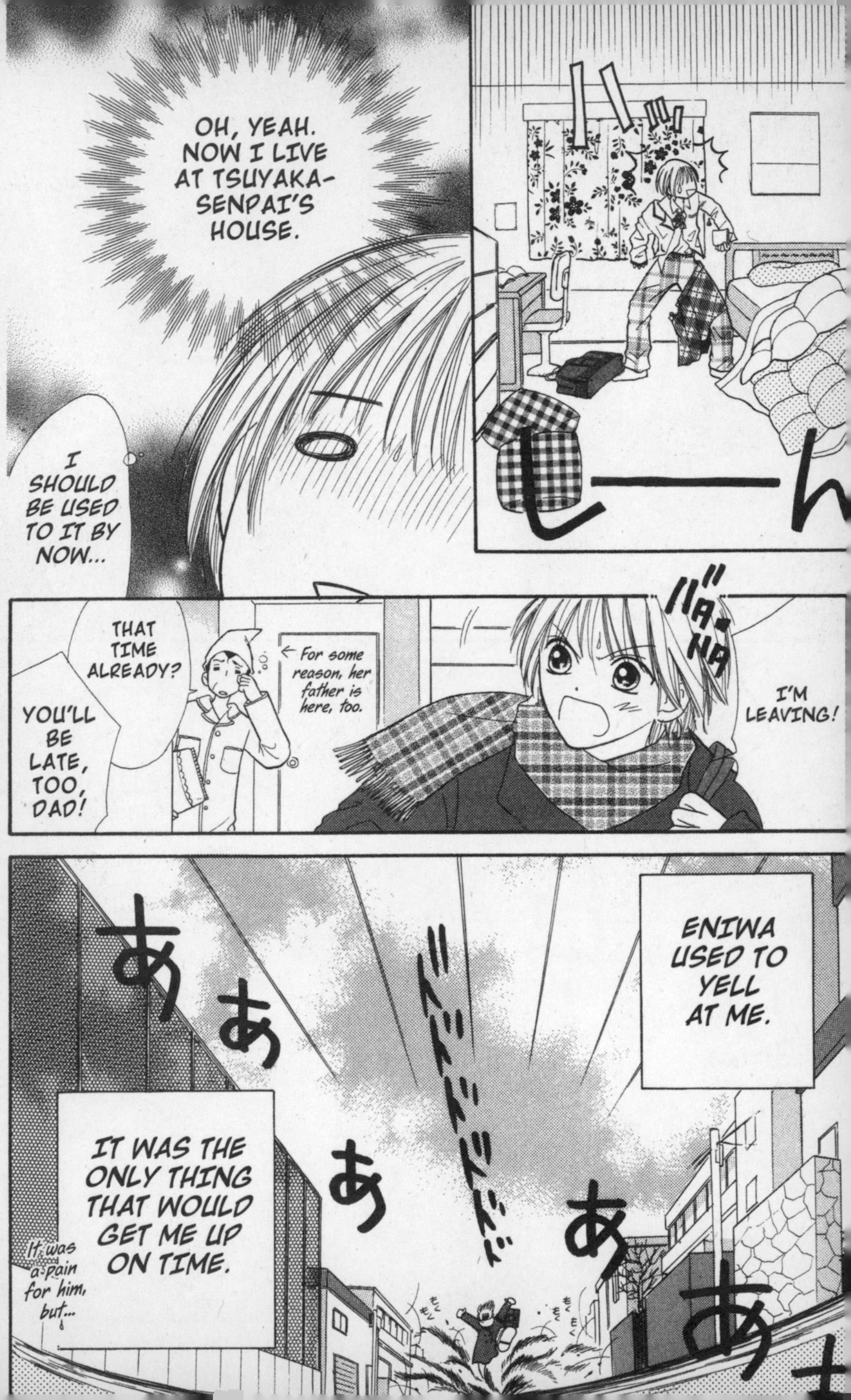
し——ん
OH, YEAH. NOW I LIVE AT TSUYAKA-SENPAI'S HOUSE.
I SHOULD BE USED TO IT BY NOW...
バタバタ
I'M LEAVING!
For some reason, her father is here, too.
THAT TIME ALREADY?
YOU'LL BE LATE, TOO, DAD!
ENIWA USED TO YELL AT ME.
ああああ
ドドドド
もく もく
IT WAS THE ONLY THING THAT WOULD GET ME UP ON TIME.
It was a pain for him, but...

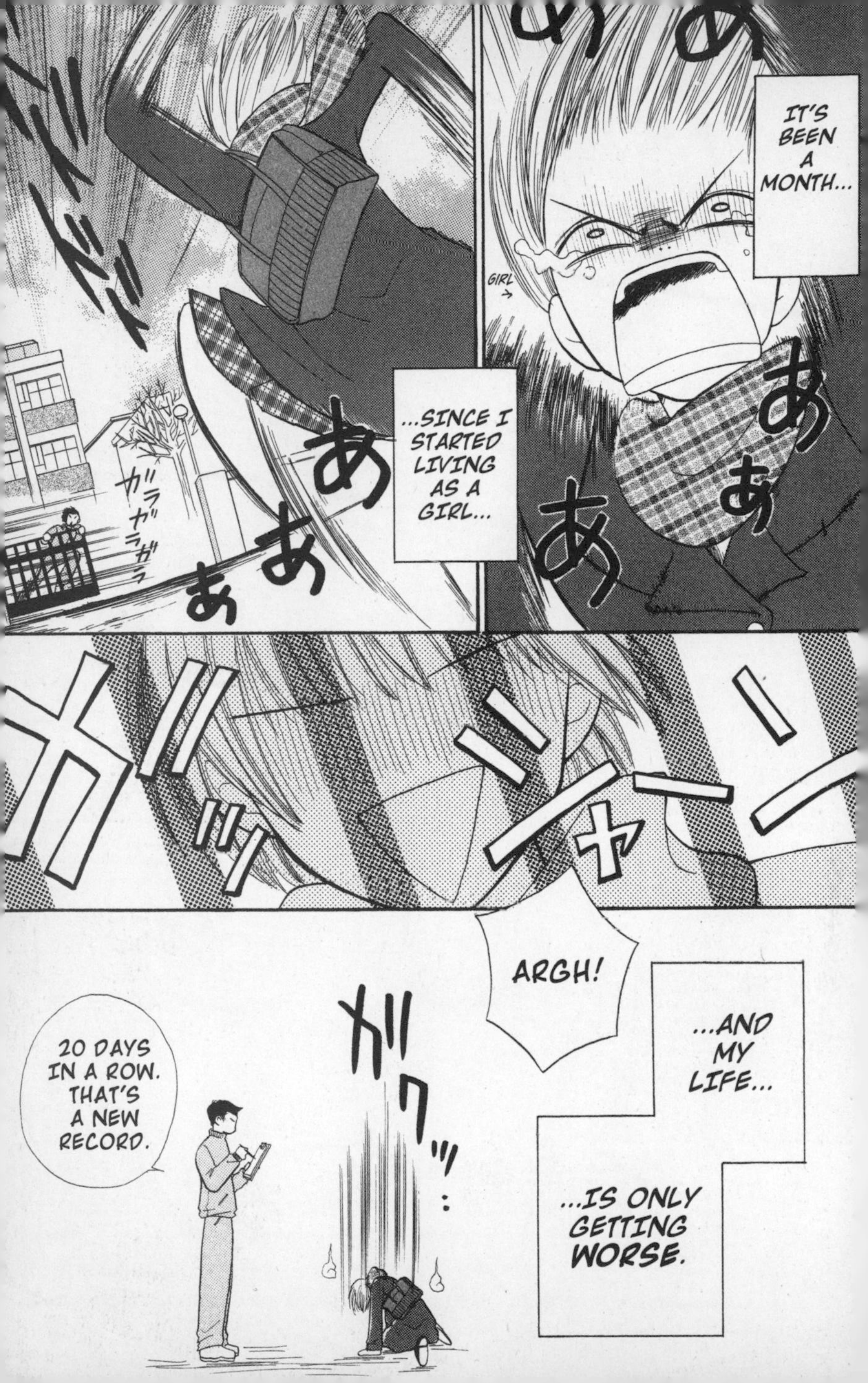
IT'S BEEN A MONTH...
GIRL →
...SINCE I STARTED LIVING AS A GIRL...
ARGH!
...AND MY LIFE...
...IS ONLY GETTING WORSE.
20 DAYS IN A ROW. THAT'S A NEW RECORD.

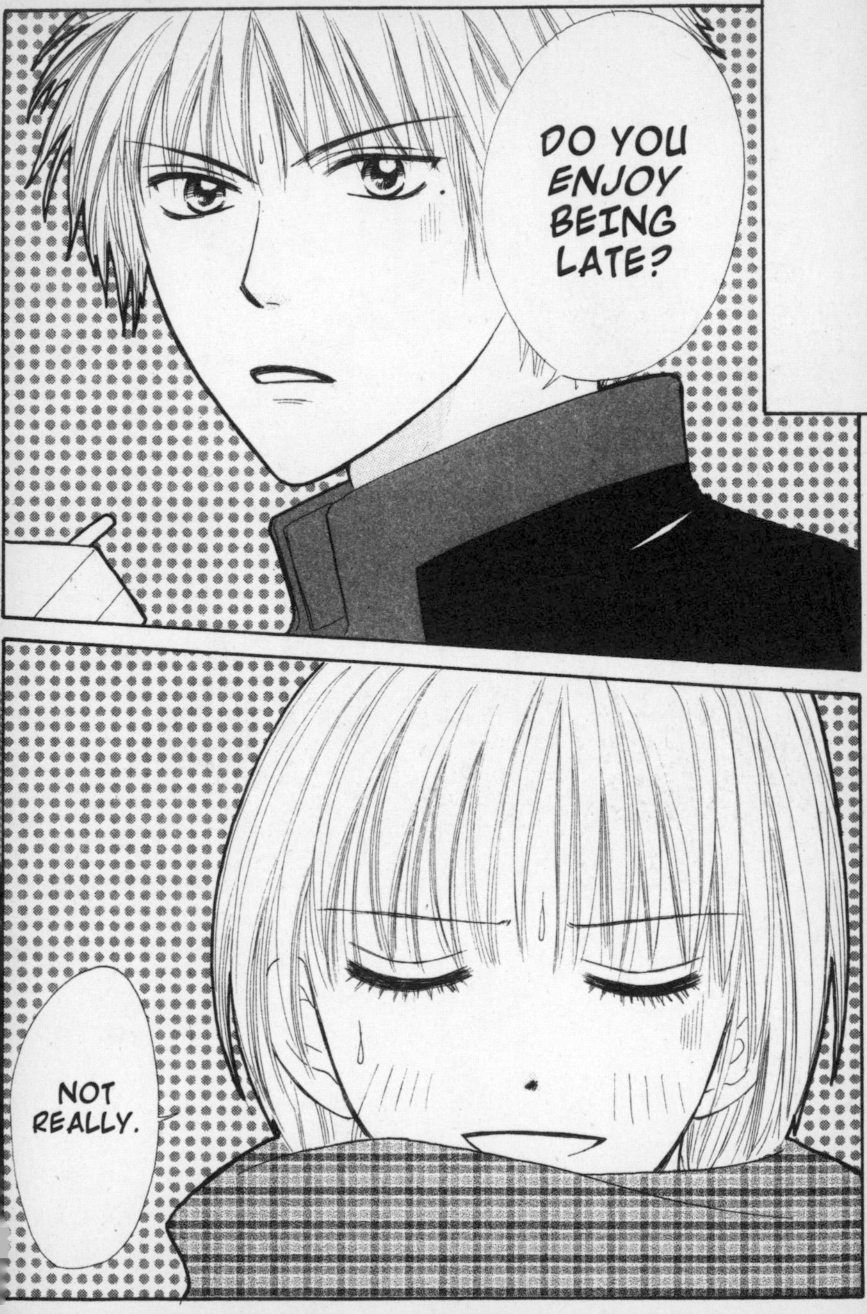
DO YOU ENJOY BEING LATE?
NOT REALLY.

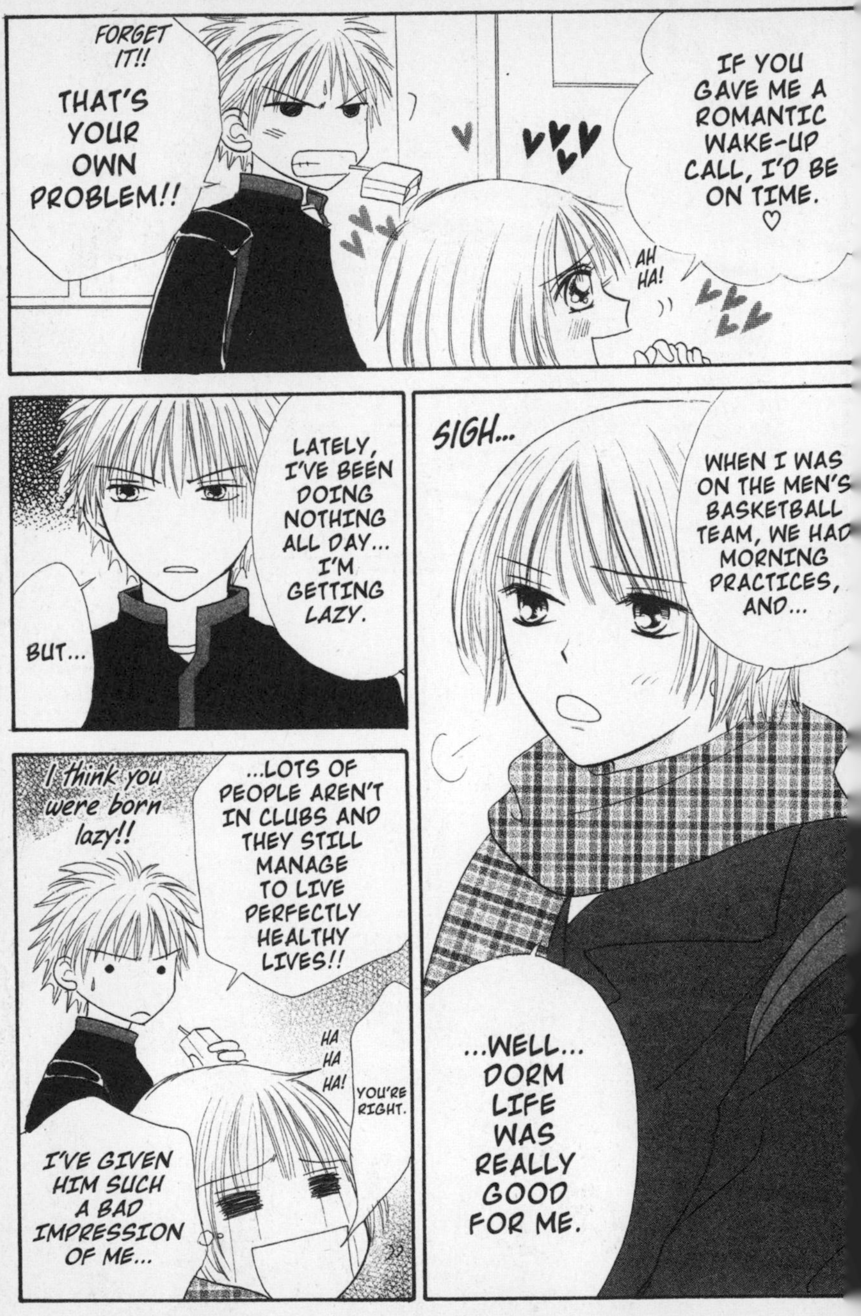
IF YOU GAVE ME A ROMANTIC WAKE-UP CALL, I'D BE ON TIME. ♡
AH HA!
FORGET IT!!
THAT'S YOUR OWN PROBLEM!!
SIGH...
WHEN I WAS ON THE MEN'S BASKETBALL TEAM, WE HAD MORNING PRACTICES, AND...
...WELL... DORM LIFE WAS REALLY GOOD FOR ME.
LATELY, I'VE BEEN DOING NOTHING ALL DAY... I'M GETTING LAZY.
BUT...
...LOTS OF PEOPLE AREN'T IN CLUBS AND THEY STILL MANAGE TO LIVE PERFECTLY HEALTHY LIVES!!
I think you were born lazy!!
HA HA HA!
YOU'RE RIGHT.
I'VE GIVEN HIM SUCH A BAD IMPRESSION OF ME...

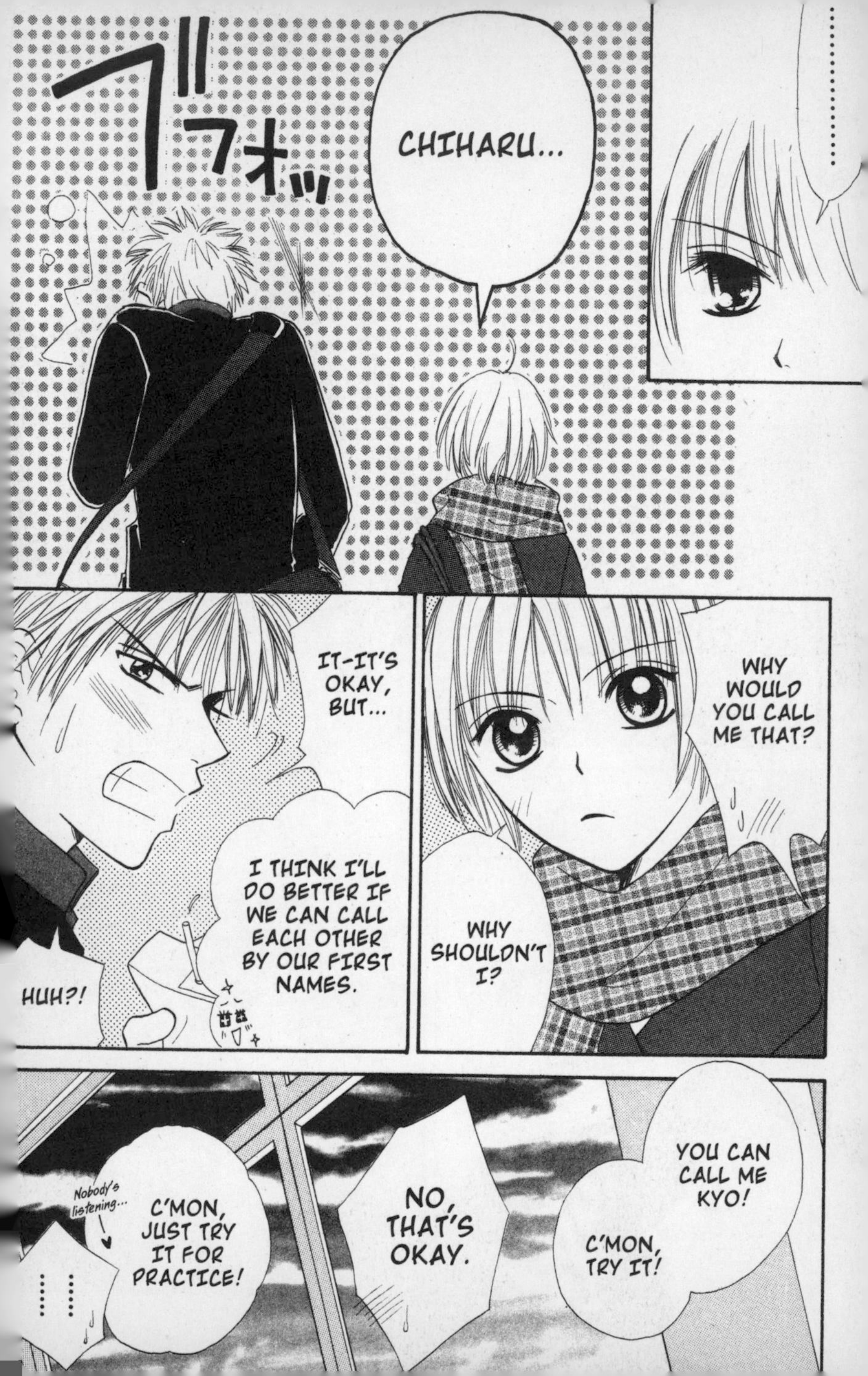
......
CHIHARU...
ブフォッ
WHY WOULD YOU CALL ME THAT?
WHY SHOULDN'T I?
IT-IT'S OKAY, BUT...
I THINK I'LL DO BETTER IF WE CAN CALL EACH OTHER BY OUR FIRST NAMES.
HUH?!
YOU CAN CALL ME KYO!
C'MON, TRY IT!
NO, THAT'S OKAY.
C'MON, JUST TRY IT FOR PRACTICE!
Nobody's listening...
......

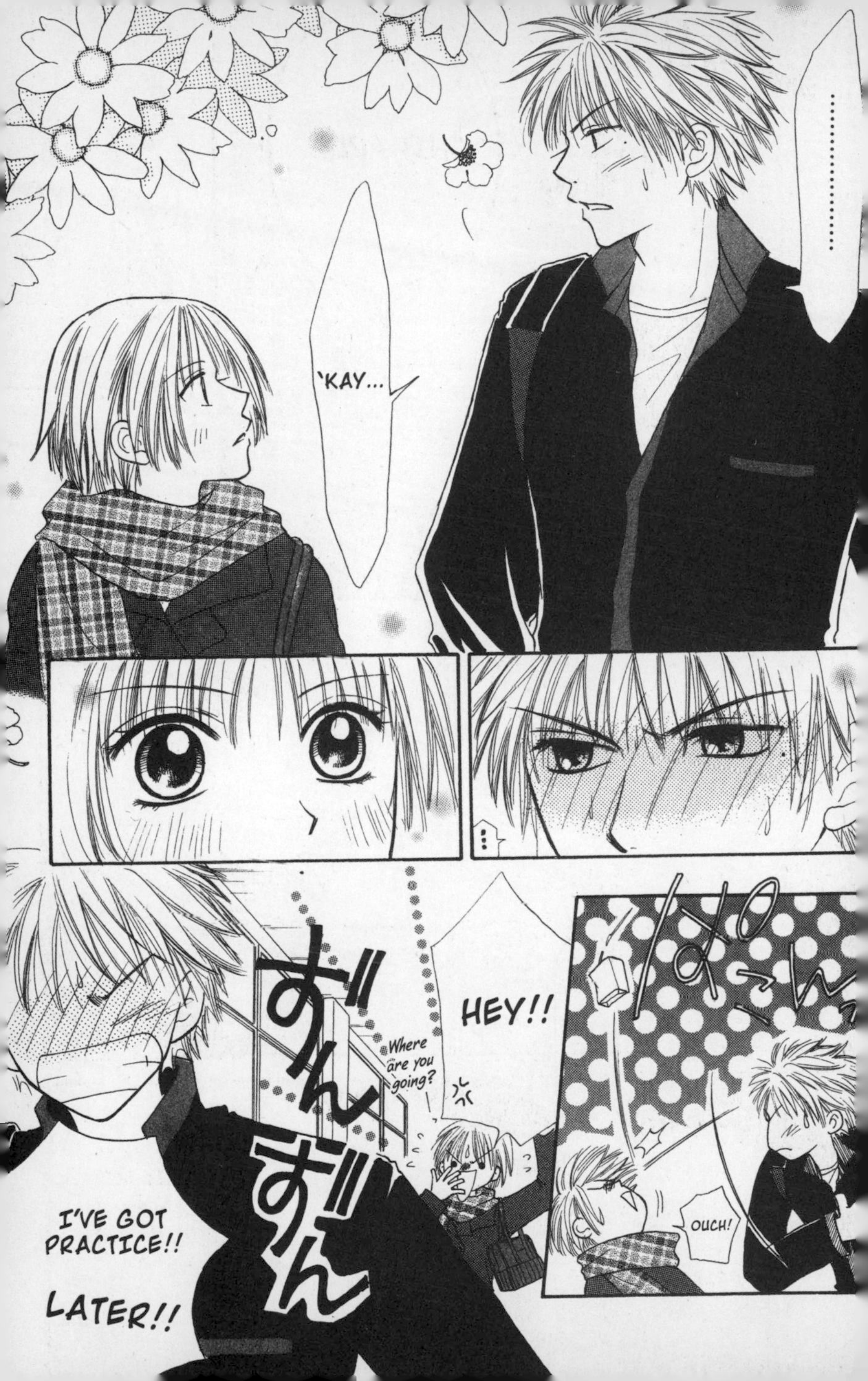
......
`KAY...
...
OUCH!
HEY!!
Where are you going?
ずんずん
I'VE GOT PRACTICE!!
LATER!!

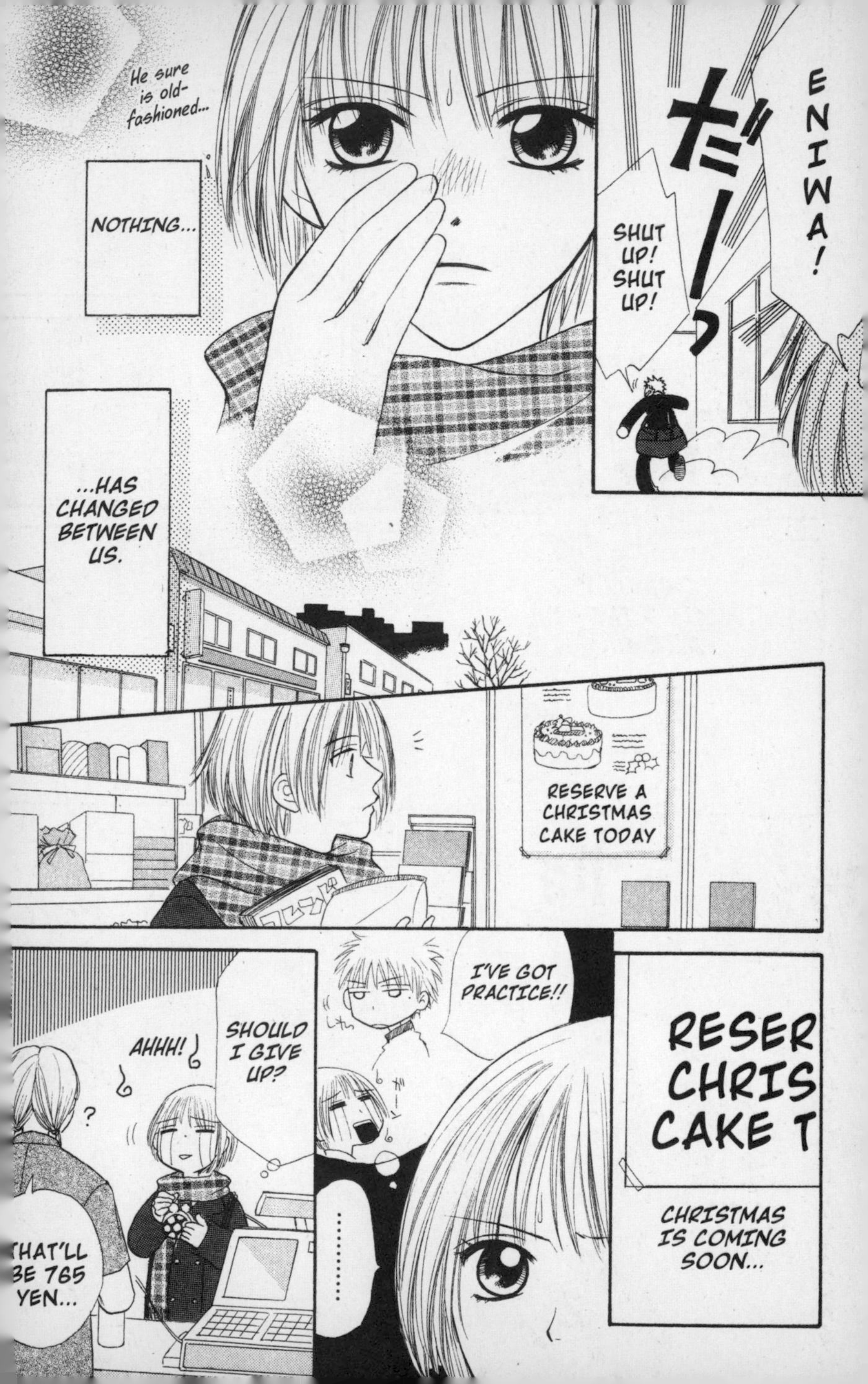
ENIWA!
だーっ
SHUT UP! SHUT UP!
He sure is old-fashioned...
NOTHING...
...HAS CHANGED BETWEEN US.
RESERVE A CHRISTMAS CAKE TODAY
RESER CHRIS CAKE T
CHRISTMAS IS COMING SOON...
I'VE GOT PRACTICE!!
......
SHOULD I GIVE UP?
AHHH!
?
THAT'LL BE 765 YEN...

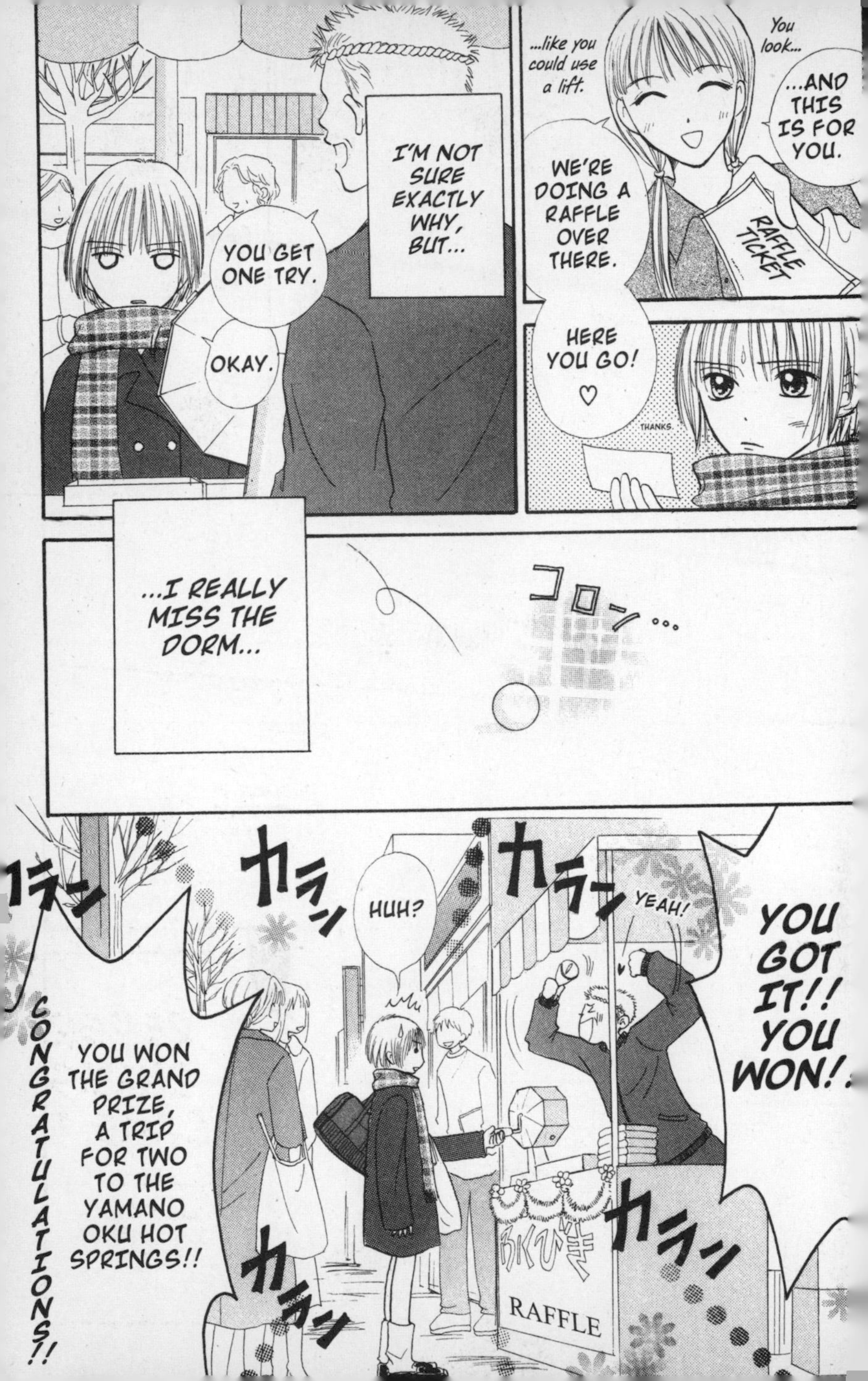
You look...
...like you could use a lift.
...AND THIS IS FOR YOU.
WE'RE DOING A RAFFLE OVER THERE.
RAFFLE TICKET
HERE YOU GO! ♡
THANKS.
I'M NOT SURE EXACTLY WHY, BUT...
YOU GET ONE TRY.
OKAY.
コロン...
...I REALLY MISS THE DORM...
YOU GOT IT!! YOU WON!
YEAH!
カラン
カラン
HUH?
CONGRATULATIONS!!
YOU WON THE GRAND PRIZE, A TRIP FOR TWO TO THE YAMANO OKU HOT SPRINGS!!
ふくびき
RAFFLE
カラン
カラン

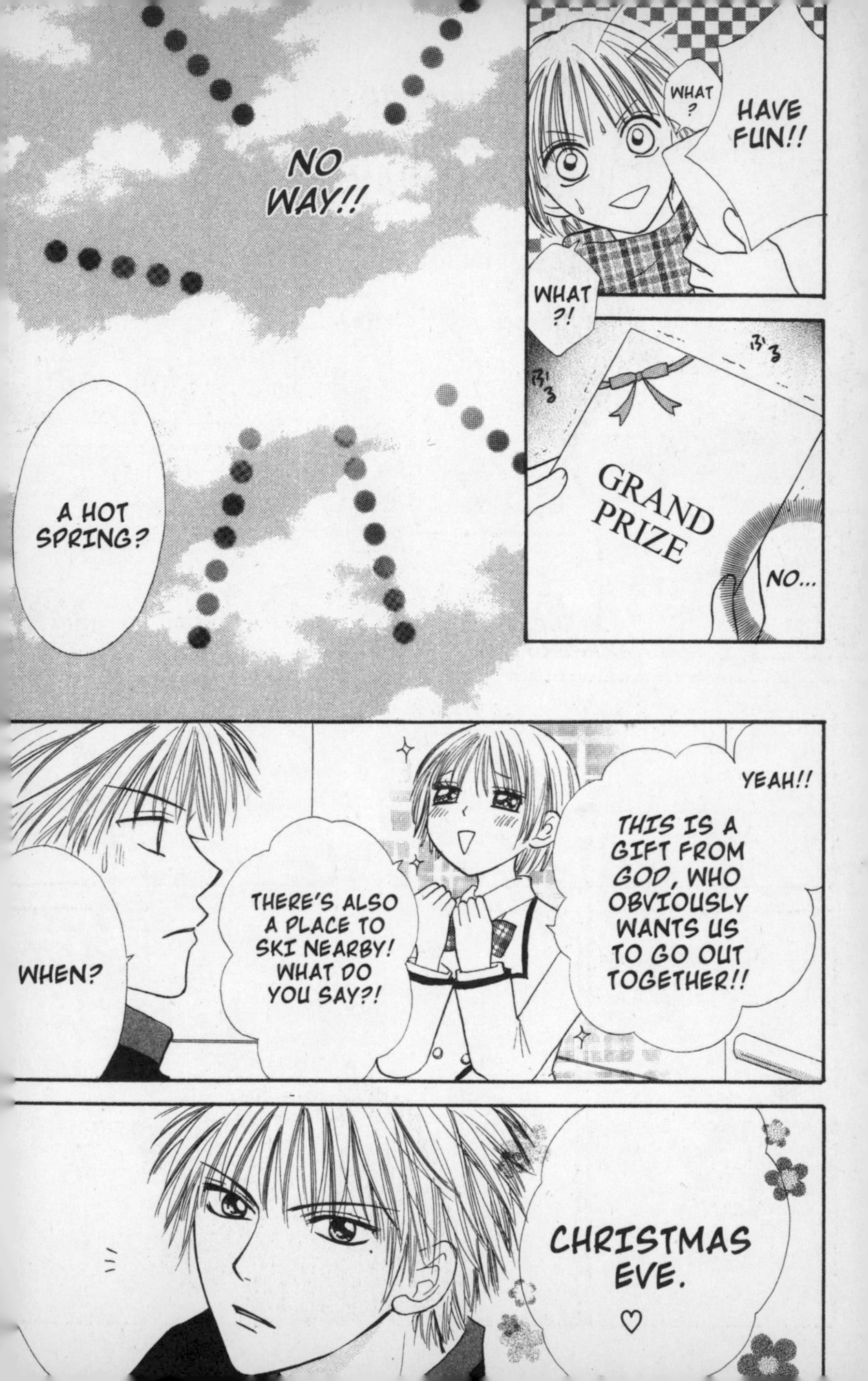
HAVE FUN!!
WHAT?
WHAT?!
ぶる
ぶる
GRAND PRIZE
NO...
NO WAY!!
A HOT SPRING?
YEAH!!
THIS IS A GIFT FROM GOD, WHO OBVIOUSLY WANTS US TO GO OUT TOGETHER!!
THERE'S ALSO A PLACE TO SKI NEARBY! WHAT DO YOU SAY?!
WHEN?
CHRISTMAS EVE. ♡

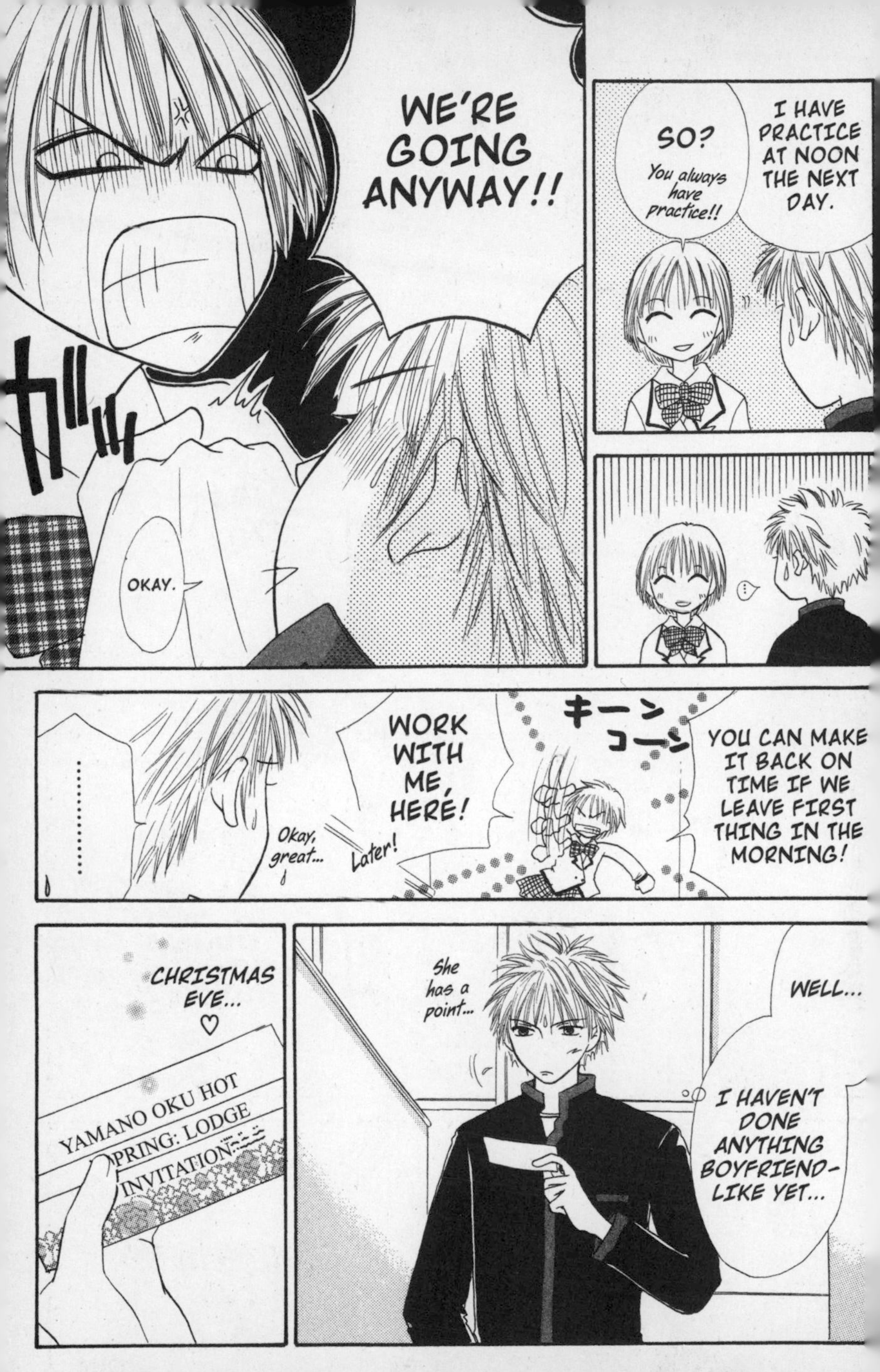
I HAVE PRACTICE AT NOON THE NEXT DAY.
SO?
You always have practice!!
…
WE'RE GOING ANYWAY!!
ガッ
OKAY.
YOU CAN MAKE IT BACK ON TIME IF WE LEAVE FIRST THING IN THE MORNING!
キーン
コーン
WORK WITH ME, HERE!
Later!
Okay, great...
......
WELL...
I HAVEN'T DONE ANYTHING BOYFRIEND-LIKE YET...
She has a point...
CHRISTMAS EVE... ♡
YAMANO OKU HOT SPRING: LODGE INVITATION

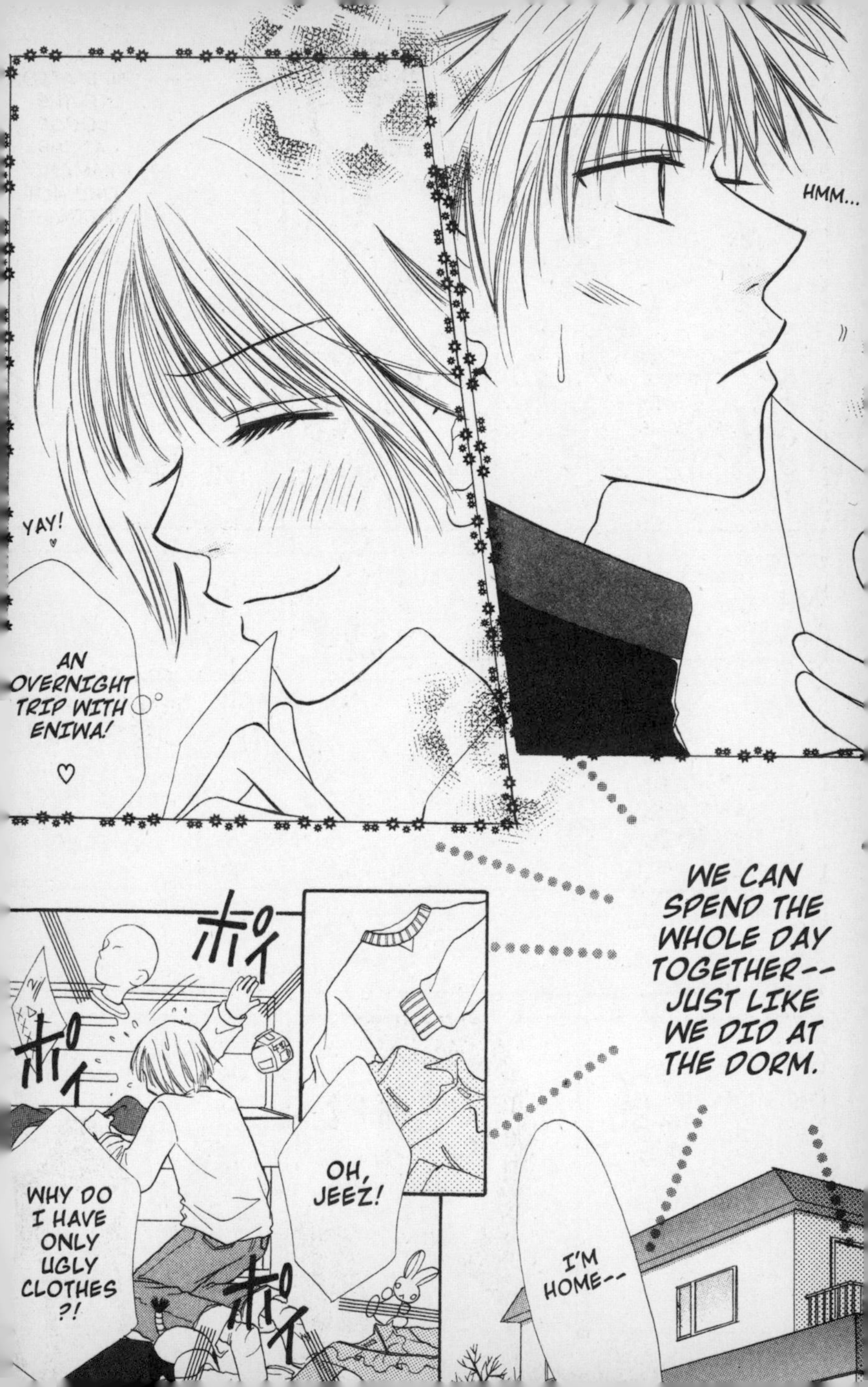
HMM...
YAY! ♡
AN OVERNIGHT TRIP WITH ENIWA! ♡
WE CAN SPEND THE WHOLE DAY TOGETHER--JUST LIKE WE DID AT THE DORM.
I'M HOME--
OH, JEEZ!
ポイ
ポイ
WHY DO I HAVE ONLY UGLY CLOTHES?!
ポイ

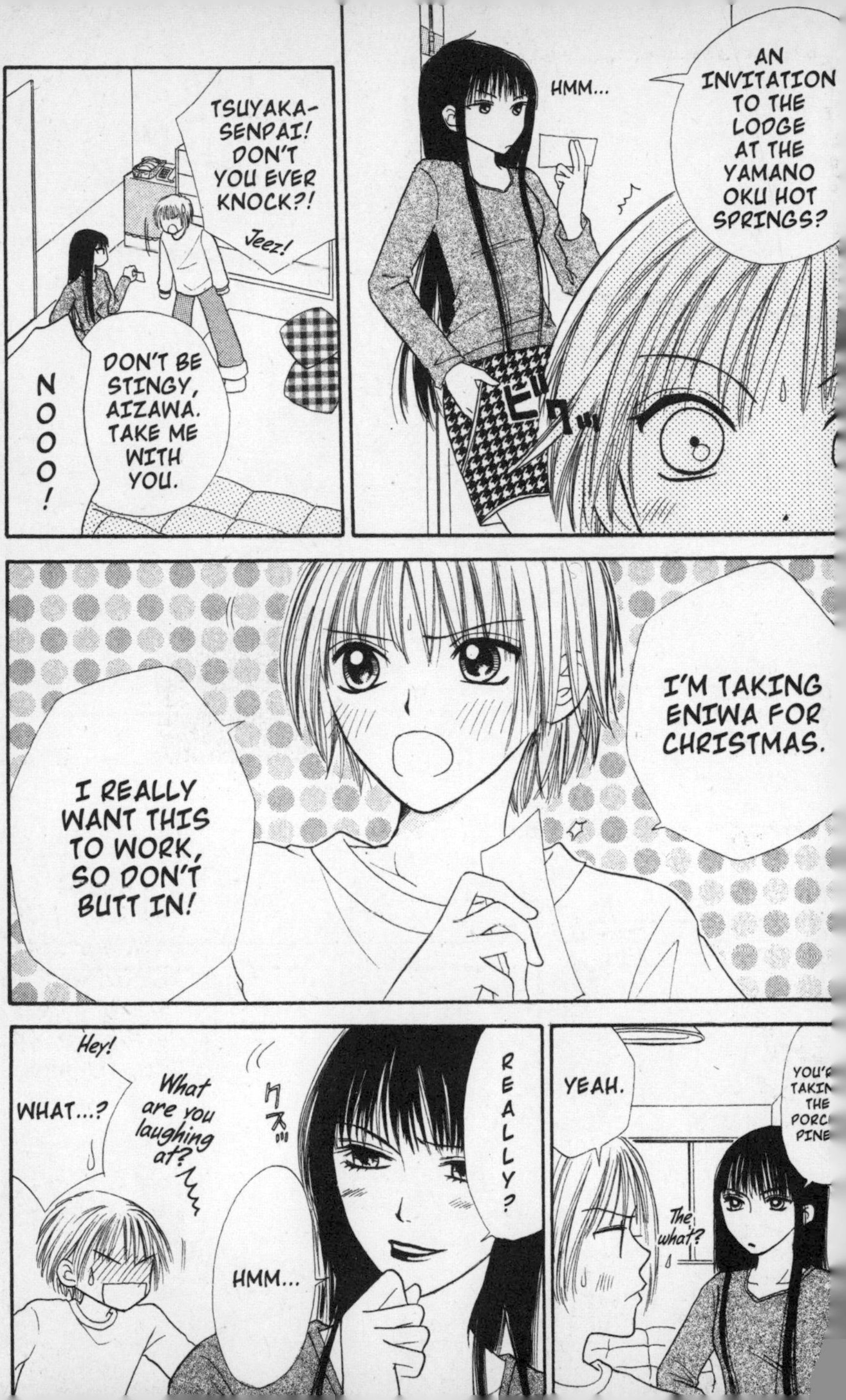
AN INVITATION TO THE LODGE AT THE YAMANO OKU HOT SPRINGS?
HMM...
TSUYAKA-SENPAI! DON'T YOU EVER KNOCK?!
Jeez!
DON'T BE STINGY, AIZAWA. TAKE ME WITH YOU.
NOOOO!
I'M TAKING ENIWA FOR CHRISTMAS.
I REALLY WANT THIS TO WORK, SO DON'T BUTT IN!
YOU'R TAKIN THE PORC PINE
YEAH.
The what?
REALLY?
HMM...
WHAT...?
Hey!
What are you laughing at?

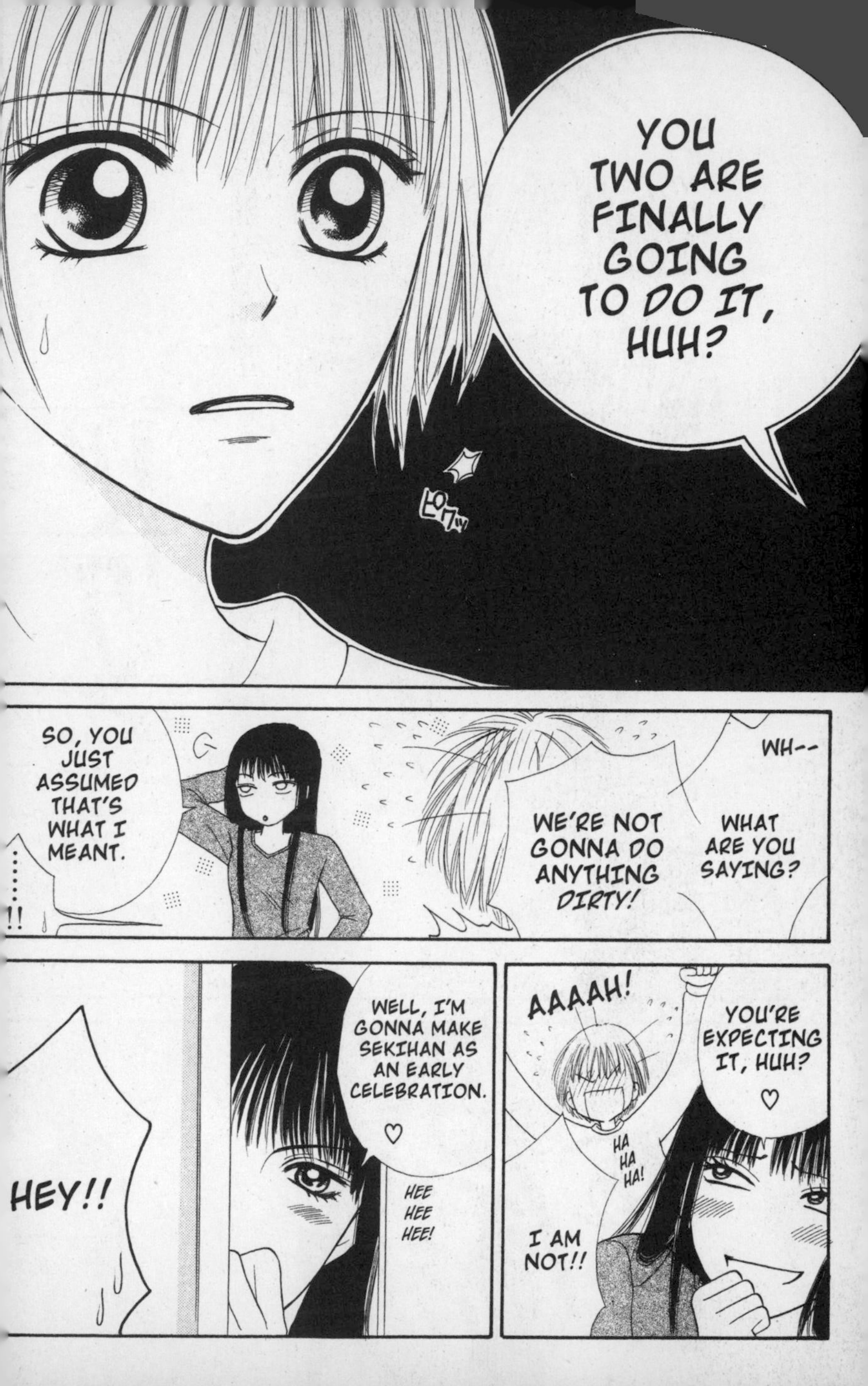
YOU TWO ARE FINALLY GOING TO *DO IT*, HUH?
ピクッ
WH--
WHAT ARE YOU SAYING?
WE'RE NOT GONNA DO ANYTHING *DIRTY!*
SO, YOU JUST ASSUMED THAT'S WHAT I MEANT.
......!!
YOU'RE EXPECTING IT, HUH? ♡
AAAAH!
HA HA HA!
I AM NOT!!
WELL, I'M GONNA MAKE SEKIHAN AS AN EARLY CELEBRATION. ♡
HEE HEE HEE!
HEY!!

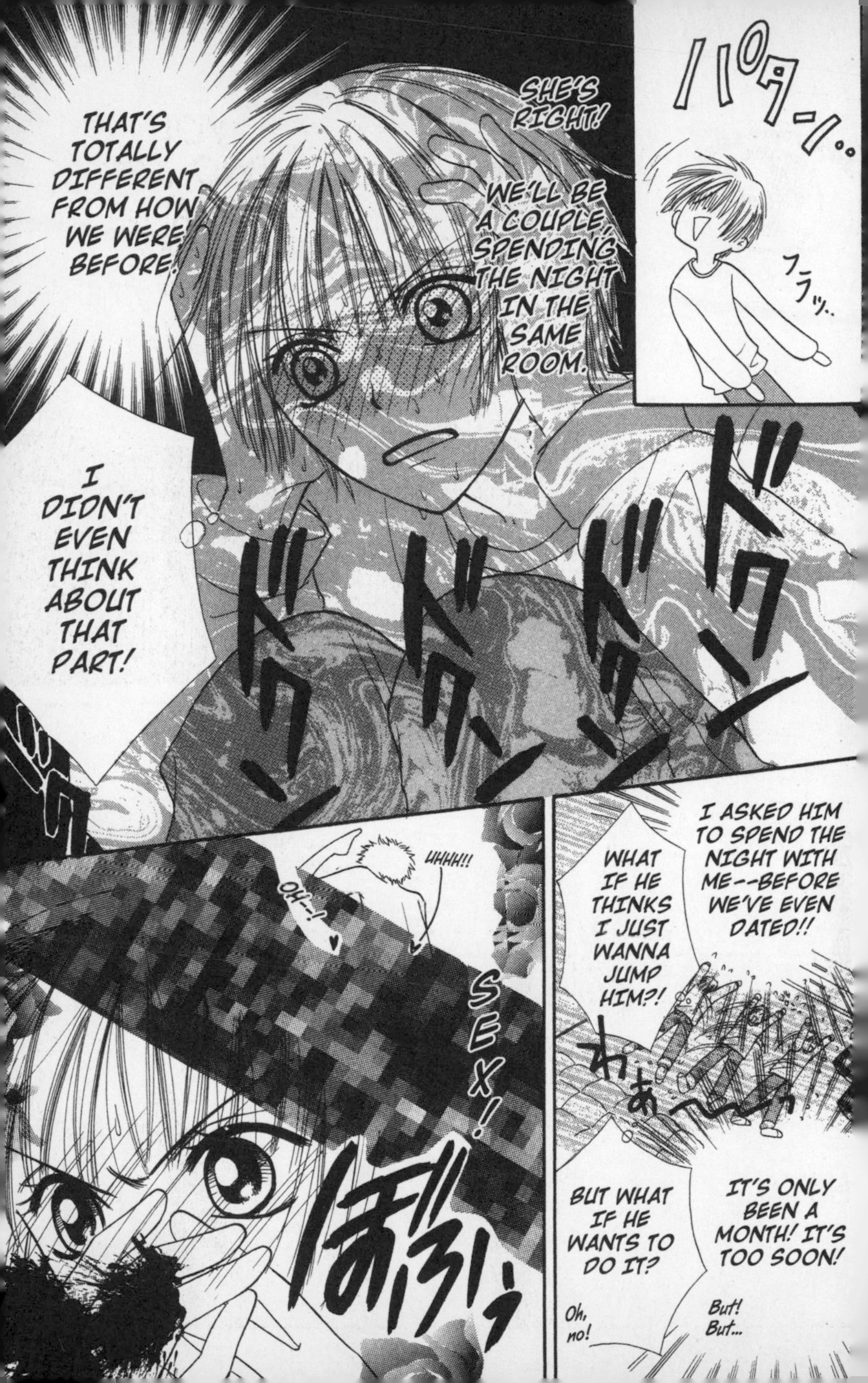
パターン。。
フラッ..
SHE'S RIGHT!
WE'LL BE A COUPLE SPENDING THE NIGHT IN THE SAME ROOM.
THAT'S TOTALLY DIFFERENT FROM HOW WE WERE BEFORE!
I DIDN'T EVEN THINK ABOUT THAT PART!
ドクン
ドクン
ドクン
I ASKED HIM TO SPEND THE NIGHT WITH ME--BEFORE WE'VE EVEN DATED!!
WHAT IF HE THINKS I JUST WANNA JUMP HIM?!
わあ〜
IT'S ONLY BEEN A MONTH! IT'S TOO SOON!
But! But...
BUT WHAT IF HE WANTS TO DO IT?
Oh, no!
UHHH!!
OH--!
SEX!

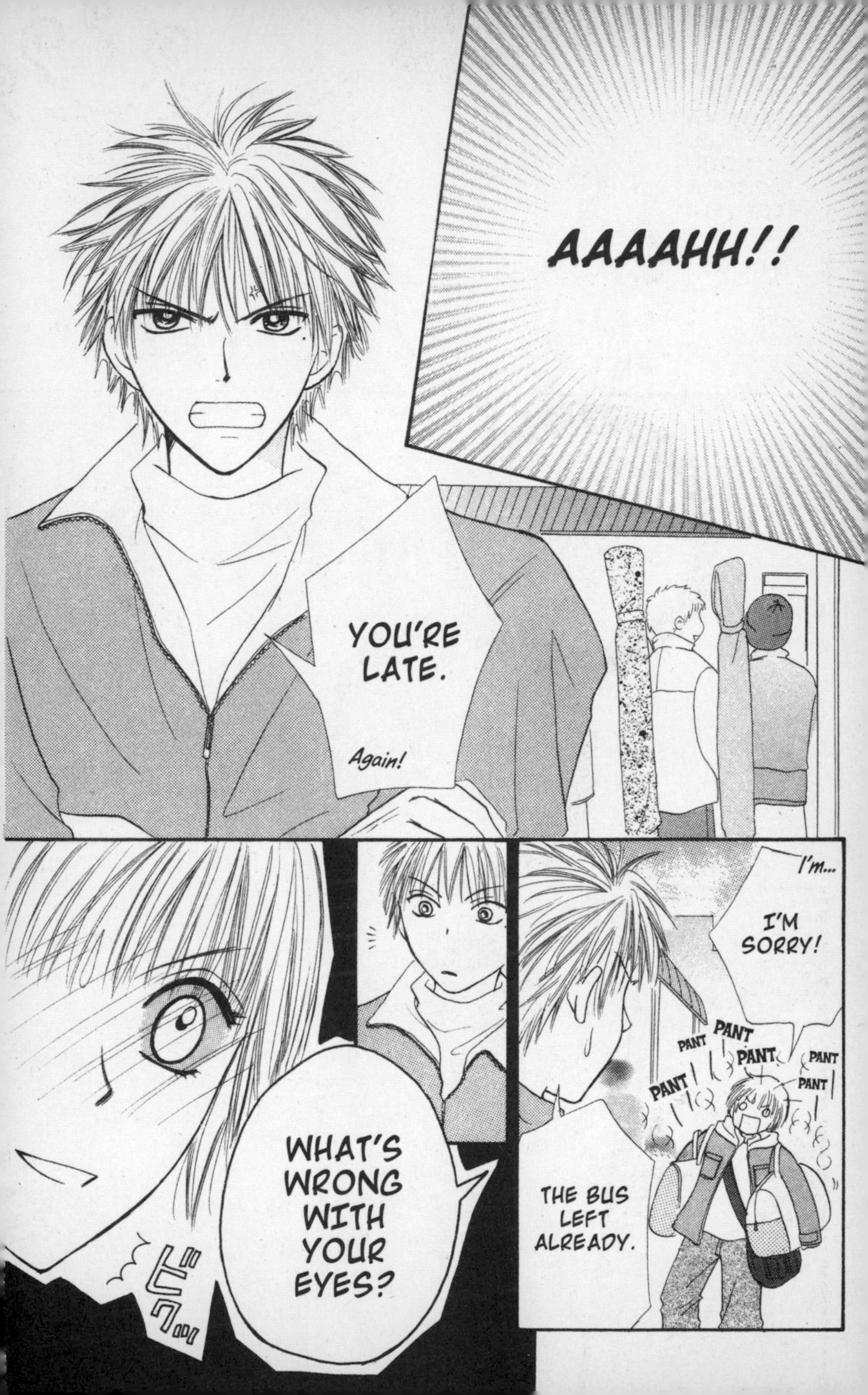
AAAAHH!!
YOU'RE LATE.
Again!
I'm...
I'M SORRY!
PANT
PANT
PANT
PANT
PANT
PANT
THE BUS LEFT ALREADY.
WHAT'S WRONG WITH YOUR EYES?

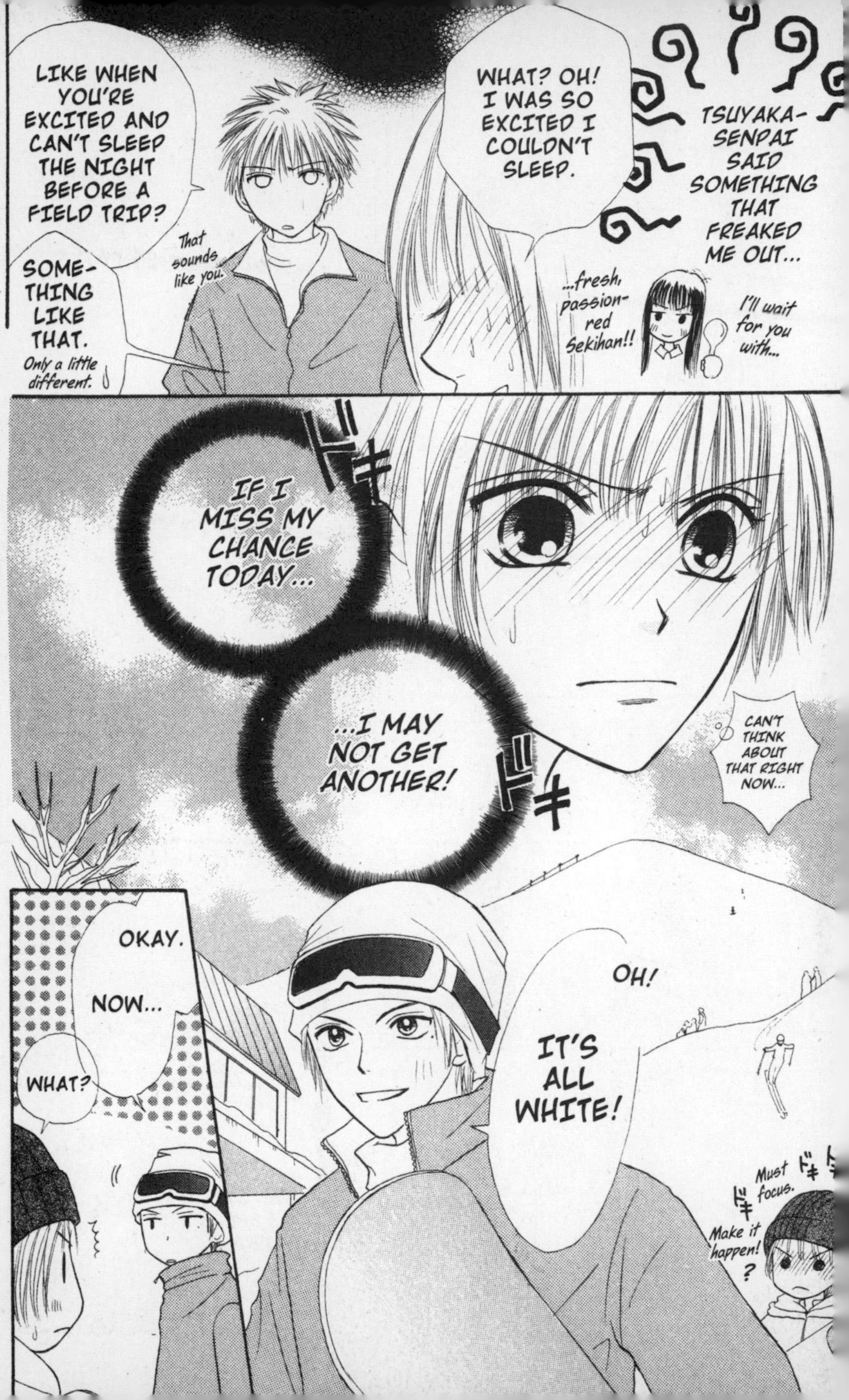
TSUYAKA-SENPAI SAID SOMETHING THAT FREAKED ME OUT...
I'll wait for you with...
...fresh, passion-red Sekihan!!
WHAT? OH! I WAS SO EXCITED I COULDN'T SLEEP.
LIKE WHEN YOU'RE EXCITED AND CAN'T SLEEP THE NIGHT BEFORE A FIELD TRIP?
That sounds like you.
SOME-THING LIKE THAT.
Only a little different.
ドキ
IF I MISS MY CHANCE TODAY...
...I MAY NOT GET ANOTHER!
ドキ
CAN'T THINK ABOUT THAT RIGHT NOW...
OH!
IT'S ALL WHITE!
ドキ
Must focus.
ドキ
Make it happen!
?
OKAY.
NOW...
WHAT?

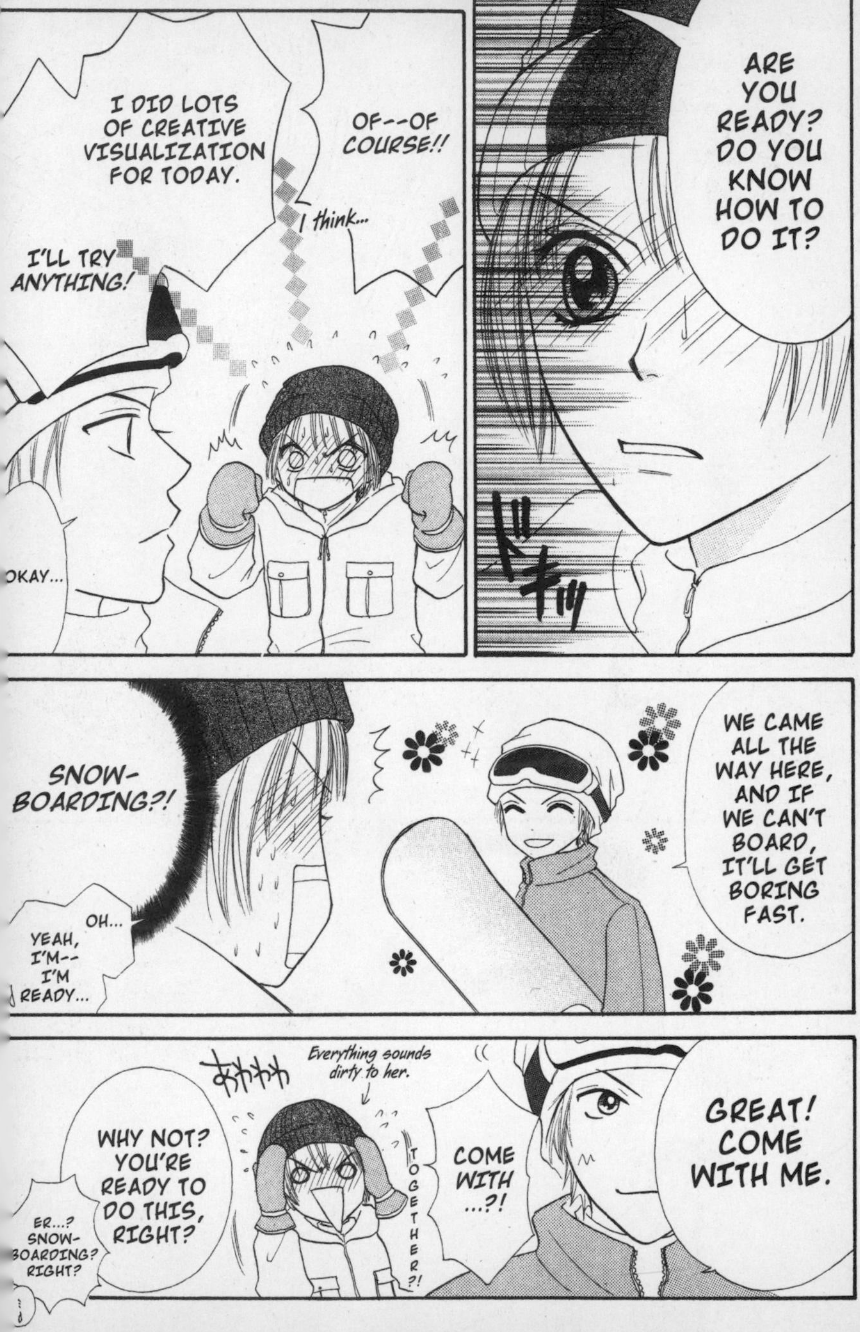
ARE YOU READY? DO YOU KNOW HOW TO DO IT?
ドキッ
OF--OF COURSE!!
I DID LOTS OF CREATIVE VISUALIZATION FOR TODAY.
I think...
I'LL TRY ANYTHING!
OKAY...
WE CAME ALL THE WAY HERE, AND IF WE CAN'T BOARD, IT'LL GET BORING FAST.
SNOW-BOARDING?!
OH... YEAH, I'M--I'M READY...
GREAT! COME WITH ME.
COME WITH ...?!
TOGETHER?!
Everything sounds dirty to her.
WHY NOT? YOU'RE READY TO DO THIS, RIGHT?
ER...? SNOW-BOARDING? RIGHT?

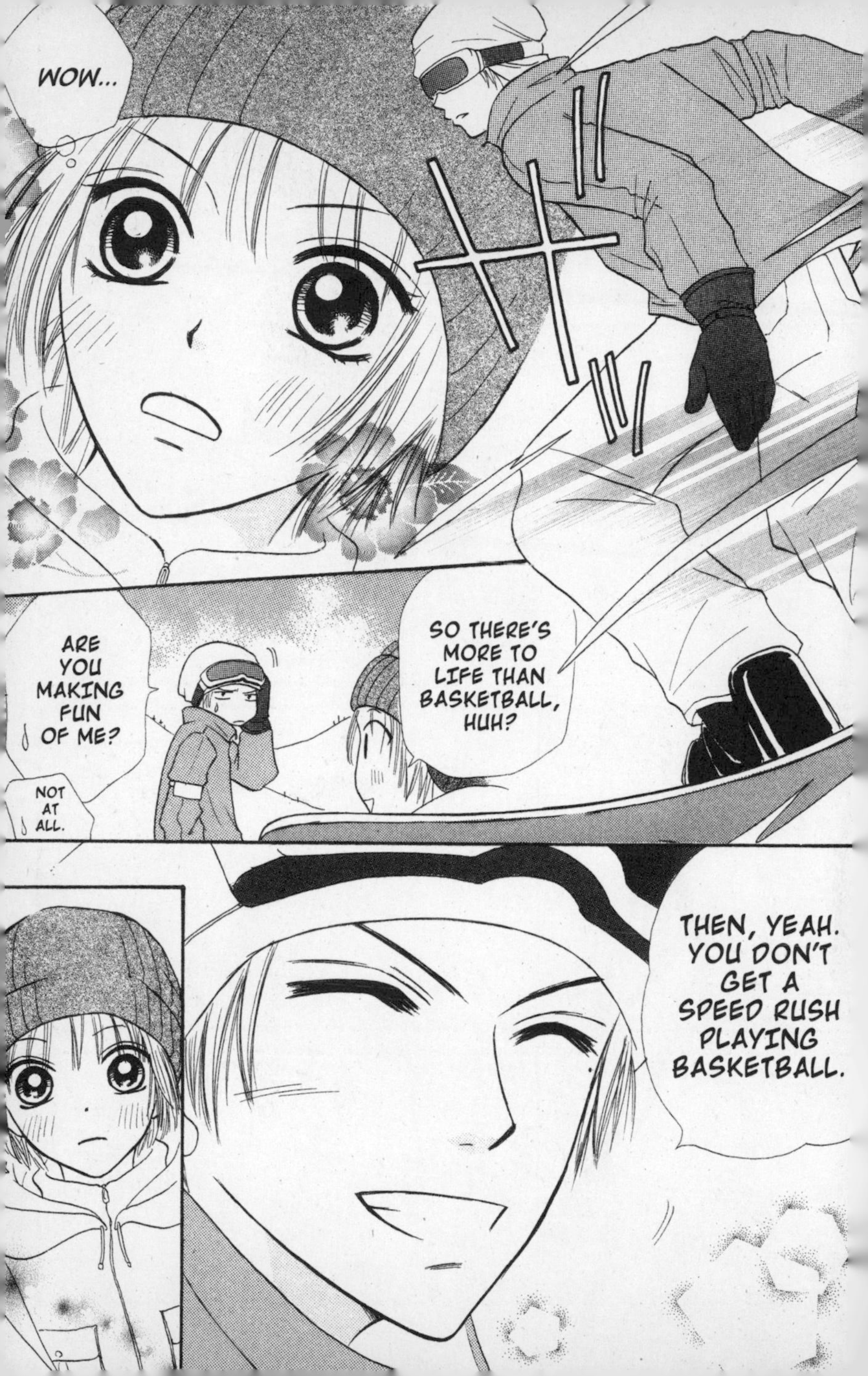
WOW...
SO THERE'S MORE TO LIFE THAN BASKETBALL, HUH?
ARE YOU MAKING FUN OF ME?
NOT AT ALL.
THEN, YEAH. YOU DON'T GET A SPEED RUSH PLAYING BASKETBALL.

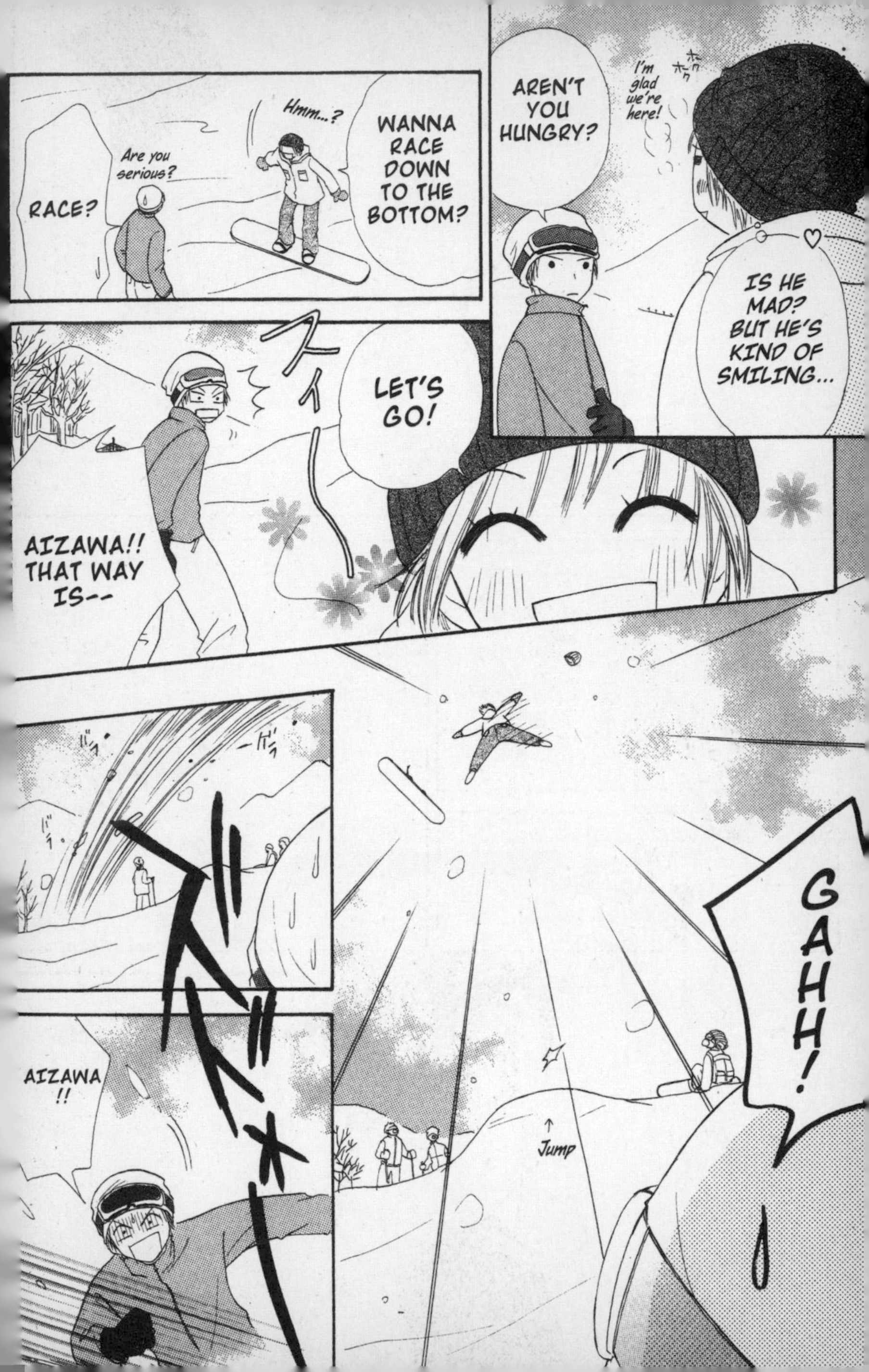
AREN'T YOU HUNGRY?
I'm glad we're here!
IS HE MAD? BUT HE'S KIND OF SMILING...
WANNA RACE DOWN TO THE BOTTOM?
Hmm...?
Are you serious?
RACE?
LET'S GO!
AIZAWA!! THAT WAY IS--
GAHH!
Jump
AIZAWA !!

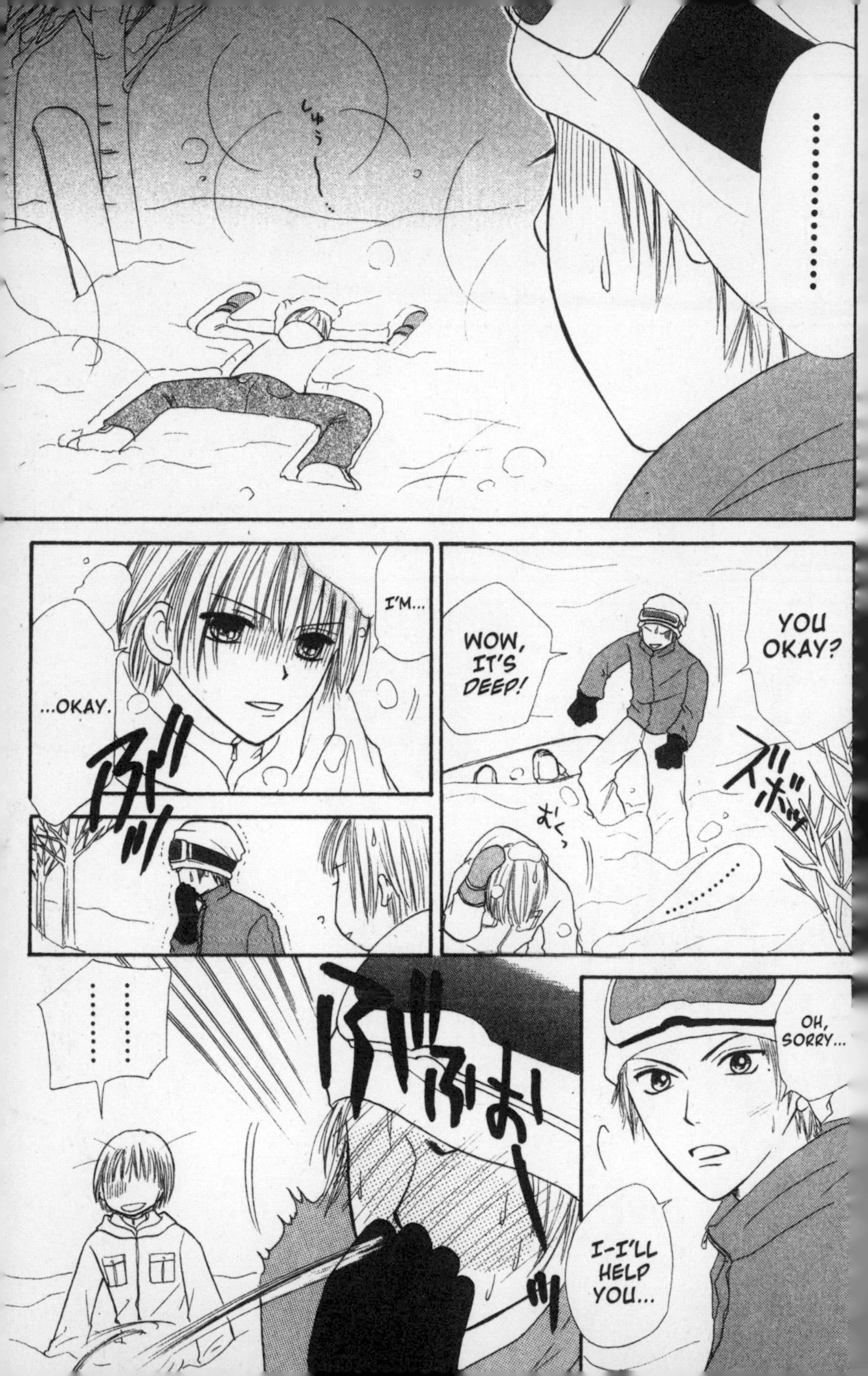
……
YOU OKAY?
WOW, IT'S DEEP!
……
I'M...
...OKAY.
OH, SORRY...
I-I'LL HELP YOU...
……

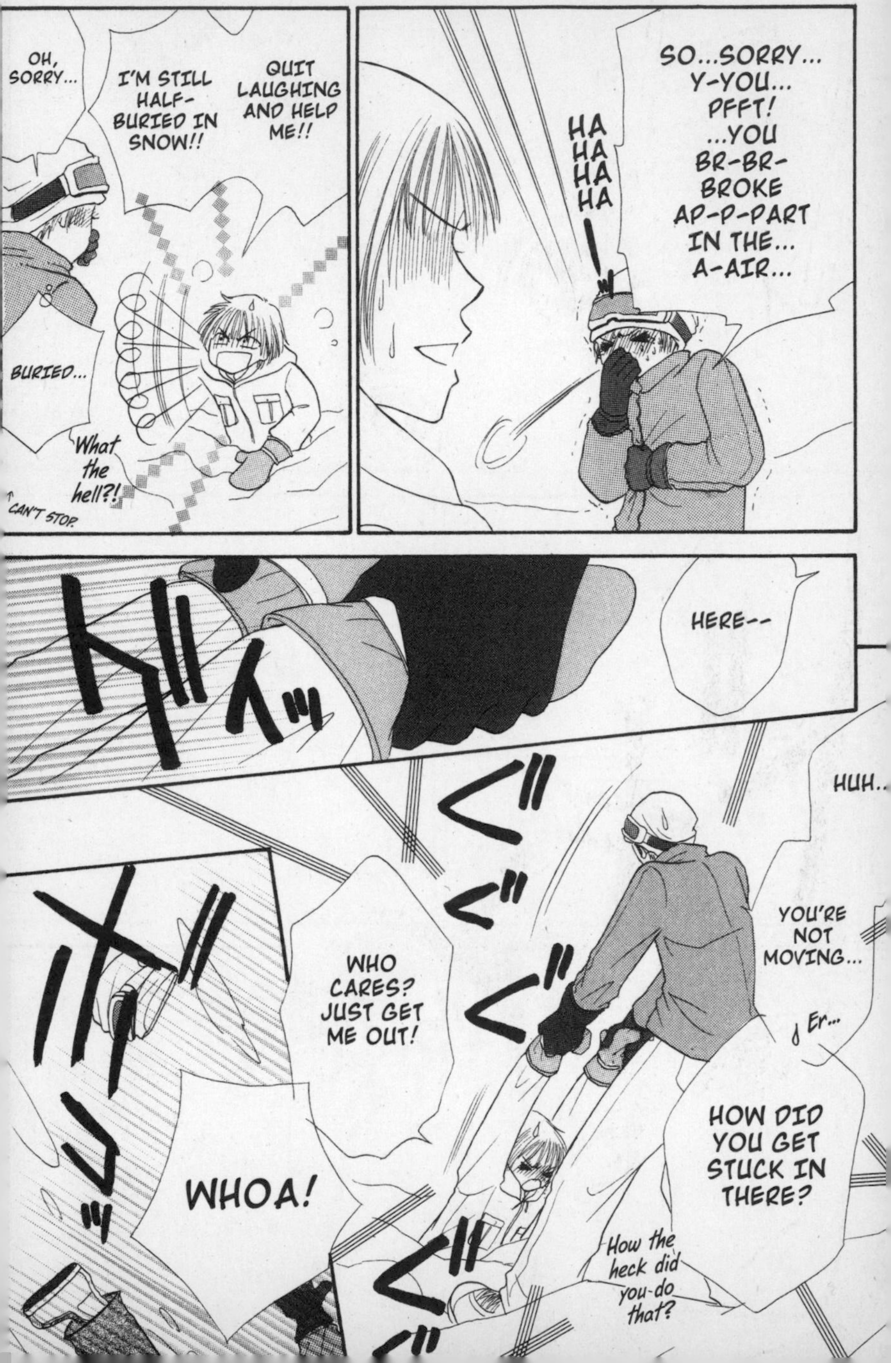
SO...SORRY... Y-YOU... PFFT! ...YOU BR-BR-BROKE AP-P-PART IN THE... A-AIR...
HA HA HA HA
QUIT LAUGHING AND HELP ME!!
I'M STILL HALF-BURIED IN SNOW!!
OH, SORRY...
BURIED...
What the hell?!
↑CAN'T STOP.
HERE--
HUH...
YOU'RE NOT MOVING...
Er...
HOW DID YOU GET STUCK IN THERE?
How the heck did you-do that?
WHO CARES? JUST GET ME OUT!
WHOA!

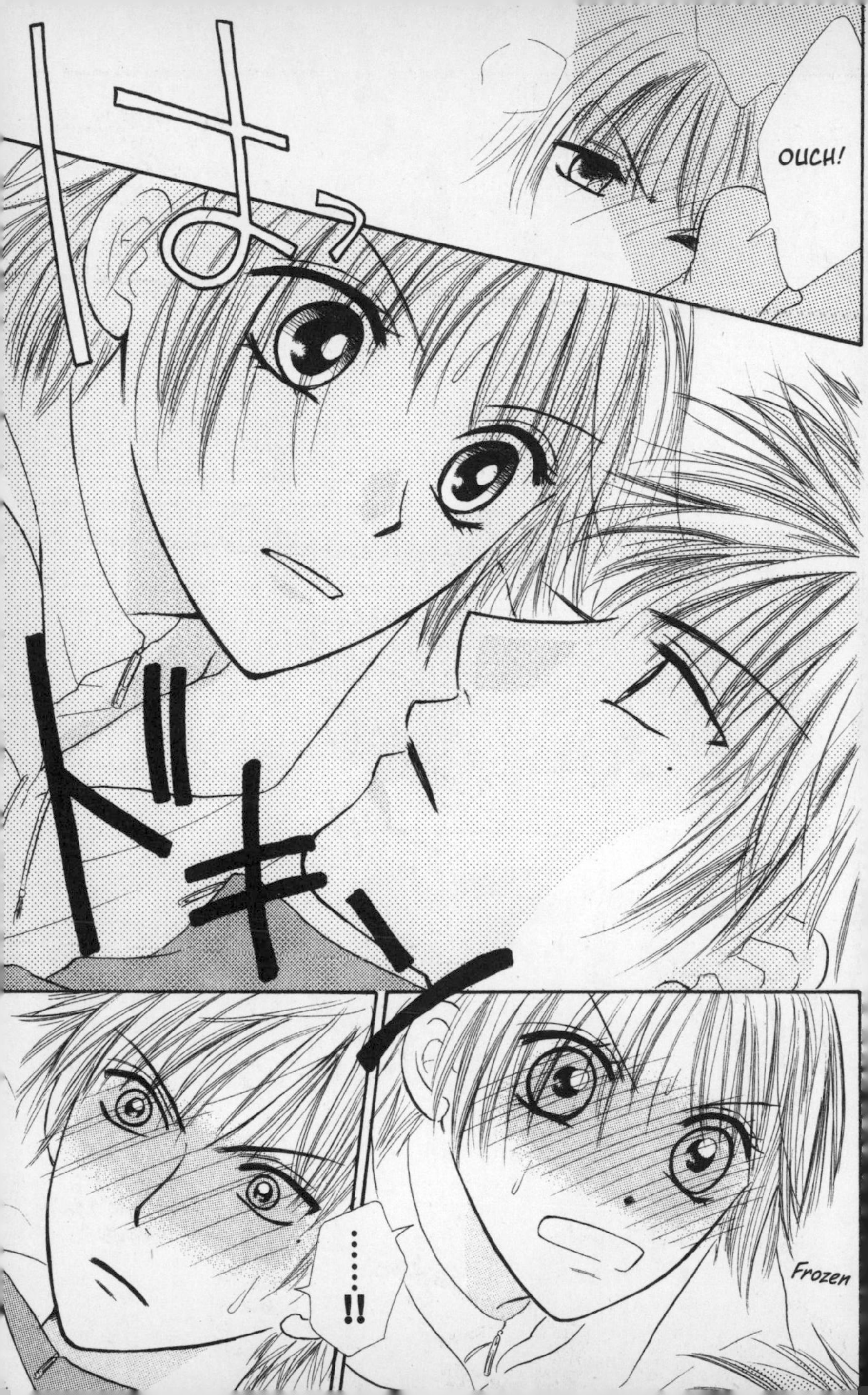
OUCH!
はっ
ドキン
Frozen
......!!

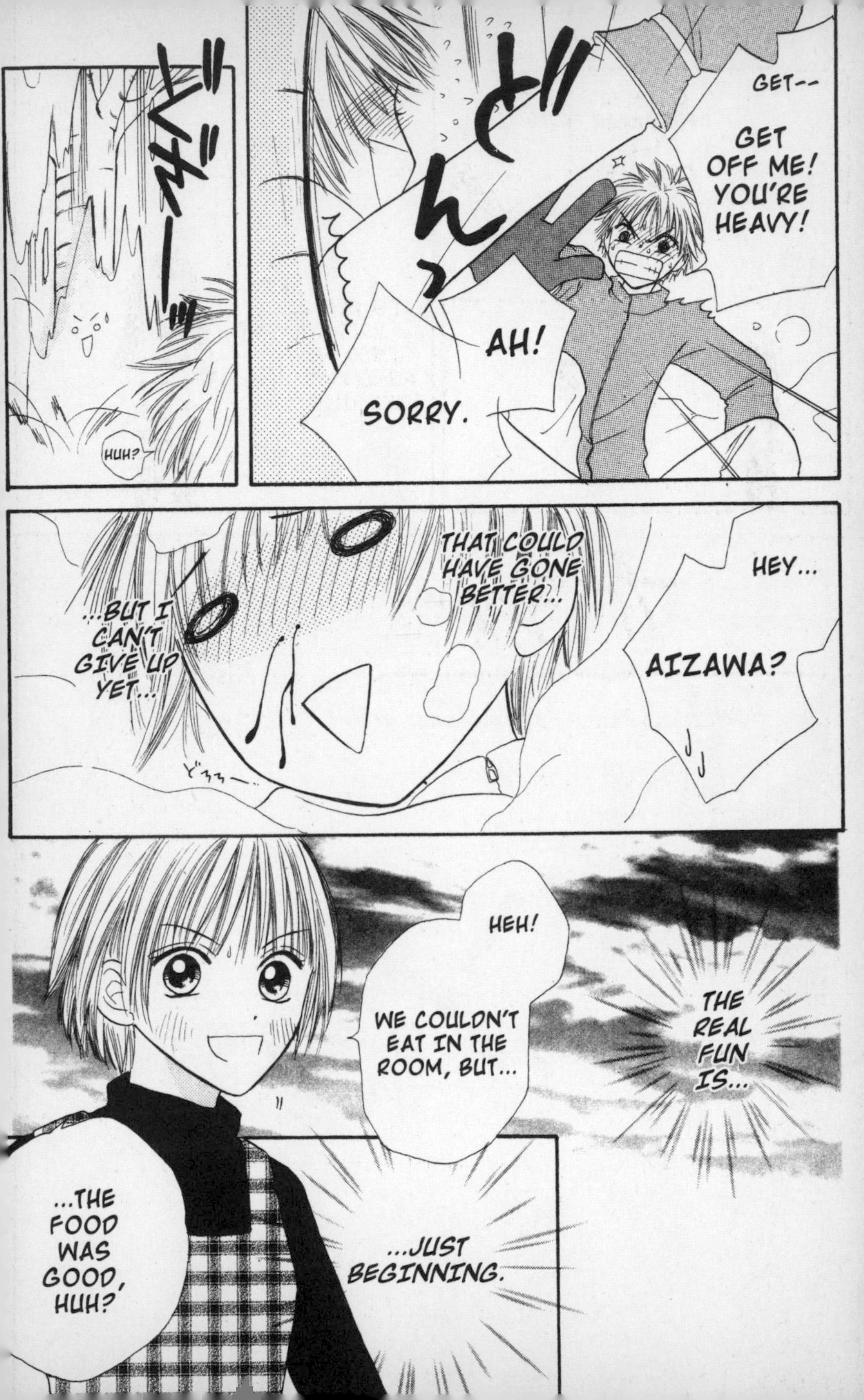
GET--
GET OFF ME! YOU'RE HEAVY!
AH!
SORRY.
HUH?
HEY...
AIZAWA?
THAT COULD HAVE GONE BETTER...
...BUT I CAN'T GIVE UP YET...
HEH!
WE COULDN'T EAT IN THE ROOM, BUT...
...THE FOOD WAS GOOD, HUH?
THE REAL FUN IS...
...JUST BEGINNING.

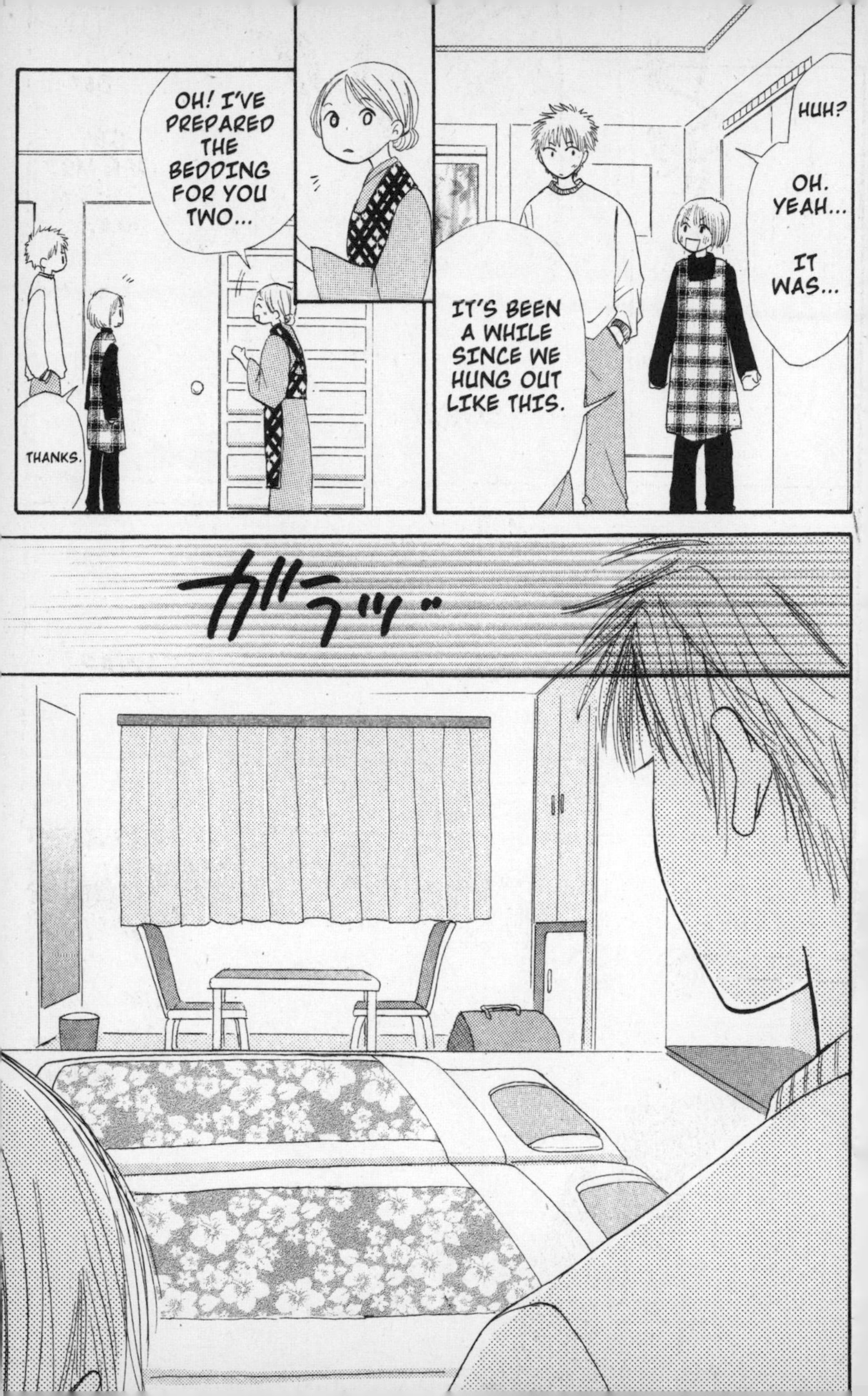
HUH?
OH. YEAH... IT WAS...
IT'S BEEN A WHILE SINCE WE HUNG OUT LIKE THIS.
OH! I'VE PREPARED THE BEDDING FOR YOU TWO...
THANKS.
ガラッ

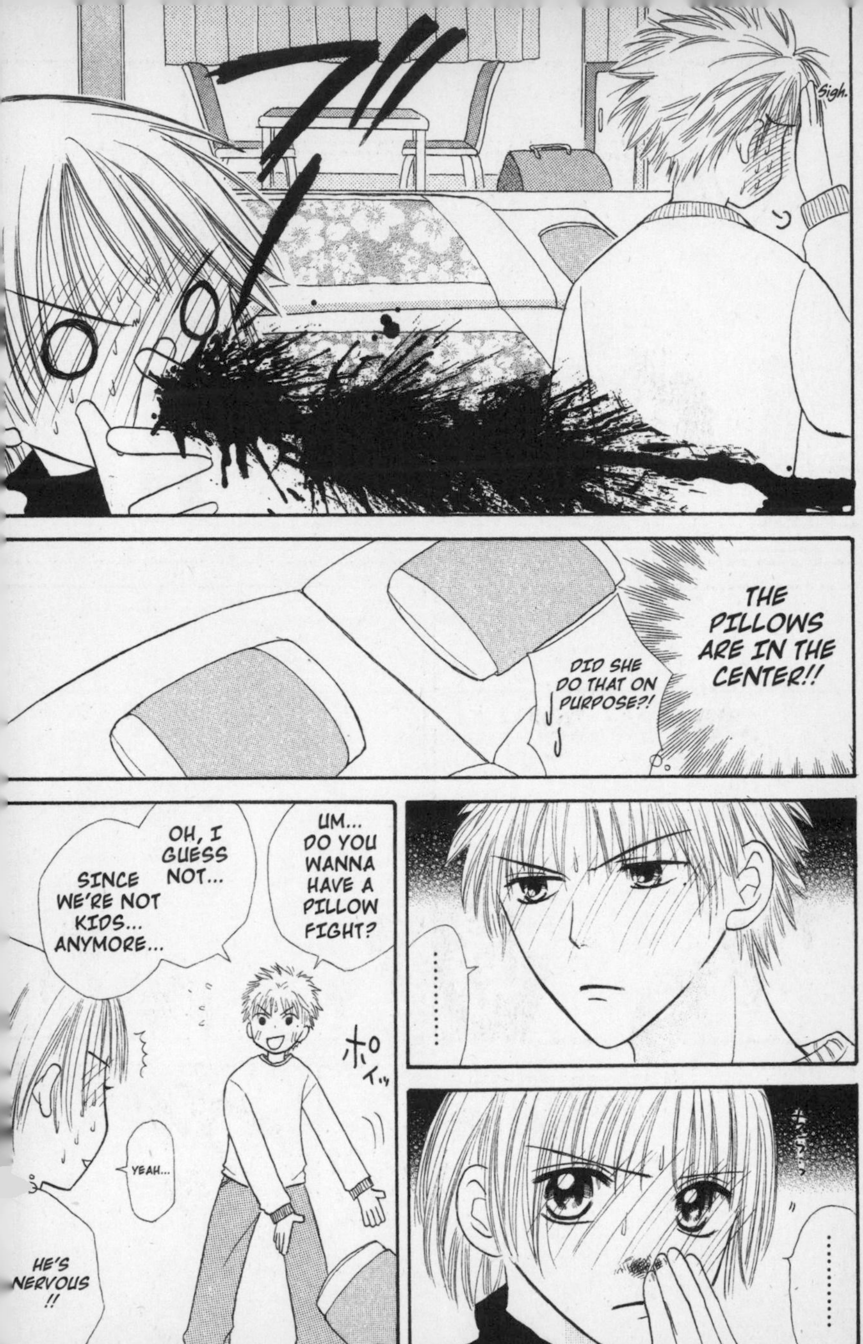
Sigh.
THE PILLOWS ARE IN THE CENTER!!
DID SHE DO THAT ON PURPOSE?!
UM... DO YOU WANNA HAVE A PILLOW FIGHT?
OH, I GUESS NOT...
SINCE WE'RE NOT KIDS... ANYMORE...
YEAH...
HE'S NERVOUS!!
....
....

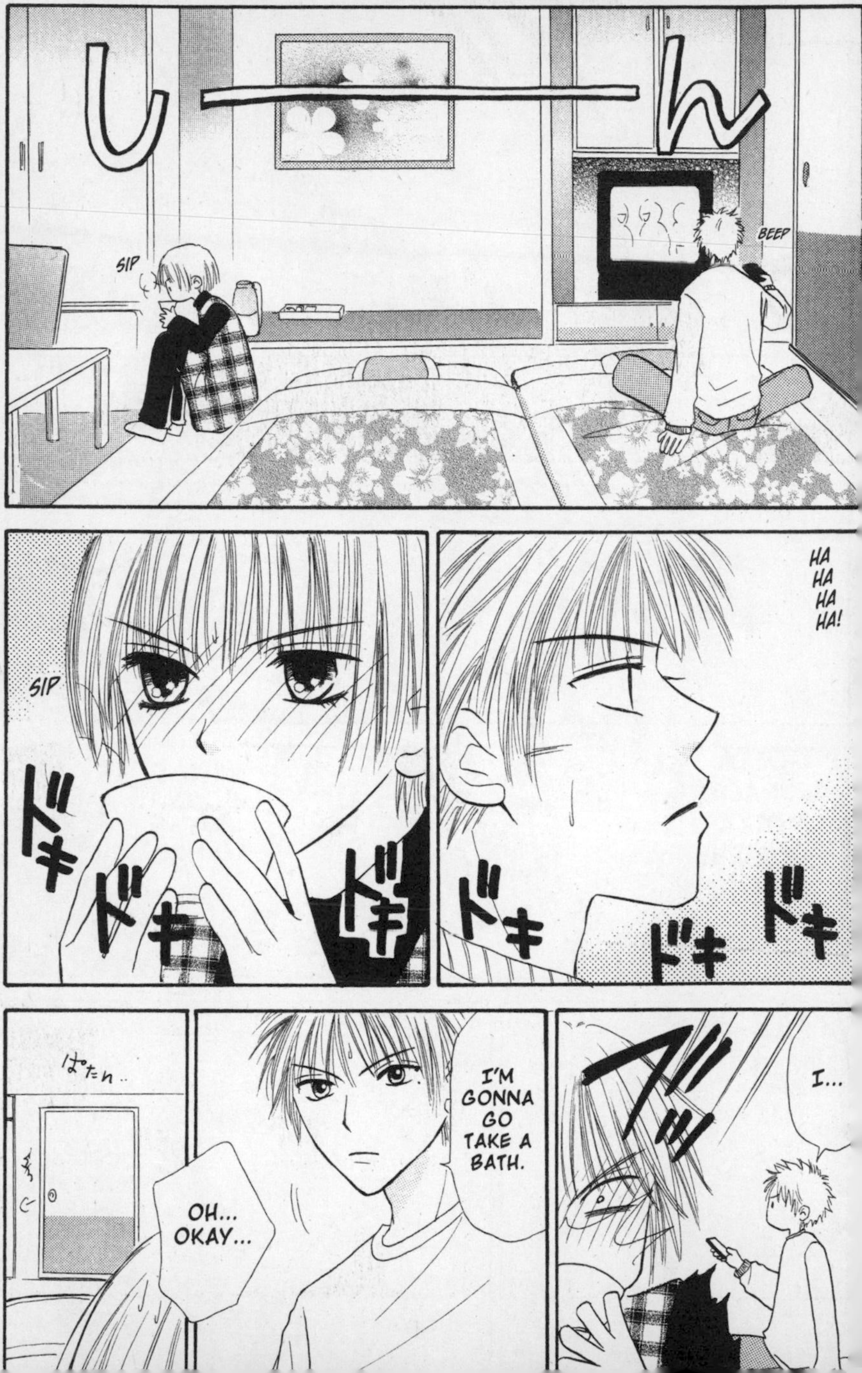
しーん
BEEP
SIP
HA HA HA HA!
ドキ ドキ ドキ
SIP
ドキ ドキ ドキ
I...
ブツッ
I'M GONNA GO TAKE A BATH.
OH... OKAY...
ぱたん..

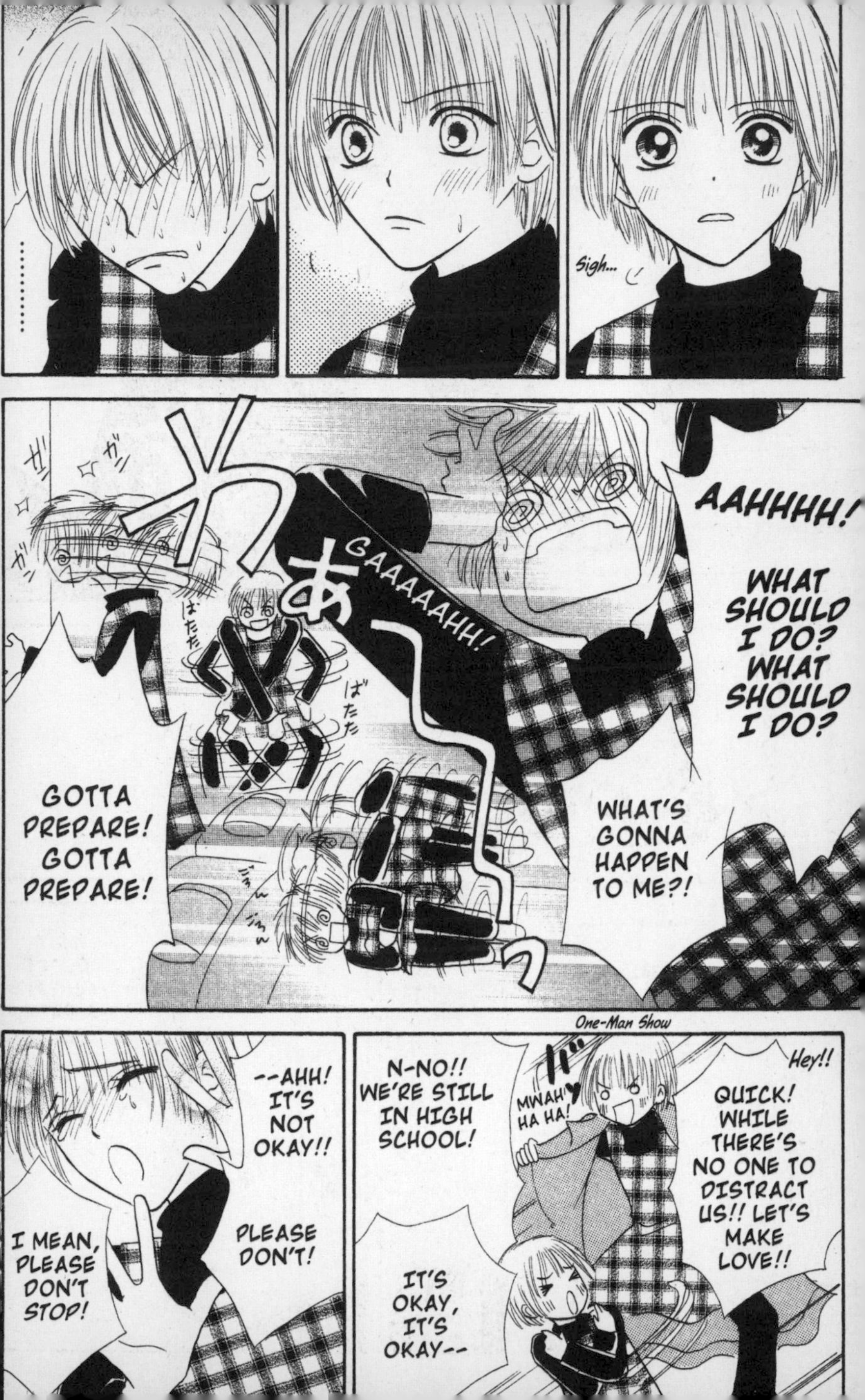
Sigh...
......
AAHHHH!
WHAT SHOULD I DO? WHAT SHOULD I DO?
GAAAAAAHH!
WHAT'S GONNA HAPPEN TO ME?!
ばたた
ばたた
GOTTA PREPARE! GOTTA PREPARE!
One-Man Show
Hey!!
QUICK! WHILE THERE'S NO ONE TO DISTRACT US!! LET'S MAKE LOVE!!
MWAH! HA HA!
N-NO!! WE'RE STILL IN HIGH SCHOOL!
IT'S OKAY, IT'S OKAY--
--AHH! IT'S NOT OKAY!!
PLEASE DON'T!
I MEAN, PLEASE DON'T STOP!

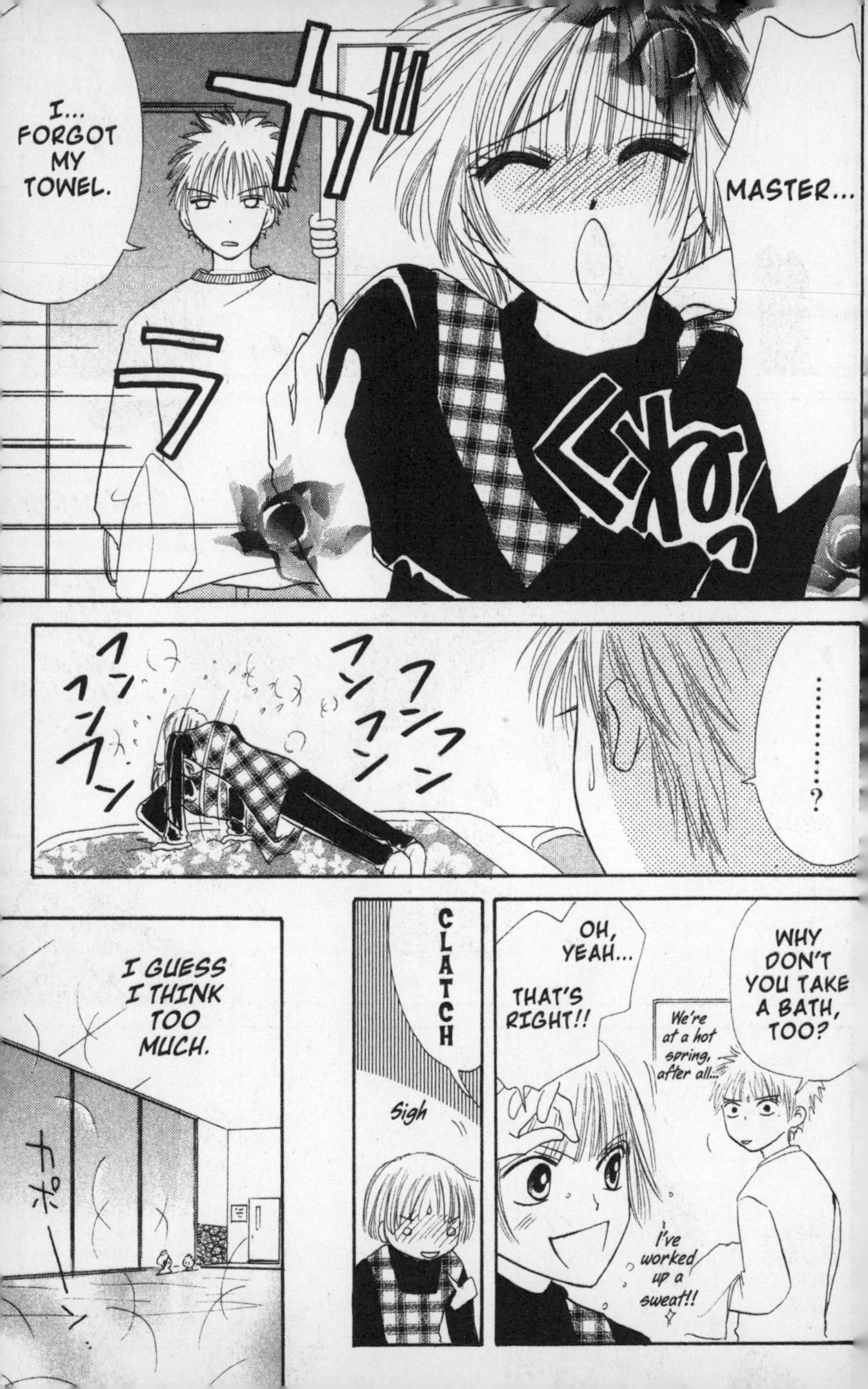
MASTER...
I... FORGOT MY TOWEL.
......?
WHY DON'T YOU TAKE A BATH, TOO?
We're at a hot spring, after all...
OH, YEAH...
THAT'S RIGHT!!
I've worked up a sweat!!
CLATCH
Sigh
I GUESS I THINK TOO MUCH.

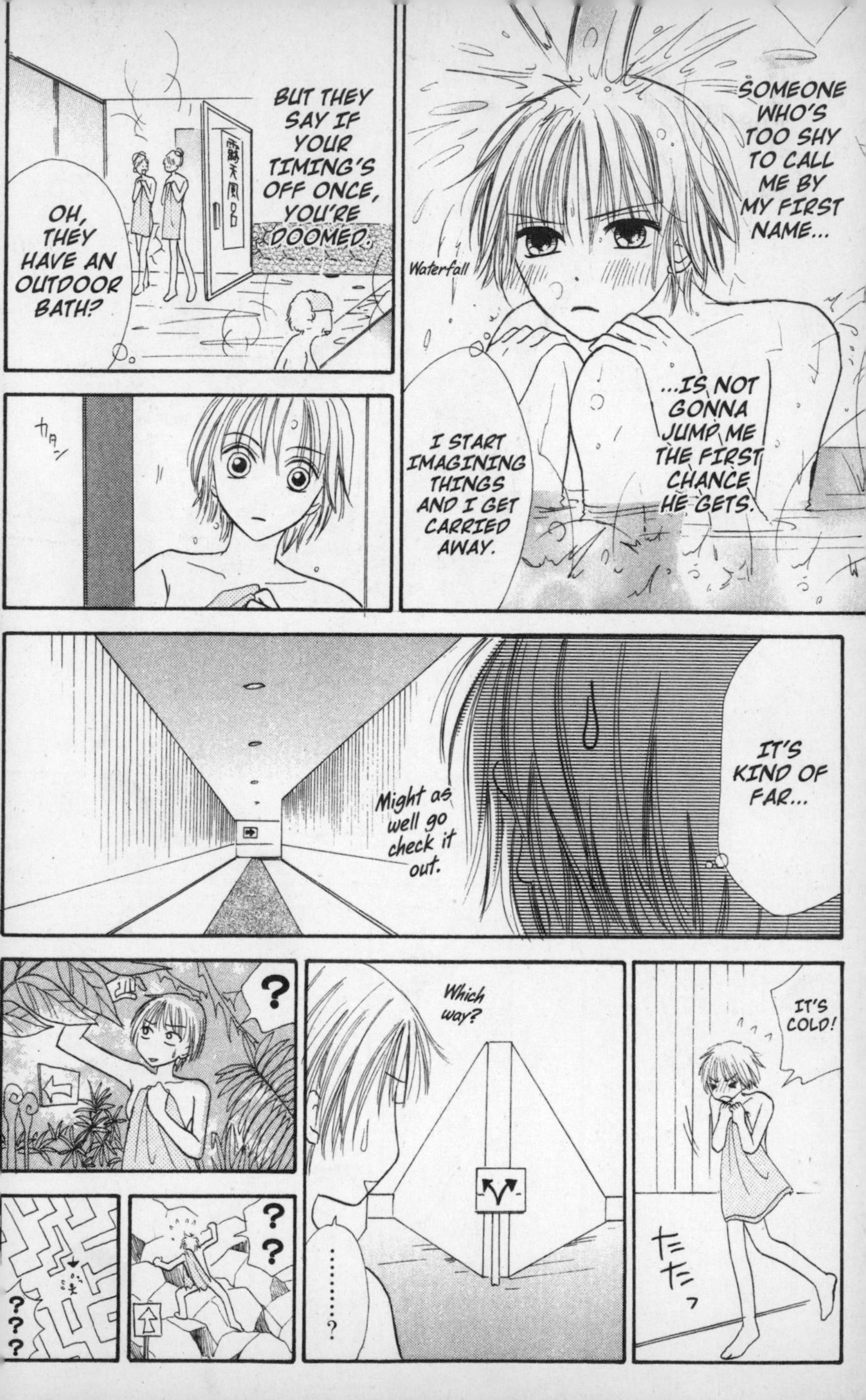
SOMEONE WHO'S TOO SHY TO CALL ME BY MY FIRST NAME...
Waterfall
...IS NOT GONNA JUMP ME THE FIRST CHANCE HE GETS.
I START IMAGINING THINGS AND I GET CARRIED AWAY.
BUT THEY SAY IF YOUR TIMING'S OFF ONCE, YOU'RE DOOMED.
露天風呂
OH, THEY HAVE AN OUTDOOR BATH?
IT'S KIND OF FAR...
Might as well go check it out.
IT'S COLD!
たたっ
Which way?
......?
?
??
???

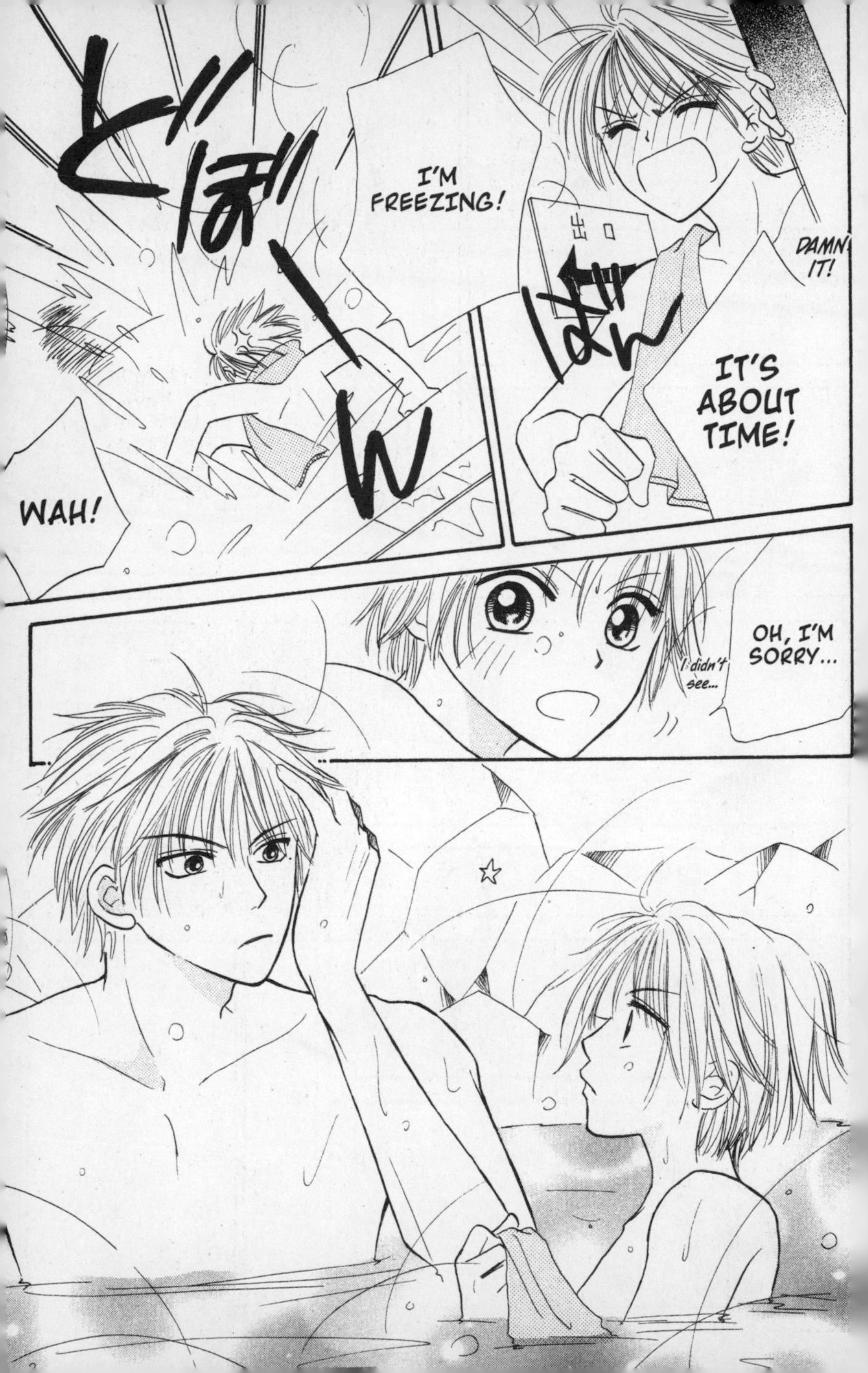
DAMN IT!
出口
ばん
IT'S ABOUT TIME!
I'M FREEZING!
どぼーん
WAH!
OH, I'M SORRY...
I didn't see...

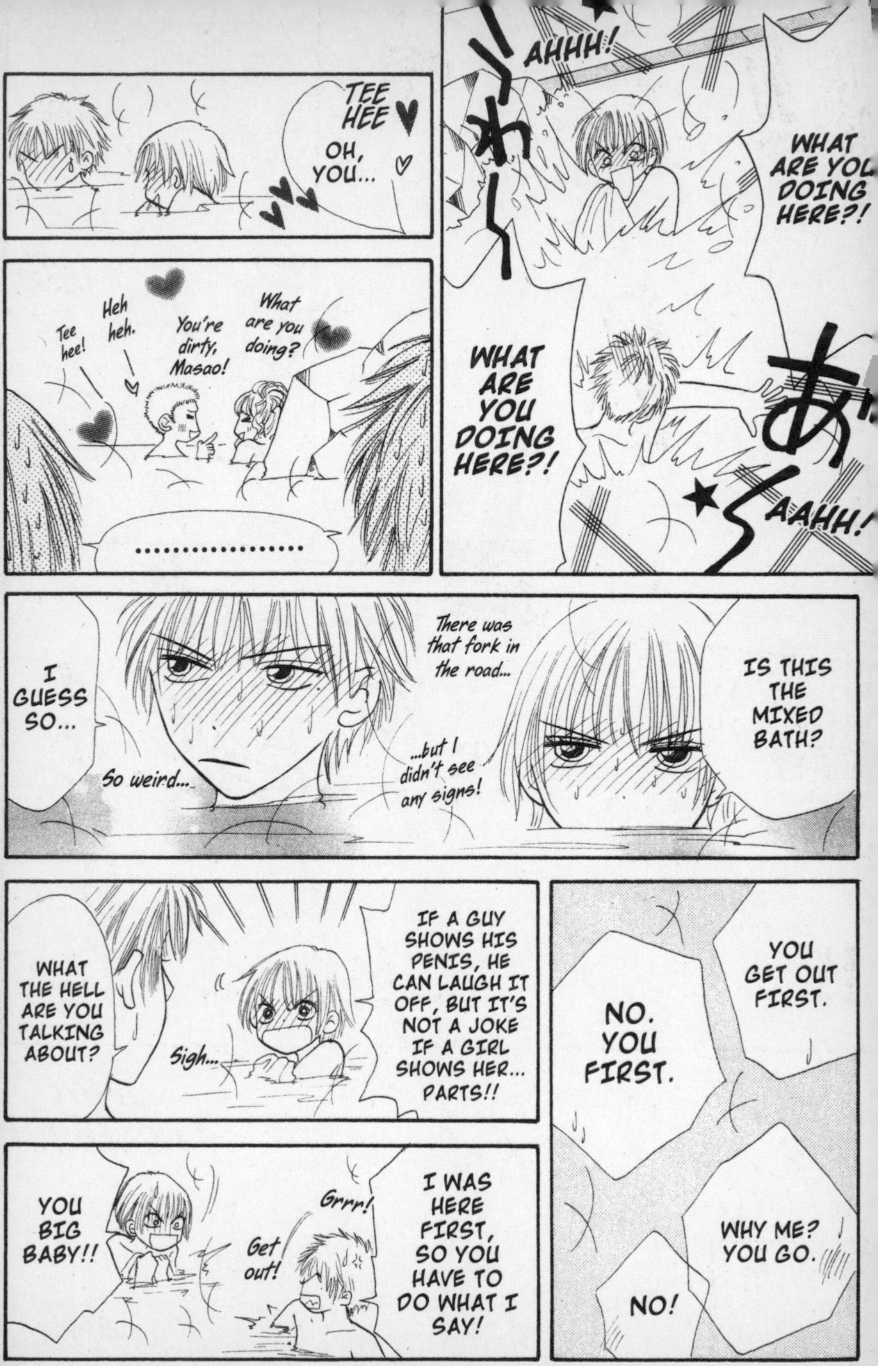
AHHH!
WHAT ARE YOU DOING HERE?!
WHAT ARE YOU DOING HERE?!
AAHH!
TEE HEE
OH, YOU...
What are you doing?
You're dirty, Masao!
Heh heh.
Tee hee!
....
IS THIS THE MIXED BATH?
There was that fork in the road...
...but I didn't see any signs!
I GUESS SO...
So weird...
YOU GET OUT FIRST.
NO. YOU FIRST.
WHY ME? YOU GO.
NO!
IF A GUY SHOWS HIS PENIS, HE CAN LAUGH IT OFF, BUT IT'S NOT A JOKE IF A GIRL SHOWS HER... PARTS!!
Sigh...
WHAT THE HELL ARE YOU TALKING ABOUT?
I WAS HERE FIRST, SO YOU HAVE TO DO WHAT I SAY!
Grrr!
Get out!
YOU BIG BABY!!

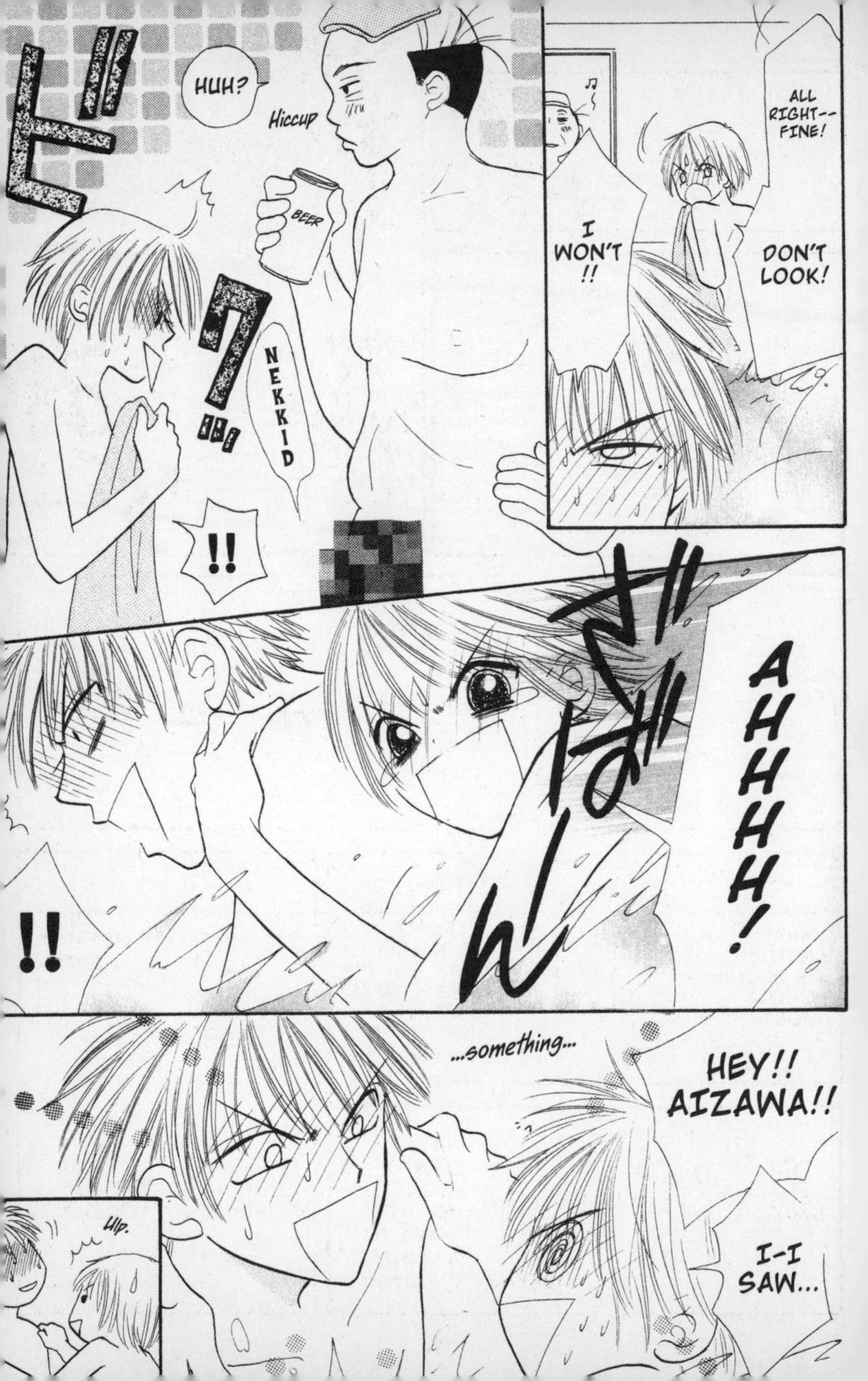
ALL RIGHT--FINE!
DON'T LOOK!
I WON'T!!
HUH?
Hiccup
BEER
NEKKID
!!
AHHHHH!
!!
HEY!! AIZAWA!!
I-I SAW...
...something...
Ulp.

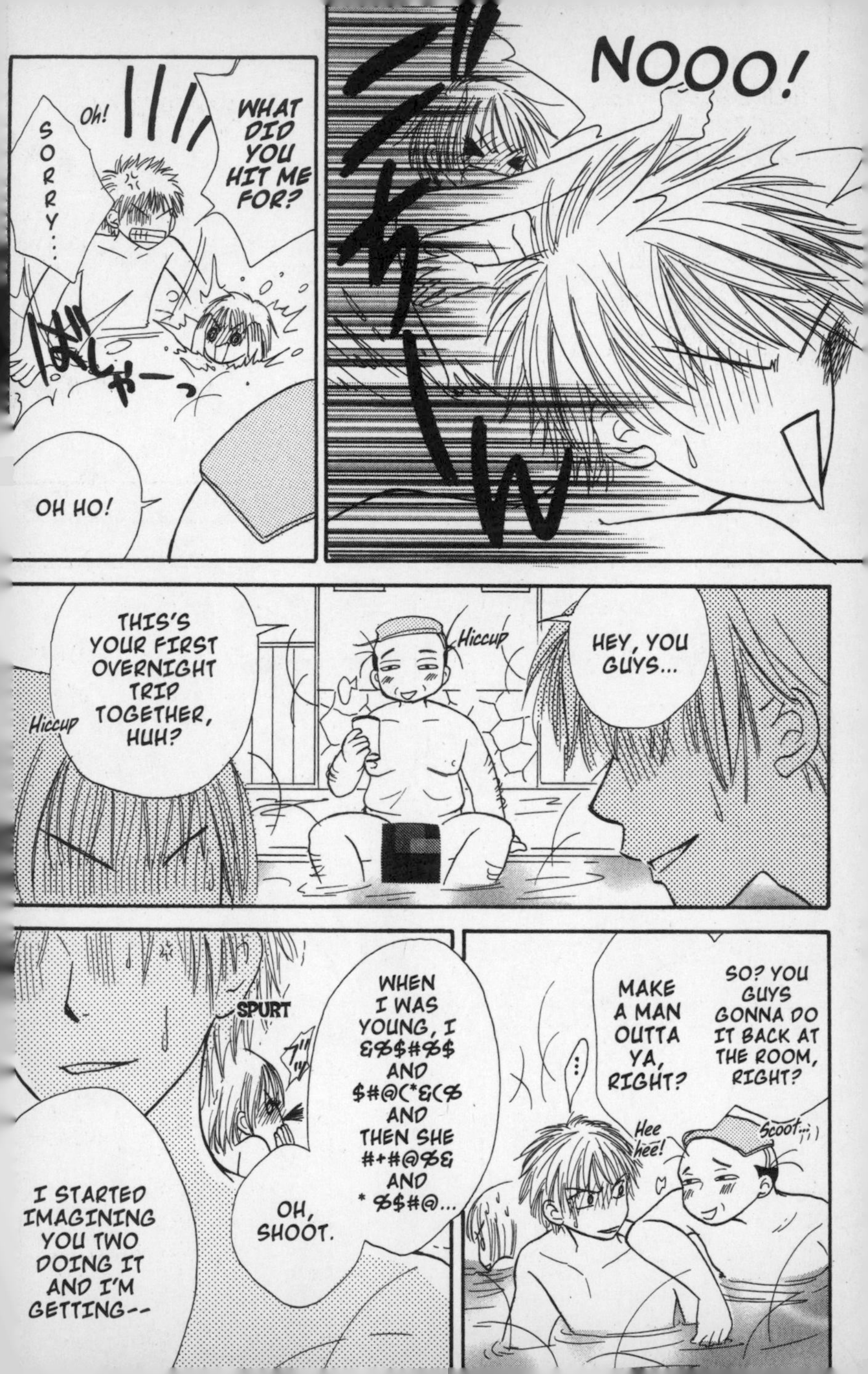
NOOO!
Oh!
SORRY...
WHAT DID YOU HIT ME FOR?
OH HO!
HEY, YOU GUYS...
Hiccup
THIS'S YOUR FIRST OVERNIGHT TRIP TOGETHER, HUH?
Hiccup
SO? YOU GUYS GONNA DO IT BACK AT THE ROOM, RIGHT?
MAKE A MAN OUTTA YA, RIGHT?
Scoot
Hee hee!
...
WHEN I WAS YOUNG, I &%$#%$ AND $#@(*&(% AND THEN SHE #+#@%& AND *%$#@...
SPURT
OH, SHOOT.
I STARTED IMAGINING YOU TWO DOING IT AND I'M GETTING--

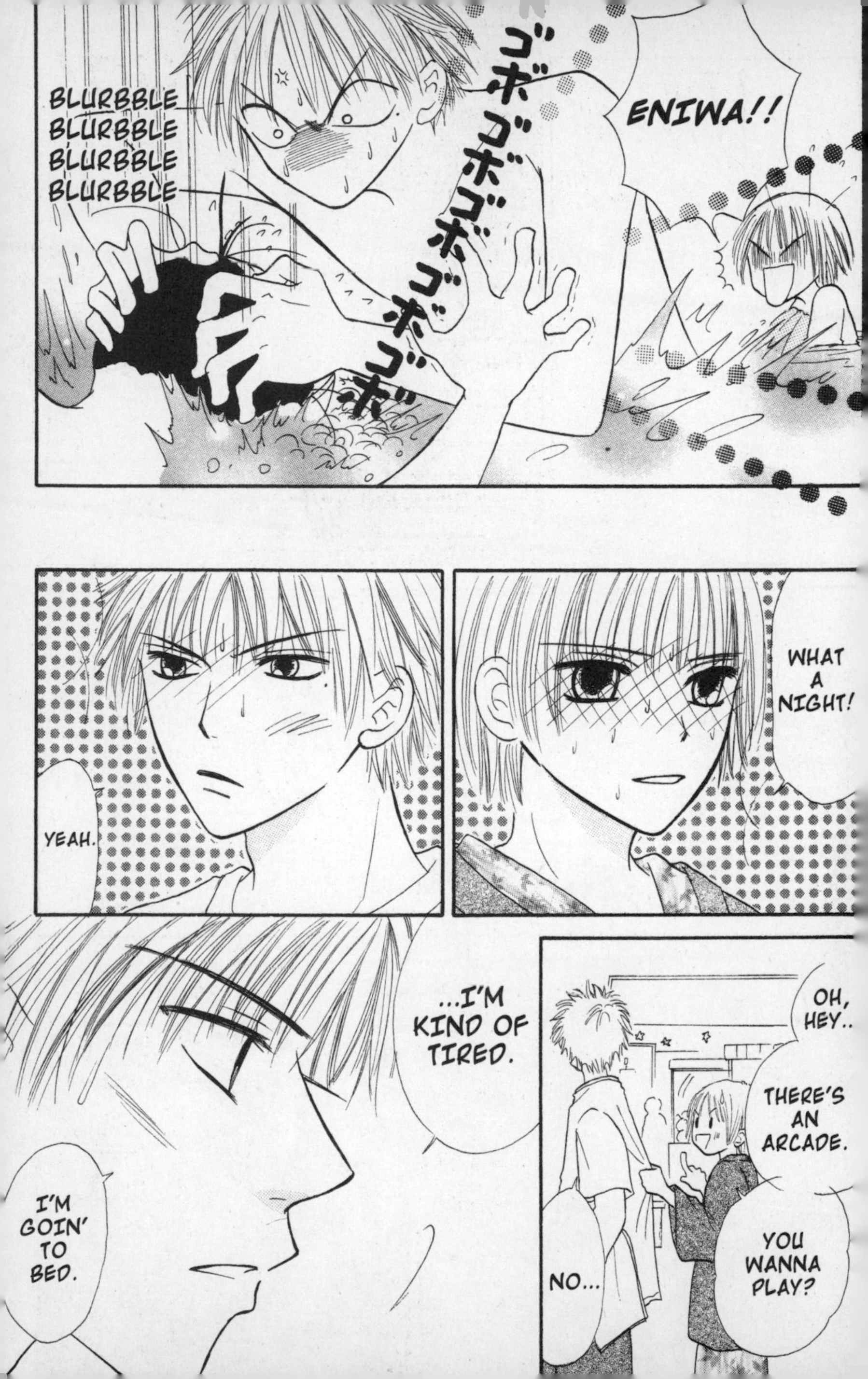
ENIWA!!
ゴボゴボゴボゴボ
BLURBBLE
BLURBBLE
BLURBBLE
BLURBBLE
WHAT A NIGHT!
YEAH.
OH, HEY..
THERE'S AN ARCADE.
YOU WANNA PLAY?
NO...
...I'M KIND OF TIRED.
I'M GOIN' TO BED.

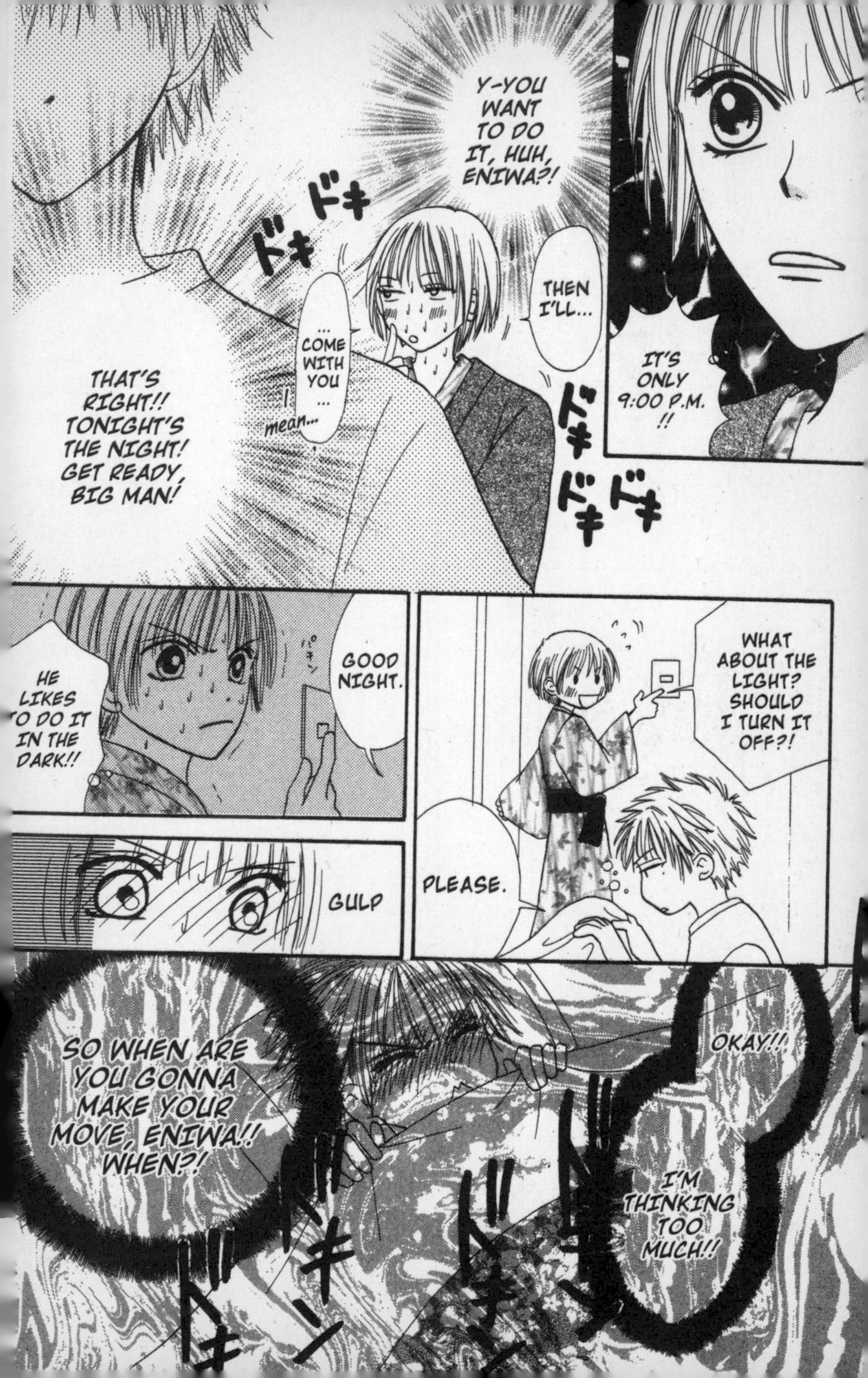
IT'S ONLY 9:00 P.M.!!
Y-YOU WANT TO DO IT, HUH, ENIWA?!
ドキ ドキ
THEN I'LL...
... COME WITH YOU ...
I mean...
ドキ ドキ ドキ
THAT'S RIGHT!! TONIGHT'S THE NIGHT! GET READY, BIG MAN!
WHAT ABOUT THE LIGHT? SHOULD I TURN IT OFF?!
PLEASE.
GOOD NIGHT.
HE LIKES TO DO IT IN THE DARK!!
GULP
OKAY!!
I'M THINKING TOO MUCH!!
SO WHEN ARE YOU GONNA MAKE YOUR MOVE, ENIWA!! WHEN?!

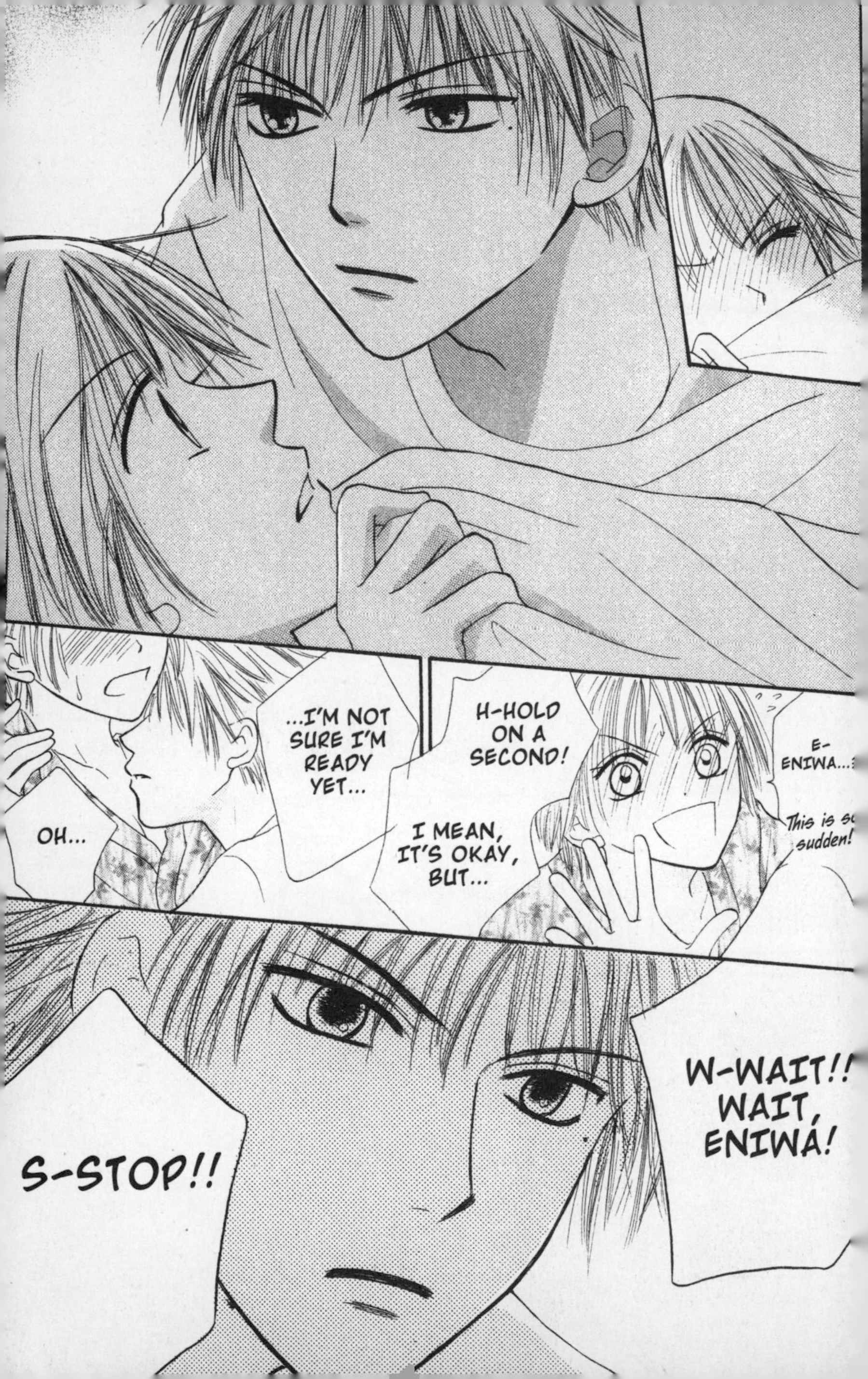
E-ENIWA...
H-HOLD ON A SECOND!
This is s sudden!
I MEAN, IT'S OKAY, BUT...
...I'M NOT SURE I'M READY YET...
OH...
W-WAIT!! WAIT, ENIWA!
S-STOP!!

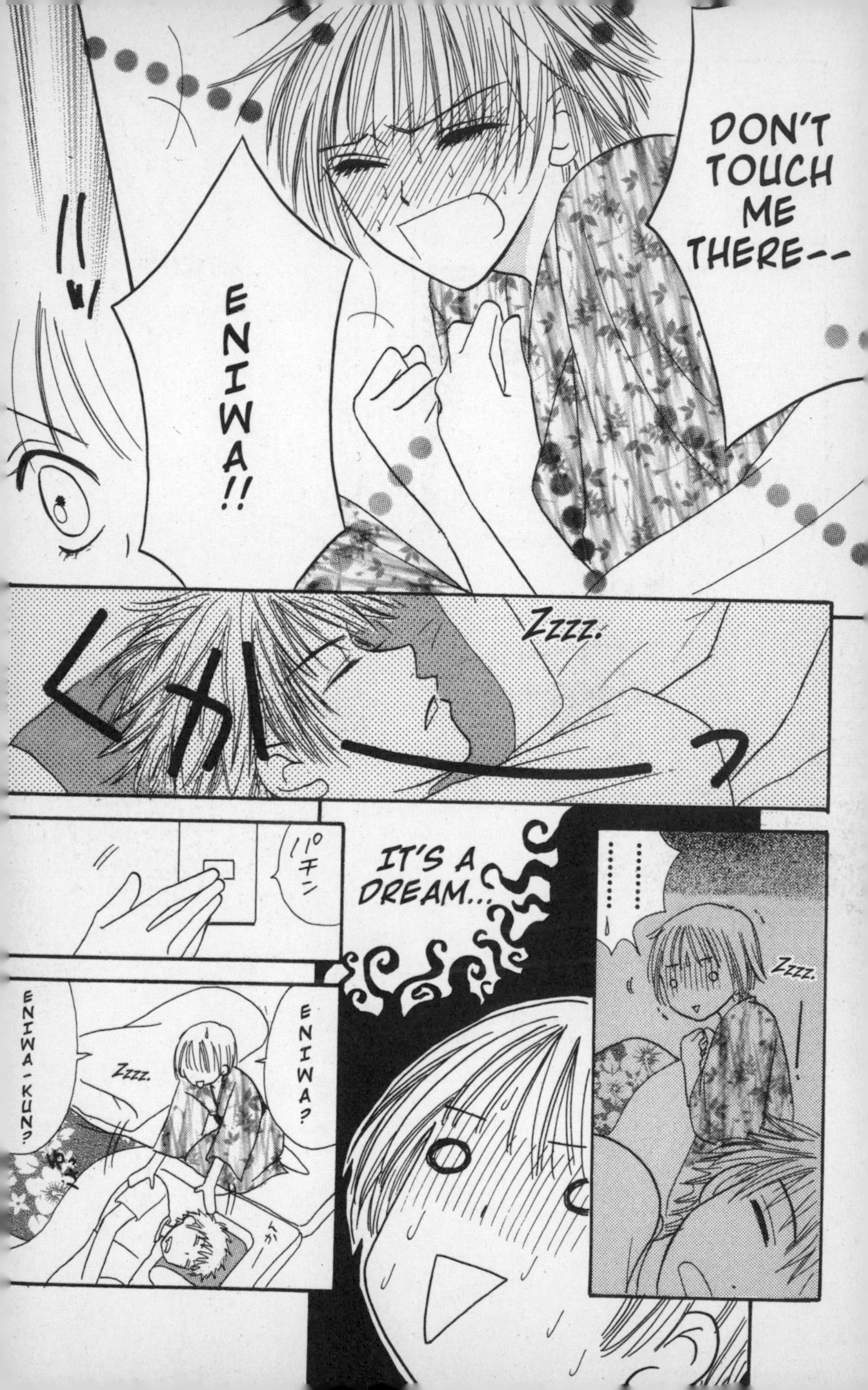
DON'T TOUCH ME THERE--
ENIWA!!
Zzzz.
ぐかーっ
......
Zzzz.
!
IT'S A DREAM...
パチン
ENIWA?
Zzzz.
ENIWA-KUN?

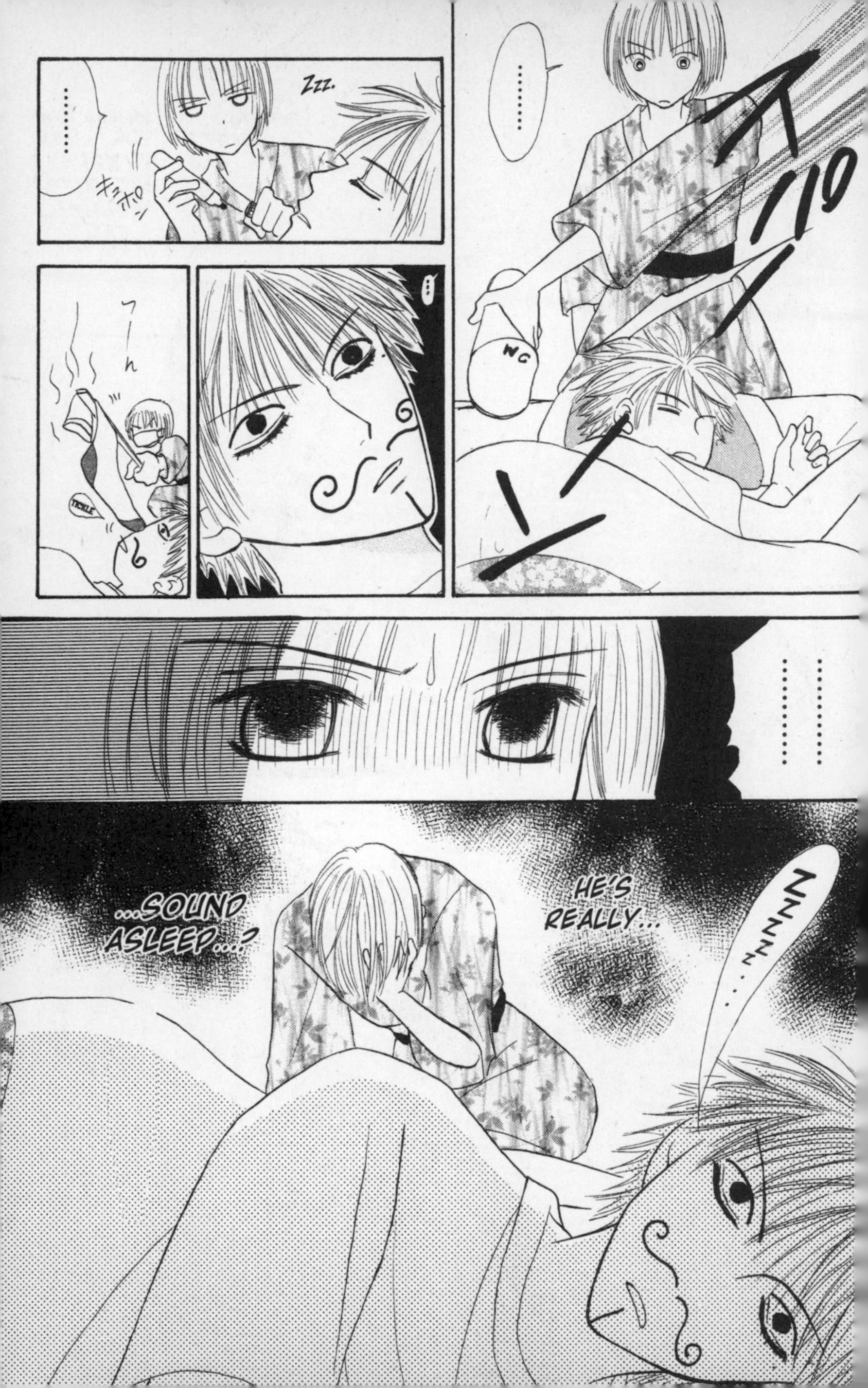
......
WC
......
Zzz.
TICKLE
......
NNNNN...
HE'S REALLY...
...SOUND ASLEEP...?

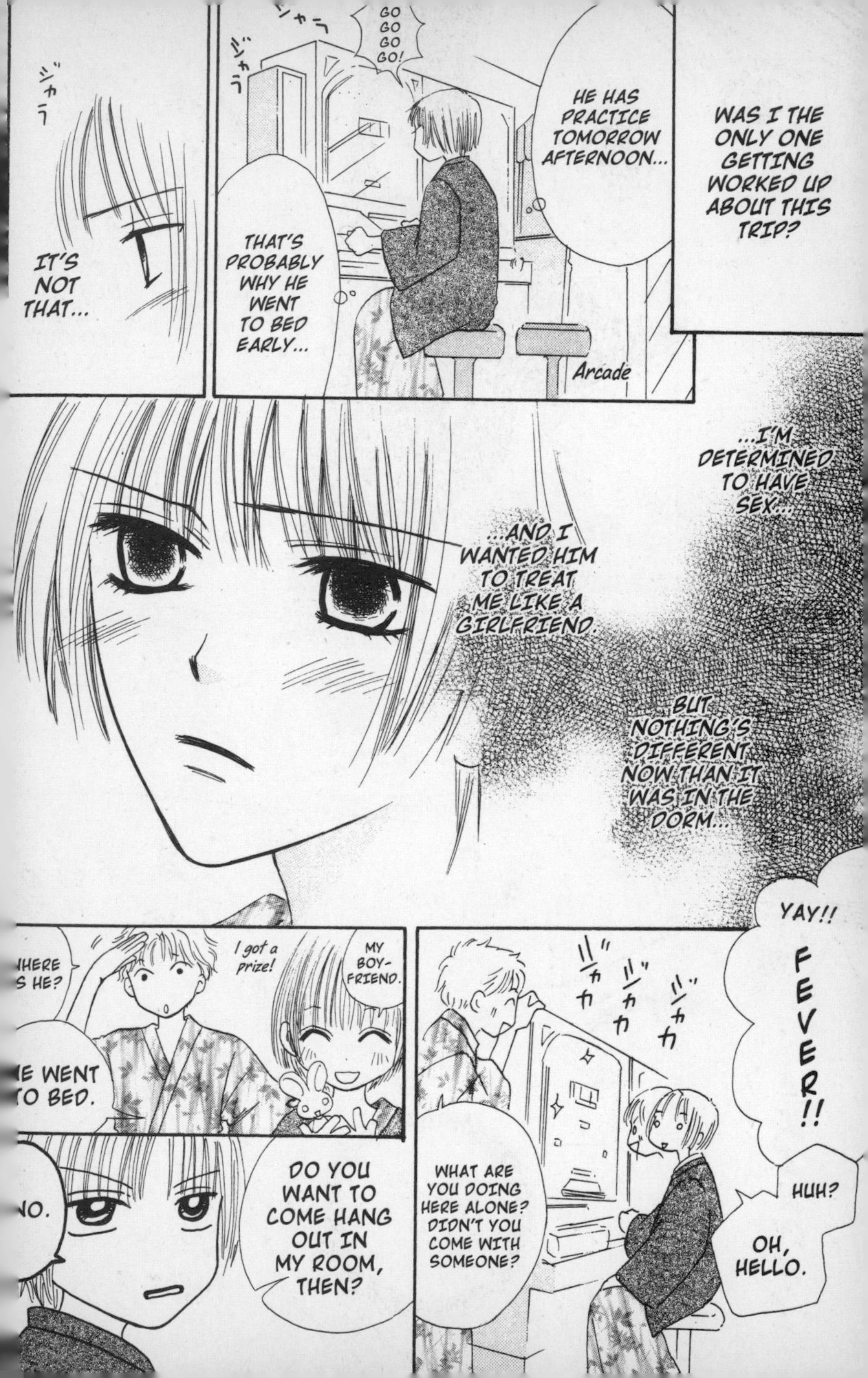
WAS I THE ONLY ONE GETTING WORKED UP ABOUT THIS TRIP?
GO GO GO GO!
HE HAS PRACTICE TOMORROW AFTERNOON...
THAT'S PROBABLY WHY HE WENT TO BED EARLY...
Arcade
IT'S NOT THAT...
...I'M DETERMINED TO HAVE SEX...
...AND I WANTED HIM TO TREAT ME LIKE A GIRLFRIEND.
BUT NOTHING'S DIFFERENT NOW THAN IT WAS IN THE DORM...
YAY!!
FEVER!!
HUH?
OH, HELLO.
WHAT ARE YOU DOING HERE ALONE? DIDN'T YOU COME WITH SOMEONE?
MY BOY-FRIEND.
I got a prize!
HERE S HE?
E WENT TO BED.
DO YOU WANT TO COME HANG OUT IN MY ROOM, THEN?
NO.

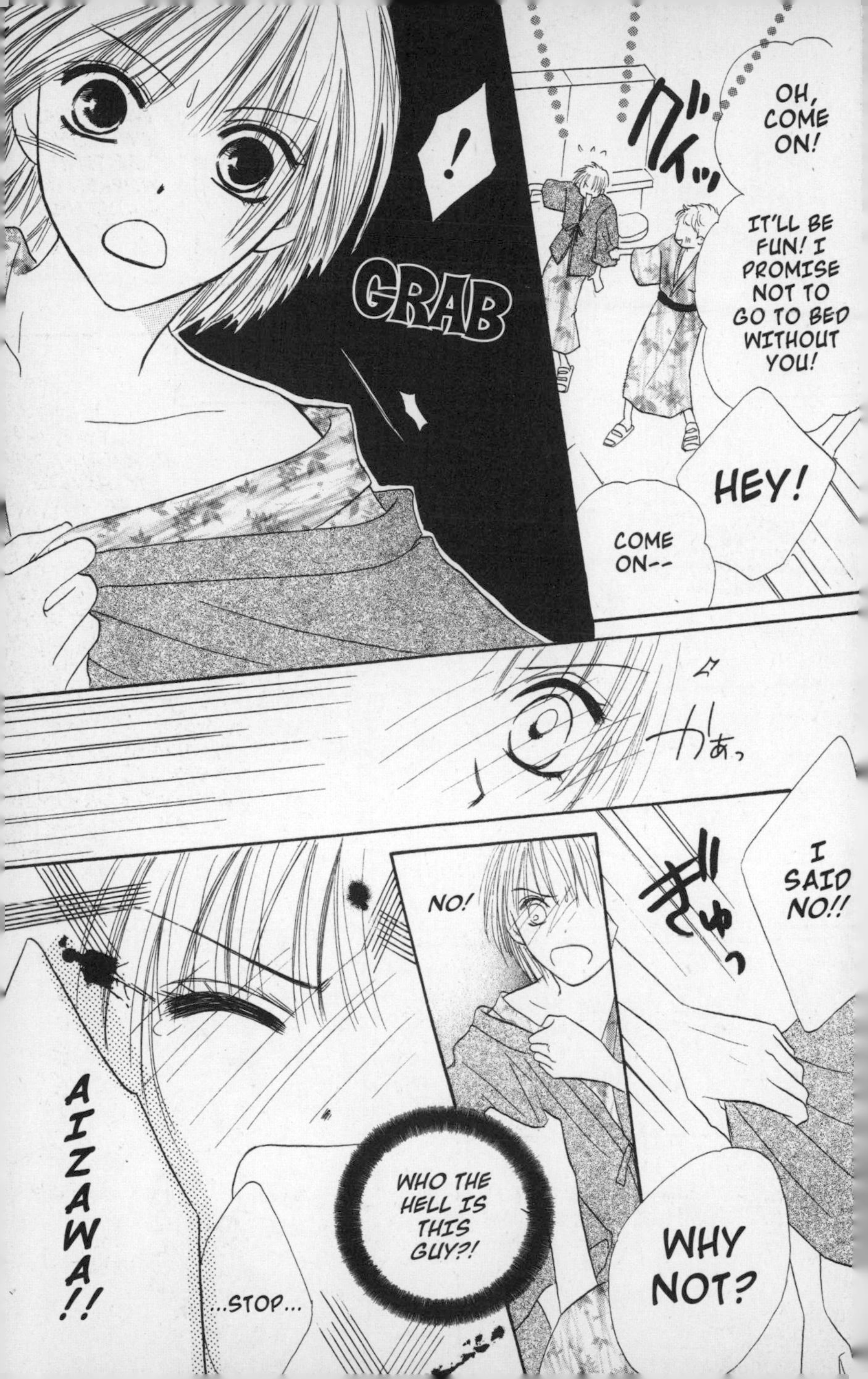
OH, COME ON!
グイッ
IT'LL BE FUN! I PROMISE NOT TO GO TO BED WITHOUT YOU!
HEY!
COME ON--
!
GRAB
かあっ
I SAID NO!!
ぎゅっ
NO!
WHY NOT?
WHO THE HELL IS THIS GUY?!
...STOP...
AIZAWA!!

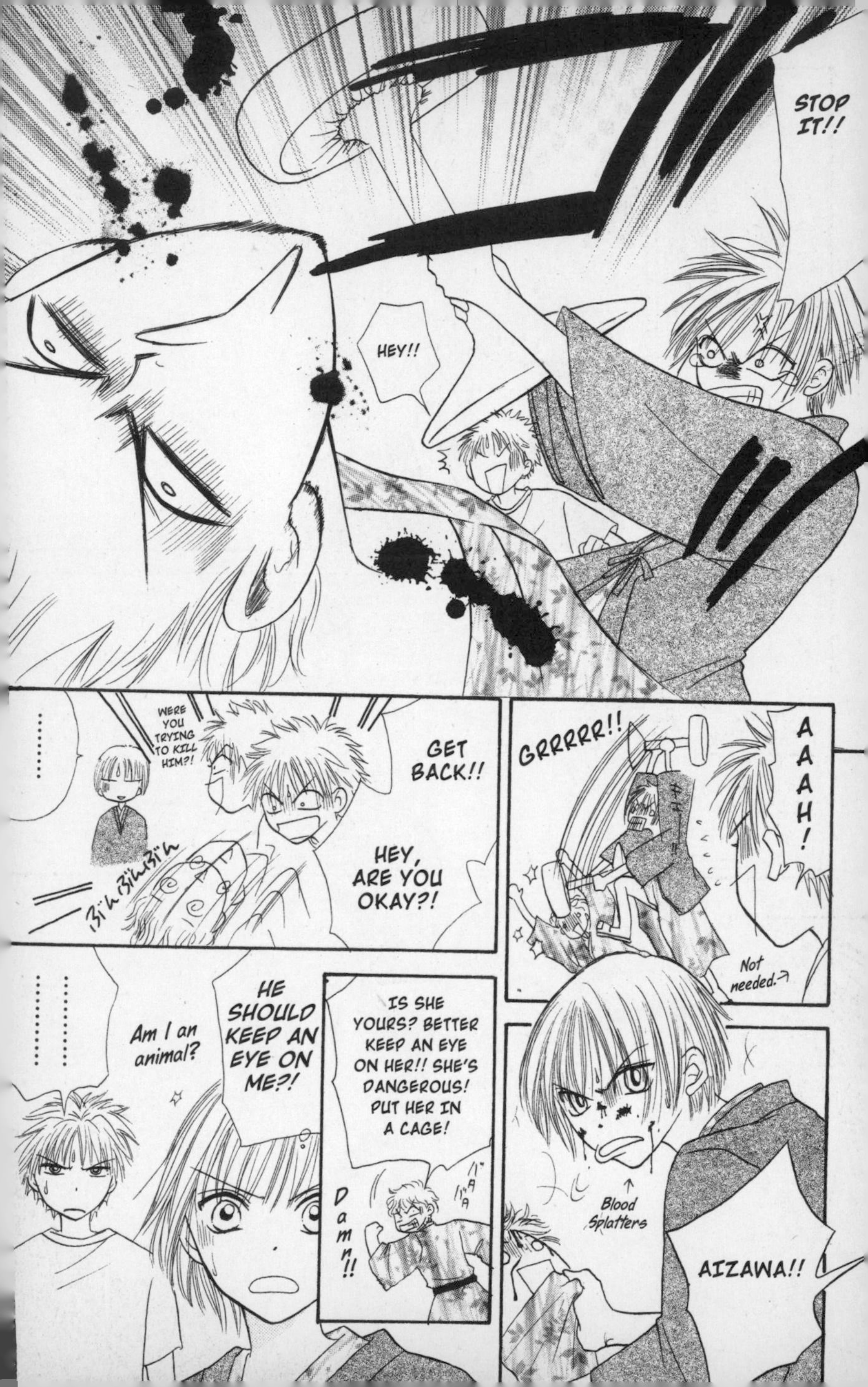
STOP IT!!
HEY!!
AAAAH!
GRRRRR!!
Not needed.
GET BACK!!
WERE YOU TRYING TO KILL HIM?!
HEY, ARE YOU OKAY?!
......
AIZAWA!!
Blood Splatters
IS SHE YOURS? BETTER KEEP AN EYE ON HER!! SHE'S DANGEROUS! PUT HER IN A CAGE!
Damn!!
HE SHOULD KEEP AN EYE ON ME?!
Am I an animal?
......

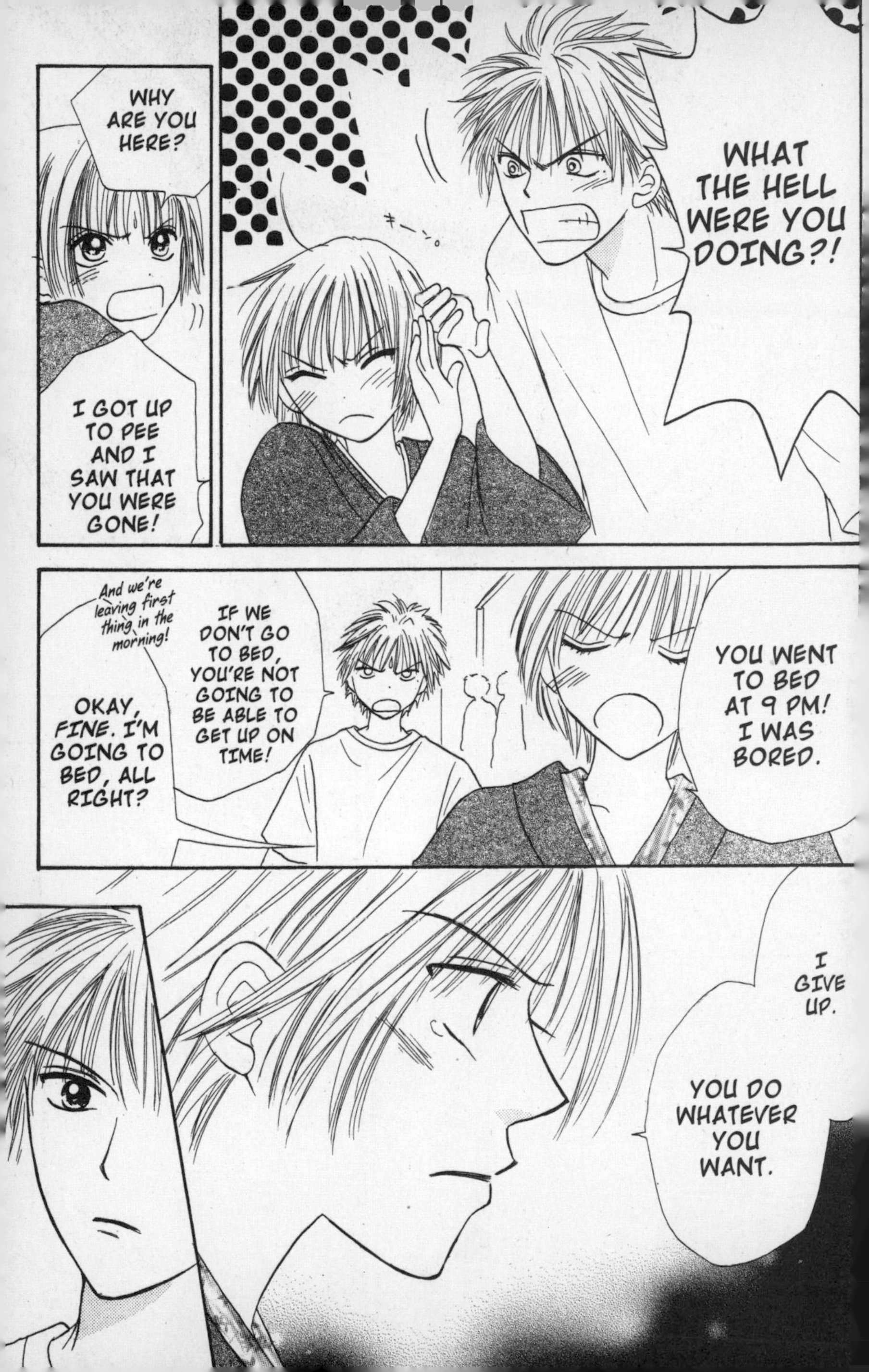
WHAT THE HELL WERE YOU DOING?!
WHY ARE YOU HERE?
I GOT UP TO PEE AND I SAW THAT YOU WERE GONE!
YOU WENT TO BED AT 9 PM! I WAS BORED.
IF WE DON'T GO TO BED, YOU'RE NOT GOING TO BE ABLE TO GET UP ON TIME!
And we're leaving first thing in the morning!
OKAY, FINE. I'M GOING TO BED, ALL RIGHT?
I GIVE UP.
YOU DO WHATEVER YOU WANT.

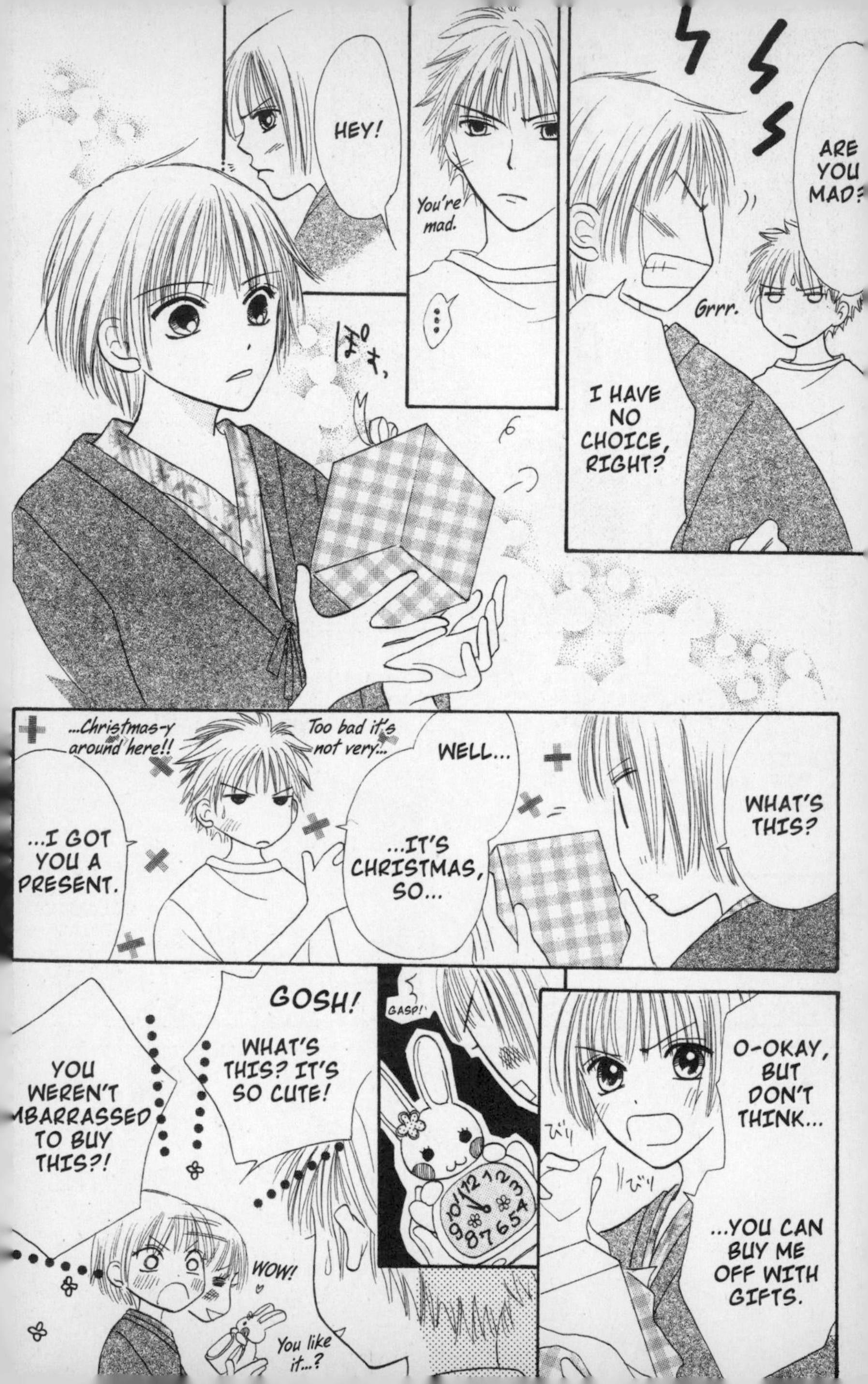
ARE YOU MAD?
Grrr.
I HAVE NO CHOICE, RIGHT?
You're mad.
...
HEY!
WHAT'S THIS?
WELL...
...IT'S CHRISTMAS, SO...
Too bad it's not very...
...Christmas-y around here!!
...I GOT YOU A PRESENT.
O-OKAY, BUT DON'T THINK...
...YOU CAN BUY ME OFF WITH GIFTS.
GASP!
GOSH!
WHAT'S THIS? IT'S SO CUTE!
YOU WEREN'T MBARRASSED TO BUY THIS?!
WOW!
You like it...?

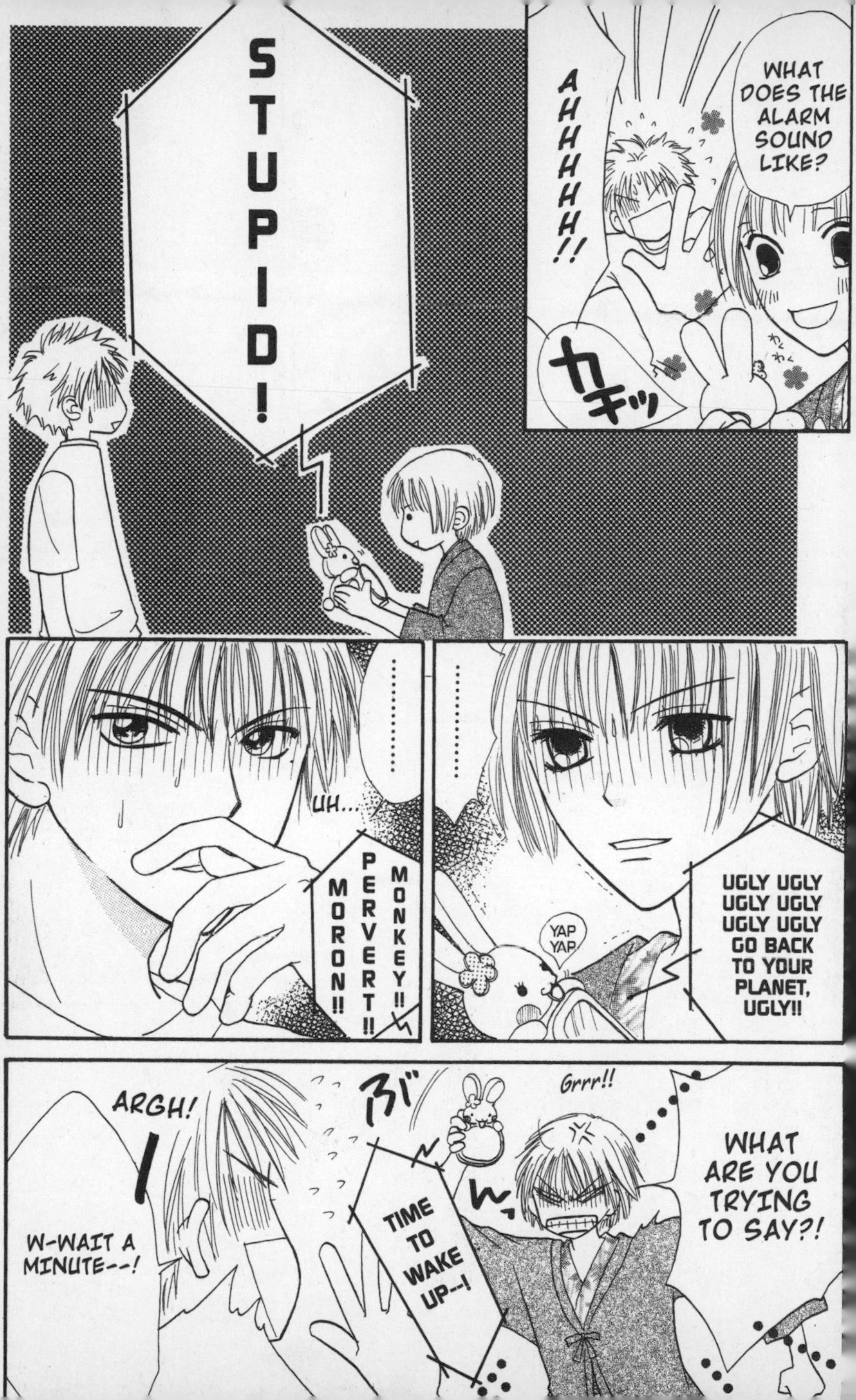
WHAT DOES THE ALARM SOUND LIKE?
わくわく
カキッ
AHHHHHH!!
STUPID!
......
UGLY UGLY UGLY UGLY UGLY UGLY GO BACK TO YOUR PLANET, UGLY!!
YAP YAP
......
UH...
MONKEY!!
PERVERT!!
MORON!!
WHAT ARE YOU TRYING TO SAY?!
Grrr!!
ん
TIME TO WAKE UP--!
ぶ
ARGH!
W-WAIT A MINUTE--!

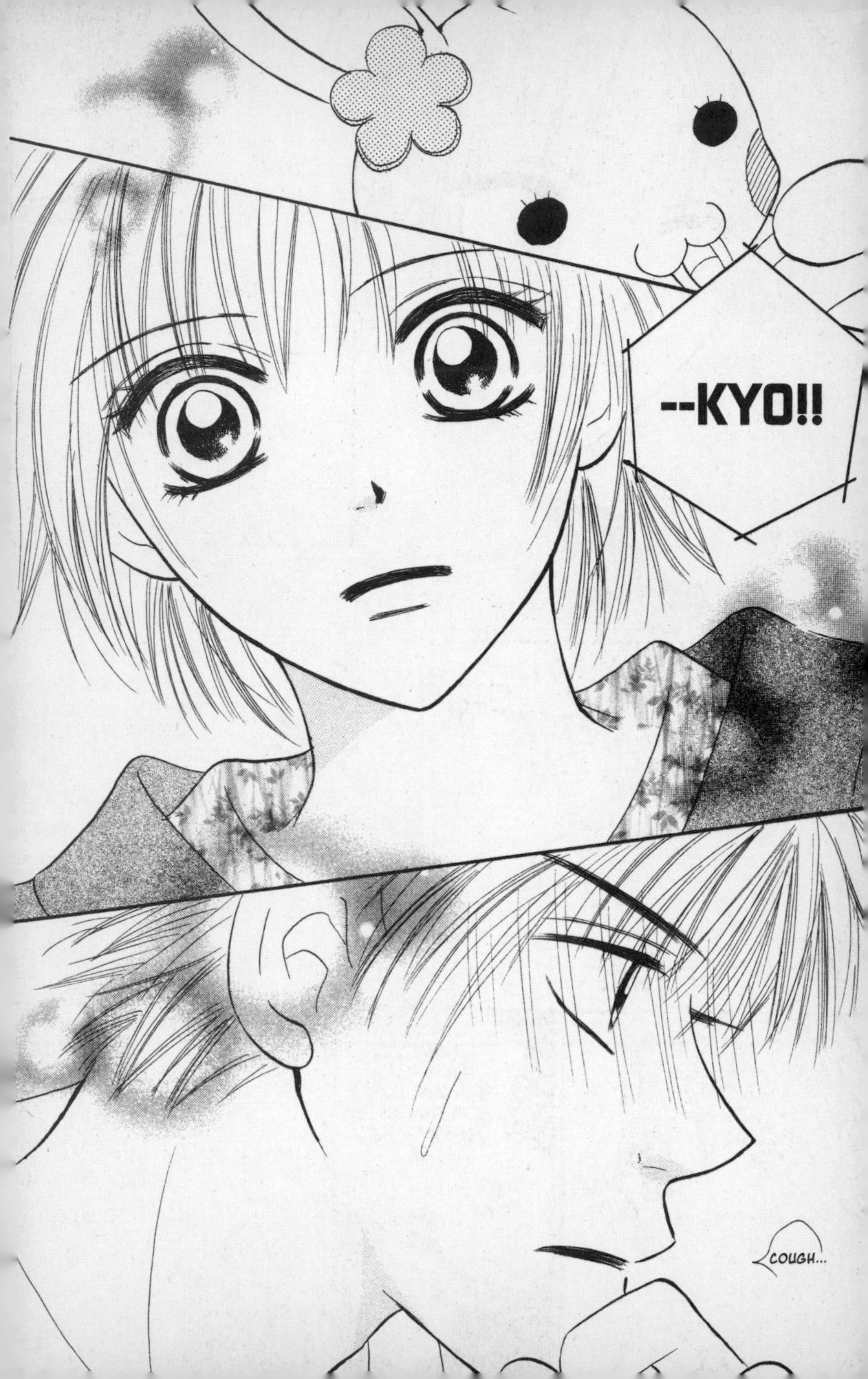
--KYO!!
COUGH...

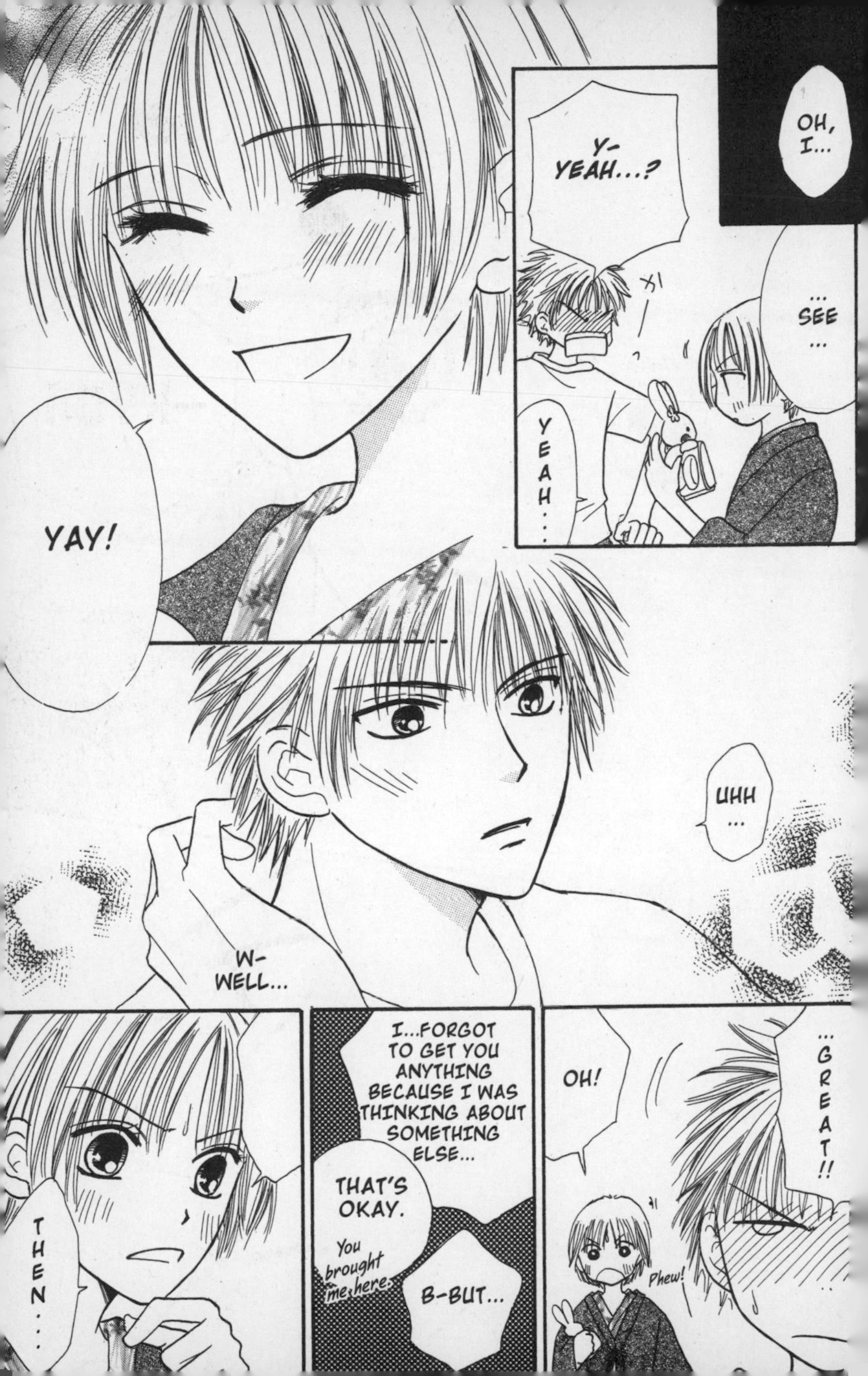
OH, I...
...SEE...
Y-YEAH...?
YEAH...
YAY!
UHH...
W-WELL...
...GREAT!!
OH!
Phew!
I...FORGOT TO GET YOU ANYTHING BECAUSE I WAS THINKING ABOUT SOMETHING ELSE...
THAT'S OKAY.
You brought me here.
B-BUT...
THEN...

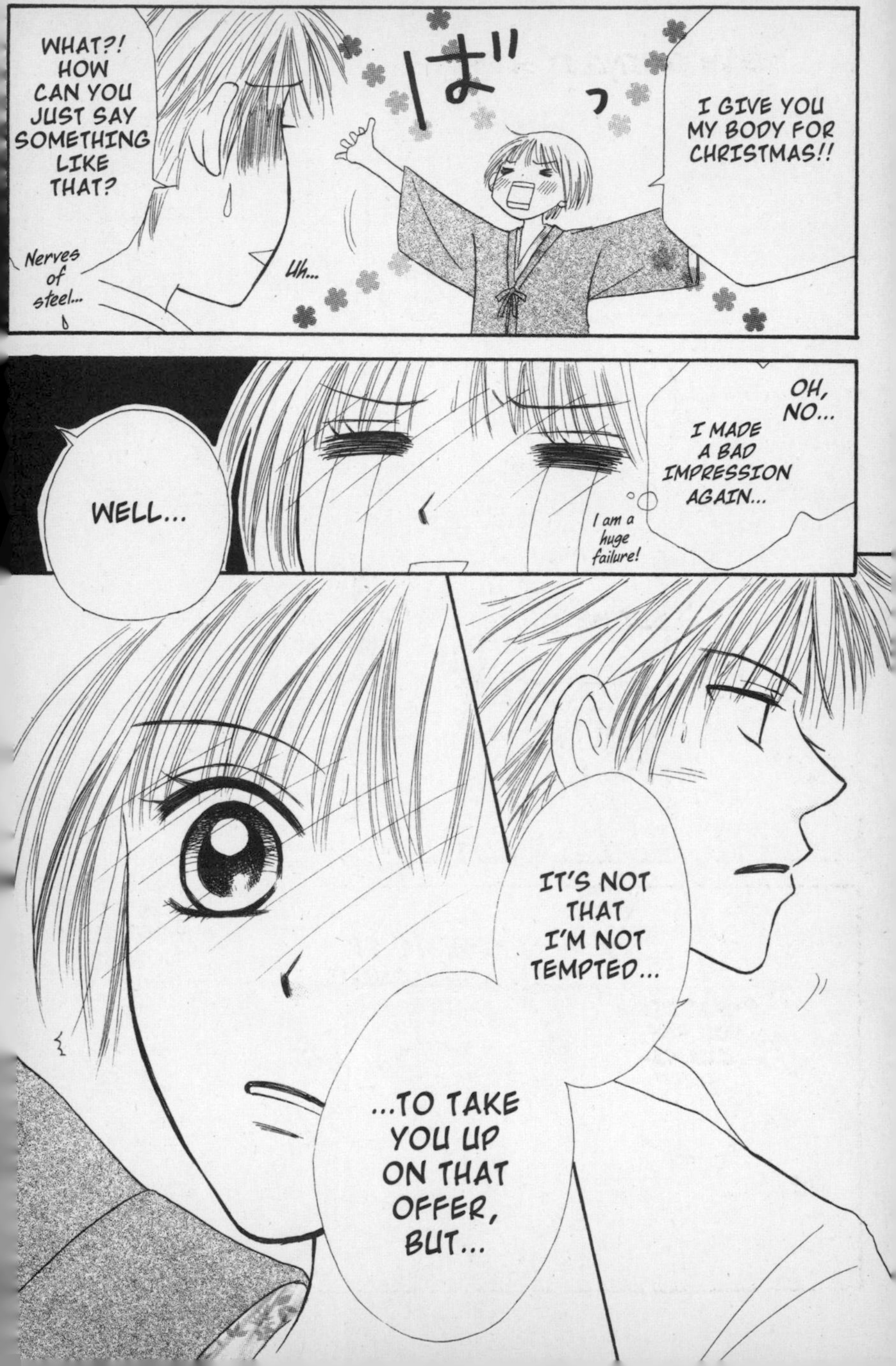
I GIVE YOU MY BODY FOR CHRISTMAS!!
ばっ
Uh...
WHAT?! HOW CAN YOU JUST SAY SOMETHING LIKE THAT?
Nerves of steel...
OH, NO... I MADE A BAD IMPRESSION AGAIN...
I am a huge failure!
WELL...
IT'S NOT THAT I'M NOT TEMPTED...
...TO TAKE YOU UP ON THAT OFFER, BUT...

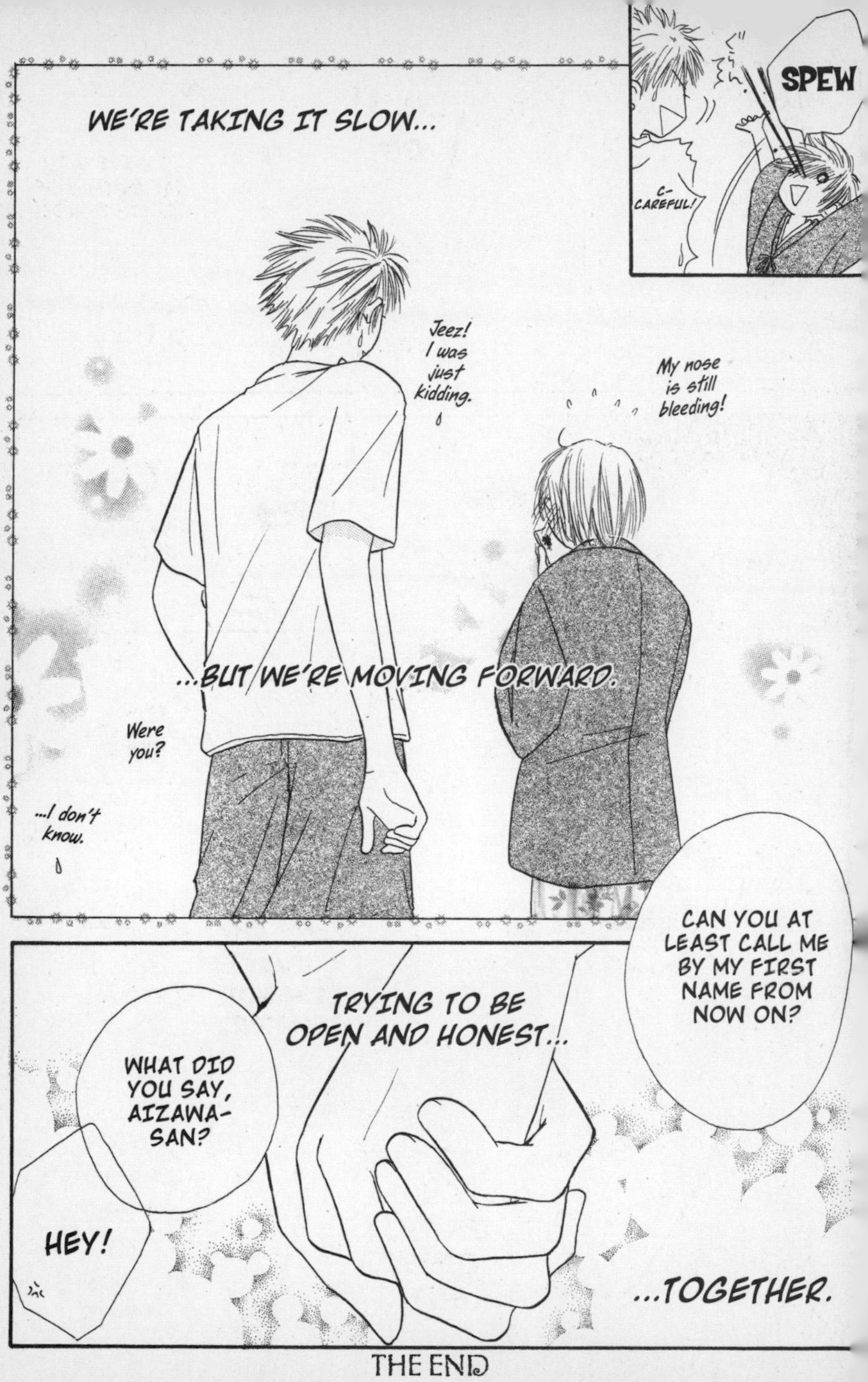
SPEW
C-CAREFUL!
WE'RE TAKING IT SLOW...
My nose is still bleeding!
Jeez! I was just kidding.
...BUT WE'RE MOVING FORWARD.
Were you?
...I don't know.
CAN YOU AT LEAST CALL ME BY MY FIRST NAME FROM NOW ON?
TRYING TO BE OPEN AND HONEST...
WHAT DID YOU SAY, AIZAWA-SAN?
HEY!
...TOGETHER.

THE END

Girl Got Game

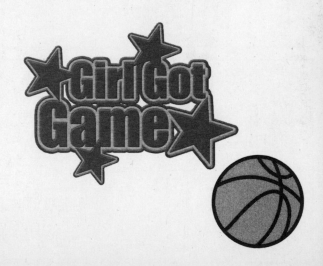

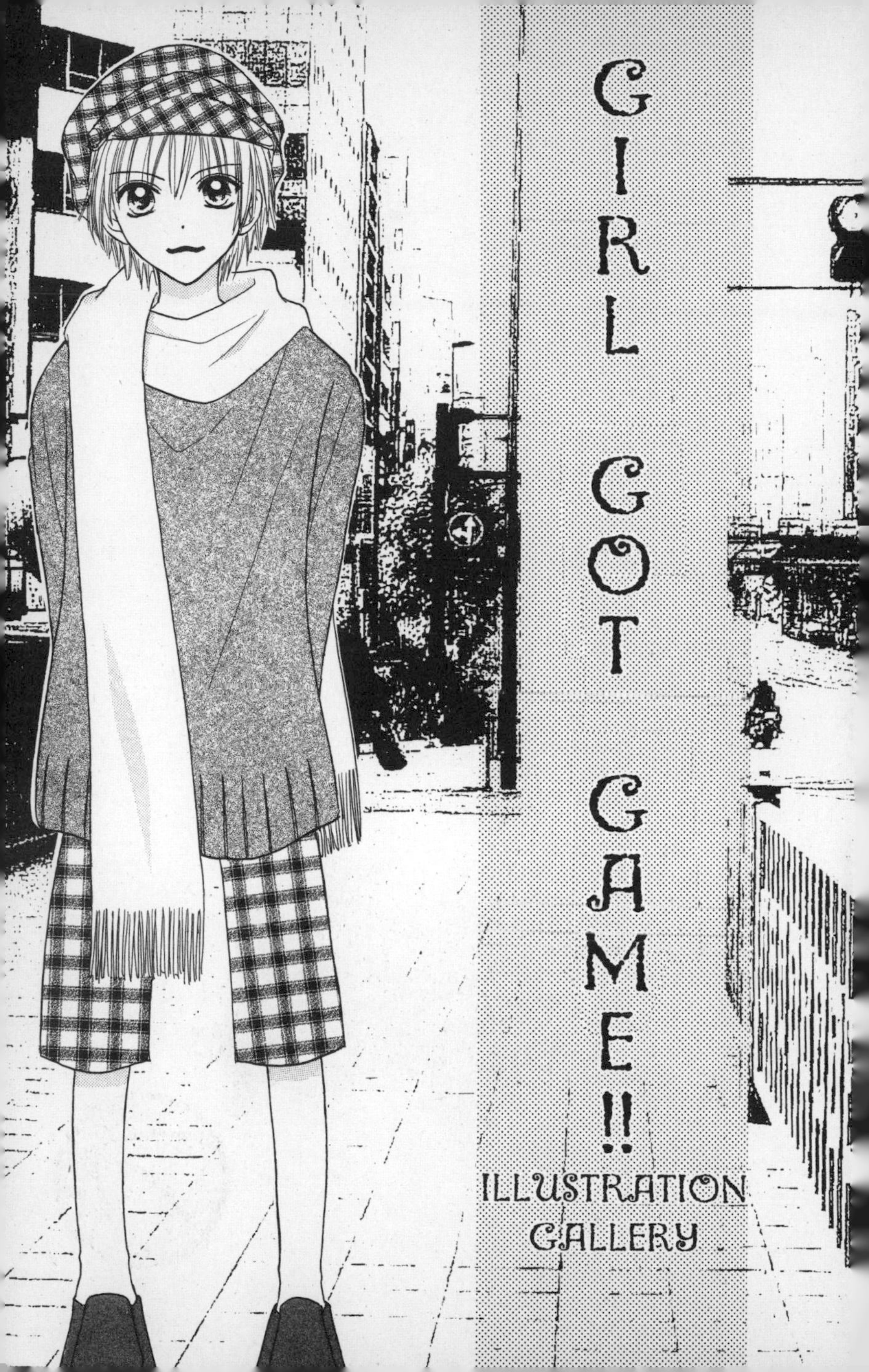
GIRL GOT GAME!!
ILLUSTRATION GALLERY

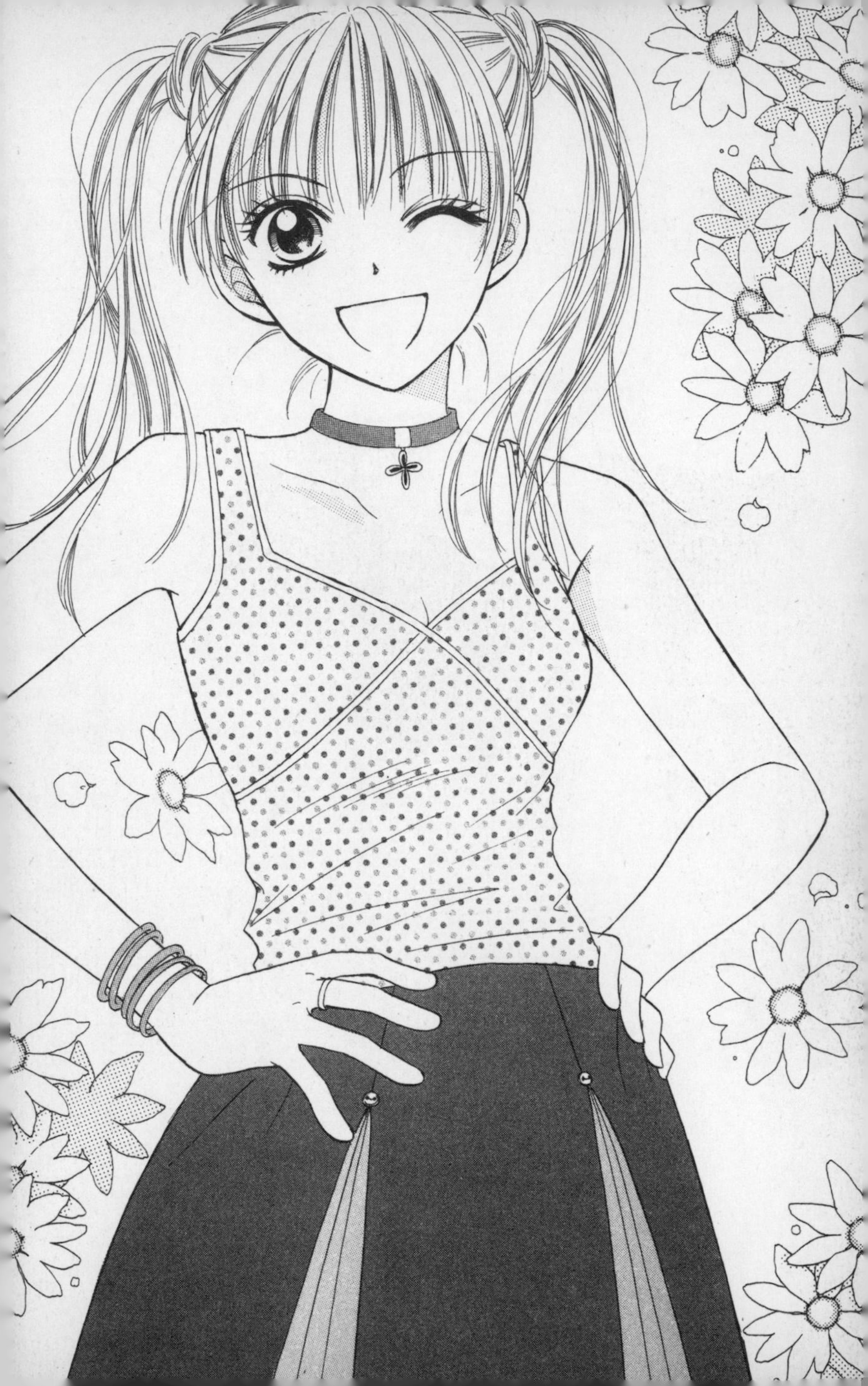

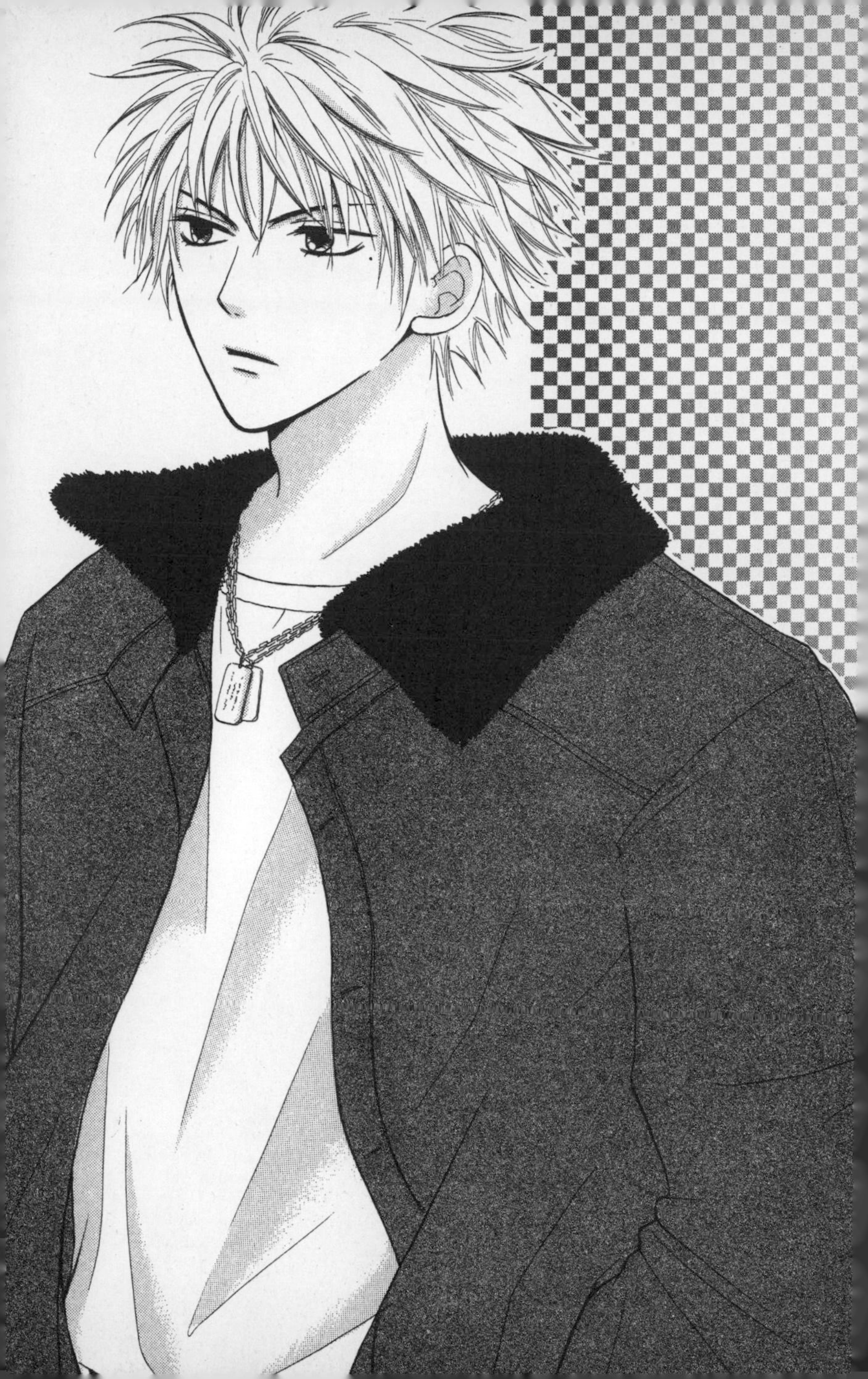

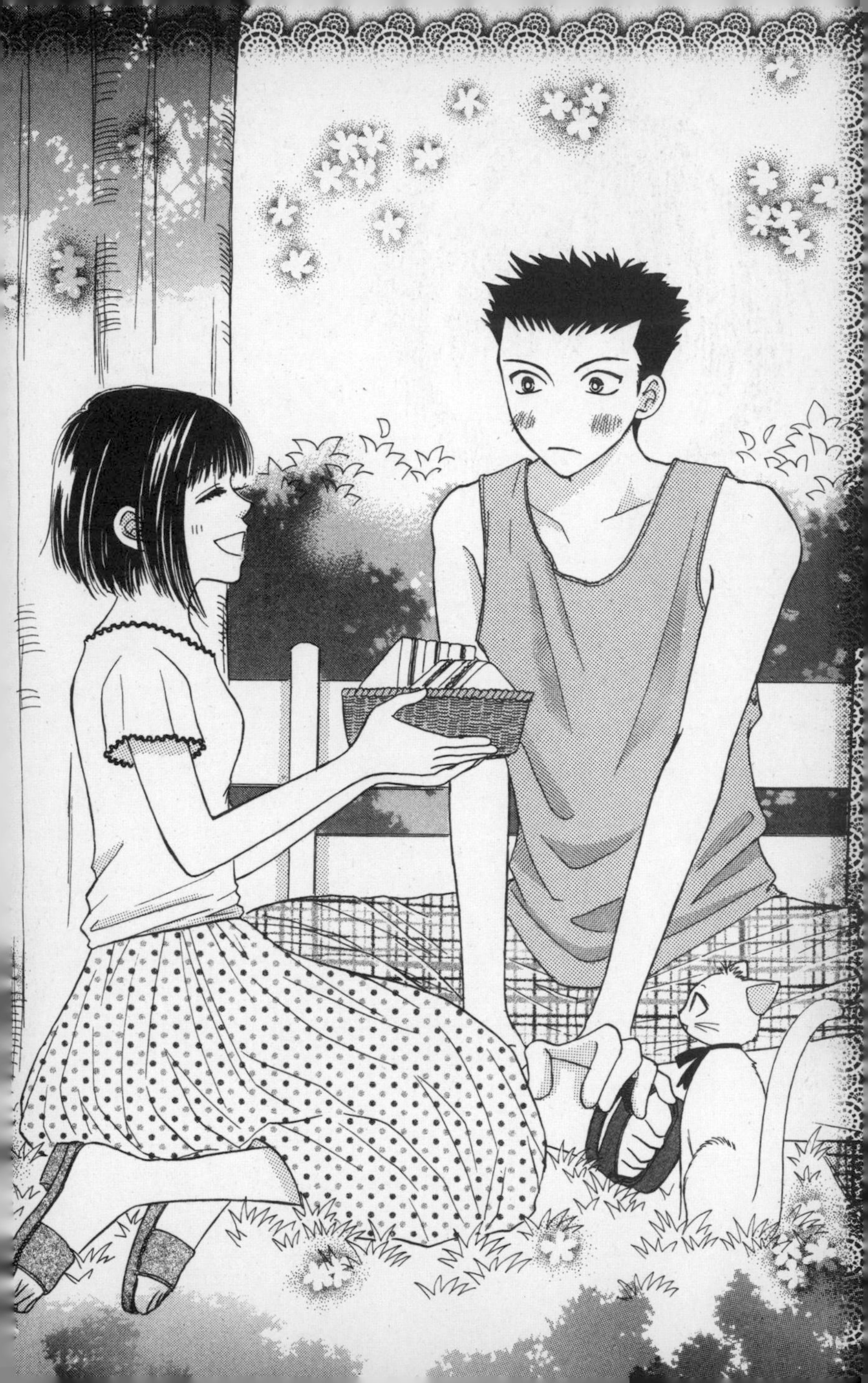

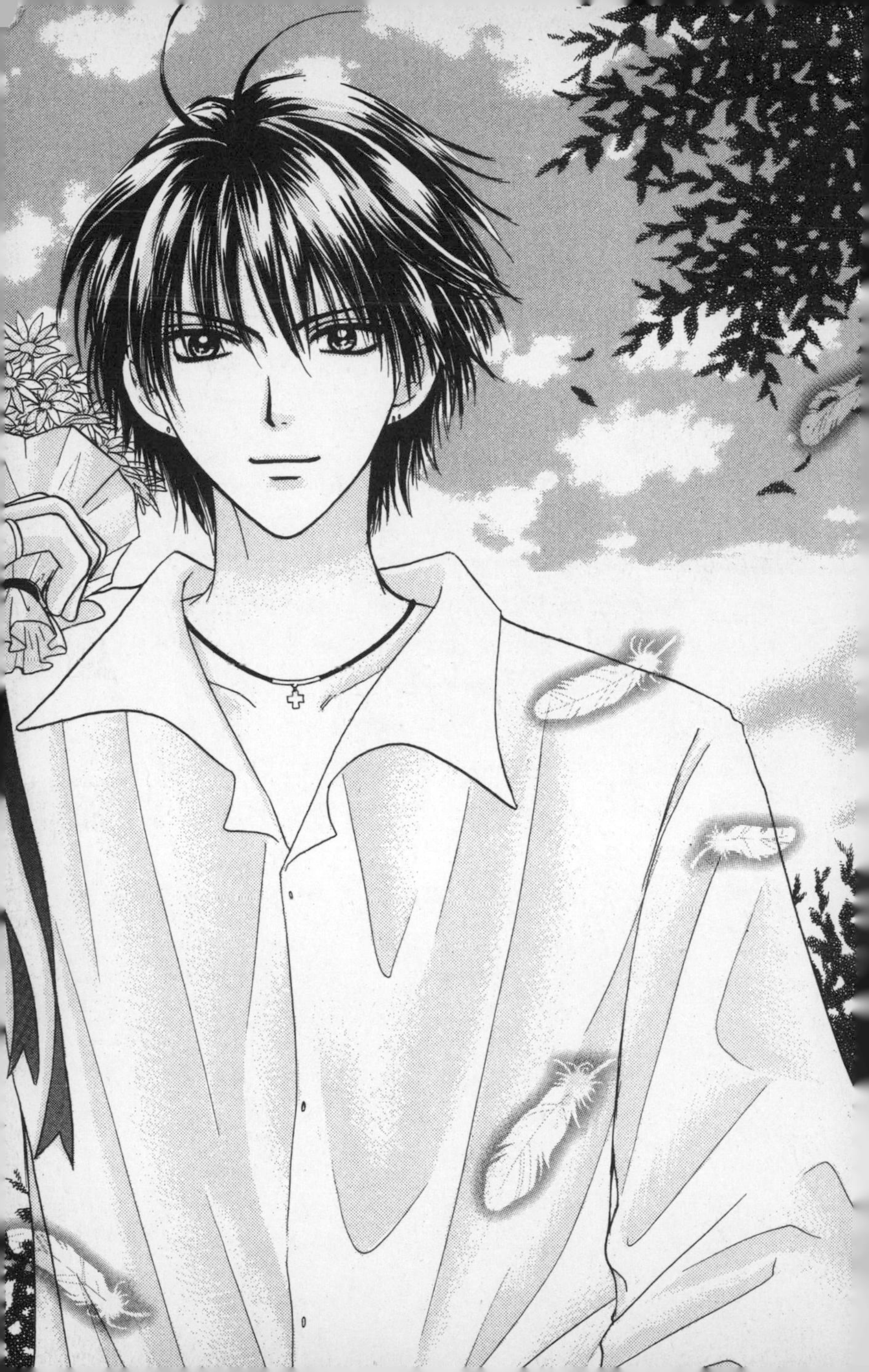

Postscript

Finally! The conclusion of the series that's been three years in the making! I'm thrilled to have it finished, although I fear I may have overdone it with the principal a little (sweat)...

I've barely managed to make deadlines on several occasions, but the three stories in this tenth volume were particularly tight and they appeared in the magazine unfinished. That inconvenienced many people--from the readers to the editing staff, and for that I am very sorry. Making this series into a book gave me a chance to make a lot of corrections but there are still time constraints and some things still didn't get fixed!
Ahhh!! (Really, I'm just lazy.)

I've totally lost that "New Artist" feeling that I had when I started this series, but I'm not sure I've gotten much better--or any faster! There'd be no end to it if I went into how pathetic I am, so I'll stop here but, in any case, I believe Girl Got Game allowed me to grow as a manga artist in many ways. (Yes. I'm trying to come up with a positive thought with which to wrap this up!) I look forward to meeting you all on my next series. When that time comes, I'll try my best to be a better Shizuru Seino.

This has become more of an apology than a postscript, but finally, I'd like to express my gratitude to the editorial staff, all of my assistants, my friends, and my family who've cheered me on, and my readers who have supported me these past three years. Thank you very much.

Shizuru Seino

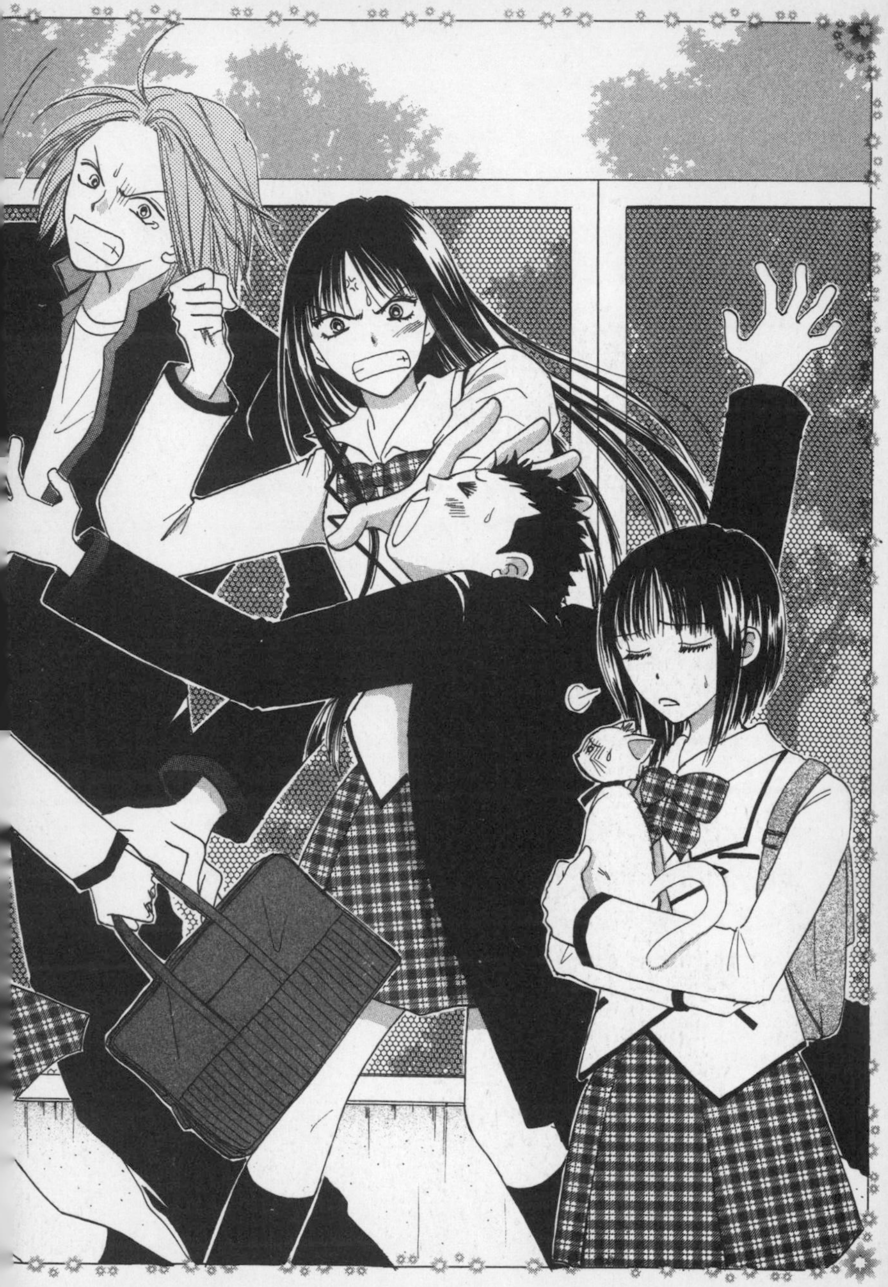

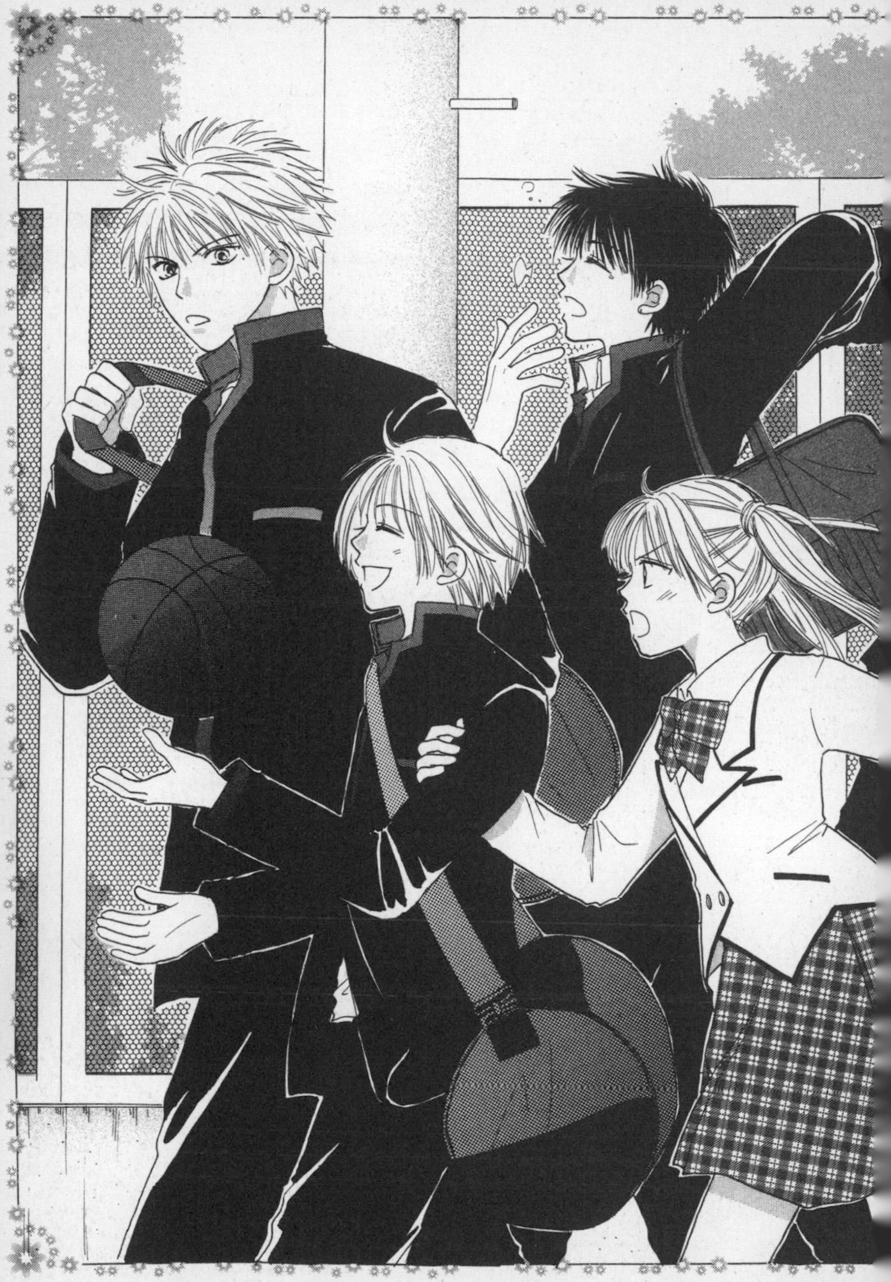

Girl Got Game

IF YOU DON'T HAVE EVERY VOLUME OF GIRL GOT GAME, YOU DON'T HAVE THE WHOLE STORY! HERE'S A QUICK PEEK AT THE OTHER VOLUMES, ALL OF WHICH CAN BE FOUND AT YOUR FAVORITE BOOKSELLER OR AT ***WWW.TOKYOPOP.COM/SHOP.***

Girl Got Game
Shizuru Seino
#1

VOLUME 1: LET THE GAMES BEGIN

THE SERIES BEGINS WITH A VERY GIRLY KYO...BUT YOU KNOW THAT DOESN'T LAST! SEE KYO'S DAD RISK HIS LIFE WHEN HE REVEALS HIS KOOKY PLAN TO ENROLL KYO AS A BOY! SEE KYO CHALLENGE CHIHARU AT BASKETBALL TRYOUTS! SEE CHIHARU BECOME KYO'S BREAST FRIEND AT THE END OF THE VOLUME!

Girl Got Game
Shizuru Seino
#2

VOLUME 2: PERSONAL FOUL

JUST WHEN CHIHARU DECIDES HE CAN HANG WITH KYO, HE ACCIDENTALLY TRIPS AND CATCHES HIMSELF--ON HER BREAST! AFRAID THAT HER NEW BOSOM BUDDY MIGHT DISCOVER HER TRUE GENDER, KYO CONCOCTS A PLAN TO MAKE HERSELF SEEM MORE LIKE ONE OF THE GUYS. UNFORTUNATELY, HER IDEA OF A MASCULINE BOY SEEMS TO BE MOST OTHER PEOPLE'S IDEA OF A SEX-CRAZED PERVERT!
ALSO INCLUDED IN THIS VOLUME ARE TWO ORIGINAL STORIES: *CHANGE* AND *FALSE GIRLFRIEND*.

Girl Got Game
Shizuru Seino
#3

VOLUME 3: GIRLS VS. BOYS

TSUYAKA HIMEJIMA IS AN OLD FRIEND AND TEAMMATE OF KYO AIZAWA. WHEN TSUYAKA TRANSFERS TO SEISYU HIGH, SHE'S SET ON PLAYING BALL WITH KYO AGAIN...UNTIL SHE DISCOVERS THAT KYO HAS SWITCHED SIDES! WILL TSUYAKA LET KYO'S DISGUISE CONTINUE? OR WILL SHE RESORT TO SOME FULL-COURT PRESSURE TO GET KYO ONTO THE GIRLS' BASKETBALL TEAM?

Girl Got Game
Shizuru Seino
#4

VOLUME 4: OUT OF BOUNDS

WHEN CHIHARU DISCOVERS KYO'S TRUE GENDER, HE TELLS HER THAT HE CAN'T BE HER ROOMMATE ANYMORE. DEVASTATED AND WITH NOWHERE TO GO, KYO MOVES INTO A CARDBOARD BOX IN THE PARK, WHERE HER HOOP DREAMS BEGIN TO TURN INTO OVERTIME NIGHTMARES!

Girl Got Game
Shizuru Seino
#5

VOLUME 5: ONE ON ONE

KENSUKE YURA IS A STAR PLAYER WITH A BASKETBALL SCHOLARSHIP WHO WON'T SHOW UP TO PRACTICE OR PLAY...UNTIL HE MEETS KYO. INTRIGUED BY KYO, YURA RETURNS TO PLAY, BUT THE REST OF THE TEAM ISN'T VERY HAPPY ABOUT IT. KYO FEELS SORRY FOR YURA, AND WANTS TO BE A GOOD TEAMMATE BY BEING HIS FRIEND. WILL YURA TAKE ADVANTAGE OF HER ASSIST? OR WILL HE JUST FOUL OUT?

Girl Got Game
Shizuru Seino
#6

VOLUME 6: TAKING ONE FOR THE TEAM

THOUGH HARASSED BY OTHERS BECAUSE OF HIS EXCELLENT GRADES, YURA AGREES TO HELP KYO WITH HER STUDIES. BUT JUST AS YURA WARMS UP TO HER, HE OVERHEARS A CONVERSATION THAT MAKES HIM WANT A REPLAY. WILL KYO PASS HER TUTOR'S NEWEST TEST...OR WILL HER FAILURE CAUSE THEIR FRIENDSHIP TO PERMANENTLY FOUL OUT?

Girl Got Game

IF YOU DON'T HAVE EVERY VOLUME OF GIRL GOT GAME, YOU DON'T HAVE THE WHOLE STORY! HERE'S A QUICK PEEK AT THE OTHER VOLUMES, ALL OF WHICH CAN BE FOUND AT YOUR FAVORITE BOOKSELLER OR AT WWW.TOKYOPOP.COM/SHOP.

VOLUME 7: REPLAY

THINGS FINALLY GET BACK TO NORMAL...BUT IS THAT A GOOD THING? CHIHARU MOVES BACK IN WITH KYO, BUT ONLY BECAUSE HE DOESN'T THINK OF HER AS A GIRL! NOT LONG AGO, KYO PUT SO MUCH TIME AND EFFORT INTO PRETENDING TO BE A BOY THAT SHE ENDED UP EARNING HERSELF A REPUTATION AS A DEPRAVED MALE PERVERT! JUST HOW FAR WILL SHE GO IN ORDER TO PROVE THAT SHE'S STILL A WOMAN TO CHIHARU? FEATURES THE BONUS STORY "HAMER."

VOLUME 8: FUNGUS AMONG US

THE PERFECT COMBINATION FOR LOVE: MAGICAL MUSHROOMS AND STEAMY HOT SPRINGS! DURING THE TRIP TO THE HOT SPRINGS, CHIHARU DISCOVERS YURA'S INTEREST IN KYO. TO MAKE MATTERS WORSE (AND A WHOLE LOT WEIRDER), KYO AND CHIHARU MISTAKENLY EAT SOME WACKY MUSHROOMS, WHICH MAKE THEM BEHAVE IN RATHER UNCHARACTERISTIC WAYS-- LIKE CONFESSING THEIR LOVE FOR EACH OTHER! IS IT LOVE BREWING OR ARE THE MUSHROOMS DOING THE TALKING?

VOLUME 9: USING TEAMWORK TO SCORE

HAMAYA'S PLAN TO KIDNAP CHIHARU'S "SISTER" IS CHALLENGED WHEN IMAI AND TSUYAKA DOUBLE TEAM THE LOVE-STRUCK YOUNG PERV. HOWEVER, THE SHARP-EYED TSUYAKA ISN'T FAZED BY KYO'S GENDER-UNBENDING FAKE OUT AND SOON REALIZES THAT KYOKO IS KYO IN DISGUISE. TSUYAKA FINDS HERSELF IN A POSITION TO GIVE KYO THE ULTIMATE ASSIST: A CHANCE TO LOCK LIPS WITH CHIHARU! FEATURES THE BONUS STORY "HAMER 2."

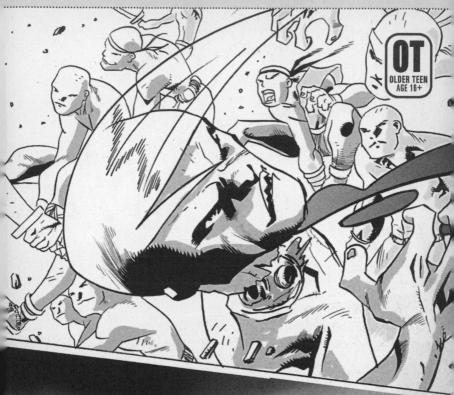

OT
OLDER TEEN
AGE 16+

In the deep South, an ancient voodoo curse unleashes the War on Flesh—a hellish plague of voracious Ew Chott hornets that raises an army of the walking dead. This undead army spreads the plague by ripping the hearts out of living creatures to make room for a Black Heart hive, all in preparation for the most awesome incarnation of evil ever imagined… An unlikely group of five mismatched individuals have to put their differences aside to try to destroy the onslaught of evil before it's too late.

VOODOO MAKES A MAN NASTY!

WAR ON FLESH

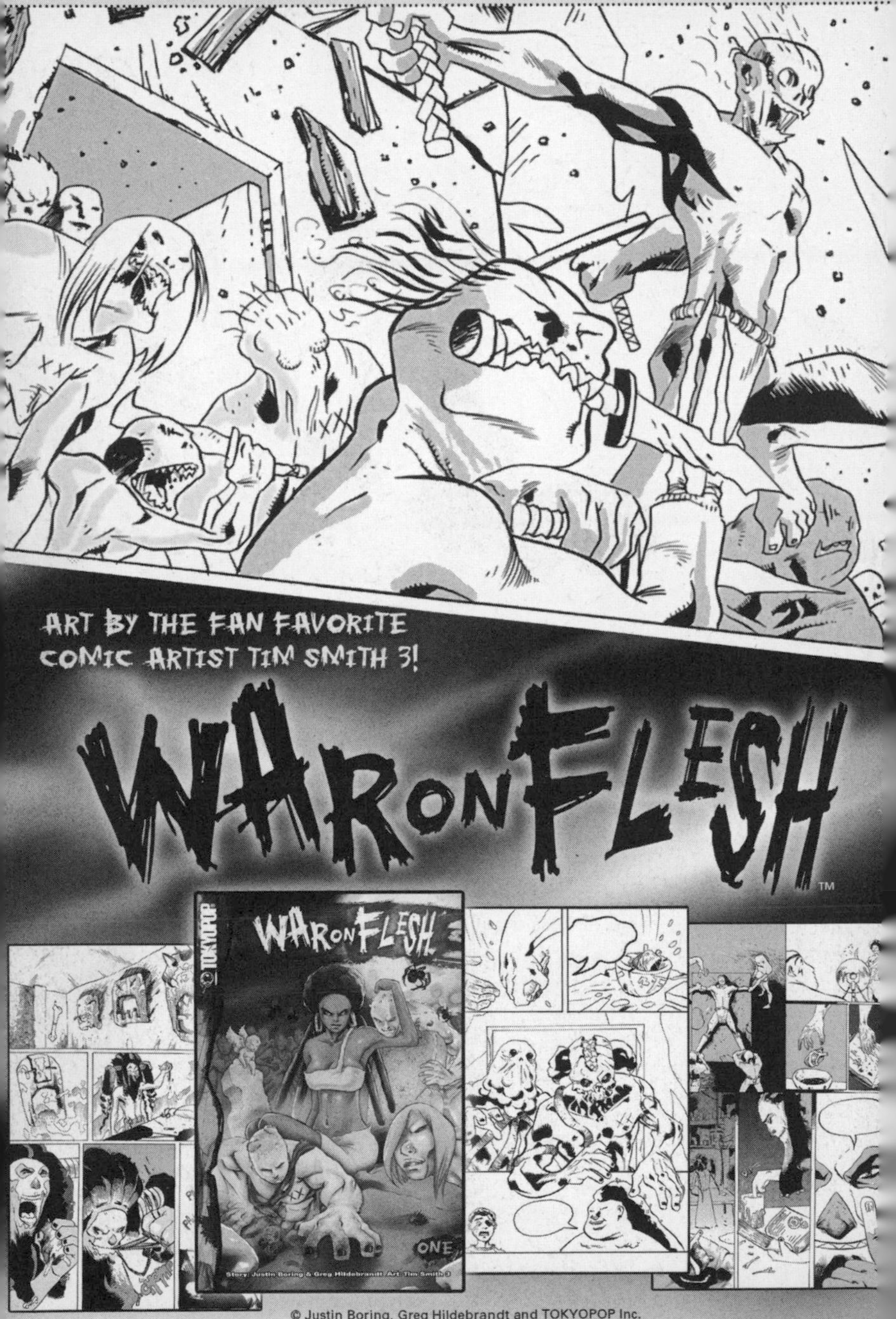
ART BY THE FAN FAVORITE
COMIC ARTIST TIM SMITH 3!
WAR ON FLESH™
TOKYOPOP
WAR ON FLESH
ONE
Story: Justin Boring & Greg Hildebrandt Art: Tim Smith 3

SPOTLIGHT **TOKYOPOP MANGA SUPPLEMENT**

GIRLS BRAVO

BY MARIO KANEDA

T TEEN AGE 13+

BOY MEETS GIRL. BOY BREAKS OUT IN HIVES. BOY STUMBLES ONTO ALIEN PLANET FULL OF GIRLS...

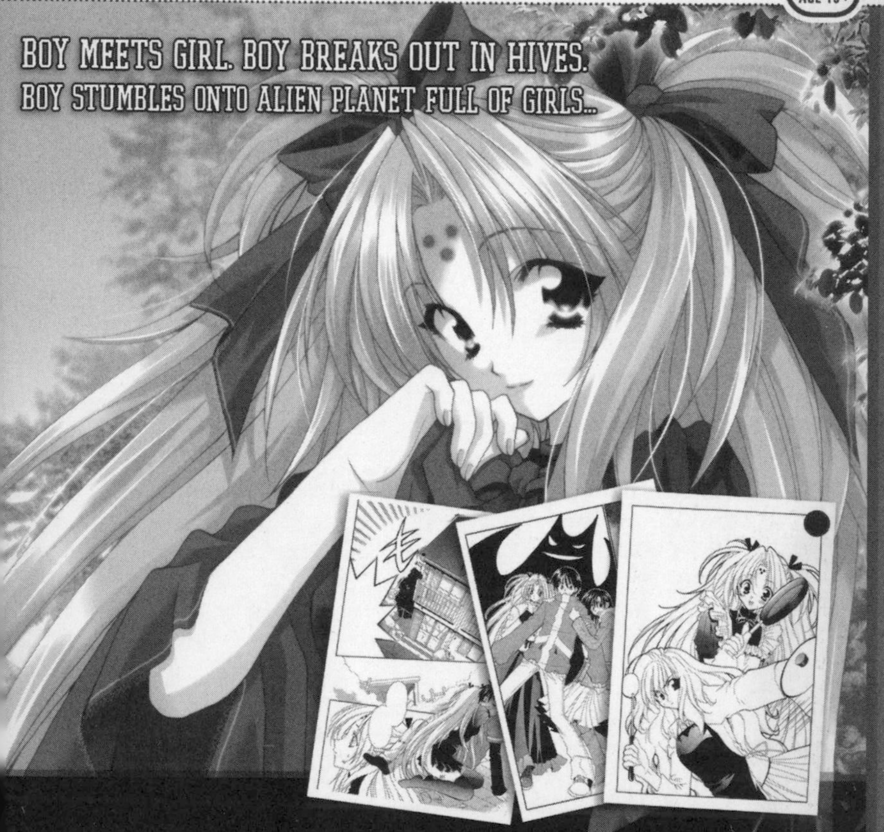

Meet Yukinari Sasaki, an average high school boy who has extreme girl phobia—and an allergic reaction when girls touch him. One day, he befriends an alien named Miharu, who comes from a planet that is inhabited by only women. Remarkably, Yukinari is able to touch Miharu, without breaking out. He returns to his own world accompanied by Miharu, but shortly thereafter, other girls follow them to his world...and his life turns into one big mess!

THE LAUGH-OUT-LOUD MANGA THAT INSPIRED THE POPULAR ANIME ADAPTATION!

FOR MORE INFORMATION VISIT: WWW.TOKYOPOP.COM

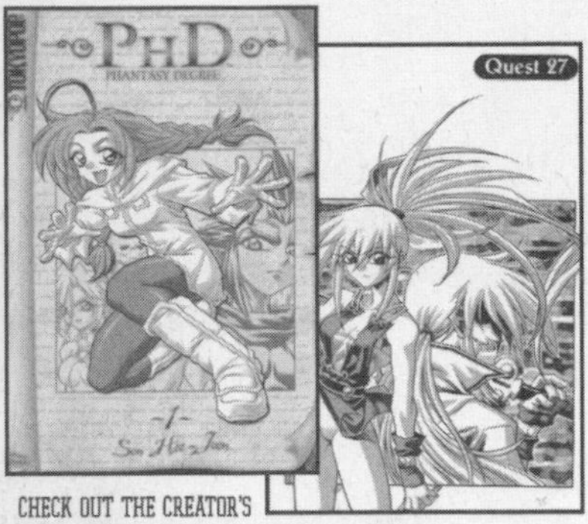
PhD
PHANTASY DEGREE
-1-
Quest 27

CHECK OUT THE CREATOR'S *iD_eNTITY*

BY SON HEE-JOON

PhD: PHANTASY DEGREE

So you think you've got it rough at *your* school? Try attending classes at Demon School Hades! When sassy, young Sang makes her monster matriculation to this arcane academy, all hell breaks loose—literally! But what would you expect when the graduating class consists of a werewolf, a mummy and demons by the score? Son Hee-Joon's underworld adventure is pure escapist fun. Always packed with action and often silly in the best sense, *PhD* never takes itself too seriously or lets the reader stop to catch his breath.

~Bryce P. Coleman, Editor

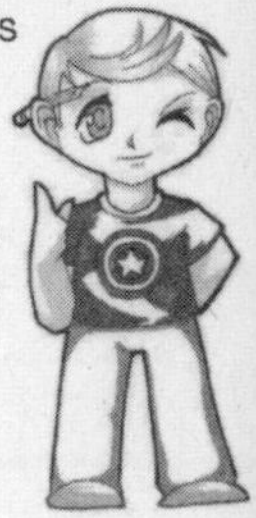

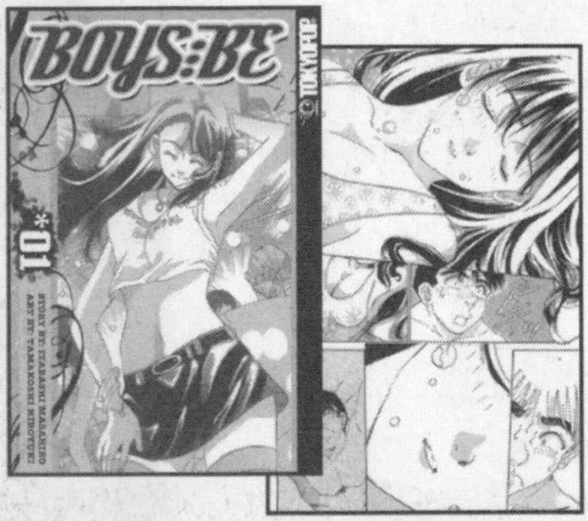
BOYS BE
TOKYOPOP
01

BY MASAHIRO ITABASHI & HIROYUKI TAMAKOSHI

BOYS BE...

Boys Be... is a series of short stories. But although the hero's name changes from tale to tale, he remains Everyboy—that dorky high school guy who'll do anything to score with the girl of his dreams. You know him. Perhaps you *are* him. He is a dirty mind with the soul of a poet, a stumblebum with a heart of sterling. We follow this guy on quest after quest to woo his lady loves. We savor his victory; we reel with his defeat...and the experience is touching, funny and above all human.

Still not convinced? I have two words for you: fan service.

~Carol Fox, Editor

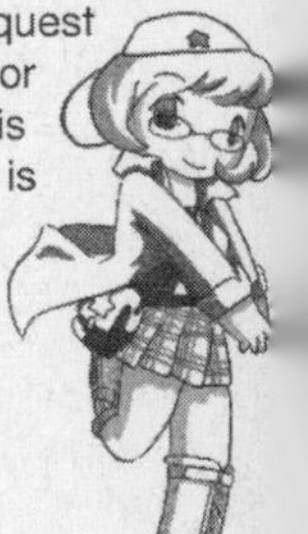

STOP!

This is the back of the book.
You wouldn't want to spoil a great ending!

This book is printed "manga-style," in the authentic Japanese right-to-left format. Since none of the artwork has been flipped or altered, readers get to experience the story just as the creator intended. You've been asking for it, so TOKYOPOP® delivered: authentic, hot-off-the-press, and far more fun!

DIRECTIONS

If this is your first time reading manga-style, here's a quick guide to help you understand how it works.

It's easy... just start in the top right panel and follow the numbers. Have fun, and look for more 100% authentic manga from TOKYOPOP®!